I0798640

Greetings from Columbus, Ohio

Robert M. Reed

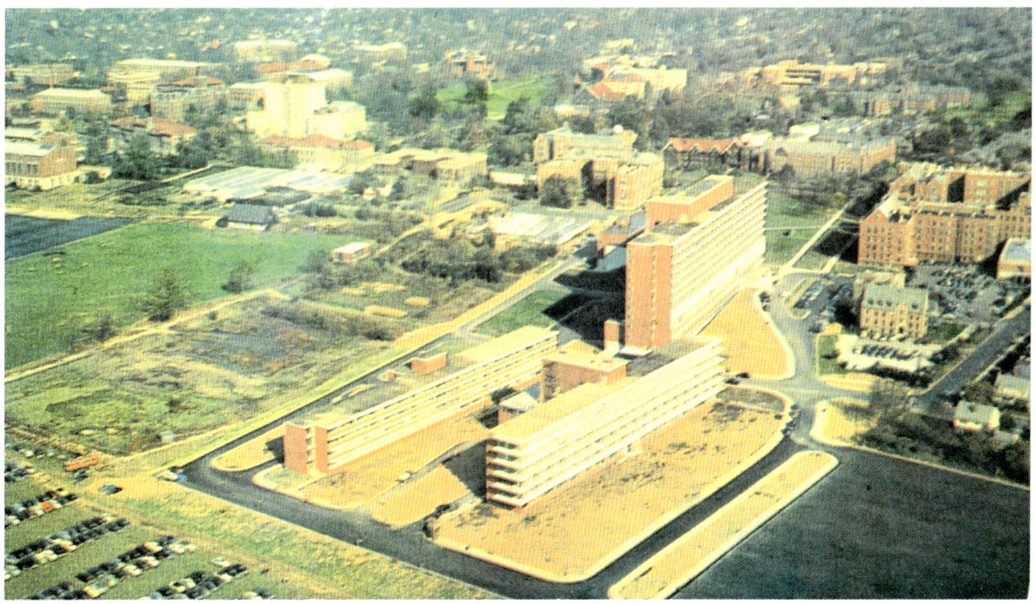

Schiffer Publishing Ltd®
4880 Lower Valley Road, Atglen, PA 19310

Acknowledgements

My deepest appreciation to the City of Columbus, *Columbus Dispatch*, Port Columbus International Airport, *Wikipedia*, Columbus Regional Airport Authority, Ohio State University, Sports Venue Technology, the Ohio Historical Society, *The Week in Columbus* (TWIC), and a generous group of postcard dealers and postcard collectors who have assisted in this effort.

Library of Congress Control Number: 2007943476

Designed by RoS
Type set in NewBskvll BT

ISBN: 978-0-7643-2885-5
Printed in China

Schiffer Books are available at special discounts for bulk purchases for sales promotions or premiums. Special editions, including personalized covers, corporate imprints, and excerpts can be created in large quantities for special needs. For more information contact the publisher:

Published by Schiffer Publishing Ltd.
4880 Lower Valley Road
Atglen, PA 19310
Phone: (610) 593-1777; Fax: (610) 593-2002
E-mail: Info@schifferbooks.com

For the largest selection of fine reference books on this and related subjects, please visit our web site at **www.schifferbooks.com**
We are always looking for people to write books on new and related subjects. If you have an idea for a book please contact us at the above address.

This book may be purchased from the publisher.
Include $3.95 for shipping.
Please try your bookstore first.
You may write for a free catalog.

In Europe, Schiffer books are distributed by
Bushwood Books
6 Marksbury Ave.
Kew Gardens
Surrey TW9 4JF England
Phone: 44 (0) 20 8392-8585; Fax: 44 (0) 20 8392-9876
E-mail: info@bushwoodbooks.co.uk
Website: www.bushwoodbooks.co.uk
Free postage in the U.K., Europe; air mail at cost.

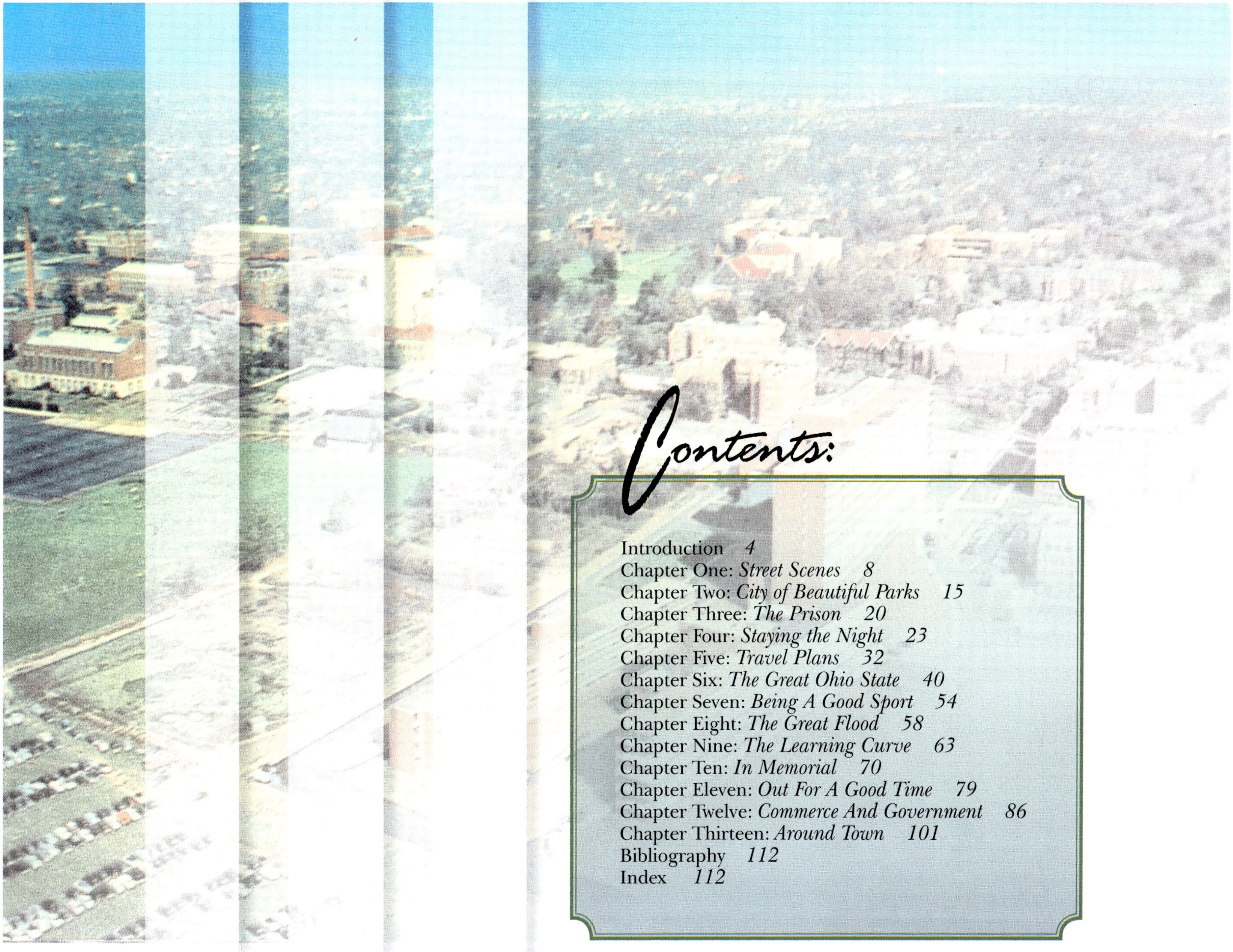

Contents:

Introduction *4*

Chapter One: *Street Scenes 8*

Chapter Two: *City of Beautiful Parks 15*

Chapter Three: *The Prison 20*

Chapter Four: *Staying the Night 23*

Chapter Five: *Travel Plans 32*

Chapter Six: *The Great Ohio State 40*

Chapter Seven: *Being A Good Sport 54*

Chapter Eight: *The Great Flood 58*

Chapter Nine: *The Learning Curve 63*

Chapter Ten: *In Memorial 70*

Chapter Eleven: *Out For A Good Time 79*

Chapter Twelve: *Commerce And Government 86*

Chapter Thirteen: *Around Town 101*

Bibliography *112*

Index *112*

Introduction

> This field, this game, is part of out past. It reminds us of all that was once good, and that could be again. Oh, people will come. People will definitely come.
>
> — *A line from "A Field of Dreams" movie*

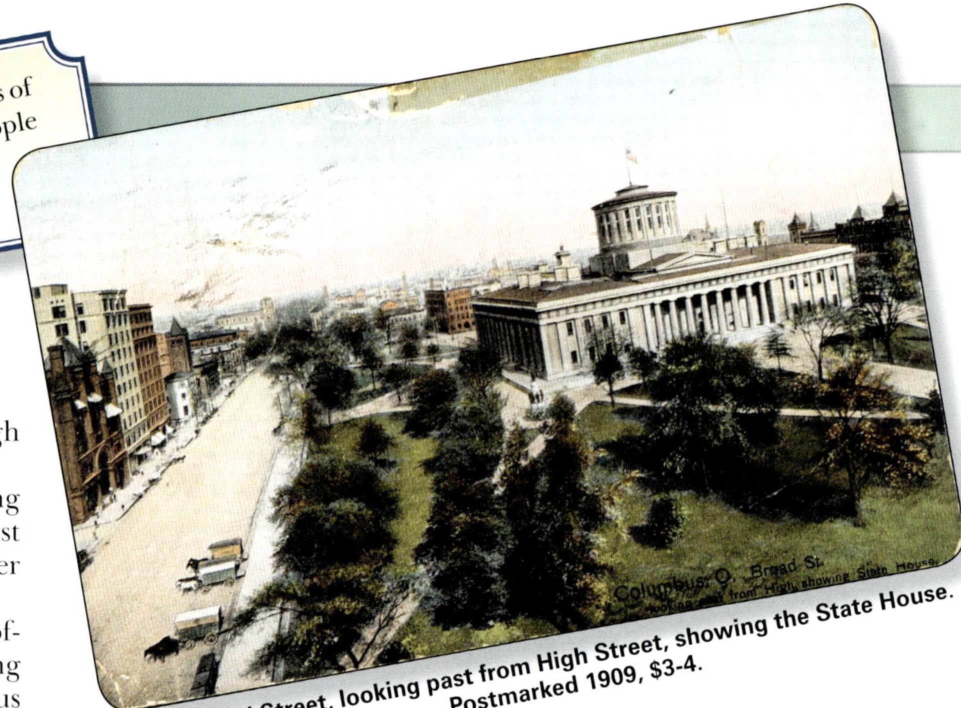

Broad Street, looking past from High Street, showing the State House. Postmarked 1909, $3-4.

Columbus began as a wilderness. When enough people and enough commerce arrived, it became a mighty city.

Early in the nineteenth century the young state of Ohio was seeking a central location for its permanent capital. After some debate, the most favorable site was determined to be a high bank east of the Scioto River directly oppose the town of Franklinton.

About seven hundred people had arrived in 1816 when Columbus officially became the state capital—and people and commerce kept coming until it became fully incorporated as a city in 1834. At the time, Columbus boasted 3,500 proud citizens.

By the late 1830s more than two hundred miles of the National Road stretched across the state of Ohio, providing still another access to the city of Columbus. Now products from within the city — and resources from places surrounding the city — would be readily available to the Eastern markets.

(Author's note: The National Road was considered to be the first highway constructed by the federal government. It had begun in Maryland and quite literally became the Gateway to the West. It paved a proud path for hundreds of miles providing settlers with westbound access to the expanding frontier. Funding for The National Road finally petered out and construction ended at the state of Illinois.)

More people came to Columbus of course. By 1850 the first railroad was serving the bustling city. Over the next two decades the number of available railroad lines quadrupled.

As the nineteenth century turned into the twentieth century, the city of Columbus had become the leading manufacturing center of the Ohio heartland. The city was even a national leader in the buggy making industry.

Early in the 1920s, a travel folder beckoning still more people to come to Columbus declared the city to be "an ideal residential community whose industrial and commercial prestige reaches to all ends of the earth."

Not bad for what was once a riverside wilderness.

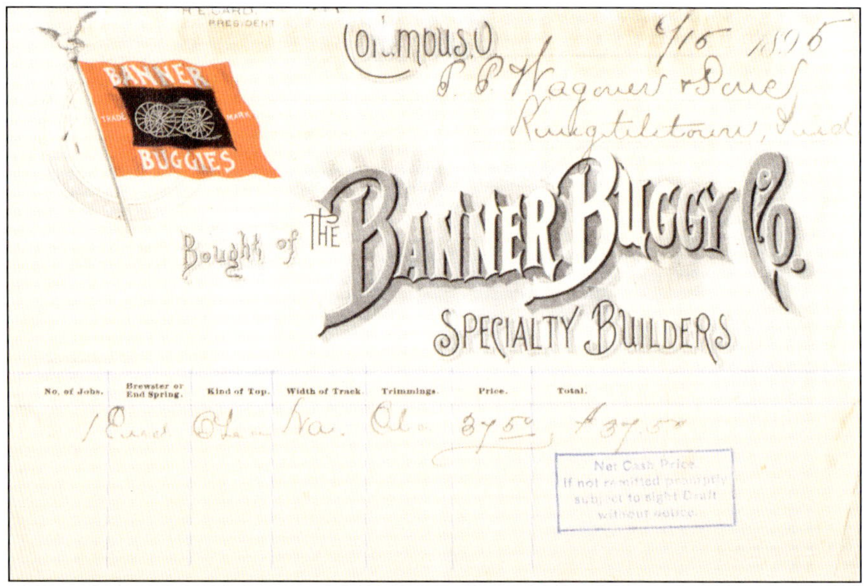

Banner Buggy Company billhead, Columbus, Ohio. Dated 1895, $5-6.

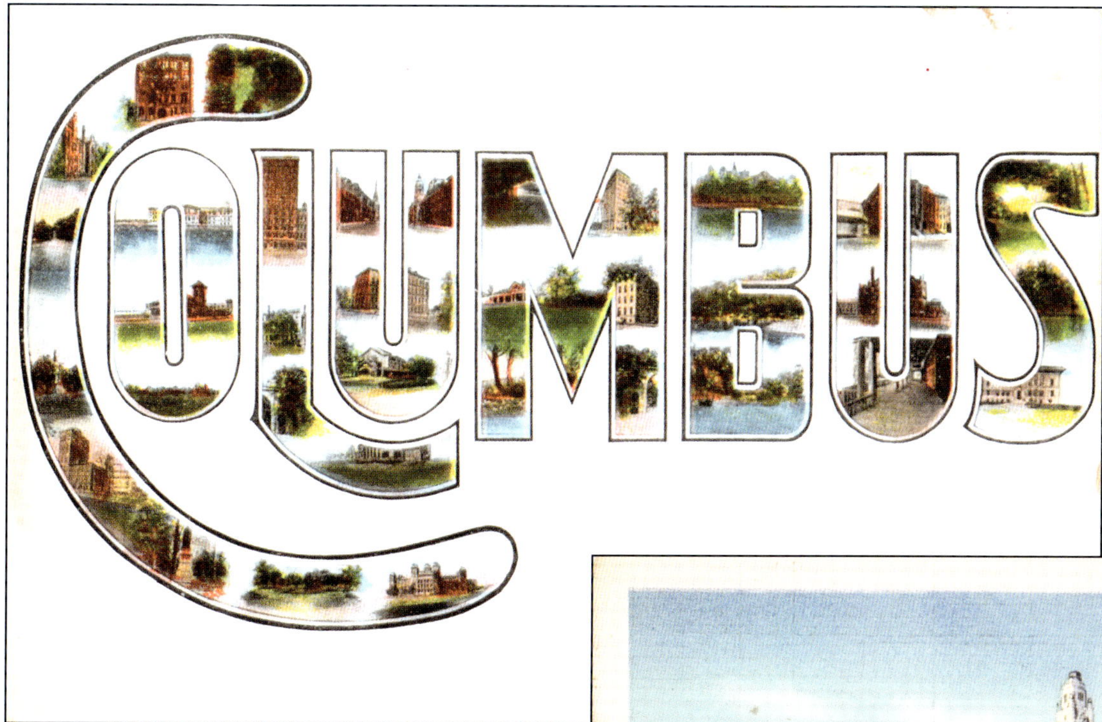

Columbus greeting postcard. Circa 1910, $2-3.

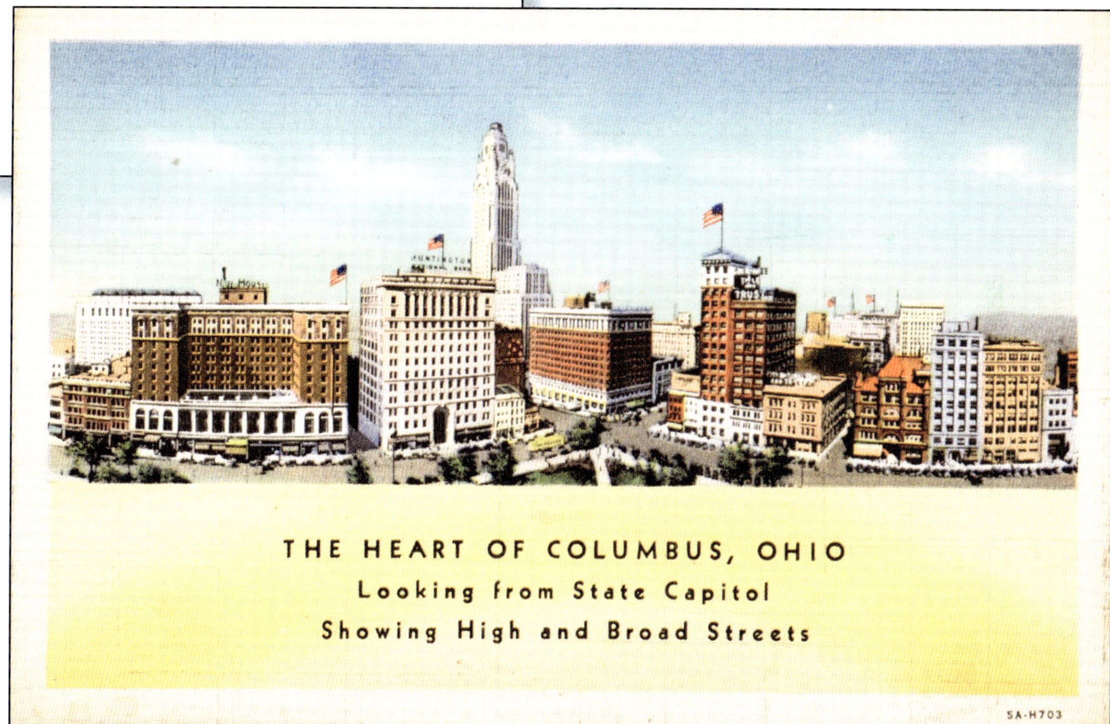

The Heart of Columbus. Postmarked 1936, $3-4. The back reads: *"I am in Columbus this week. I am missing the first week of school but can make that up. I am at the 4-H Club Congress. They chose me as a delegate from Van Wert and paid my expenses so I couldn't miss such an opportunity. We are staying at the Mack Hall. Sure having a swell time."*

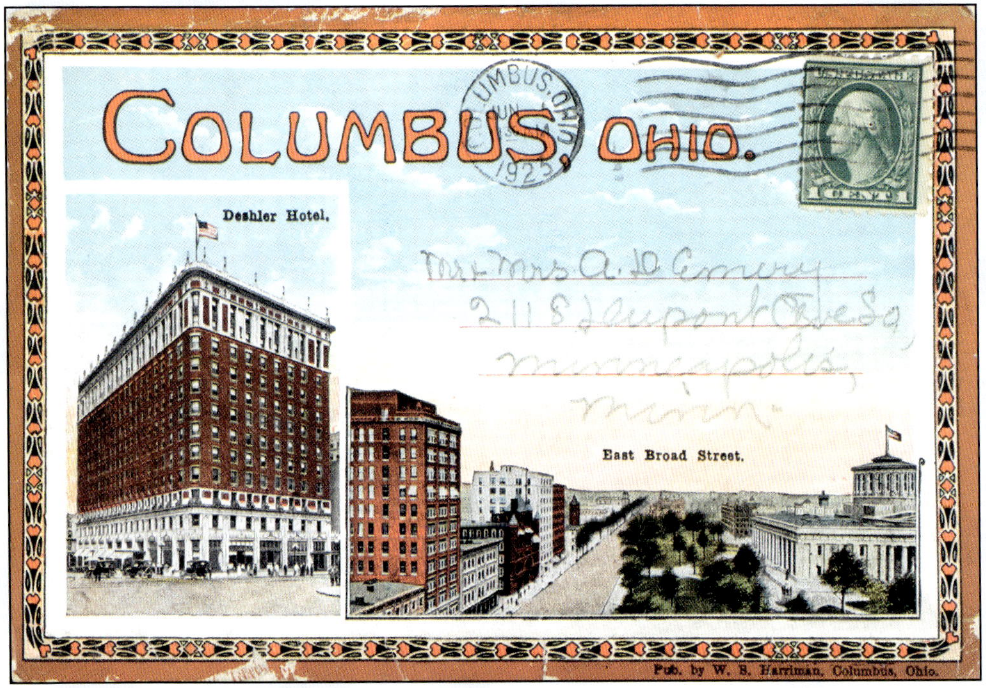

Columbus, Ohio postcard folder. Postmarked 1925, $3-4.

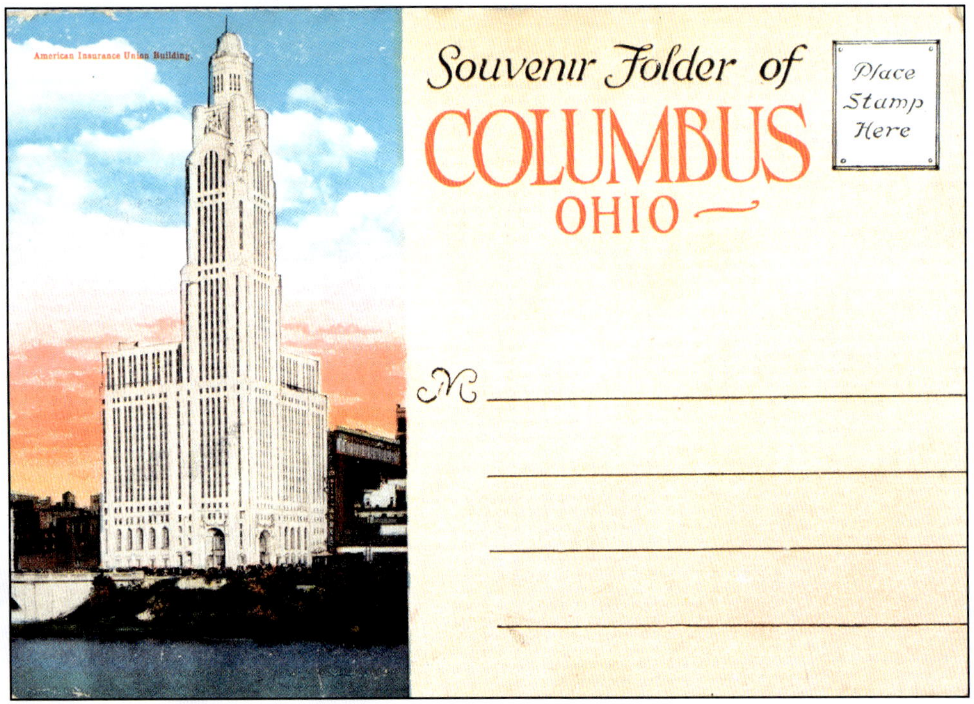

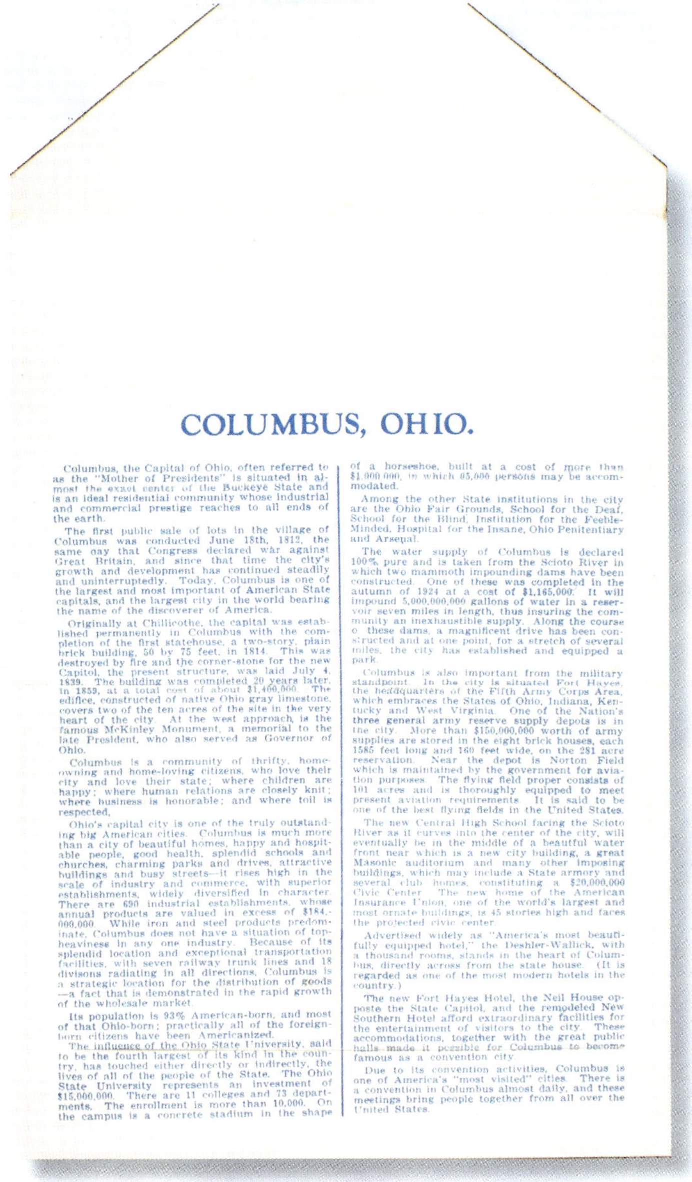

COLUMBUS, OHIO.

Columbus, the Capital of Ohio, often referred to as the "Mother of Presidents" is situated in almost the exact center of the Buckeye State and is an ideal residential community whose industrial and commercial prestige reaches to all ends of the earth.

The first public sale of lots in the village of Columbus was conducted June 18th, 1812, the same day that Congress declared war against Great Britain, and since that time the city's growth and development has continued steadily and uninterruptedly. Today, Columbus is one of the largest and most important of American State capitals, and the largest city in the world bearing the name of the discoverer of America.

Originally at Chillicothe, the capital was established permanently in Columbus with the completion of the first statehouse, a two-story, plain brick building, 50 by 75 feet, in 1814. This was destroyed by fire and the corner-stone for the new Capitol, the present structure, was laid July 4, 1839. The building was completed 20 years later, in 1859, at a total cost of about $1,400,000. The edifice, constructed of native Ohio gray limestone, covers two of the ten acres of the site in the very heart of the city. At the west approach, is the famous McKinley Monument, a memorial to the late President, who also served as Governor of Ohio.

Columbus is a community of thrifty, home-owning and home-loving citizens, who love their city and love their state; where children are happy; where human relations are closely knit; where business is honorable; and where toil is respected.

Ohio's capital city is one of the truly outstanding big American cities. Columbus is much more than a city of beautiful homes, happy and hospitable people, good health, splendid schools and churches, charming parks and drives, attractive buildings and busy streets—it rises high in the scale of industry and commerce, with superior establishments, widely diversified in character. There are 690 industrial establishments, whose annual products are valued in excess of $184,000,000. While iron and steel products predominate, Columbus does not have a situation of top-heaviness in any one industry. Because of its splendid location and exceptional transportation facilities, with seven railway trunk lines and 18 divisons radiating in all directions, Columbus is a strategic location for the distribution of goods—a fact that is demonstrated in the rapid growth of the wholesale market.

Its population is 93% American-born, and most of that Ohio-born; practically all of the foreign-born citizens have been Americanized.

The influence of the Ohio State University, said to be the fourth largest of its kind in the country, has touched either directly or indirectly, the lives of all of the people of the State. The Ohio State University represents an investment of $15,000,000. There are 11 colleges and 73 departments. The enrollment is more than 10,000. On the campus is a concrete stadium in the shape of a horseshoe, built at a cost of more than $1,000,000, in which 65,000 persons may be accommodated.

Among the other State institutions in the city are the Ohio Fair Grounds, School for the Deaf, School for the Blind, Institution for the Feeble-Minded, Hospital for the Insane, Ohio Penitentiary and Arsenal.

The water supply of Columbus is declared 100% pure and is taken from the Scioto River in which two mammoth impounding dams have been constructed. One of these was completed in the autumn of 1924 at a cost of $1,165,000. It will impound 5,000,000,000 gallons of water in a reservoir seven miles in length, thus insuring the community an inexhaustible supply. Along the course o these dams, a magnificent drive has been constructed and at one point, for a stretch of several miles, the city has established and equipped a park.

Columbus is also important from the military standpoint. In the city is situated Fort Hayes, the headquarters of the Fifth Army Corps Area, which embraces the States of Ohio, Indiana, Kentucky and West Virginia. One of the Nation's three general army reserve supply depots is in the city. More than $150,000,000 worth of army supplies are stored in the eight brick houses, each 1585 feet long and 160 feet wide, on the 281 acre reservation. Near the depot is Norton Field which is maintained by the government for aviation purposes. The flying field proper consists of 101 acres and is thoroughly equipped to meet present aviation requirements. It is said to be one of the best flying fields in the United States.

The new Central High School facing the Scioto River as it curves into the center of the city, will eventually be in the middle of a beautful water front near which is a new city building, a great Masonic auditorium and many other imposing buildings, which may include a State armory and several club homes, constituting a $20,000,000 Civic Center. The new home of the American Insurance Union, one of the world's largest and most ornate buildings, is 45 stories high and faces the projected civic center.

Advertised widely as "America's most beautifully equipped hotel," the Deshler-Wallick, with a thousand rooms, stands in the heart of Columbus, directly across from the state house. (It is regarded as one of the most modern hotels in the country.)

The new Fort Hayes Hotel, the Neil House opposte the State Capitol, and the remodeled New Southern Hotel afford extraordinary facilities for the entertainment of visitors to the city. These accommodations, together with the great public halls made it possible for Columbus to become famous as a convention city.

Due to its convention activities, Columbus is one of America's "most visited" cities. There is a convention in Columbus almost daily, and these meetings bring people together from all over the United States.

Souvenir Folder of Columbus, Ohio. Circa 1920s, $3-4.

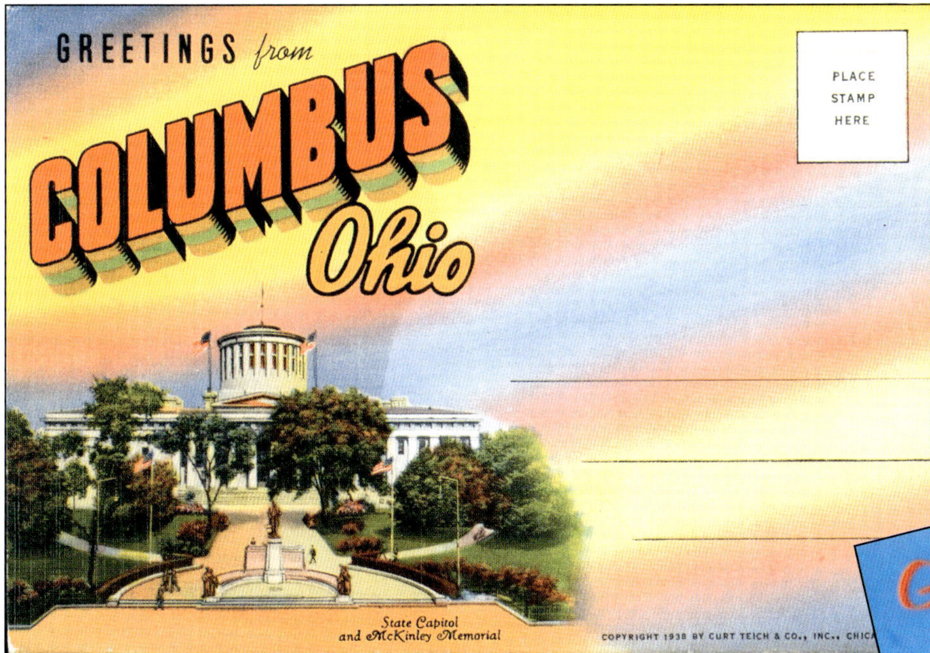

Greetings From Columbus, Ohio. Copyright 1938, $3-4.

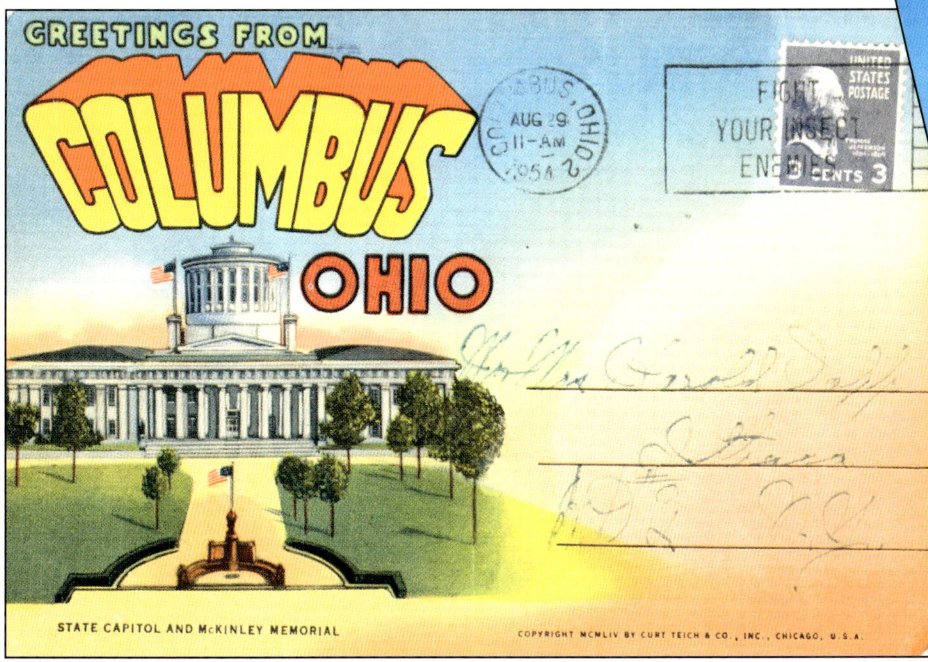

Greetings From Columbus, Ohio. Copyright 1954, $3-4.

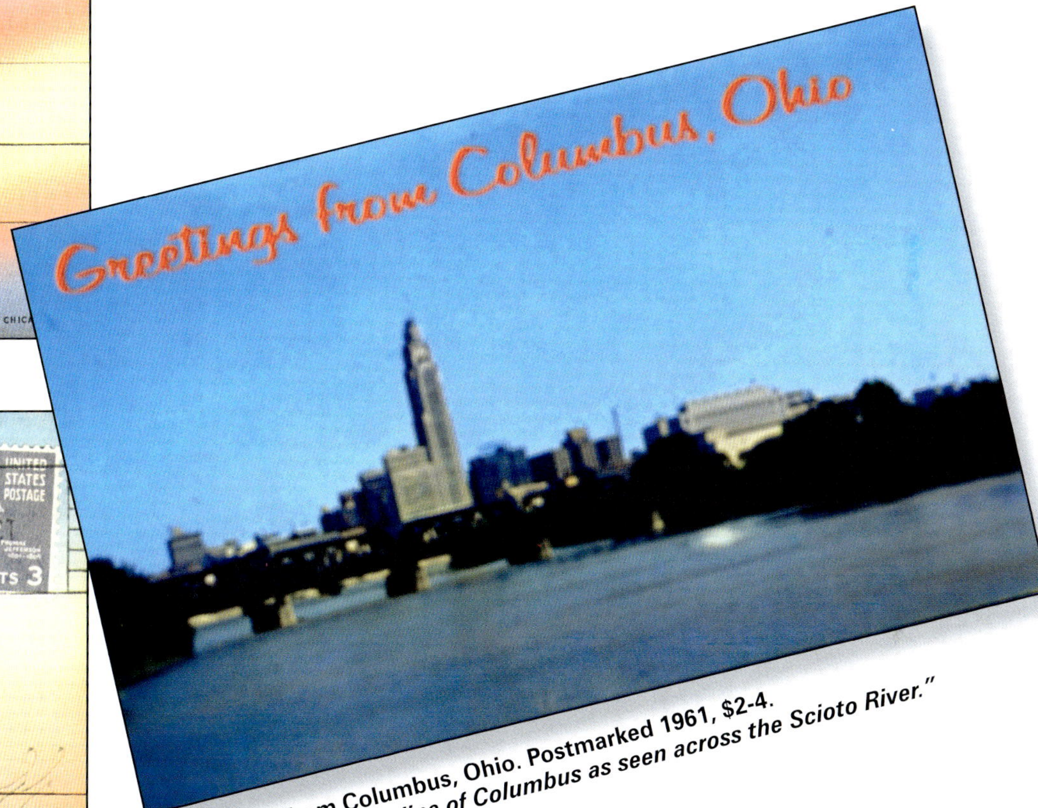

Greetings From Columbus, Ohio. Postmarked 1961, $2-4. The back reads, *"Skyline of Columbus as seen across the Scioto River."*

Chapter One: Street Scenes

Just follow this street straight out of town.
—*A line from the movie, "American Graffiti"*

Just as postcards were gaining popularity in the early twentieth century, the streets of downtown Columbus were becoming busy thoroughfares.

Horse and buggies dodged not only trolley cars, but also the occasional automobile. Signs advertised the "new idea in millinery" for ladies of fashion. Other signs, meanwhile, offered the hungry masses meals for twenty-five cents each.

Along High Street was travel agencies offering European tours, dentists' offices, dry goods stores, beer taverns, and a laundromat or two.

Columbus gradually expanded from its virtually bustling High, Broad, Gay, Front, and State streets to more business, more social intercourse, and more traffic in other distant locations.

"Columbus is much more than a city of attractive buildings and busy streets," noted a colorful postcard folder of city scenes in the early 1920s, "it rises high in the scale of industry and commerce, with superior establishments widely diversified in character."

Still, the city maintained its appreciation for its thriving and numerous streets.

During World War II, a booklet was mailed to some soldiers courtesy of a Columbus department store to remind them of their good old hometown. Complete with photographs of the downtown area, the narrative read in part:

"Hello...from Broad and High! Here are the true crossroads of Central Ohio...The Broad and High you have kept tucked in your memories. The Broad and High with those passing bevies of pretty girls heralding spring as they parade along in their bright, gay clothes...the bumper-to-bumper summer tourist traffic streaming past Deshler corner...the throngs of fans converging on the day of an Ohio State-Michigan football game...the Holiday shoppers bustling by with arms full of gifts at Christmas time... Yes, it's your Broad and High."

It added, bitter-sweetly:

"Wherever you are, and whatever you are doing...remember, these spots still stand. There is Griggs Dam, the Zoo, High School, your favorite Dine & Dance stop, and even the Theatres. They are all here...they'll be here when you return."

Best-selling author John Gunther wrote in the book, *Inside U.S.A.*, of his personal visit to the city:

"Columbus today is a spacious and friendly town," he commented, adding that, "a big issue is apt to be whether or not to cut down the trees as so make a street broader."

The year was 1947.

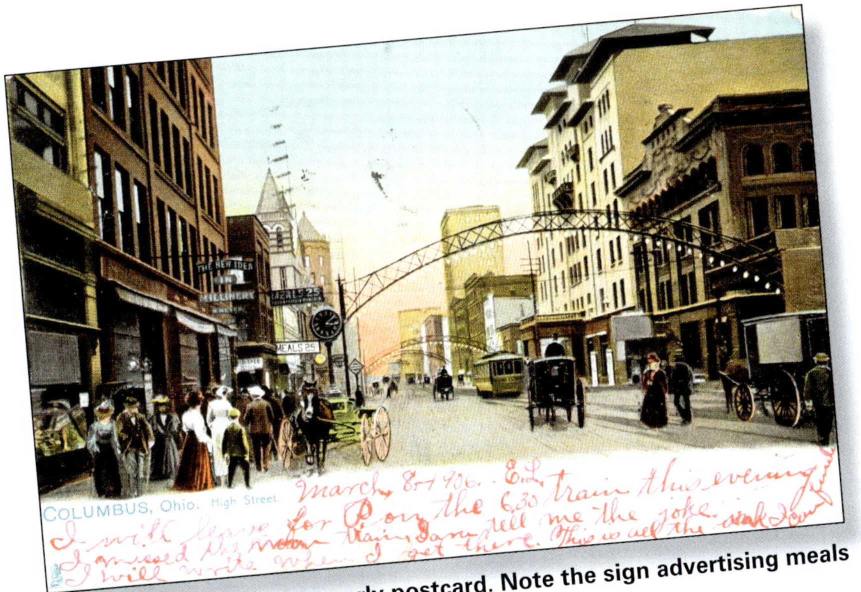

High Street depicted on early postcard. Note the sign advertising meals for twenty-five cents. Postmarked 1906, $5-6.

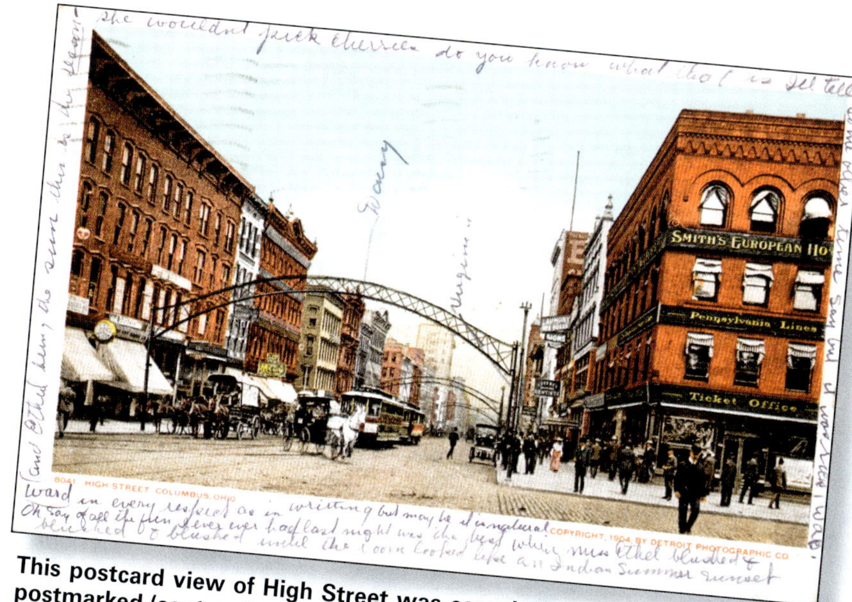

This postcard view of High Street was copyrighted in 1904, but wasn't postmarked (sent out) until 1906, $5-6.

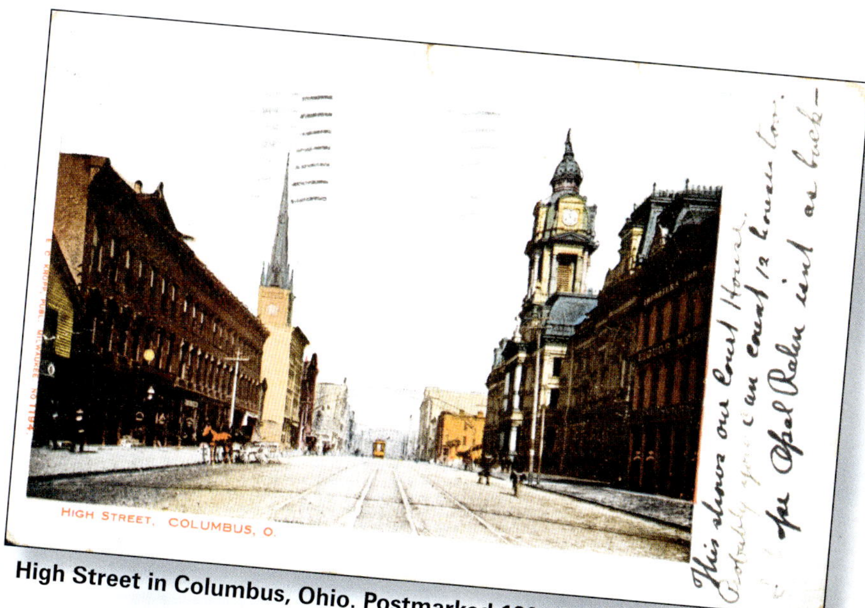

High Street in Columbus, Ohio. Postmarked 1906, $4-5.

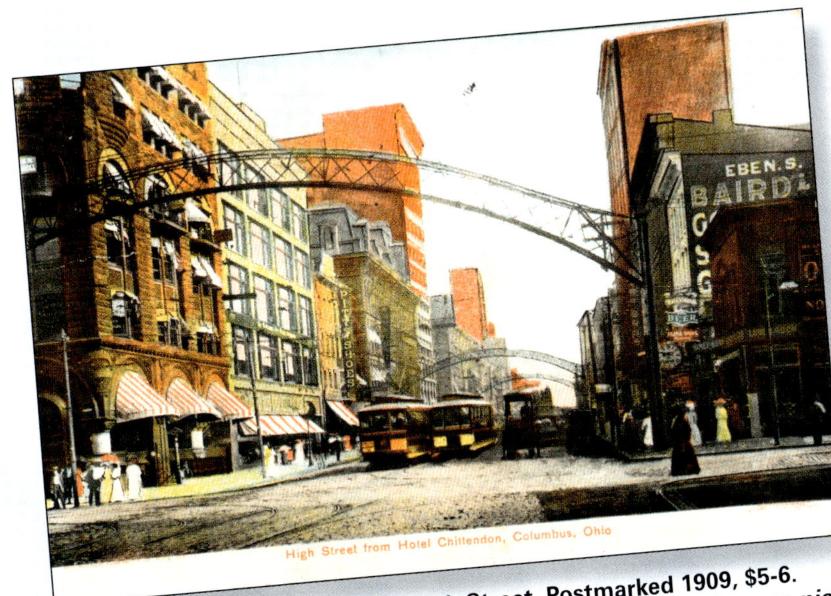

View from Hotel Chittendon on High Street. Postmarked 1909, $5-6. The hand-written message on back reads: *"This street looks very nice at night, all these arches over the street are electric lights and make the street very light."*

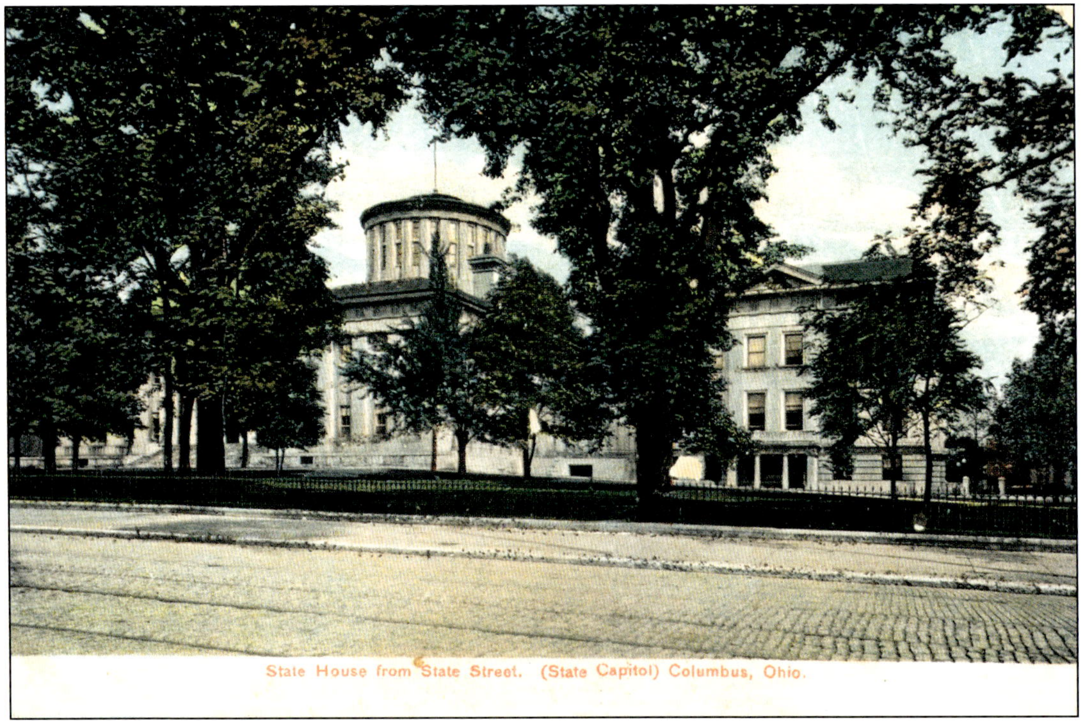

State House from State Street, Columbus, Ohio. Circa 1910, $3-4.

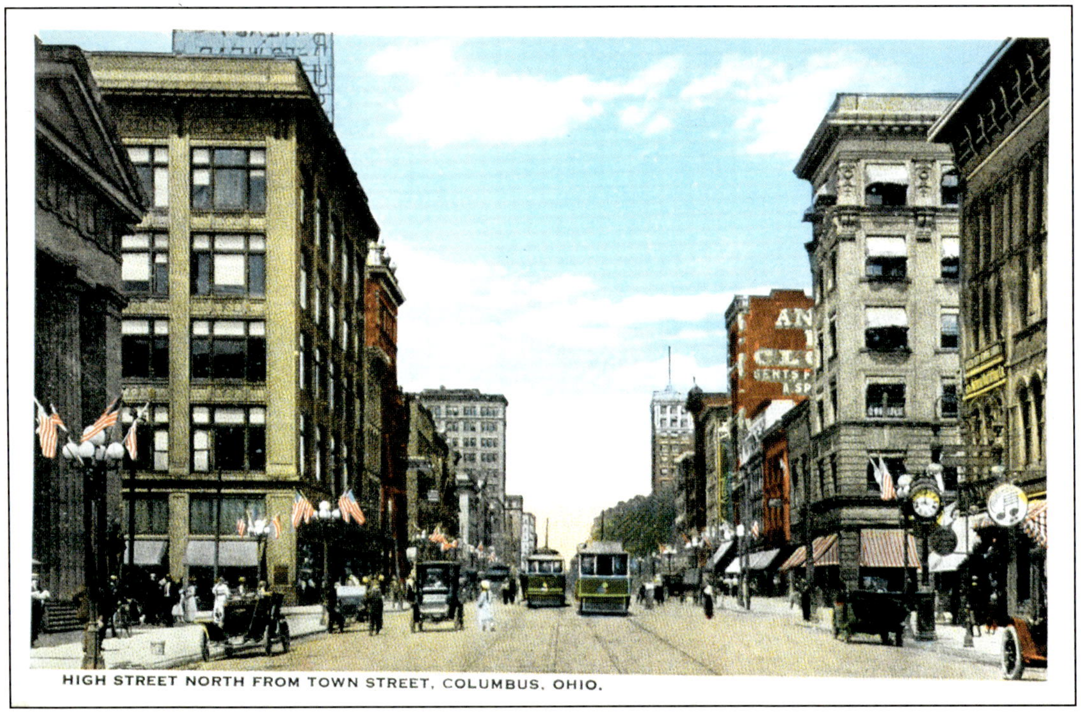

High Street north from Town Street. Circa 1915, $4-5.

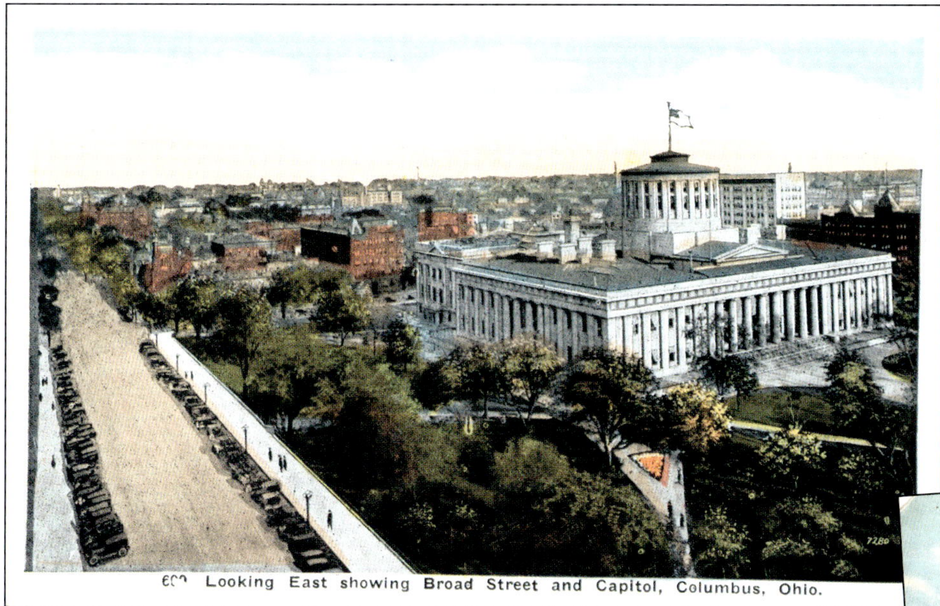

A view of Broad Street looking east. Postmarked 1921, $3-4. Hand-written message on the back reads: *"I am spending the weekend at Buckeye Lake and have wished frequently that you were here. I enjoy watching tem dance in the big pavilion over the lake. The beautiful lighting effect reacts on a person."*

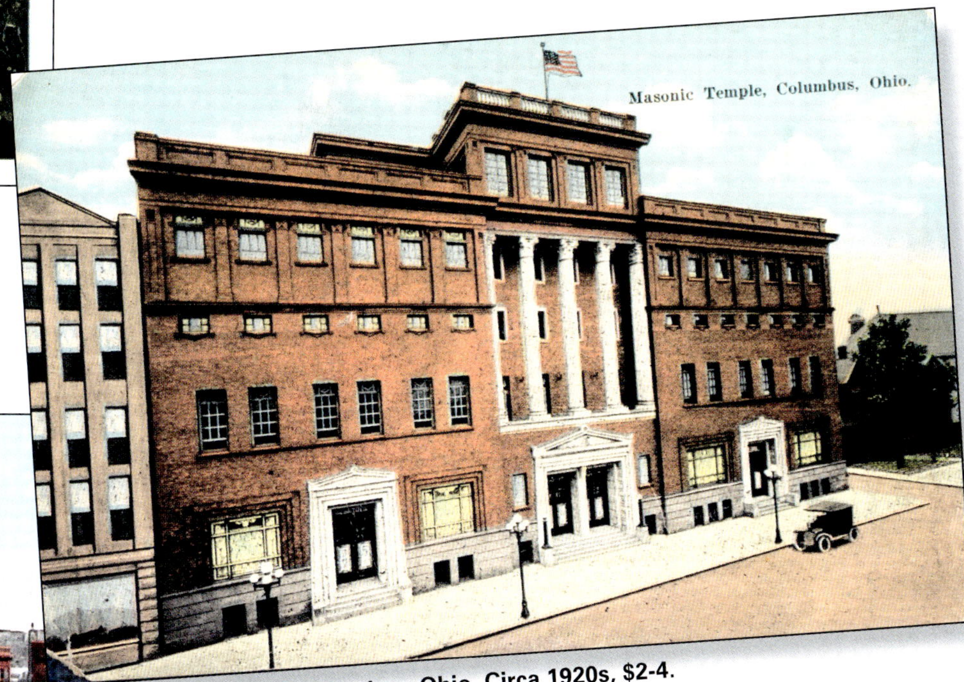

Masonic Temple, Columbus, Ohio. Circa 1920s, $2-4.

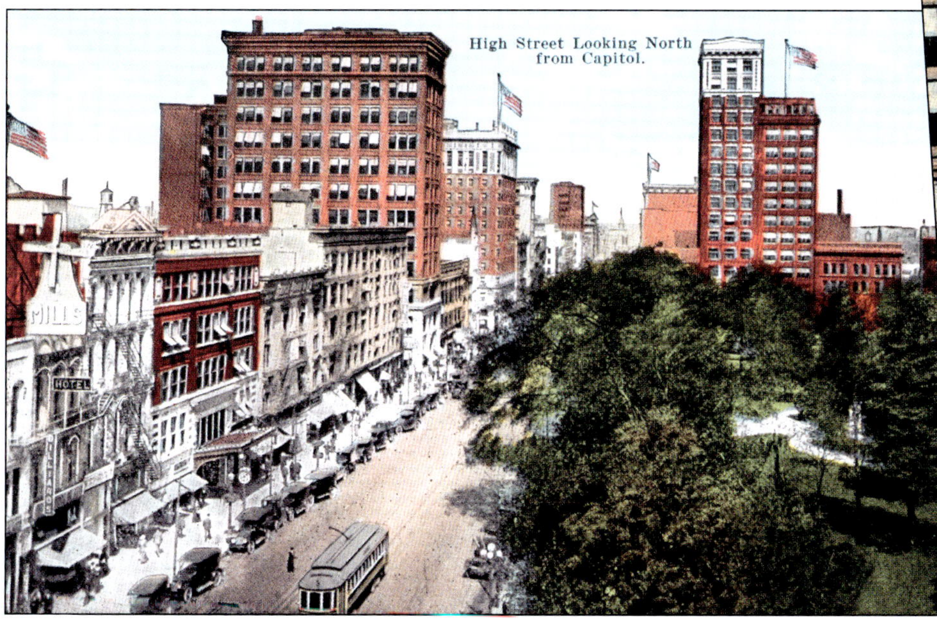

High Street looking north from Capitol. Postmarked 1925, $2-3.

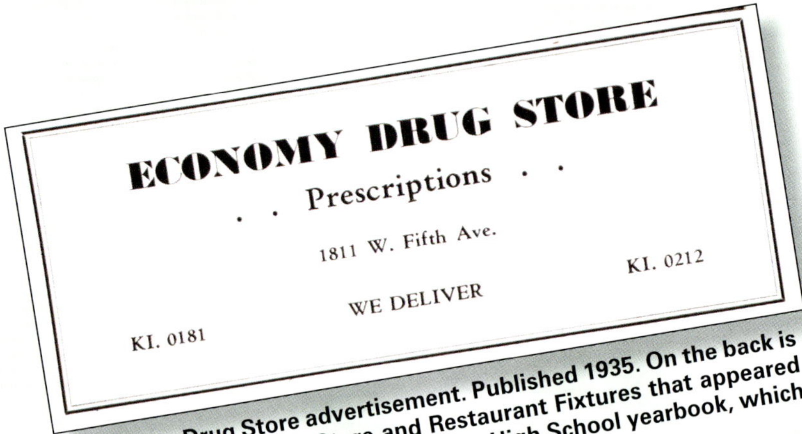

Economy Drug Store advertisement. Published 1935. On the back is an advertisement for Store and Restaurant Fixtures that appeared in the back of the Grandview Heights High School yearbook, which was also published in 1935.

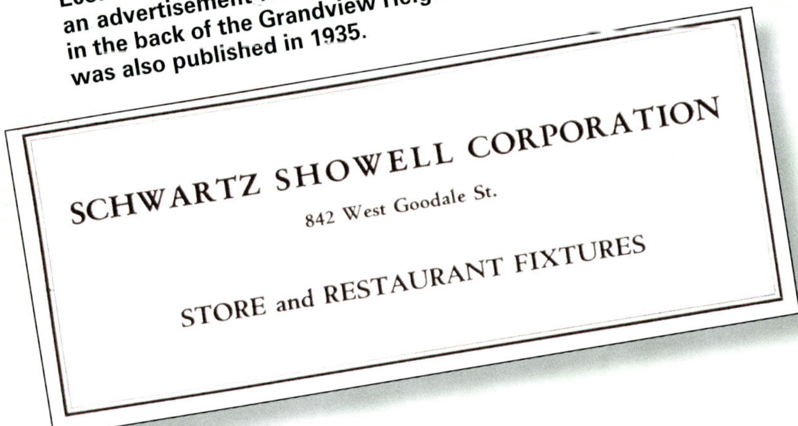

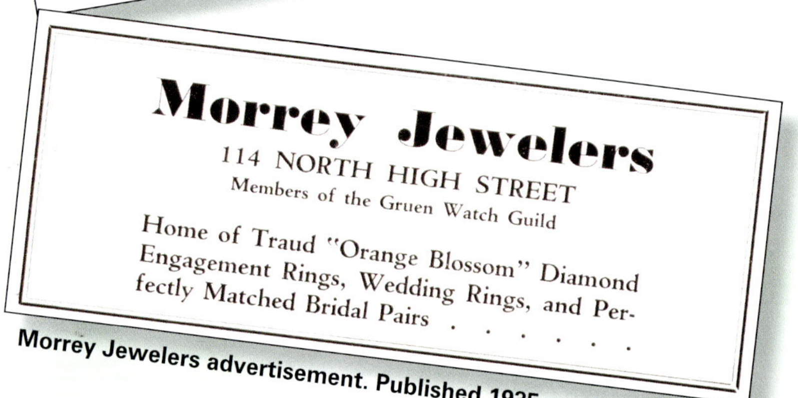

Morrey Jewelers advertisement. Published 1935.

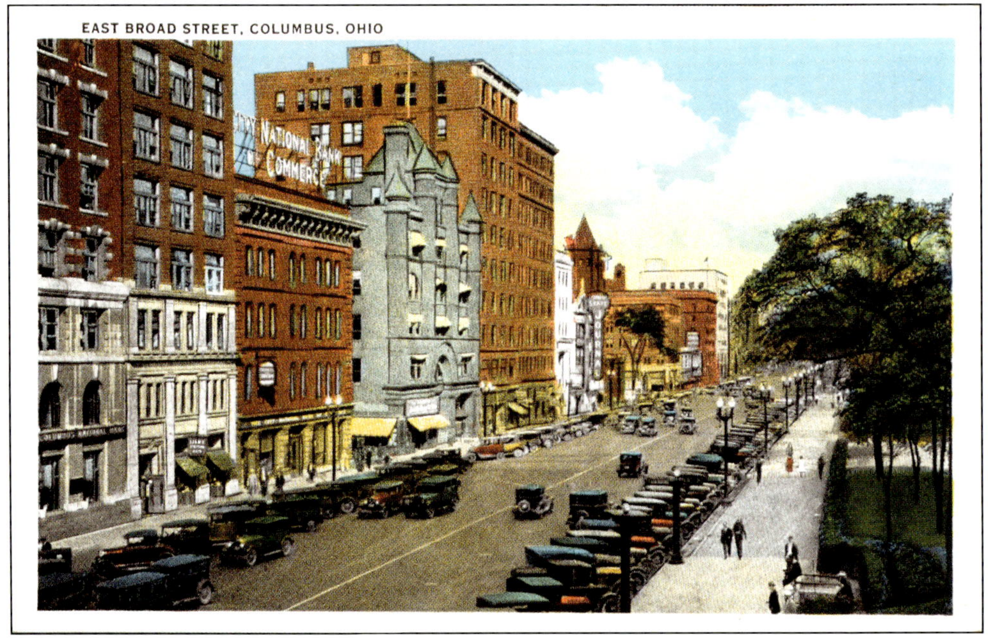

East Broad Street, Columbus, Ohio. Circa 1930s, $3-4.

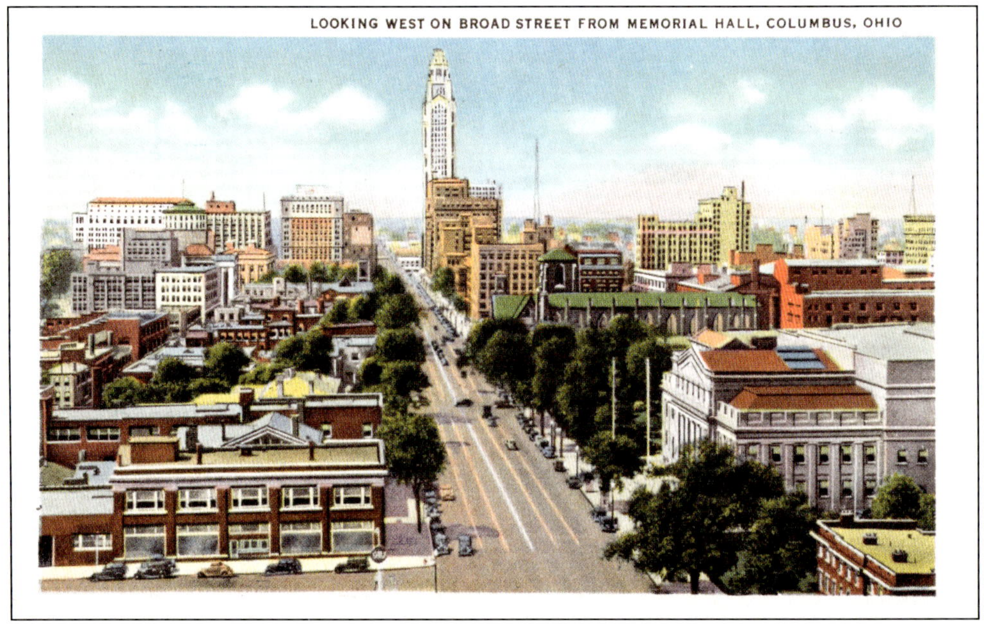

Looking west on Broad Street from Memorial Hall. Circa 1950s, $3-4.

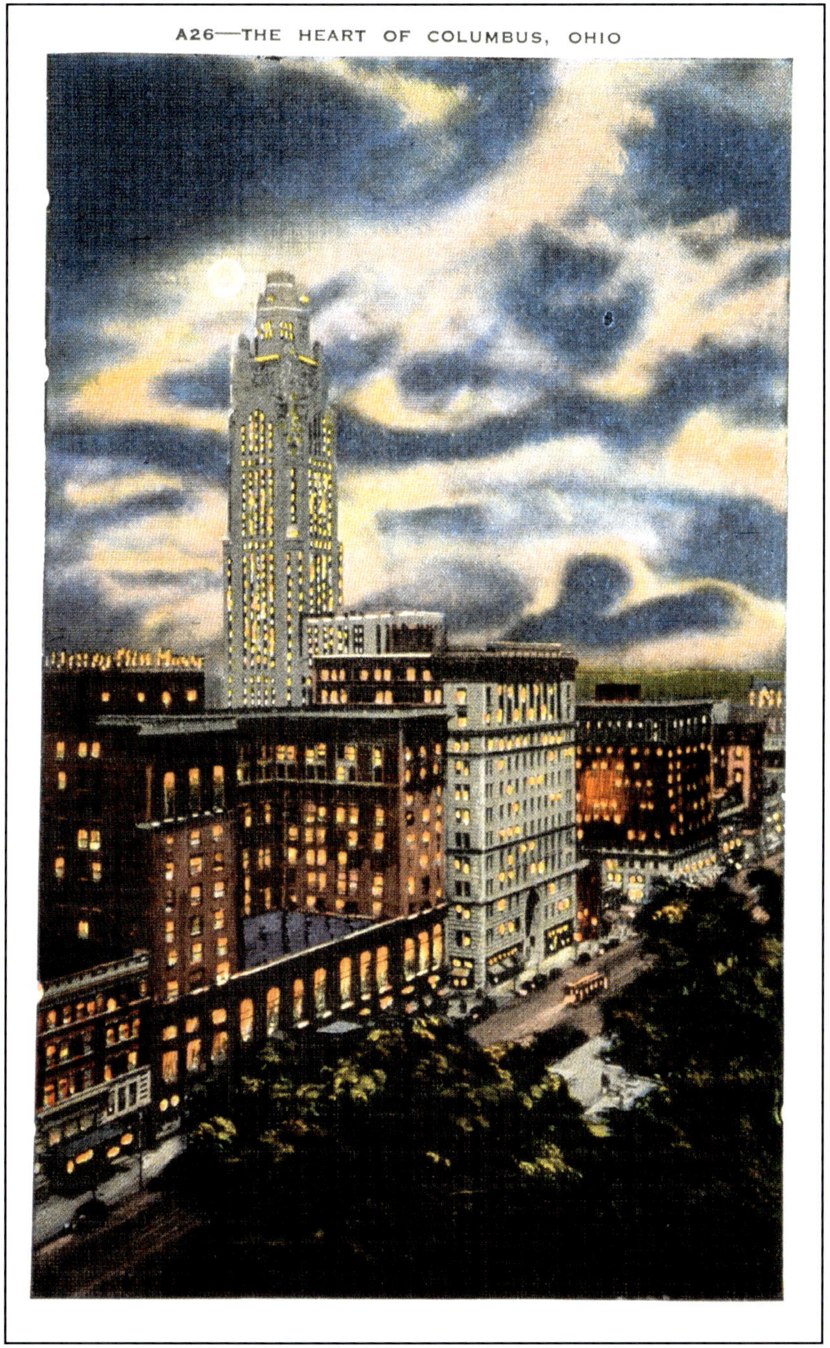

High Street in "heart of Columbus." Circa 1940s, $2-3.

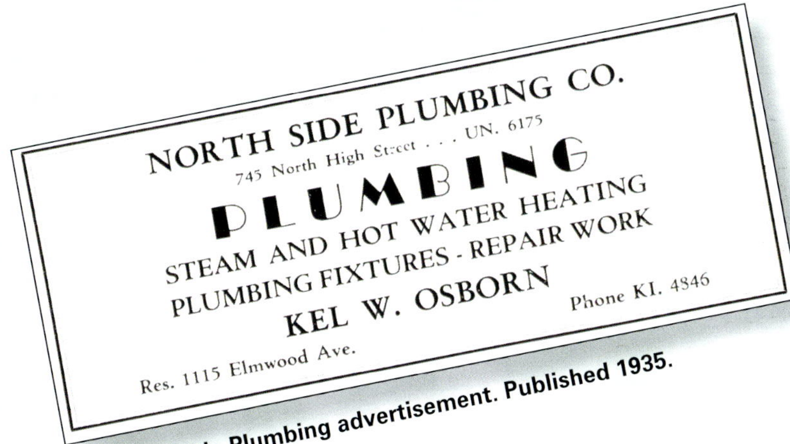

North Side Plumbing advertisement. Published 1935.

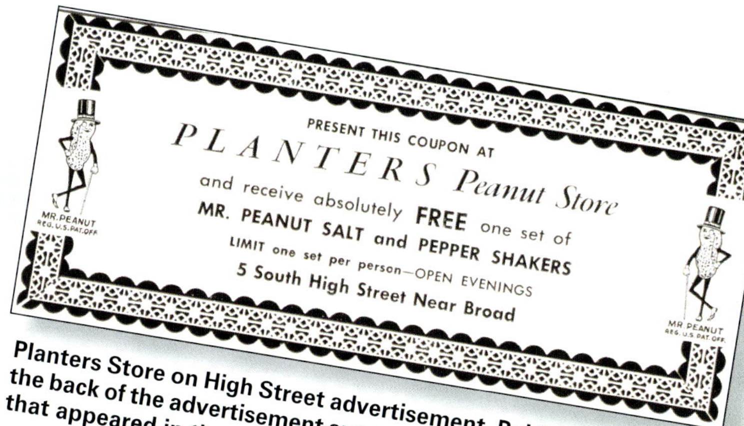

Planters Store on High Street advertisement. Published in 1954. On the back of the advertisement appears snippets from a daily column that appeared in the *Columbus Citizen* published also in 1954.

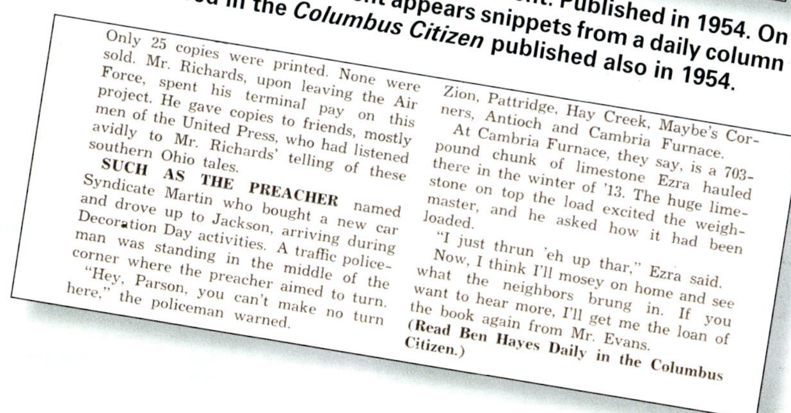

Only 25 copies were printed. None were sold. Mr. Richards, upon leaving the Air Force, spent his terminal pay on this project. He gave copies to friends, mostly men of the United Press, who had listened avidly to Mr. Richards' telling of these southern Ohio tales.

SUCH AS THE PREACHER named Syndicate Martin who bought a new car and drove up to Jackson, arriving during Decoration Day activities. A traffic policeman was standing in the middle of the corner where the preacher aimed to turn.

"Hey, Parson, you can't make no turn here," the policeman warned.

Zion, Pattridge, Hay Creek, Maybe's Corners, Antioch and Cambria Furnace.

At Cambria Furnace, they say, is a 703-pound chunk of limestone Ezra hauled there in the winter of '13. The huge limestone on top the load excited the weighmaster, and he asked how it had been loaded.

"I just thrun 'eh up thar," Ezra said.

Now, I think I'll mosey on home and see what the neighbors brung in. If you want to hear more, I'll get me the loan of the book again from Mr. Evans.

(Read Ben Hayes Daily in the Columbus Citizen.)

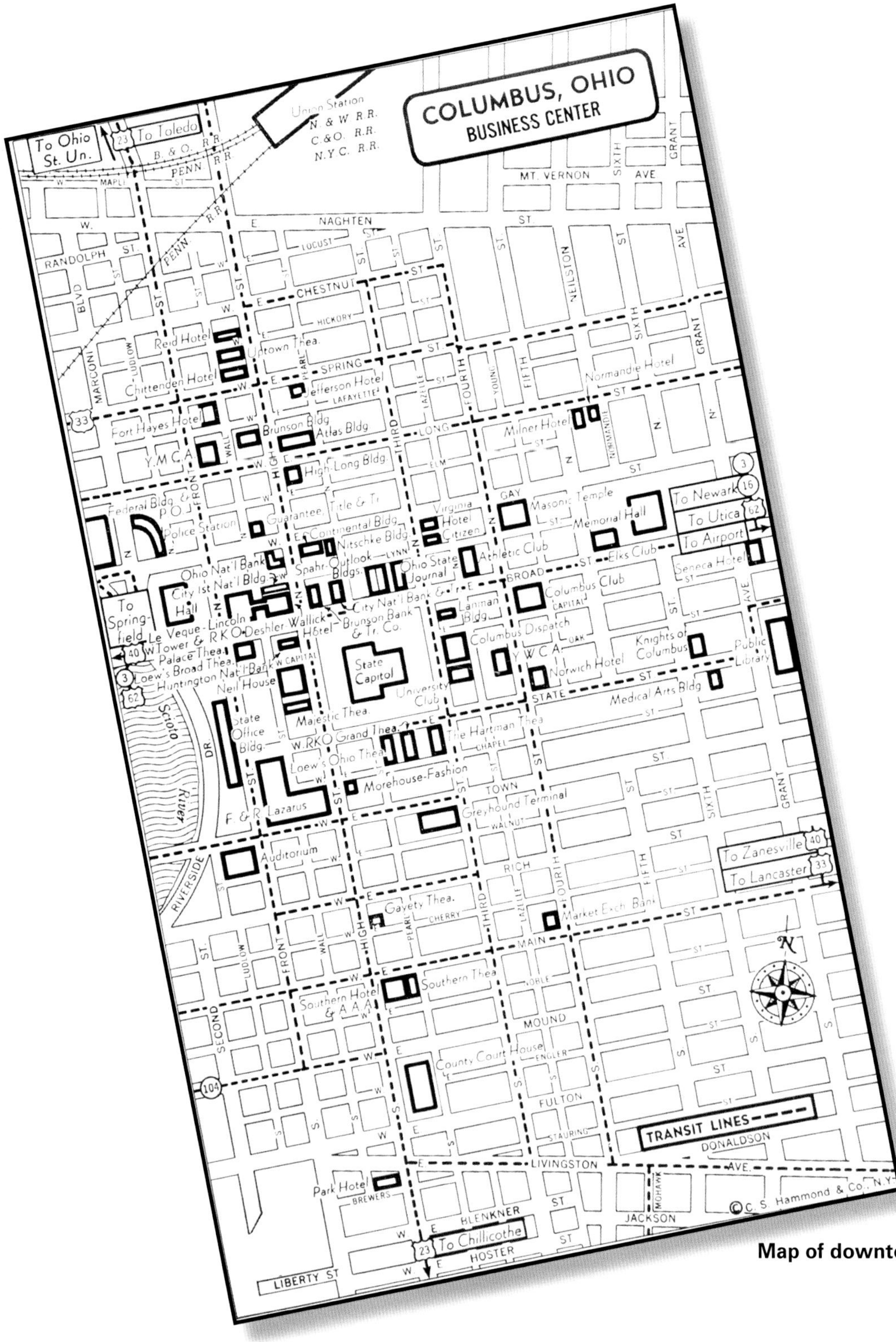

Map of downtown Columbus. Circa 1950s, $3-4.

Chapter Two: City of Beautiful Parks

> When you look at a city, it's like reading the hopes, aspirations, and pride of everyone who built it.
>
> — *Architect Hugh Newell Jacobsen*

Columbus was many things during the twentieth century — including being a city of beautiful parks.

Several early promotional documents made reference to the city's "charming parks." By the 1970s the city officially listed more than one hundred parks and playgrounds in active use, covering nearly 5,500 acres. Among them were the familiar names of Goodale, Fairwood, and Wolfe.

One endearing name that was missing from the list was Olentangy Park.

Vintage postcards are about all that remains of the legendary site that at one time was considered to be the largest amusement park in America.

Technically, the grand park was about five miles north of Columbus in nearby Clintonville. Originally it had been a wooded land at the edge of the Olentangy River. Late in the nineteenth century it became known as The Villa, where it attracted riders on the trolley lines.

The place was renamed Olentangy Park in the late 1890s and began steadily adding attractions for visitors. Early in the twentieth century the continuing number of crowd lures at the park included one of the country's largest theaters, a boat house, a mill ride, and of course a tunnel of love.

Olentangy Park also featured a wild water ride known as Shoot-the-Chutes. It was popular at other parks as well, including Indianola Park, which was also in Columbus. For all of this amusement park glory, Olentangy Park finally closed in early autumn of 1938. The marvelous rides were sold and the grounds were cleared to make way for the Olentangy Village apartment complex. Although the impressive theater building briefly survived, it was destroyed by fire in 1940.

Perhaps the last vestige of the mighty Olentangy Park, an enormous swimming pool, disappeared for good early in the twenty-first century so that the Olentangy Village apartment complex could expand.

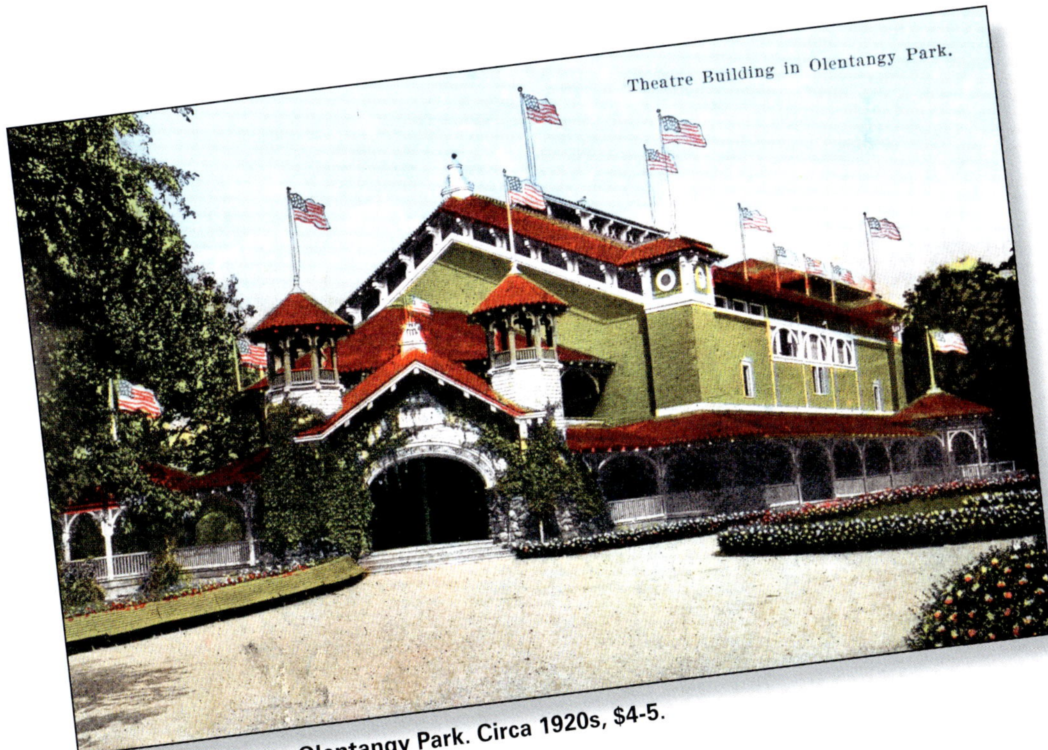

Theatre building in Olentangy Park. Circa 1920s, $4-5.

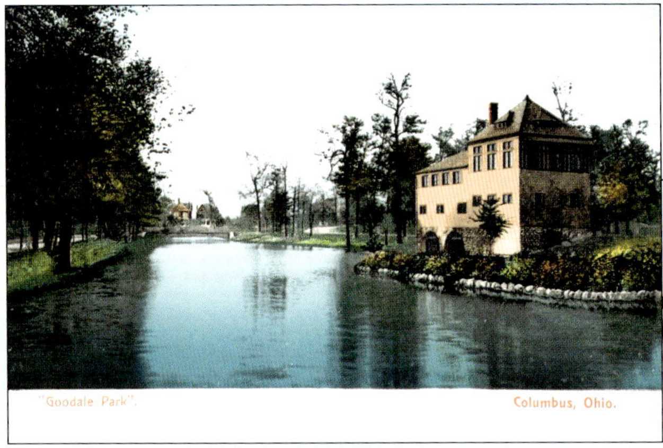

Goodale Park, Columbus, Ohio. Circa 1910, $3-4.

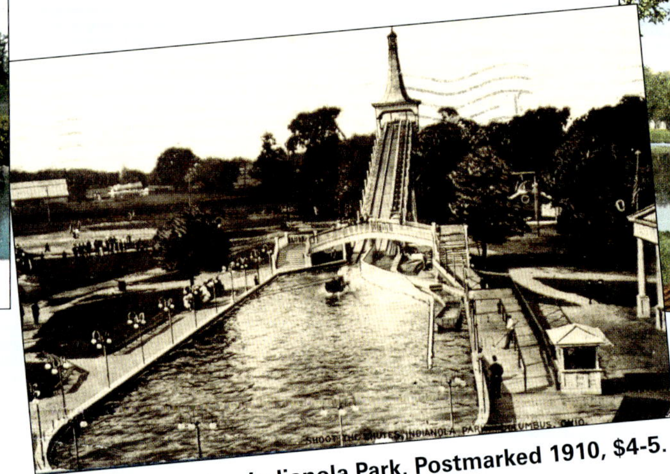

Shoot the Chutes, Indianola Park. Postmarked 1910, $4-5.

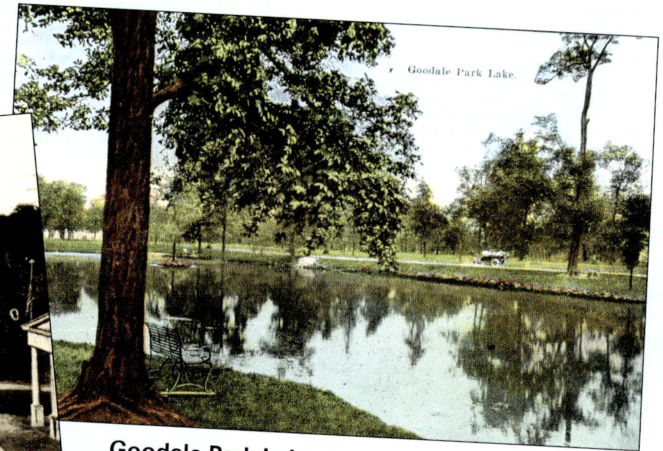

Goodale Park Lake scene. Circa 1920s, $2-3.

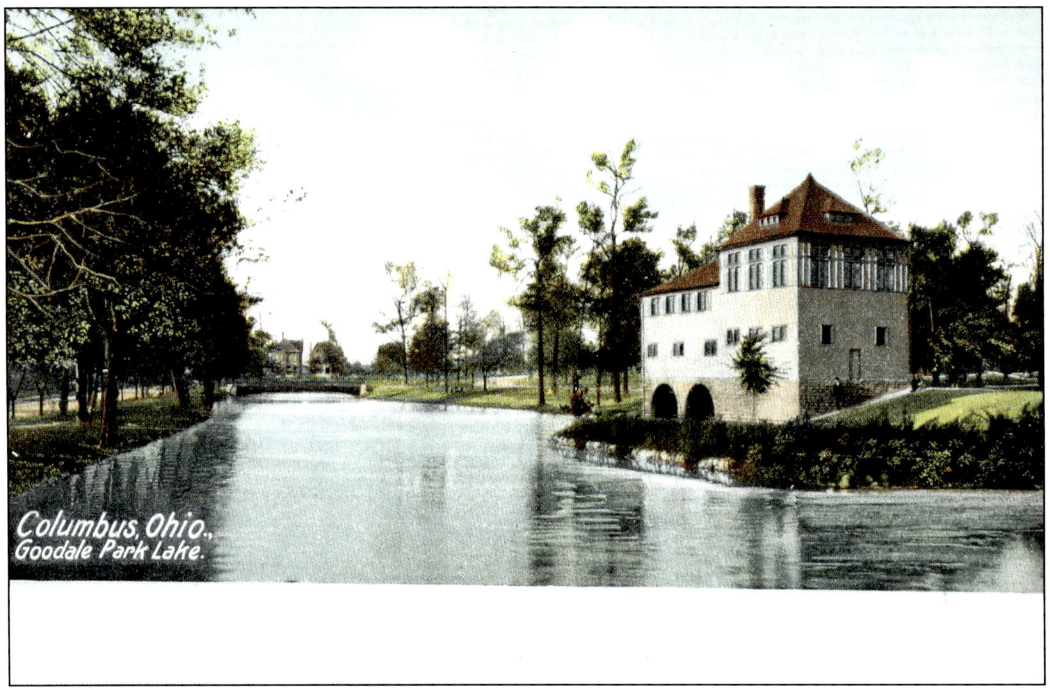

View of Goodale Park Lake. Circa 1910, $3-4.

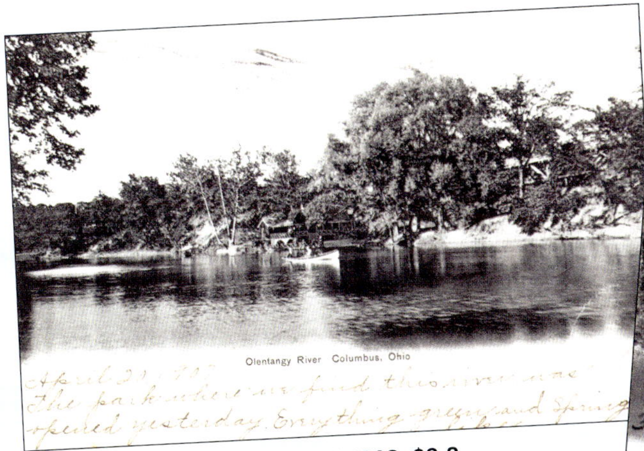

Olentangy River. Postmarked 1908, $2-3. Hand-written message on the back is dated 1907: *"The park where we find this river was opened yesterday. Everything green and Spring-like."*

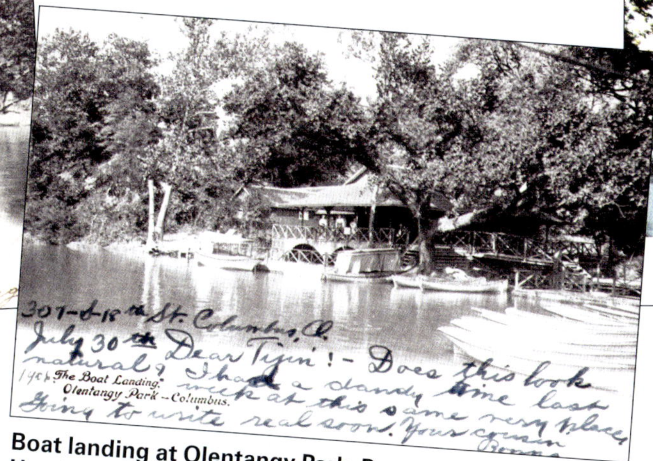

Boat landing at Olentangy Park. Postmarked 1906, $3-4. Hand-written message on back reads: *"Does this look natural? I had a dandy time last week at this same very place."*

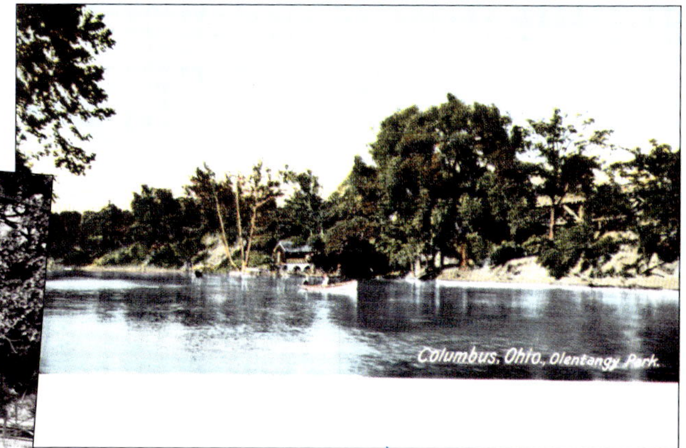

Lake scene at Olentangy Park. Circa 1910, $3-4.

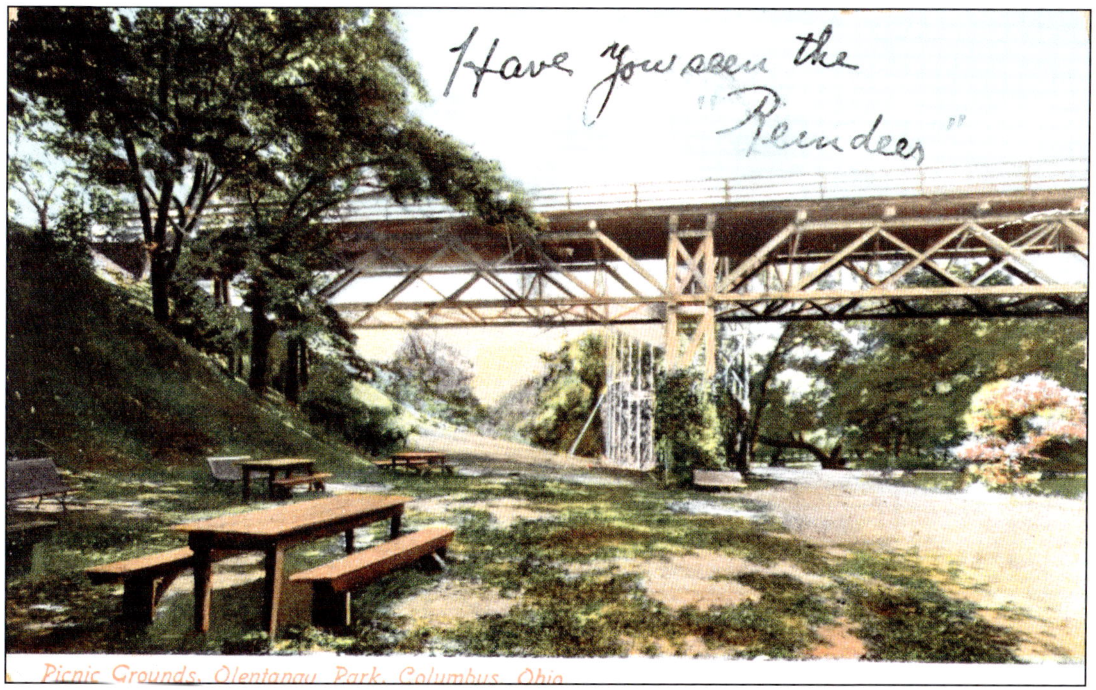

Picnic grounds at Olentangy Park. Postmarked 1909, $4-5.

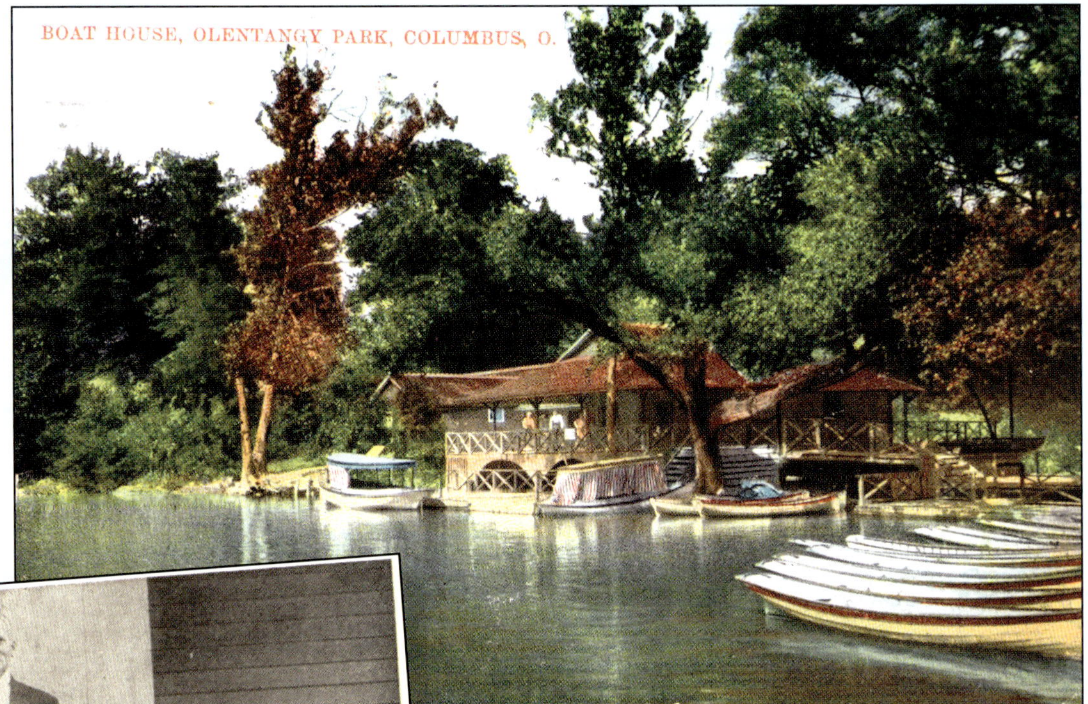

Boat House, Olentangy Park. Postmarked 1907, $3-4.

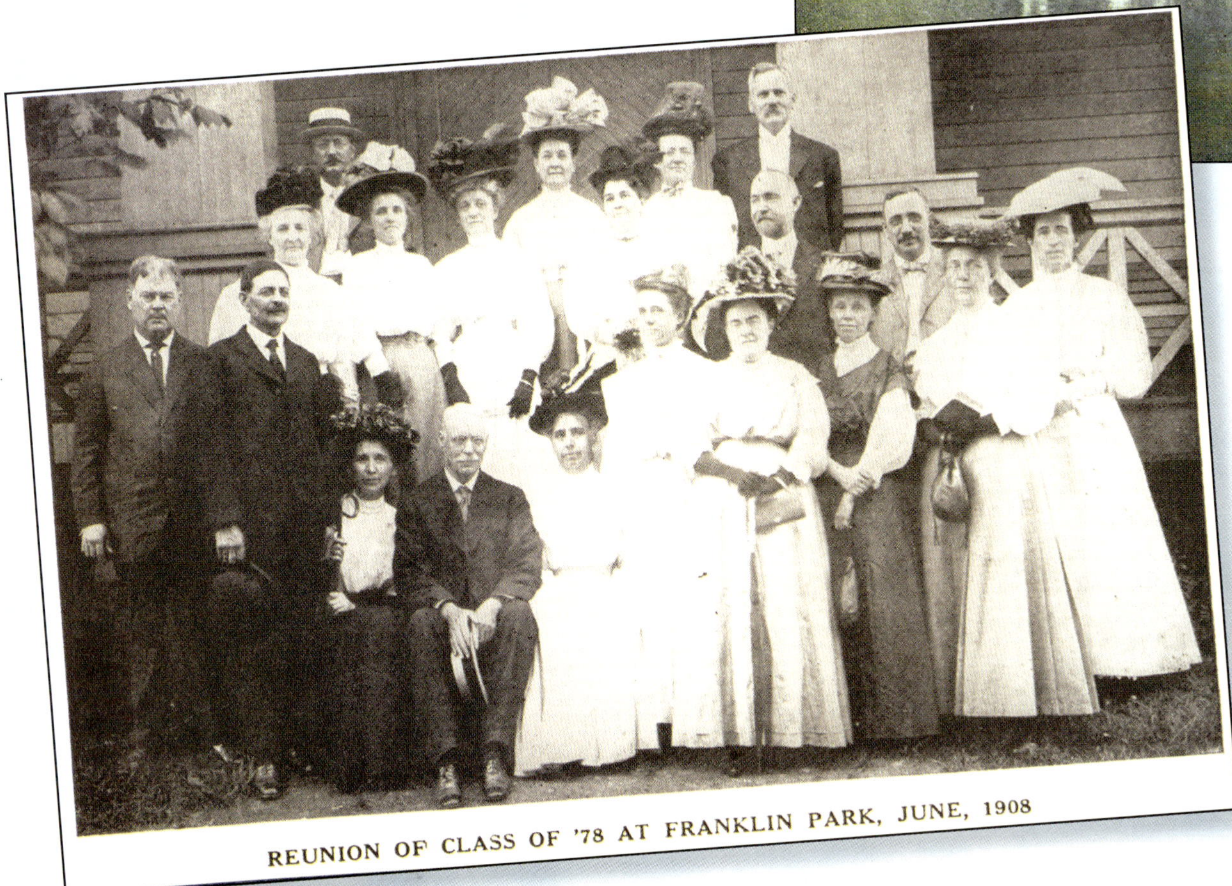

Reunion of class of 1878 at Franklin Park. Dated June of 1908, $8-10.

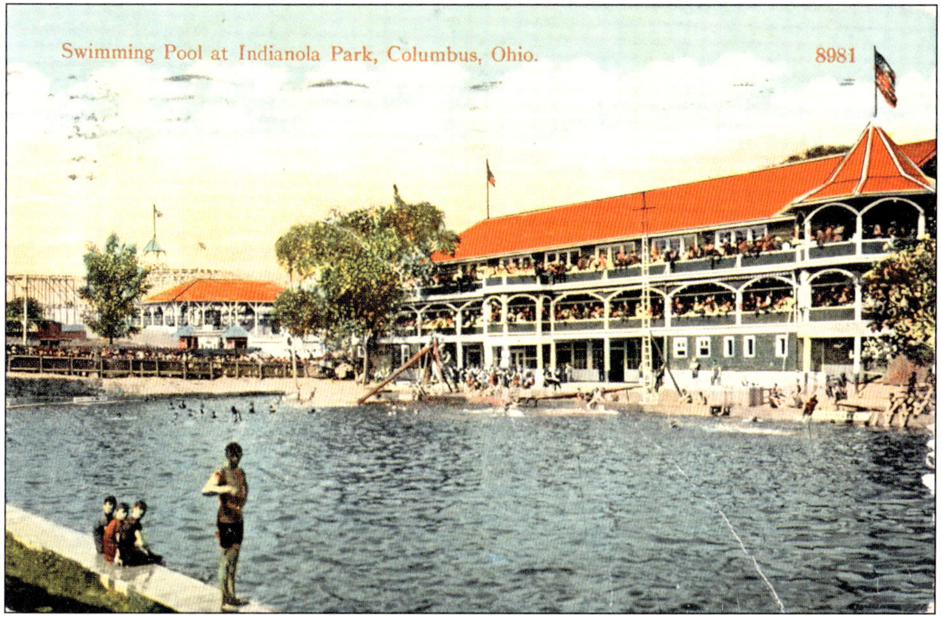

Swimming pool at Indianola Park. Postmarked 1916, $3-5.

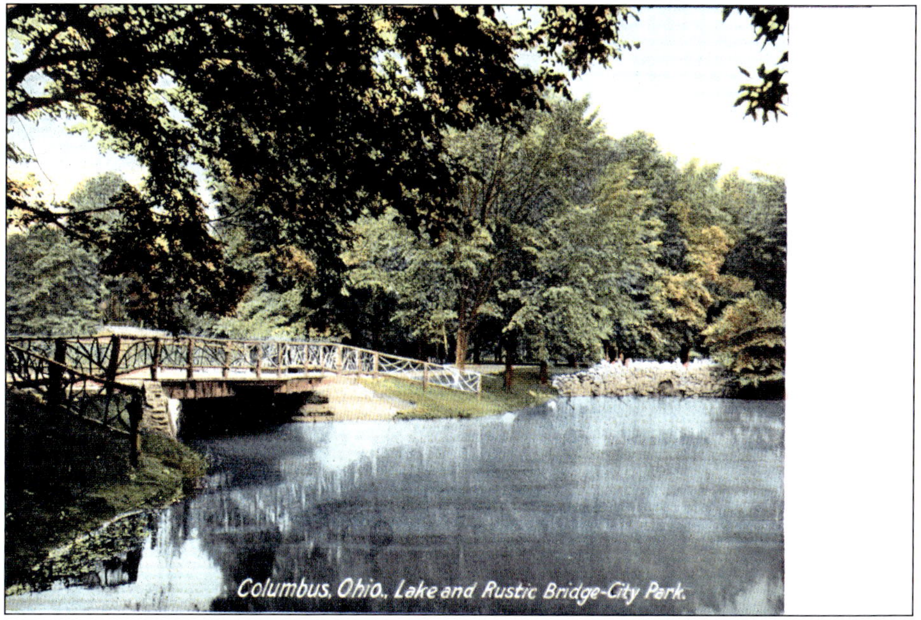

Lake and Rustic Bridge, City Park. Circa 1908, $3-4.

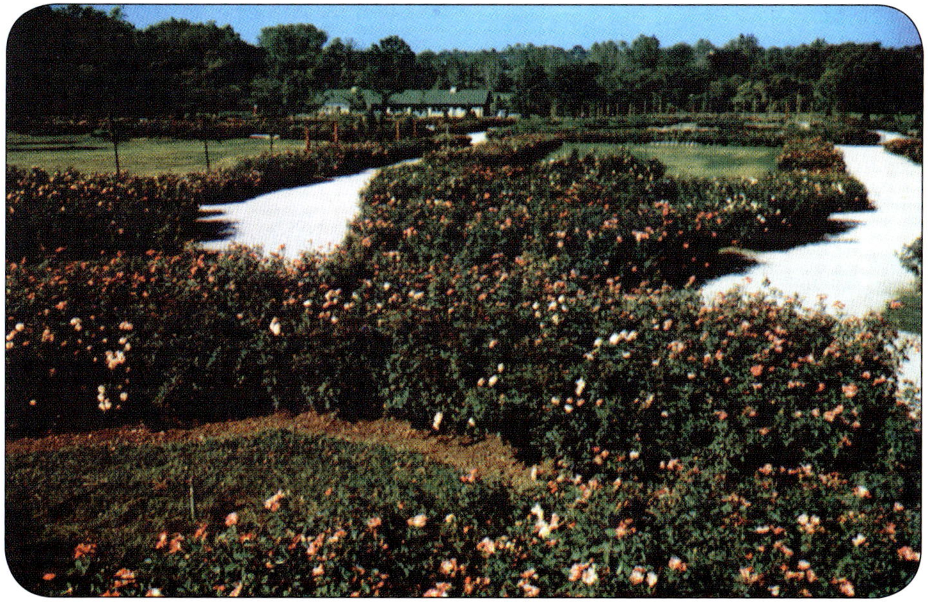

Park of Roses, North High Street. Circa 1960s, $1-2.

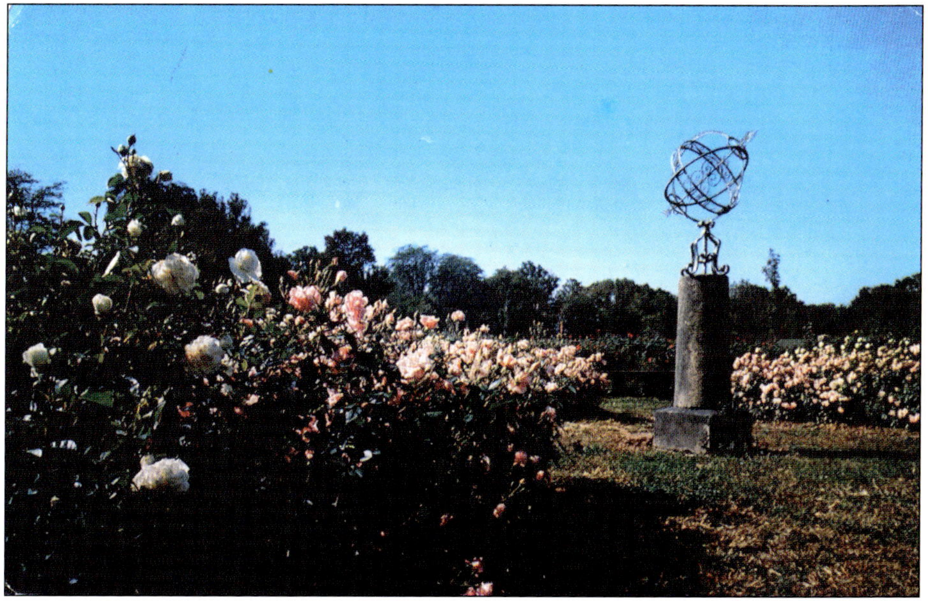

Garden view of Park of Roses. Postmarked 1963, $1-2.

Chapter Three: The Prison

> Our penitentiary, compared to the one in Michigan, is an oubliette out of the Dark Ages.
> — *A Columbus newspaper editor in 1947*

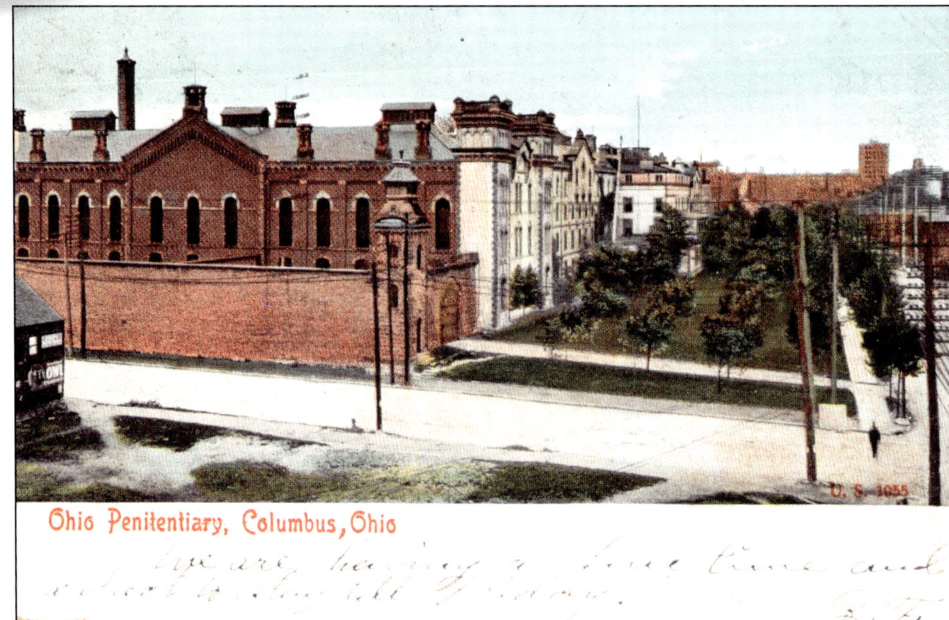

Ohio Penitentiary, Columbus, Ohio. Postmarked 1907, $5-7 Hand-written message on back reads: ***"We are having a fine time and expected to stay till Friday."***

For those not familiar with the term "oubliette," it was pretty much a reference to a dungeon. It is derived from the French word meaning a place of forgetting. In European countries, it conjures up the image of a cell that can only be reached by a trap door in the ceiling.

The unidentified newspaper editor quoted in the beginning of this chapter compared the Ohio Penitentiary to an oubliette while talking to best-selling author John Gunther in the late 1940s. Gunther was writing a book based on his travels around the United States.

The grim, gray Ohio Penitentiary opened in Columbus in 1834—the same year that Columbus officially became a city. At the time many of the prison buildings were still under construction. In just a few years the prison was fully completed and included a special section for female prisoners.

Two things of historical note took place in the prison during the late 1890s: in 1897, an electric chair was installed to replace the gallows that had been used for hanging prisoners for more than a decade; and in 1898 a federal prisoner was transferred to the prison under sentence of embezzlement. The inmate's name was William Porter. Later he would become a famed short-story writer known as "O. Henry."

By most accounts, Porter avoided what was otherwise a fairly harsh life in the Ohio Penitentiary. He was a licensed pharmacist and therefore drew duty in the prison hospital. Rather than a prison cell, his minimum-security status allowed him to have a room in the hospital wing itself. There are some reports that the prisoner actually wrote many of his short stories while locked in the familiar prison.

The origin of the "O. Henry" pseudonym was never fully revealed by the author who penned such enduring stories as "The Ransom of Red Chief" and "The Gift of the Magi." Some said it was taken from the name of one of the prison guards at Columbus while others say it was the name of a friend's cat.

At any rate Porter or O. Henry was freed in 1901 after serving only three years. The bleak prison remained however, and in 1930 one of the worst fires in penitentiary history took more than three hundred lives in the Columbus facility.

In the mid-1950s, the prison population reached an all-time high of more than 5,200 inmates. A fierce riot in 1968 killed five convicts and resulted in damage to numerous prison buildings. By the early 1970s, the exodus from the Ohio Penitentiary had begun—an increasing number of prisoners were transferred to the Southern Ohio Correctional Facility in Lucasville, Ohio. Federal courts ordered the existing prison to close in 1979, however the prison continued operations in a limited capacity until 1984.

In 1995 the city of Columbus purchased the prison from the state of Ohio. Eventually it was demolished, clearing the land for other projects.

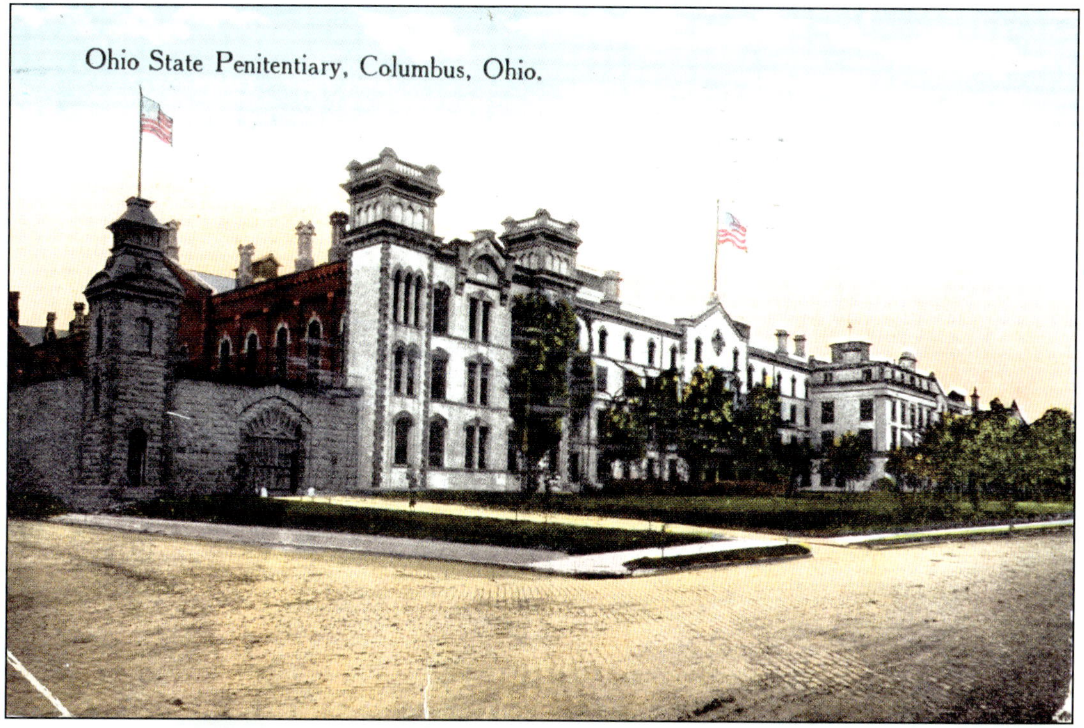

View of Ohio Prison. Postmarked 1916, $3-4. Handwritten message on the back reads: *"If you need me call Bell Main 3104. Harry."*

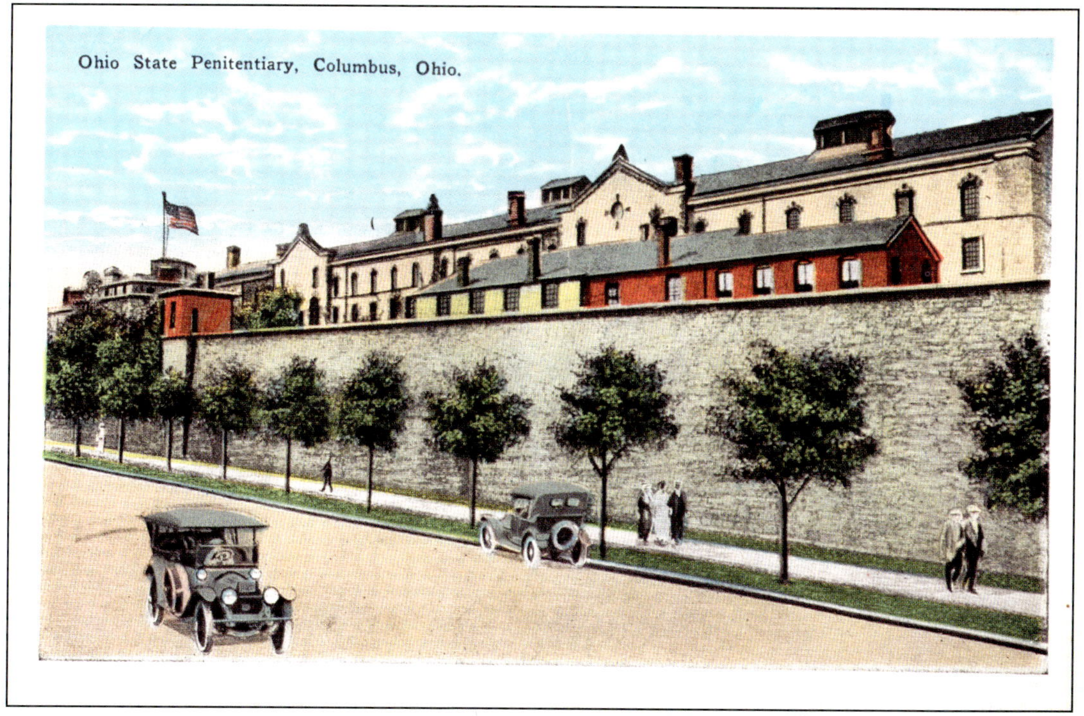

Traffic in front of the penitentiary. Circa 1920, $5-7.

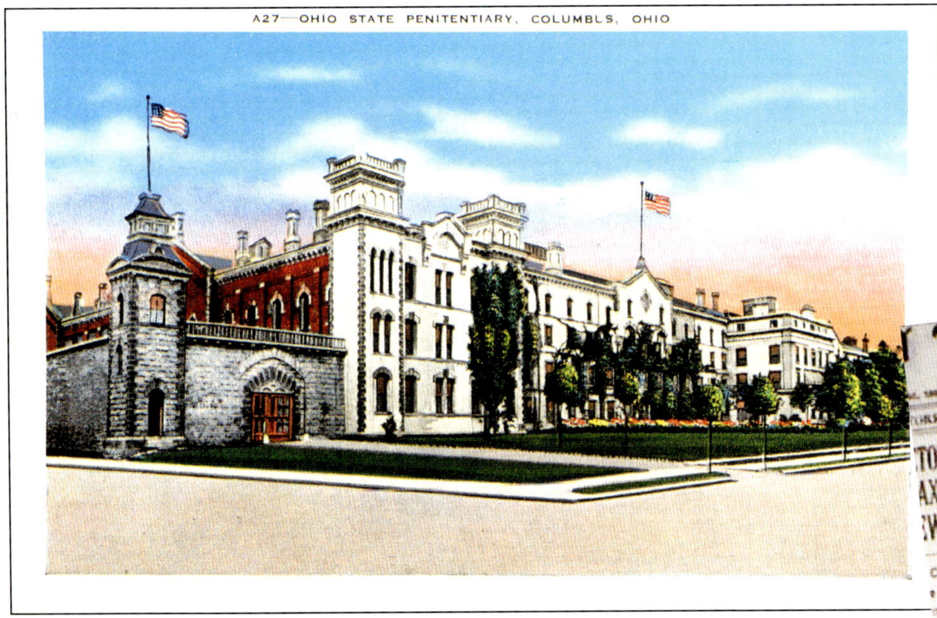

Ohio State Penitentiary. Circa 1920s, $4-6. The back reads: *"Here all Ohio auto license tags are made. The first penitentiary buildings were erected on this site in 1833 but many additions and alterations have been made since, covers an area of 23 acres, surrounded by a thick stone wall 33 feet high."*

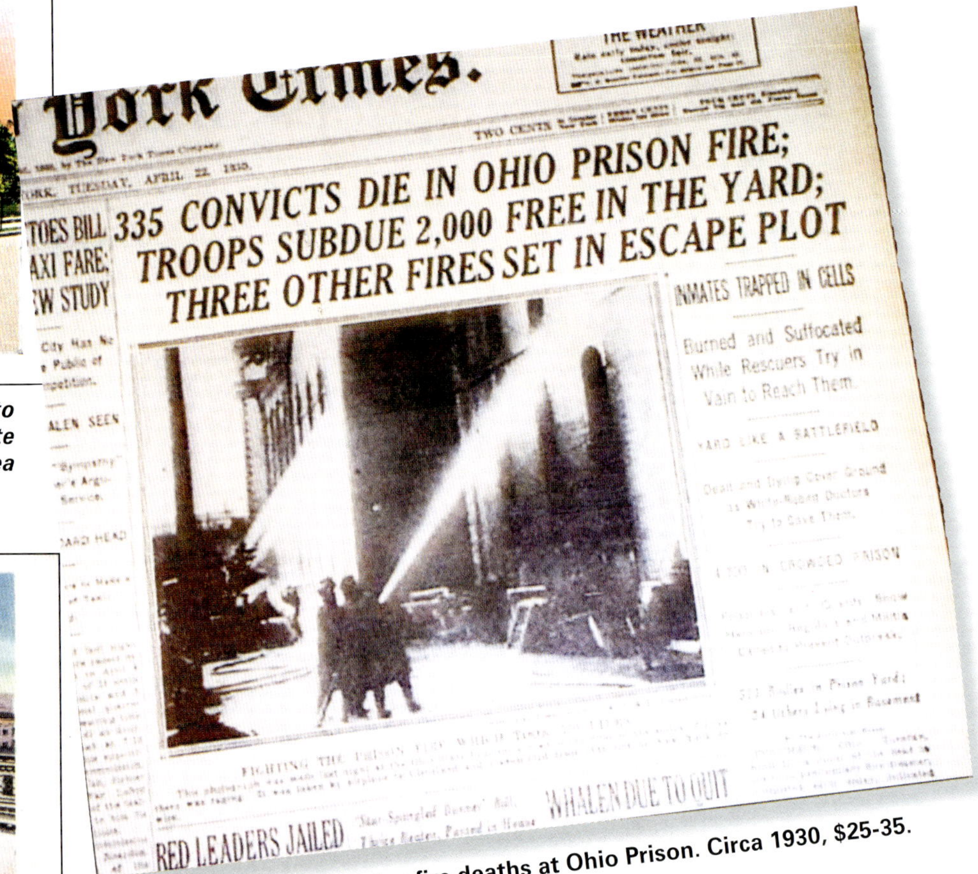
York Times.

335 CONVICTS DIE IN OHIO PRISON FIRE; TROOPS SUBDUE 2,000 FREE IN THE YARD; THREE OTHER FIRES SET IN ESCAPE PLOT

INMATES TRAPPED IN CELLS

Burned and Suffocated While Rescuers Try in Vain to Reach Them.

YARD LIKE A BATTLEFIELD

RED LEADERS JAILED

WHALEN DUE TO QUIT

New York Times headlining fire deaths at Ohio Prison. Circa 1930, $25-35.

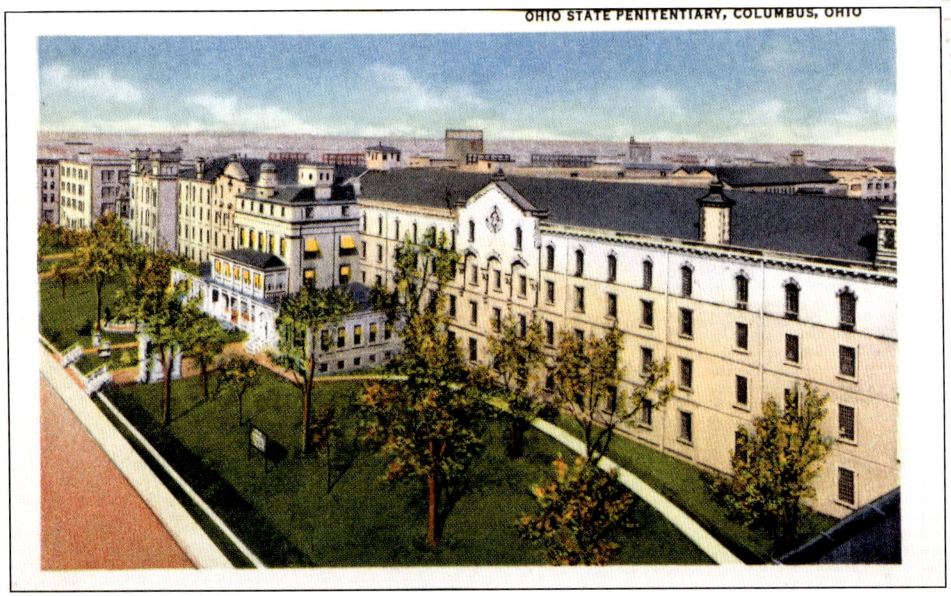

Tree-lined view of the prison. Circa 1950, $3-4.

Chapter Four: Staying the Night

Columbus is one of America's most visited cities. There is a convention in Columbus almost daily, and these meetings bring people together from all over the United States.

—A 1920s travel brochure

The travel brochures and postcard folders of the Roaring Twenties absolutely gushed with glowing words about hotels in downtown Columbus.

A reference to the one thousand-room Deshler-Wallick unflinchingly called it "America's most beautifully equipped hotel." Travelers were told to find it standing in the heart of Columbus, directly across from the state house.

Then, too, tourists could also turn to the "new" Fort Hayes Hotel, the Neil House opposite the state capitol, and the "remodeled" New Southern Hotel. A revised brochure from the W. E. Ayres Company of Columbus later substituted the Chittenden Hotel for the Southern.

However it still joyfully proclaimed, "These accommodations together with the great public halls made it possible for Columbus to become famous as a convention city."

Staying the night in Columbus however didn't always mean a hotel. Sometimes it meant going to one of the city's many hospitals. Even as late as the 1970s, the city had a surprising fifteen hospitals. Included among them were the familiar names of Grant, Mt. Carmel, Mercy, Children's Riverside Methodist, St. Ann's, and St. Anthony's.

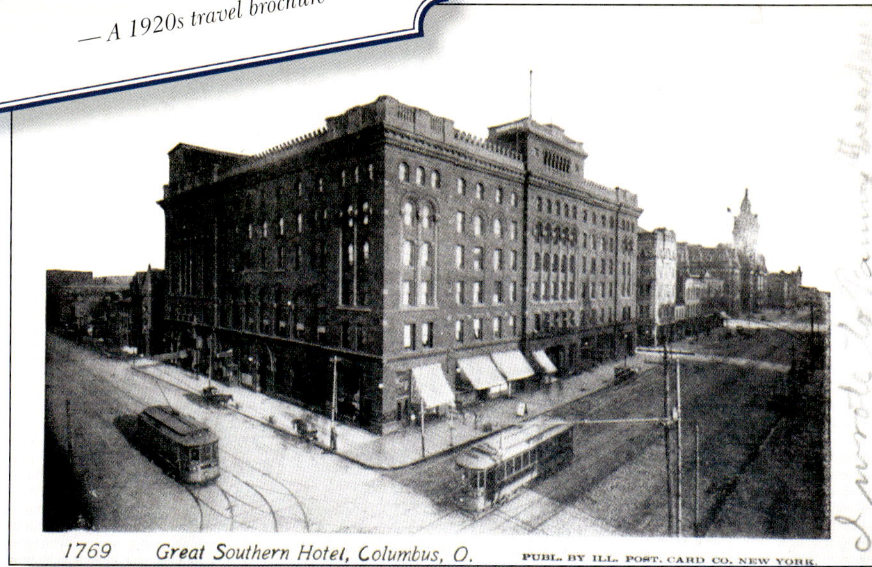

Great Southern Hotel, Columbus, Ohio. Postmarked 1906, $5-6.

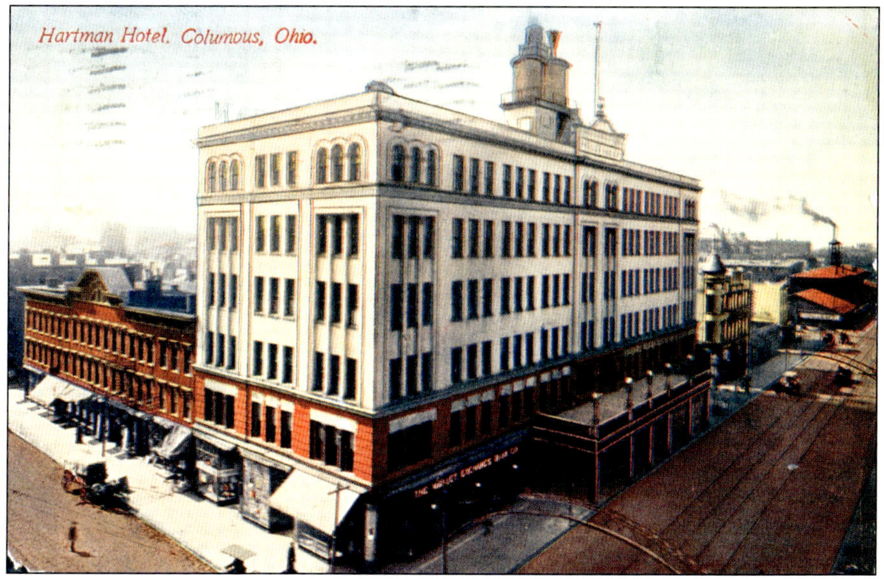

Hartman Hotel, Columbus, Ohio. Circa 1911, $4-5. Hand-written message on the back reads: "We are all right, stayed here last night. Ready to start for Cleveland. Found the markers waiting for the men."

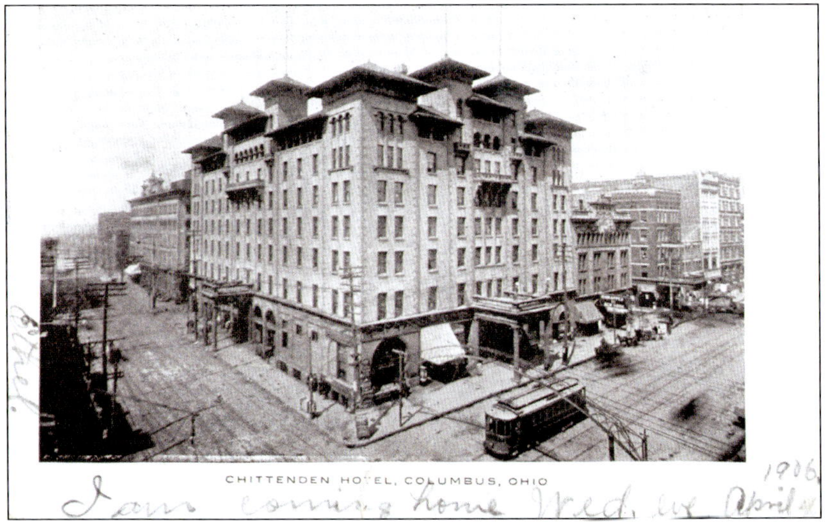

Chittenden Hotel, Columbus, Ohio. Postmarked 1906, $4-5.

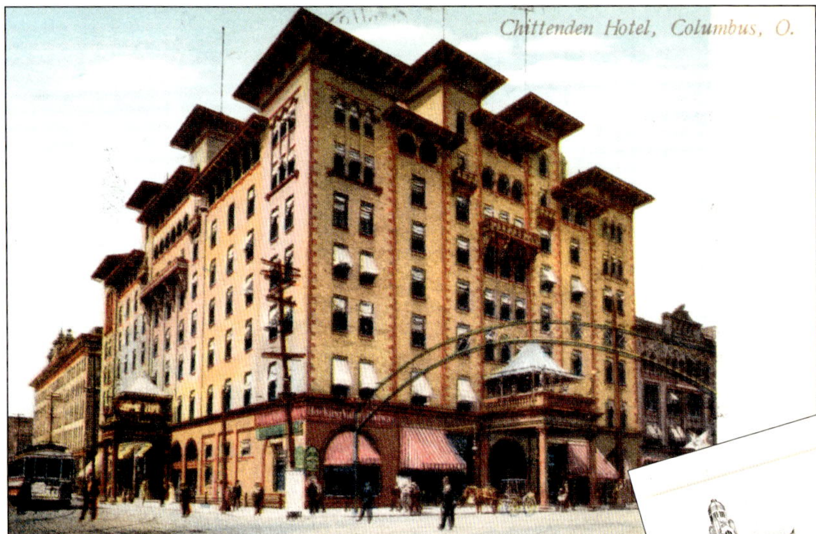

Traffic at the Chittenden Hotel.
Postmarked 1908, $5-6.

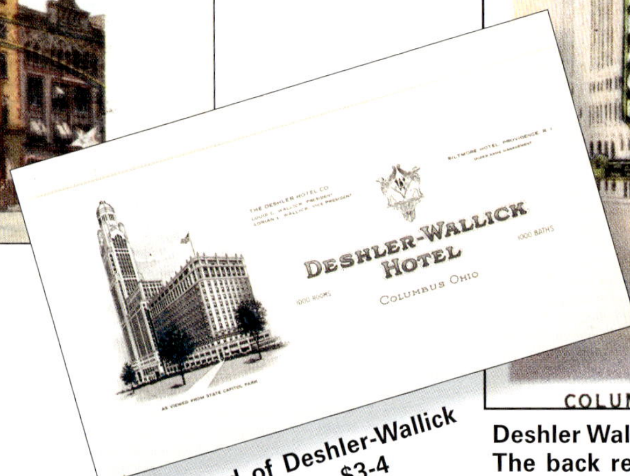

Letterhead of Deshler-Wallick Hotel. Circa 1920s, $3-4

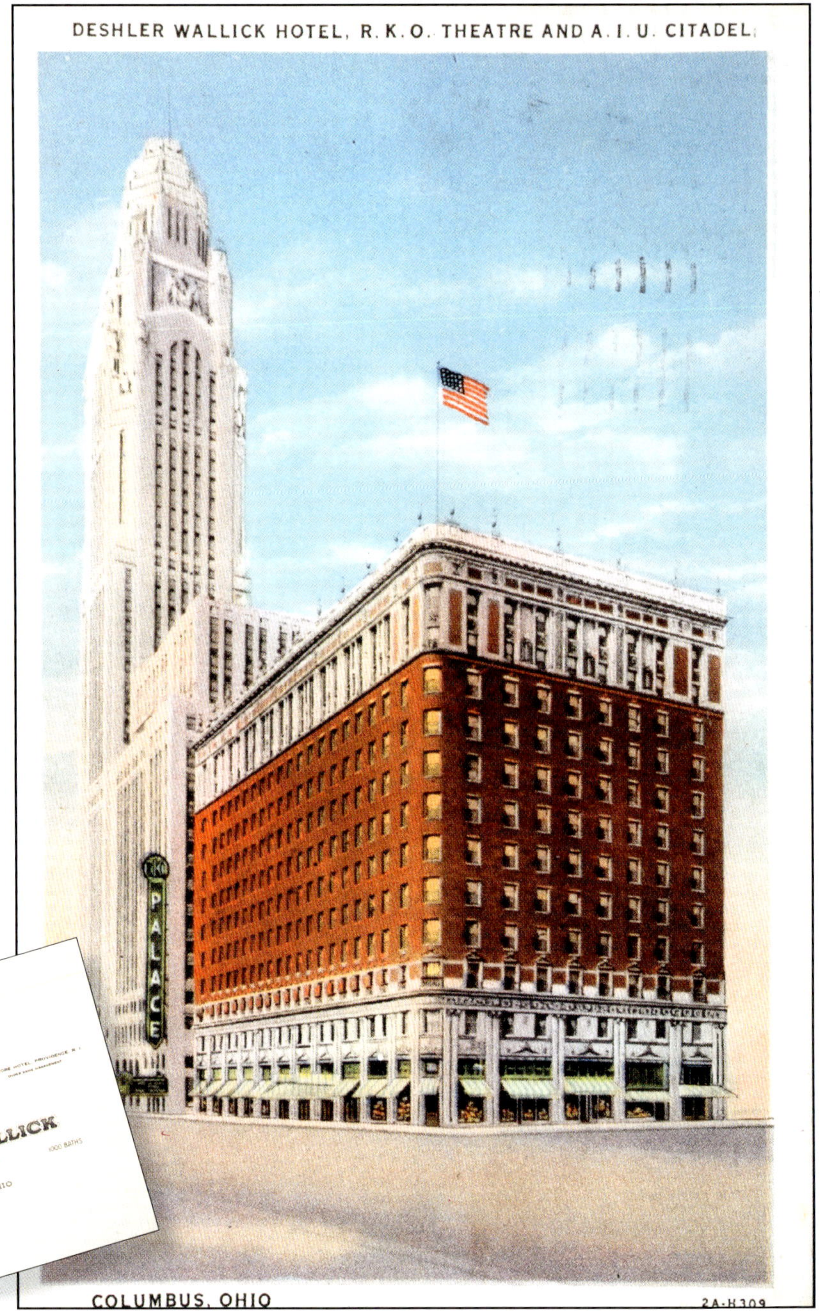

Deshler Wallick Hotel, R.K.O. Theatre and Citadel. Postmarked 1933, $3-4. The back reads: *"The Deshler Wallick Hotel is one of Columbus' most modern hotels. It contains 1,000 rooms and baths, 600 of these rooms are located in the new 45-story A. I. U. Citadel."*

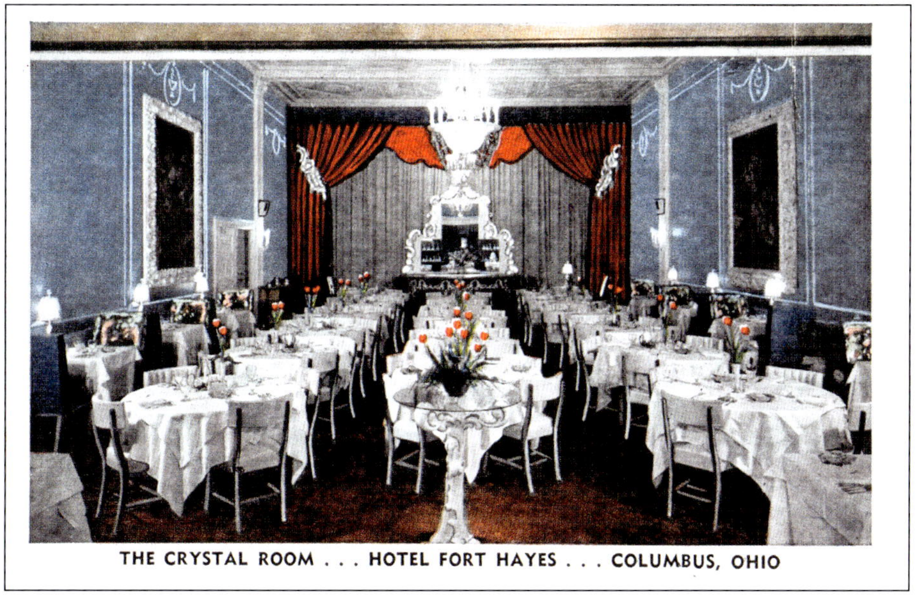

The Crystal Room, Hotel Fort Hayes.Circa 1920s, $5-6.
The back reads: *"Adventures in good eating, lodging for a night."*

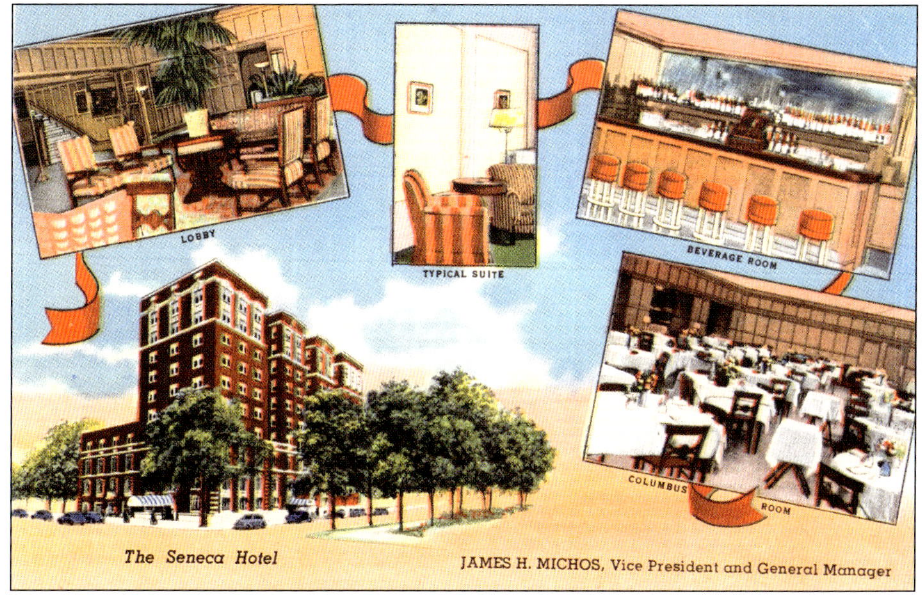

The Seneca Hotel. Circa 1940s, $3-4.
The back reads: *"Exceptional but not expensive."*

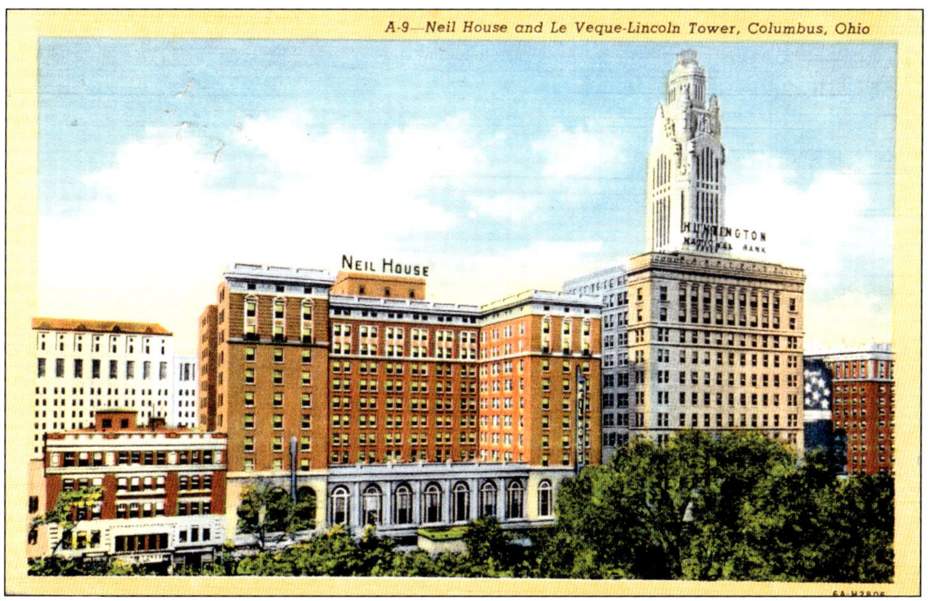

Neil House and Le Veque-Lincoln Tower. Postmarked 1948, $2-3.

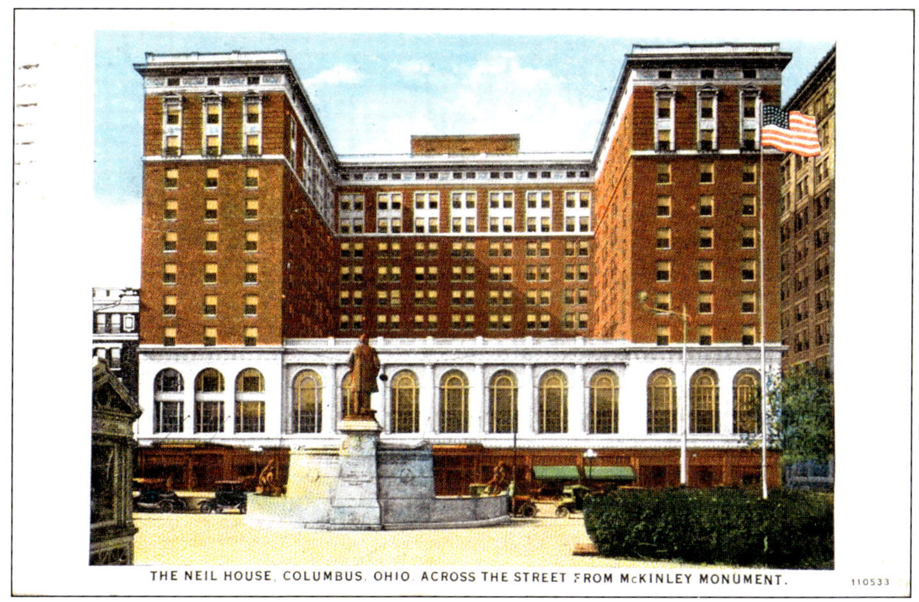

Neil House, Across from the McKinley monument. Postmarked 1926, $2-3.
Hand-written message on back reads: *"Drove 200 miles to Columbus today."*

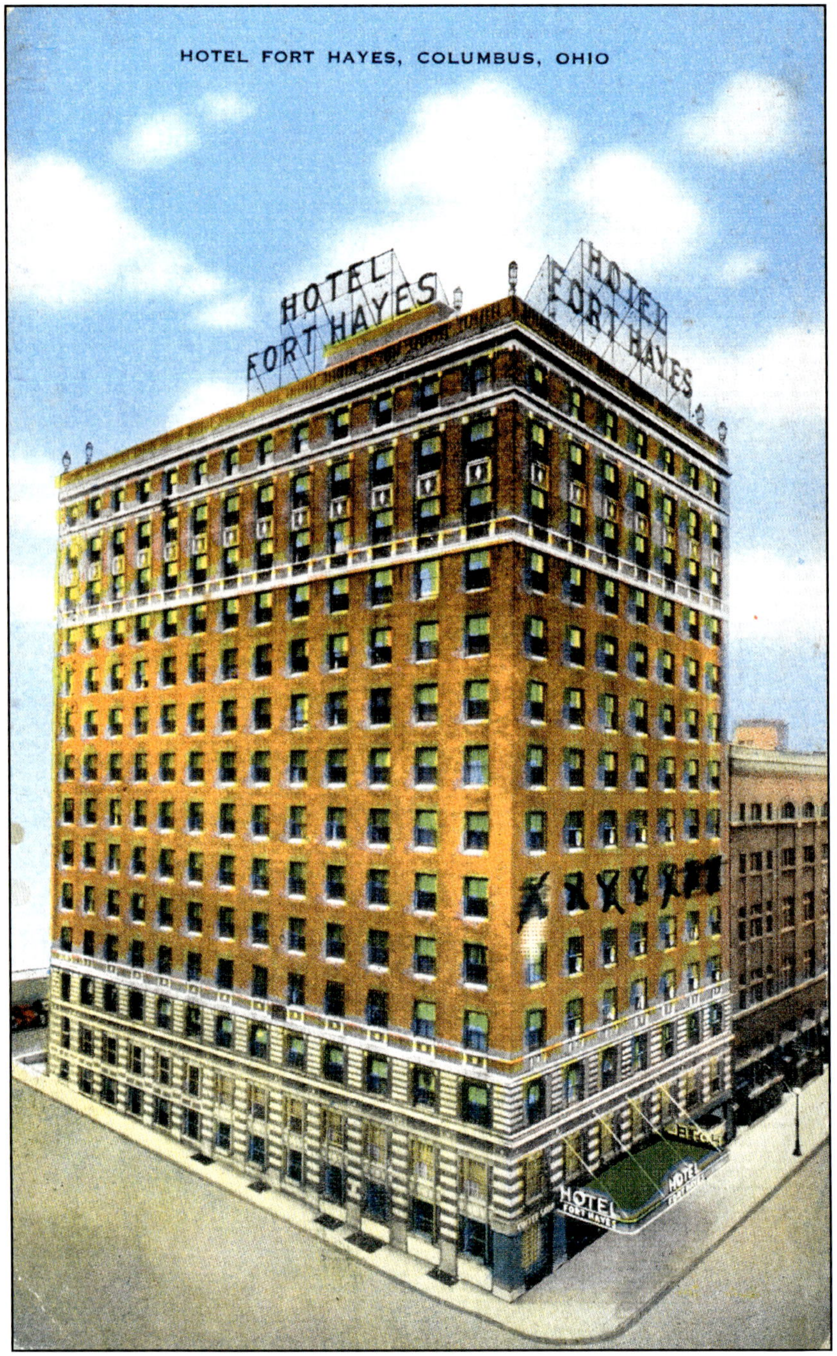

Hotel Fort Hayes. Circa 1940s, $2-3.

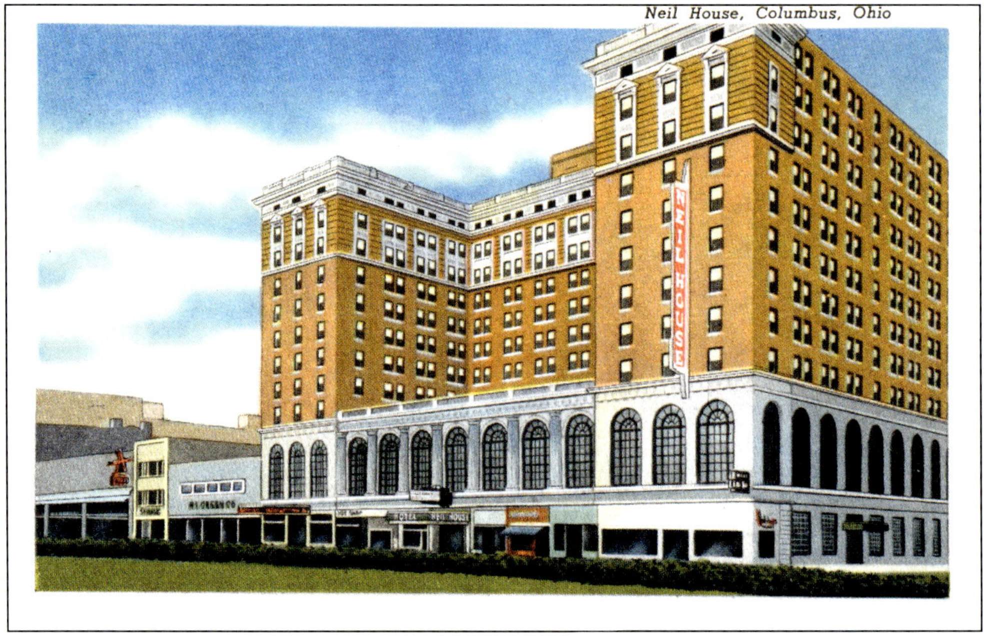

Neil House, Columbus, Ohio. Circa 1950, $2-3.

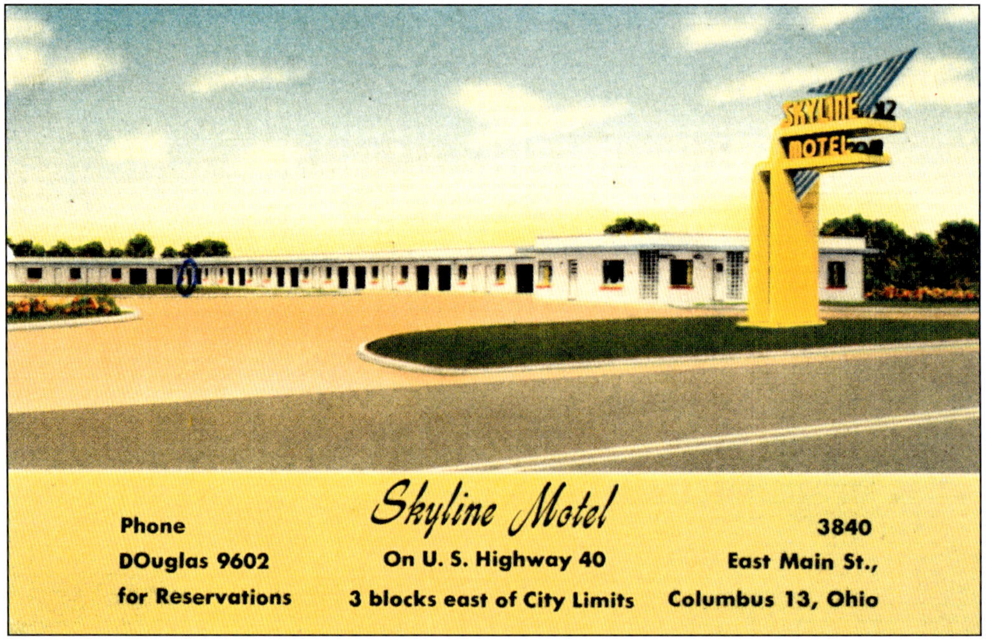

Skyline Motel on U.S. Highway 40. The fifteen-unit motel was completed in 1950. Postmarked 1953, $4-5.

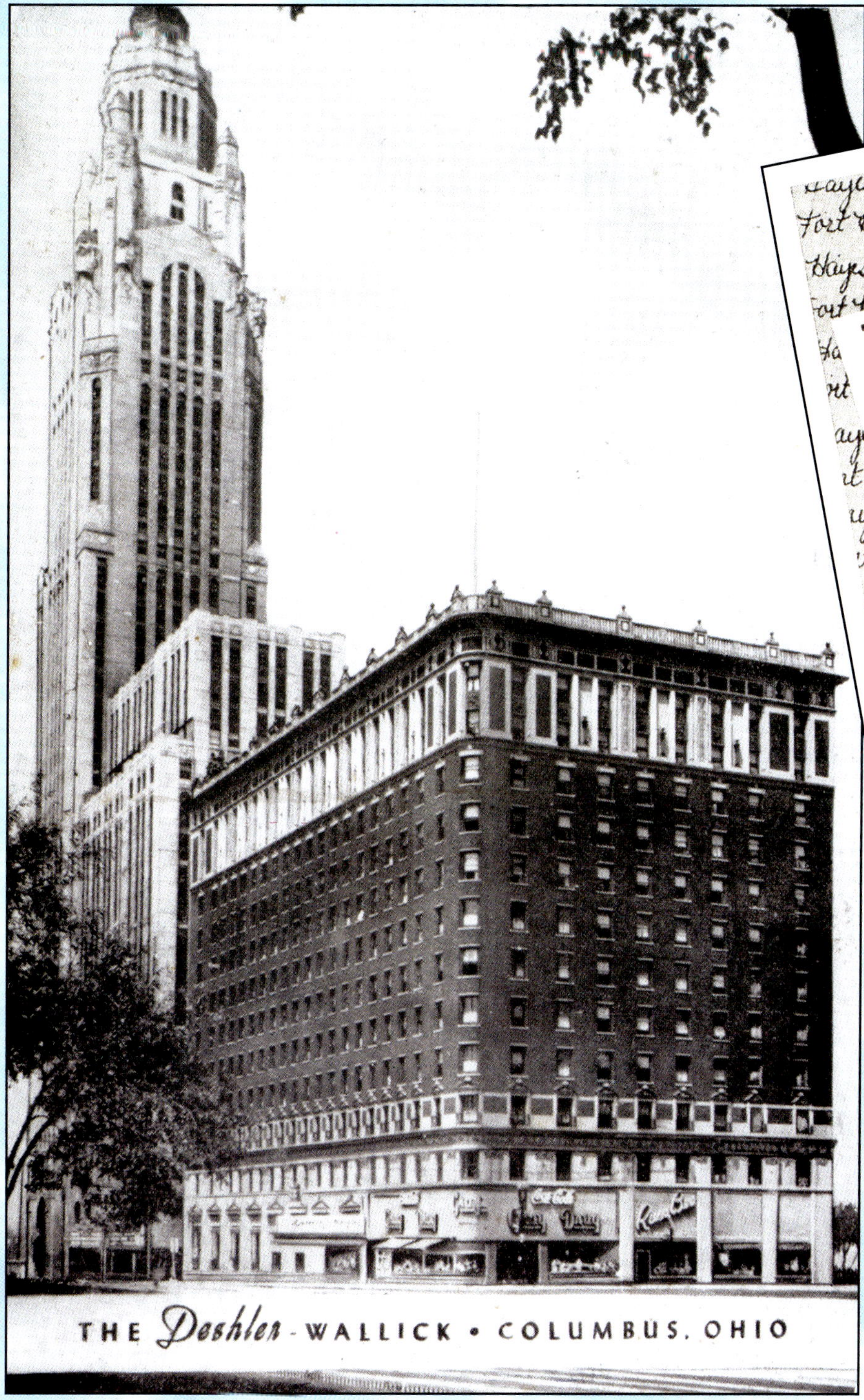

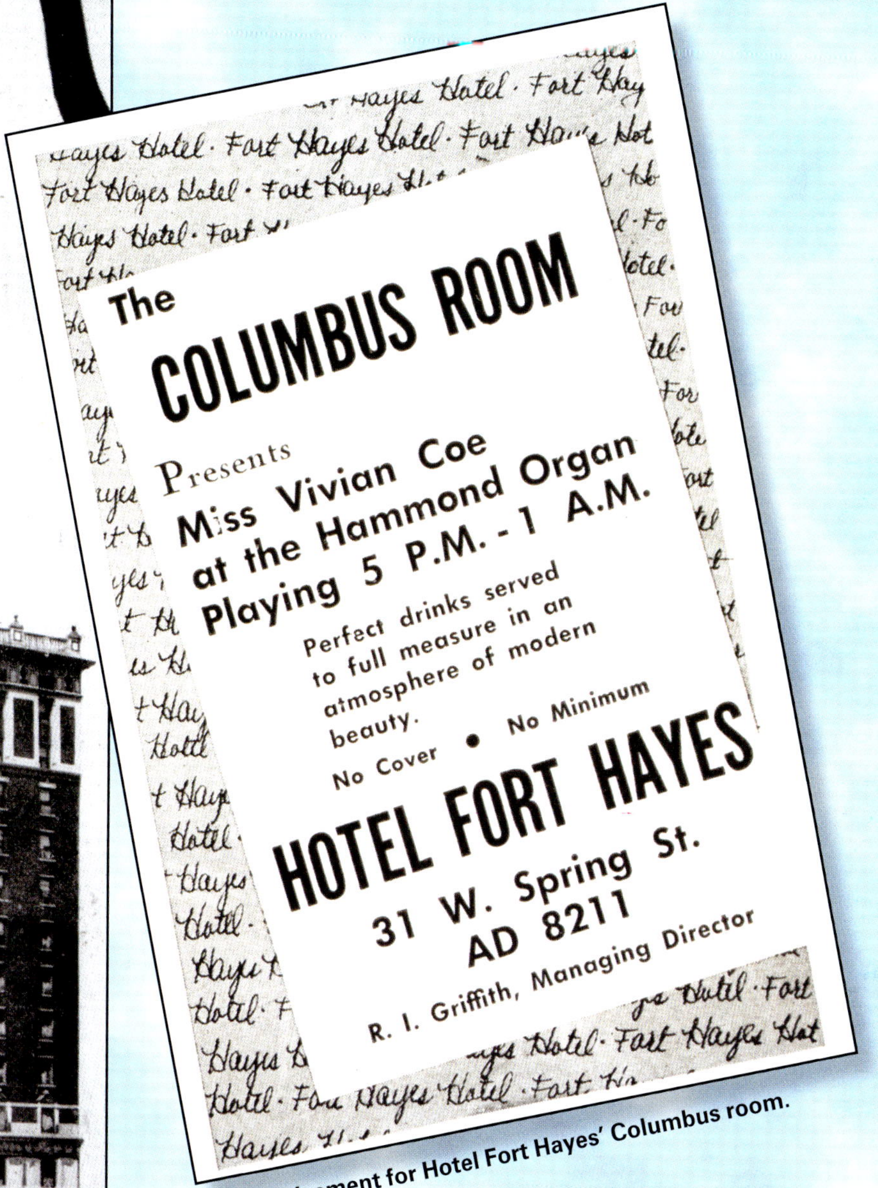

Advertisement for Hotel Fort Hayes' Columbus room. Dated 1954.

The Dashler-Wallick. Postmarked 1950, $2-4.

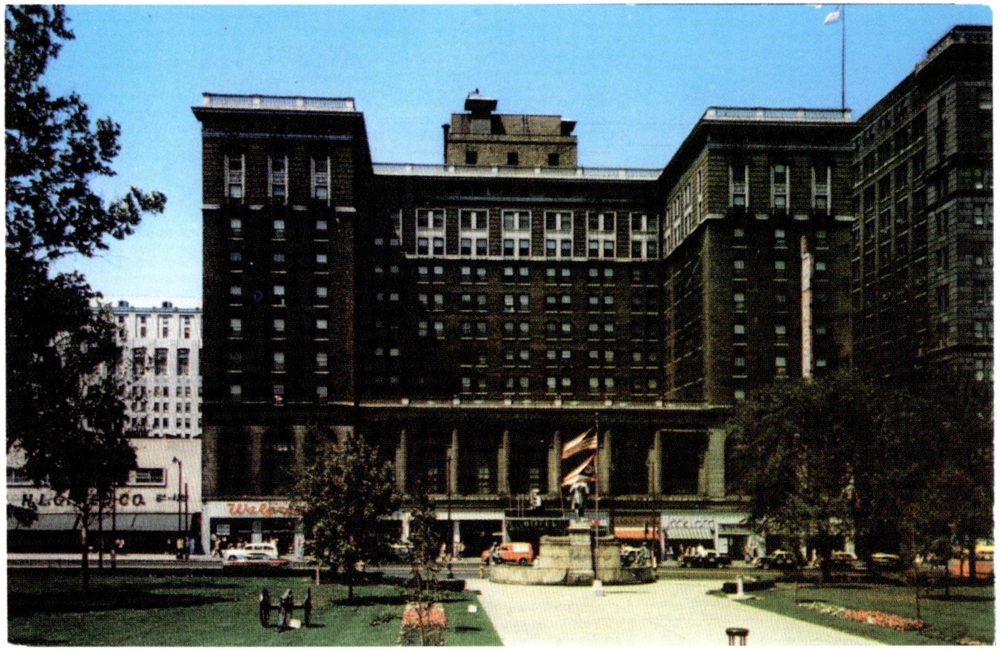

The Neil House. Circa 1950s, $2-3.

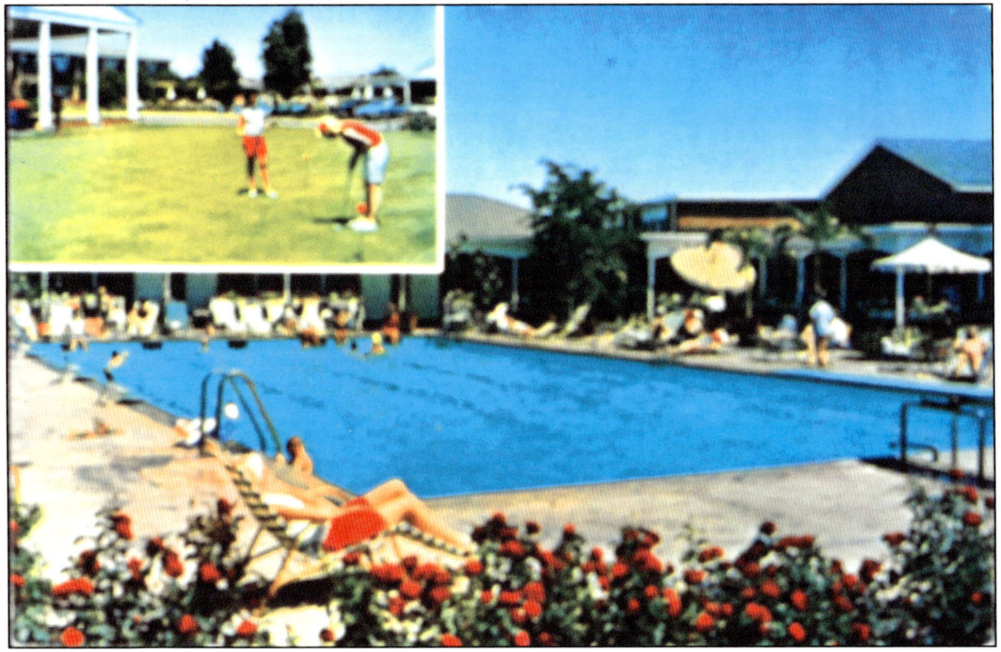

Lincoln Lodge. Circa 1960s, $2-3.

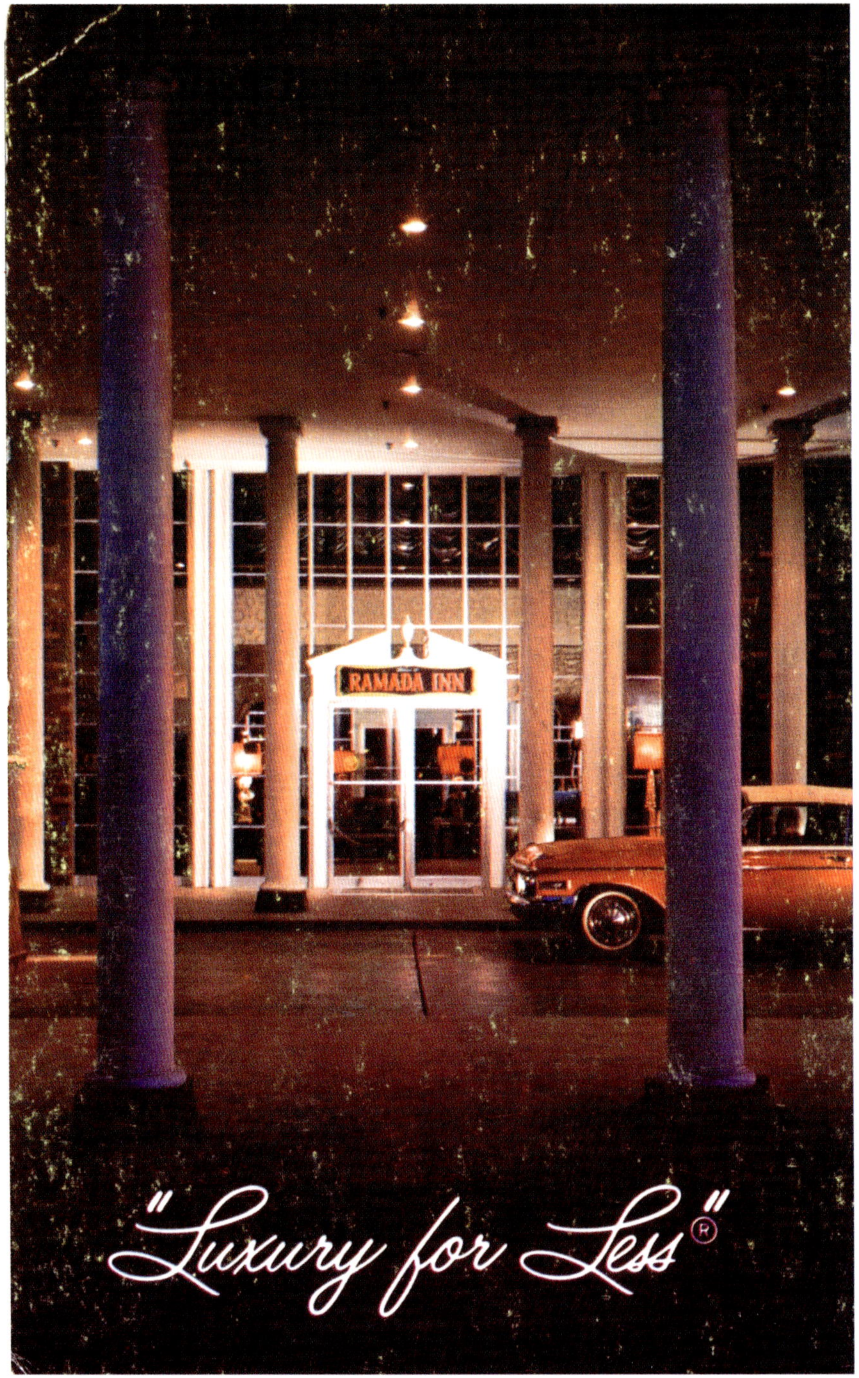

The Ramada Inn. Located at I-71 and Highway 161. Circa 1970s, $2-3.

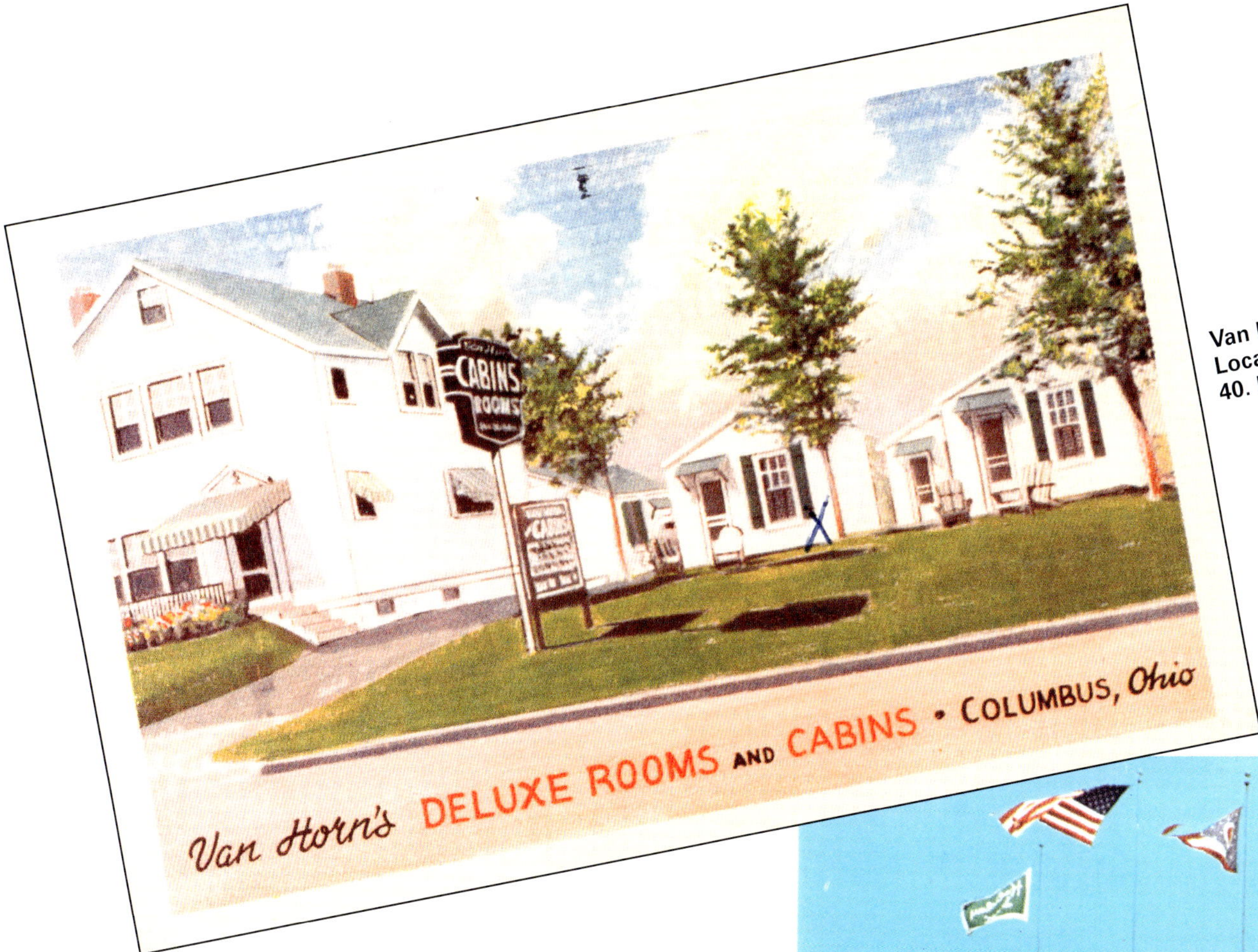

Van Horn's Deluxe rooms and cabins. Located at 3257 East Main Street on U.S. 40. Postmarked 1950, $4-6.

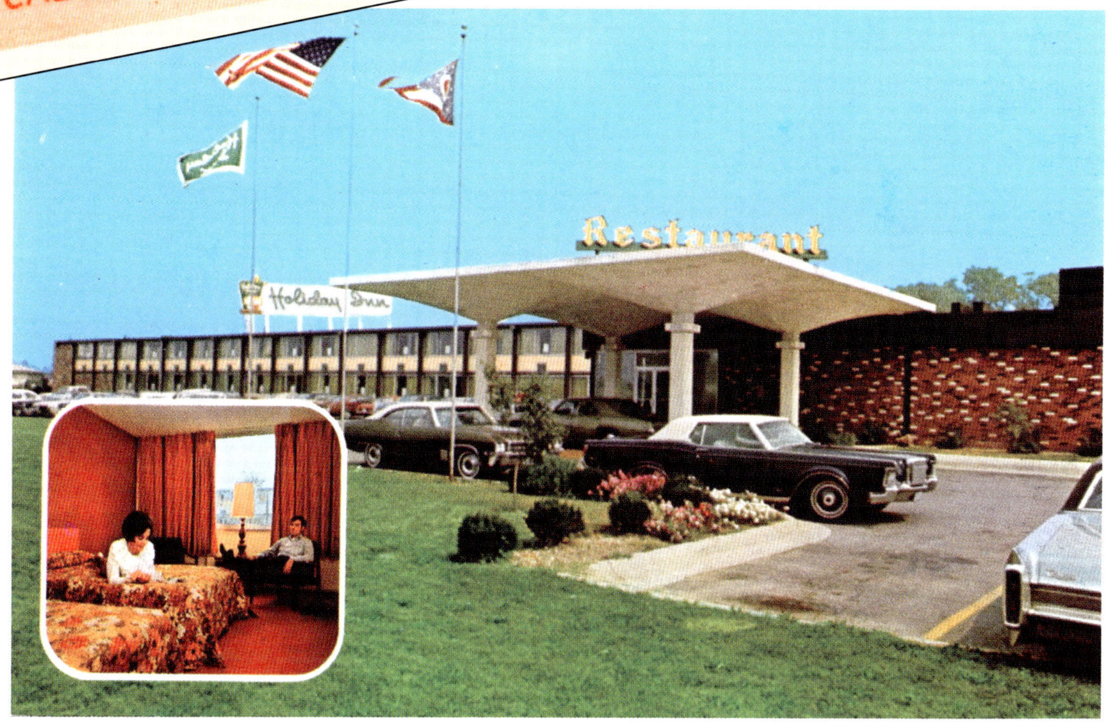

Holiday Inn North, Columbus, Ohio. Circa 1970s, $2-3.

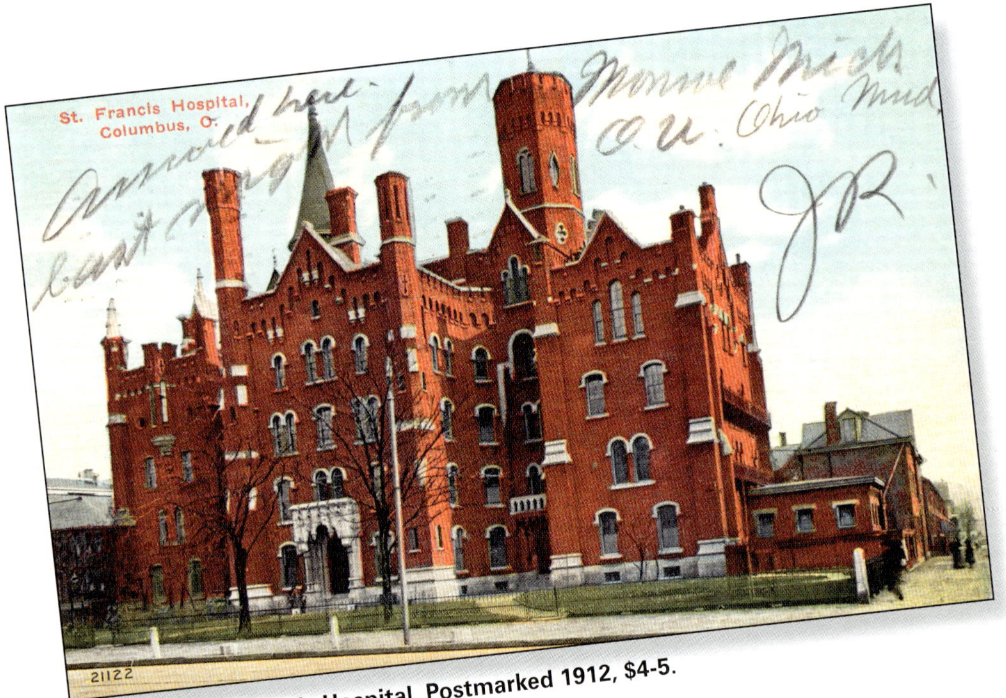

St. Francis Hospital. Postmarked 1912, $4-5.

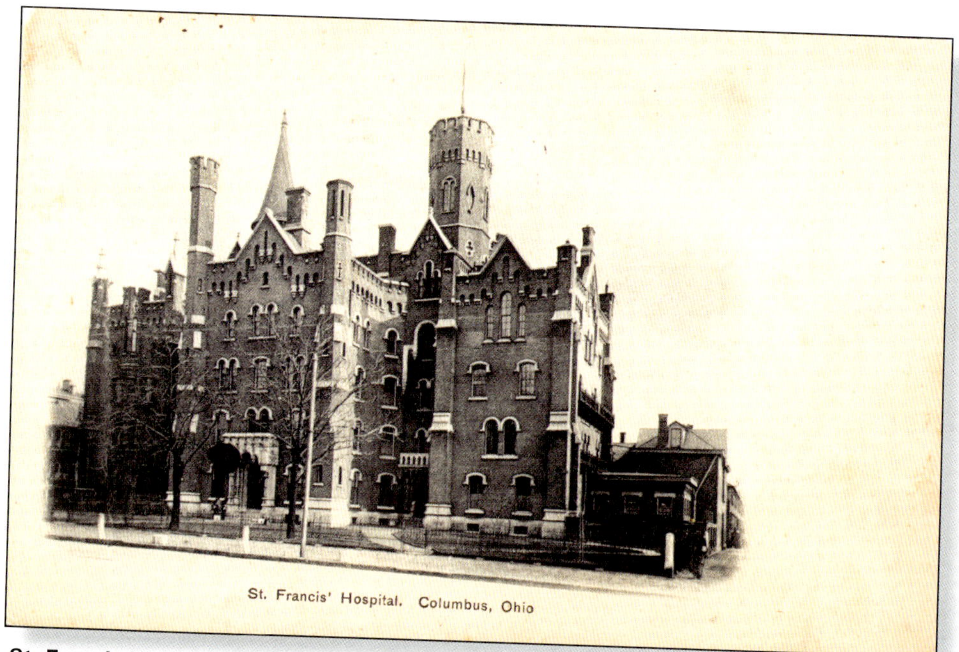

St. Francis Hospital. Postmarked 1908, $5-6.

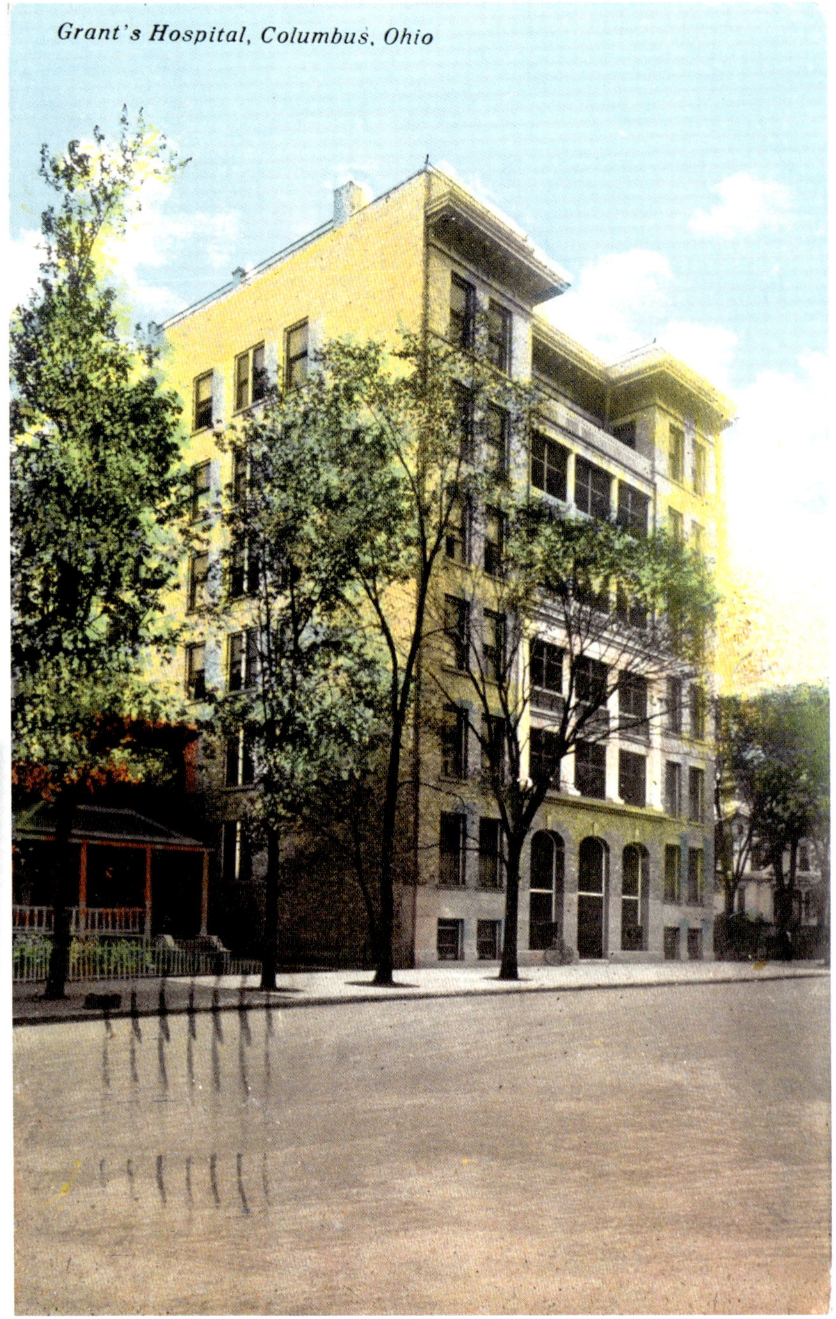

Grant's Hospital, Columbus, Ohio. Postmarked 1911, $4-5.

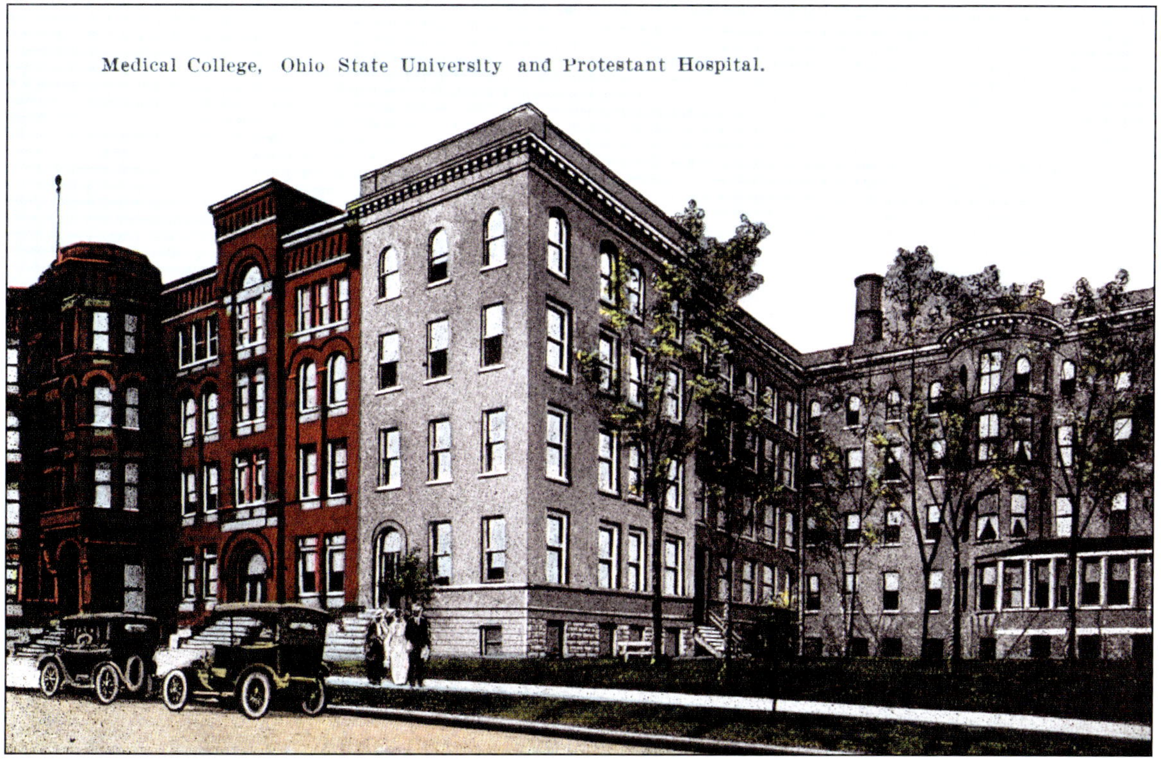

Medical college and Protestant Hospital. Circa 1920s, $4-6.

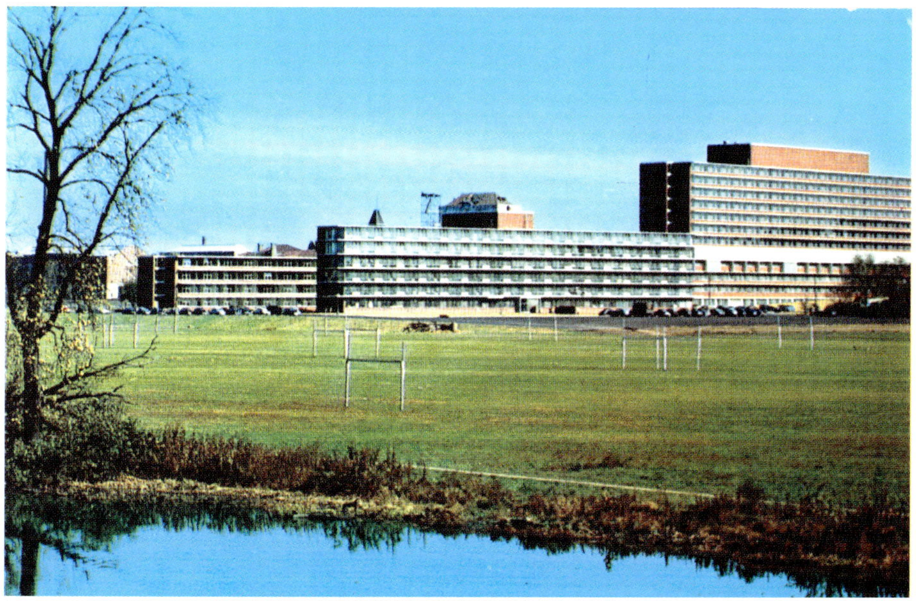

"Newly completed" Medical Health Center. Circa 1960, $2-3.

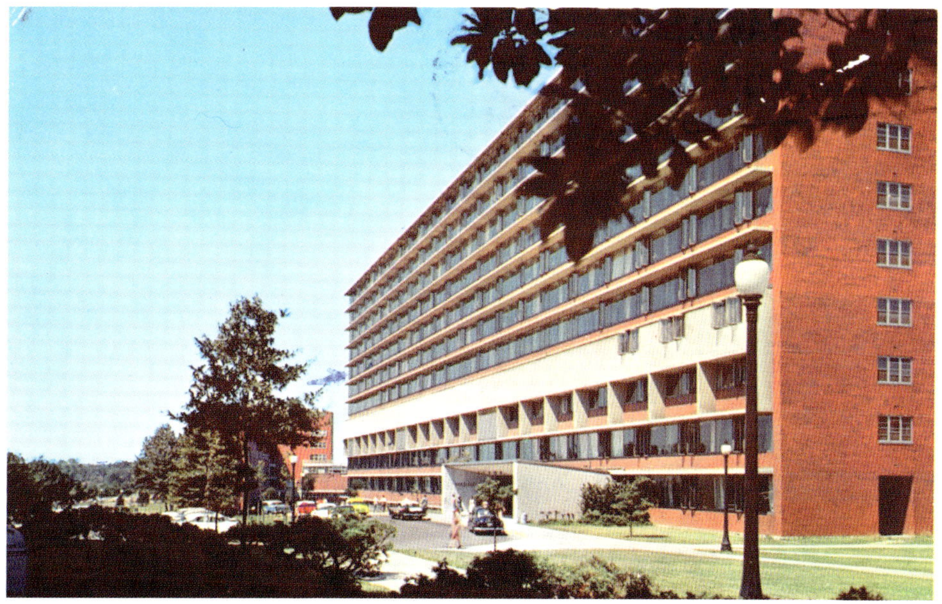

Ohio State University Hospital. Postmarked 1969, $2-3.

Chapter Five:
Travel Plans

> The time will come when people will travel in stages moved by steam engines, from one city to another, almost as fast as birds fly, 15 or 20 miles an hour.
>
> — *Engineer Oliver Evans in 1813*

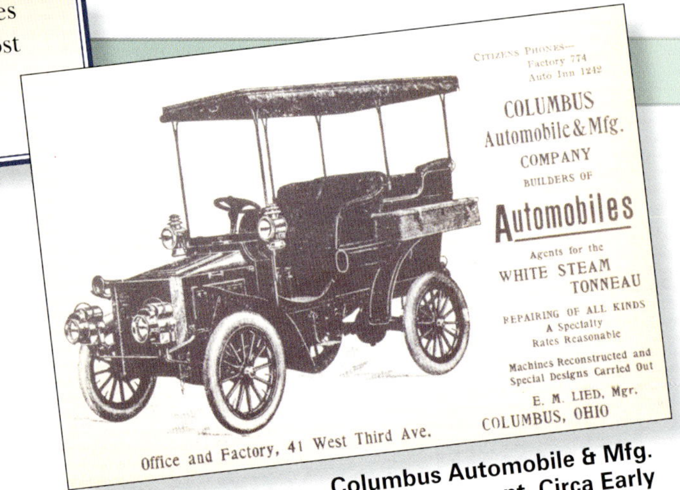

Columbus Automobile & Mfg. advertisement. Circa Early 1900s, $3-4.

Travel plans in early twentieth century Columbus likely involved a horse and buggy. Bigger plans might have involved the railroad and the sleek and new Union Station. The ultimate trip to the lucky and elite few could be in the luxury of the automobile.

Union Station was a popular starting point for travel plans in the early 1900s and similarly a popular postcard image. The "new" station had opened just a few years earlier as the exciting architectural creation of the Daniel Burnham & Company. Two striking features of this railroad station — actually the third for the city — were its viaduct and its Arcade.

The road viaduct over the tracks provided an immediate solution to the traffic problem that regularly snarled High Street. The Arcade, meanwhile, also on the cutting edge of commerce, involved locating offices and stores atop the viaduct facing busy High Street.

Another occupant of High Street at about the same time the gleam was still on all of Union Station was the Columbus Motor Vehicle Company. In 1903, this company offered its first Santos Dumont automobile for buyers in the Columbus vicinity. The vehicle drew its name from a famed airship flyer named Alberto Santos-Dumont. Among other things Santos-Dumont was the first to fly around the Eiffel Tower in Paris, France.

Back in Columbus the two-cylinder Santos-Dumont automobile was first priced at $1,800 and later lowered to $1,500. It was advertised by the Columbus Motor Vehicle Company as being, "in appearance, power and general results (it is) fully the equal of any $6,000 French car on the market."

Meanwhile, on Gay Street, the firm of Seed and Evans offered many other automobile choices including the Studebaker Stanhope, the Sandusky Runabout, and the Packard Touring Car. On West Third Avenue were agents for the White Steam Tonneau under the supervision of the Columbus Automobile and Manufacturing Company.

Columbus travel took to the air in 1929 when the Port Columbus Airport was finally opened to the public. The grand opening festivities turned out to actually be the ultimate in planes and trains.

Transcontinental Air Transport (TAT) included Port Columbus in their grand coast-to-coast inaugural that July. Columbus in fact became the eastern transfer point of the historic journey. A group of passengers including Amelia Earhart and Charles Lindbergh made the trip. Starting in New York City, the passengers traveled westward by railroad arriving the following day in Columbus. From Port Columbus, they departed on the Ford Tri-Motor 'City of Columbus' and a second plane for a town in Oklahoma. Once on the ground there, they again boarded a train that sped on westward to California. The entire trip took about forty-eight hours, which was a travel record at that time.

By the late 1930s Port Columbus was handling fourteen flights daily. Transcontinental and Western Airline boarded a heady twenty-one passengers per day.

During that same period, railroad passenger traffic was declining. Part of the Arcade had been demolished to make room for automobiles, and train sheds had been replaced with an enclosed concourse. By 1956 the station was down to forty-two daily passenger trains—a fraction of the number during is zenith half a century earlier. Finally, rail passenger service ended in the 1970s, and the once proud Arcade was demolished in 1976. A single arch of the famed structure was saved, however; it was displayed in the Arena District's Dimon McPherson Park, directly across Nationwide Boulevard from the Nationwide Arena.

The land on which the historic Arcade arch now sits was once the site of the Ohio Penitentiary *(See Chapter Three)*.

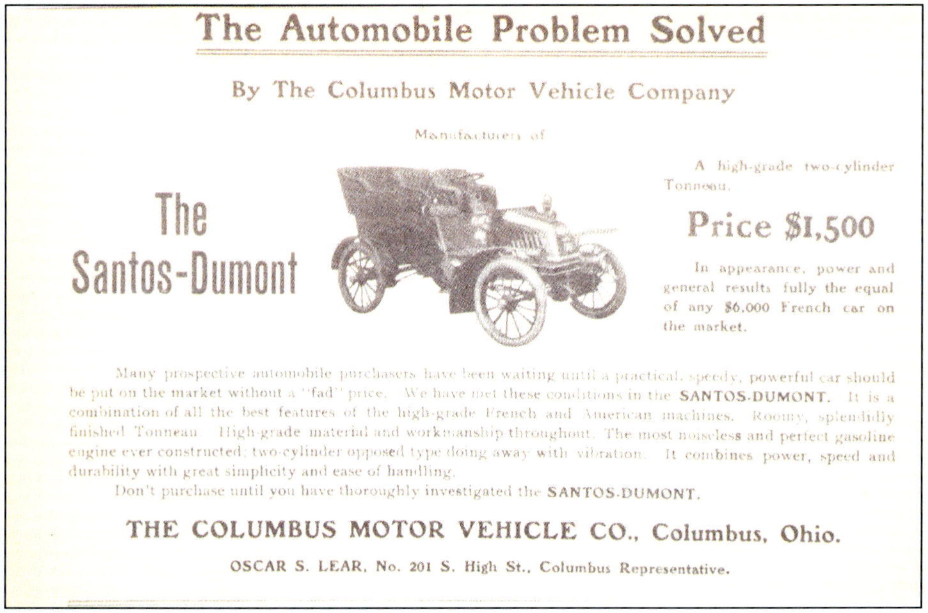

Columbus Motor Vehicle Company advertisement. Circa Early 1900s, $3-4.

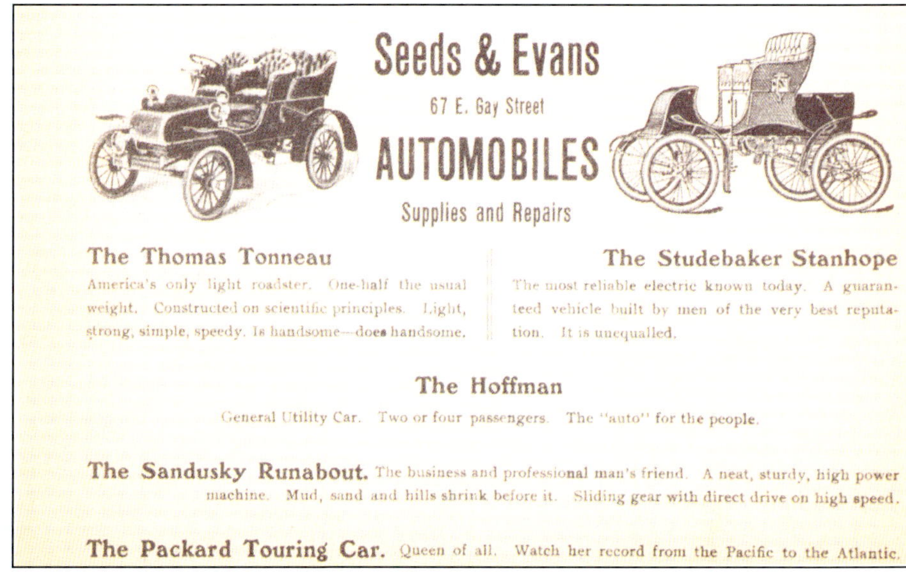

Seeds & Evans Automobiles advertisement. Circa Early 1900s, $3-5.

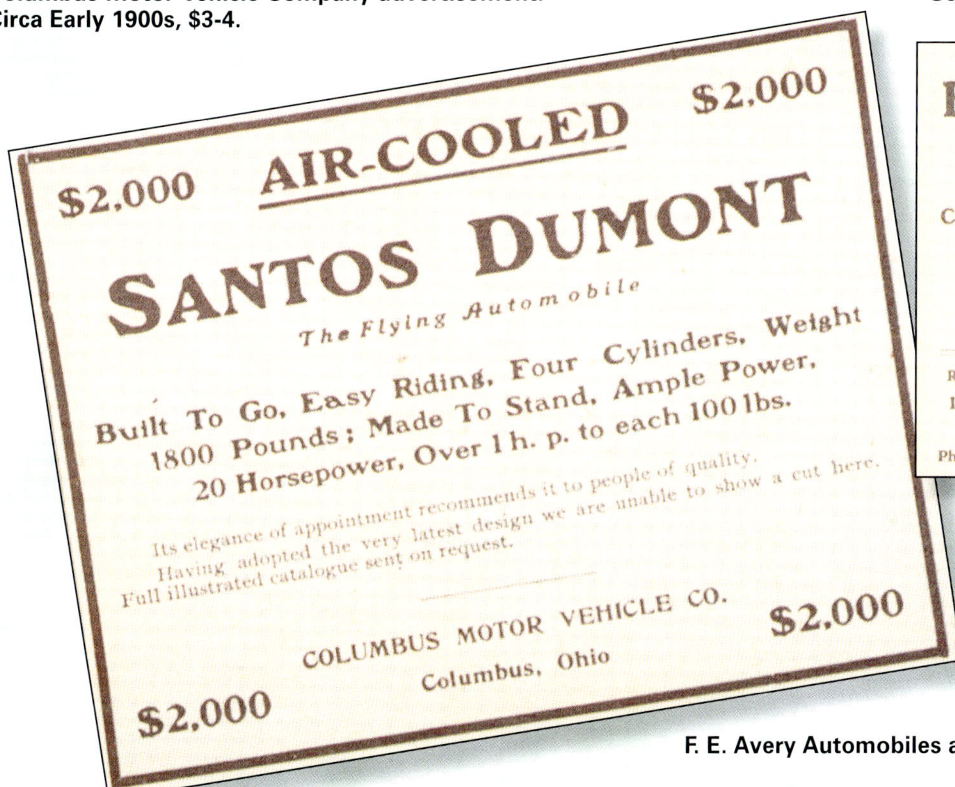

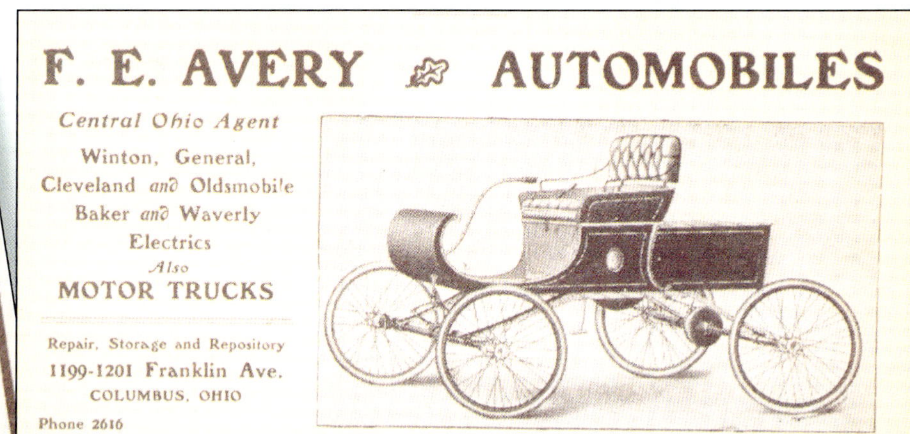

Santos Dumont advertisement. "The Flying Automobile." Published 1904, $3-4.

F. E. Avery Automobiles advertisement. Circa Early 1900s, $3-5.

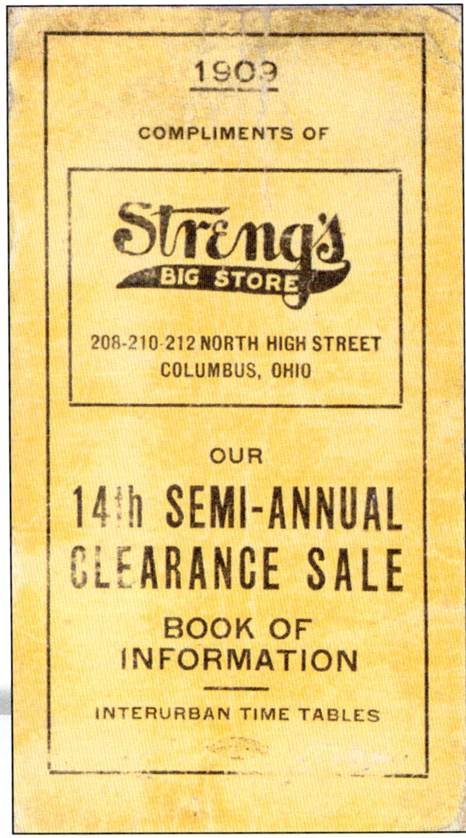

Book of interurban time tables. Dated 1909, $10-12.

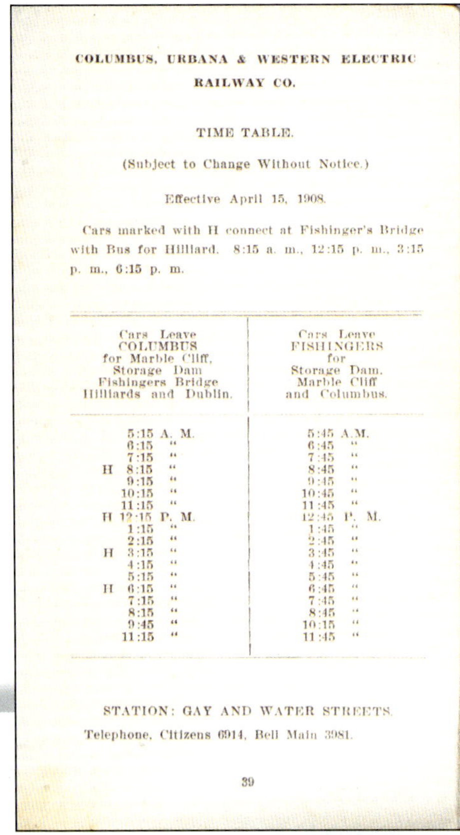

COLUMBUS, URBANA & WESTERN ELECTRIC RAILWAY CO.

TIME TABLE.

(Subject to Change Without Notice.)

Effective April 15, 1908.

Cars marked with H connect at Fishinger's Bridge with Bus for Hillard. 8:15 a. m., 12:15 p. m., 3:15 p. m., 6:15 p. m.

Cars Leave COLUMBUS for Marble Cliff, Storage Dam, Fishingers Bridge, Hilliards and Dublin.	Cars Leave FISHINGERS for Storage Dam, Marble Cliff and Columbus.
5:15 A. M.	5:45 A. M.
6:15 "	6:45 "
7:15 "	7:45 "
H 8:15 "	8:45 "
9:15 "	9:45 "
10:15 "	10:45 "
11:15 "	11:45 "
H 12:15 P. M.	12:45 P. M.
1:15 "	1:45 "
2:15 "	2:45 "
H 3:15 "	3:45 "
4:15 "	4:45 "
5:15 "	5:45 "
H 6:15 "	6:45 "
7:15 "	7:45 "
8:15 "	8:45 "
9:45 "	10:15 "
11:15 "	11:45 "

STATION: GAY AND WATER STREETS.

Telephone, Citizens 6914, Bell Main 3981.

39

Columbus, Urbana & Western Electric Railway time-table. Effective 1908.

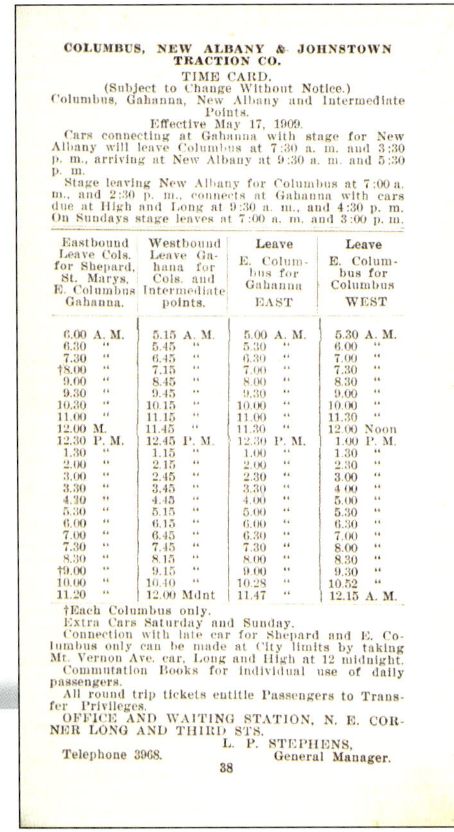

COLUMBUS, NEW ALBANY & JOHNSTOWN TRACTION CO.

TIME CARD.

(Subject to Change Without Notice.)

Columbus, Gahanna, New Albany and Intermediate Points.

Effective May 17, 1909.

Cars connecting at Gahanna with stage for New Albany will leave Columbus at 7:30 a. m. and 3:30 p. m., arriving at New Albany at 9:30 a. m. and 5:30 p. m.

Stage leaving New Albany for Columbus at 7:00 a. m., and 2:30 p. m., connects at Gahanna with cars due at High and Long at 9:30 a. m., and 4:30 p. m. On Sundays stage leaves at 7:00 a. m. and 3:00 p. m.

Eastbound Leave Cols. for Shepard, St. Marys, E. Columbus Gahanna.	Westbound Leave Gahana for Cols. and Intermediate points.	Leave E. Columbus for Gahanna EAST	Leave E. Columbus for Columbus WEST
6.00 A. M.	5.15 A. M.	5.00 A. M.	5.30 A. M.
6.30 "	5.45 "	5.30 "	6.00 "
7.30 "	6.45 "	6.30 "	7.00 "
†8.00 "	7.15 "	7.00 "	7.30 "
9.00 "	8.45 "	8.00 "	8.30 "
9.30 "	9.45 "	9.30 "	9.00 "
10.30 "	10.15 "	10.00 "	10.00 "
11.00 "	11.15 "	11.00 "	11.30 "
12.00 M.	11.45 "	11.30 "	12.00 Noon
12.30 P. M.	12.45 P. M.	12.30 P. M.	1.00 P. M.
1.30 "	1.15 "	1.00 "	1.30 "
2.00 "	2.15 "	2.00 "	2.30 "
3.00 "	2.45 "	2.30 "	3.00 "
3.30 "	3.45 "	3.30 "	4.00 "
4.30 "	4.45 "	4.00 "	5.00 "
5.30 "	5.15 "	5.00 "	5.30 "
6.00 "	6.15 "	6.00 "	6.30 "
7.00 "	6.45 "	6.30 "	7.00 "
7.30 "	7.45 "	7.30 "	8.00 "
8.30 "	8.15 "	8.00 "	8.30 "
†9.00 "	9.15 "	9.00 "	9.30 "
10.00 "	10.40 "	10.28 "	10.52 "
11.20 "	12.00 Mdnt	11.47	12.15 A. M.

†Each Columbus only.

Extra Cars Saturday and Sunday.

Connection with late car for Shepard and E. Columbus only can be made at City limits by taking Mt. Vernon Ave. car, Long and High at 12 midnight.

Commutation Books for individual use of daily passengers.

All round trip tickets entitle Passengers to Transfer Privileges.

OFFICE AND WAITING STATION, N. E. CORNER LONG AND THIRD STS.

L. P. STEPHENS, General Manager.

Telephone 3968.

38

Columbus, New Albany & Johnstown Traction Co. Effective 1909.

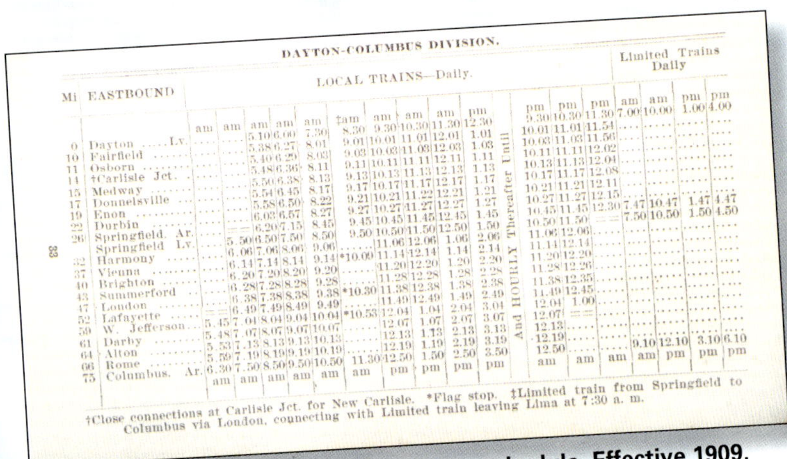

DAYTON-COLUMBUS DIVISION.

EASTBOUND — LOCAL TRAINS—Daily. — Limited Trains Daily

†Close connections at Carlisle Jct. for New Carlisle. *Flag stop. ‡Limited train from Springfield to Columbus via London, connecting with Limited train leaving Lima at 7:30 a. m.

Eastbound Dayton-Columbus interurban schedule. Effective 1909.

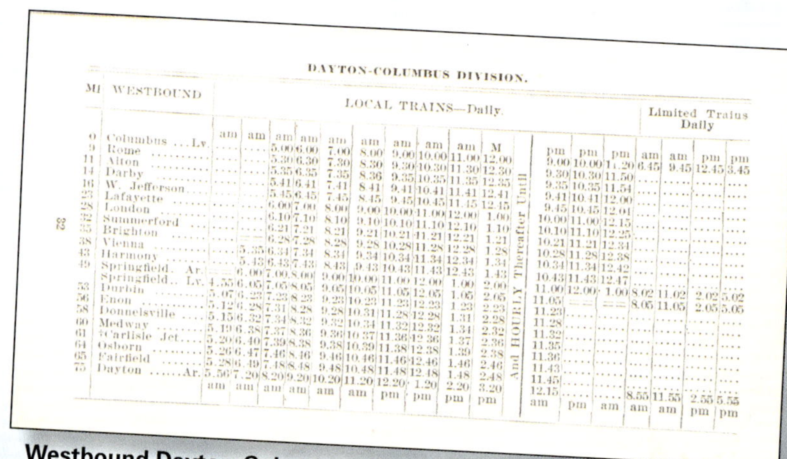

DAYTON-COLUMBUS DIVISION.

WESTBOUND — LOCAL TRAINS—Daily. — Limited Trains Daily

Westbound Dayton-Columbus inter-urban schedule. Effective 1909.

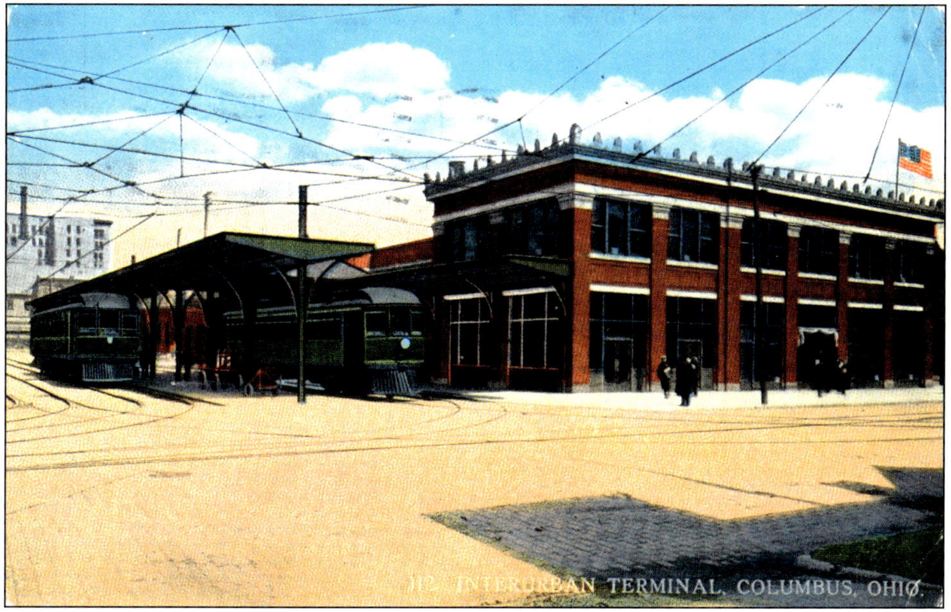

Interurban terminal, Columbus, Ohio. Postmarked 1916, $6-8.

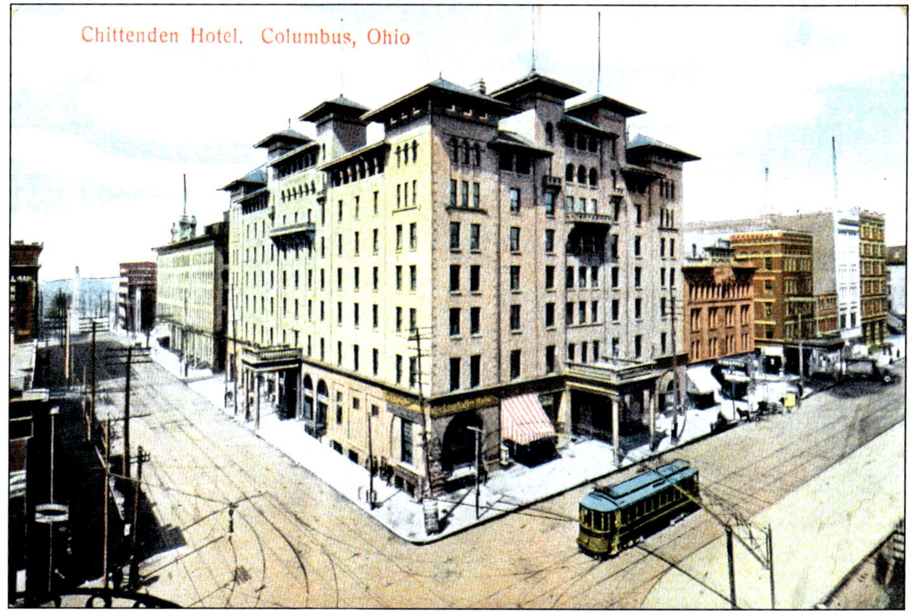

Interurban traveling next to the Chittenden Hotel. Circa 1916, $4-6.

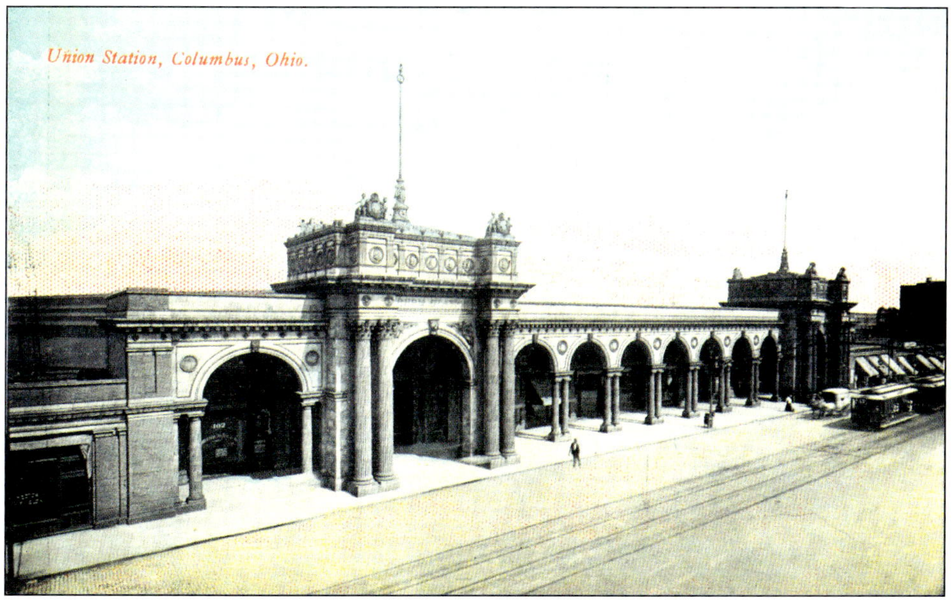

Union Station, Columbus, Ohio. Circa 1908, $4-6.

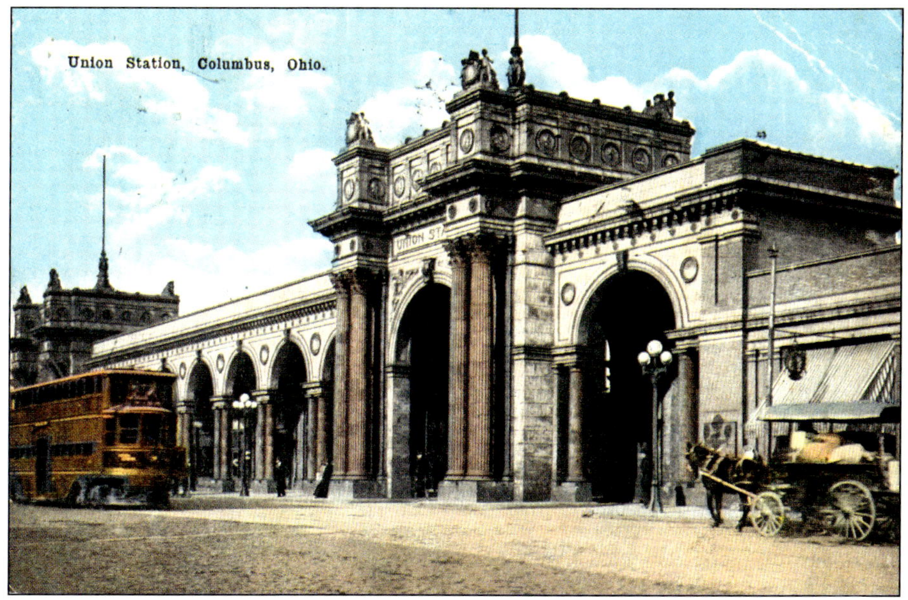

Union Station and interurban. Postmarked 1920, $6-7.

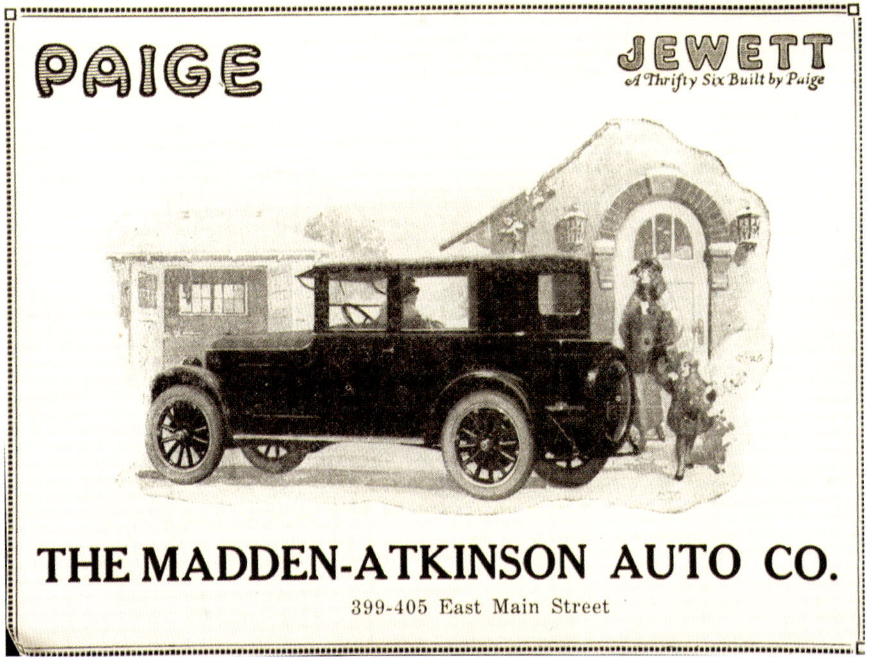

Madden-Atkinson Auto Co. advertisement. Published 1924, $2-4.

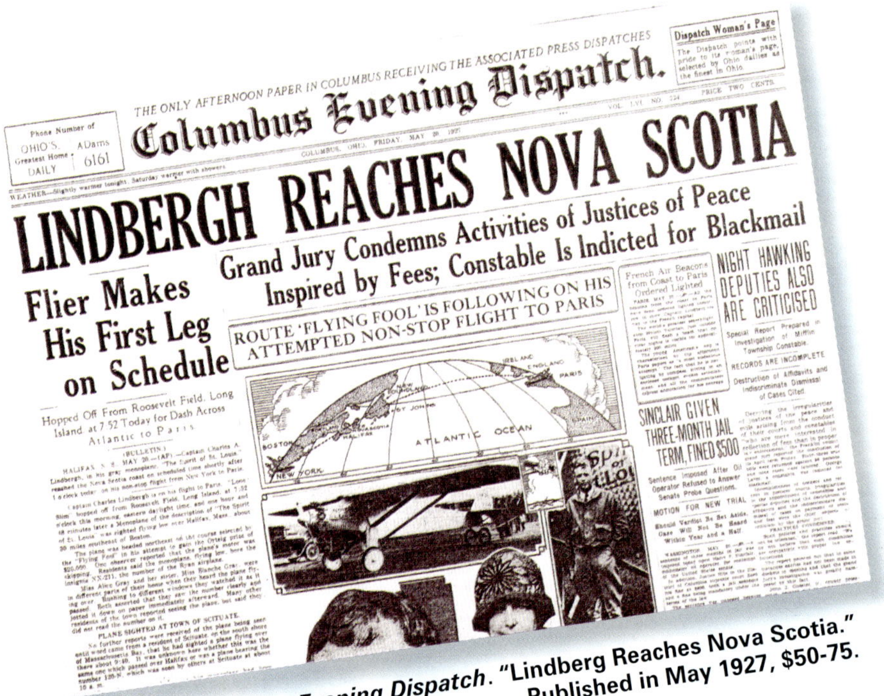

THE ONLY AFTERNOON PAPER IN COLUMBUS RECEIVING THE ASSOCIATED PRESS DISPATCHES

Columbus Evening Dispatch.

Dispatch Woman's Page

LINDBERGH REACHES NOVA SCOTIA

Grand Jury Condemns Activities of Justices of Peace Inspired by Fees; Constable Is Indicted for Blackmail

Flier Makes His First Leg on Schedule

Hopped Off From Roosevelt Field, Long Island, at 7:52 Today for Dash Across Atlantic to Paris

ROUTE 'FLYING FOOL' IS FOLLOWING ON HIS ATTEMPTED NON-STOP FLIGHT TO PARIS

NIGHT HAWKING DEPUTIES ALSO ARE CRITICISED

SINCLAIR GIVEN THREE-MONTH JAIL TERM, FINED $500

Columbus Evening Dispatch. "Lindberg Reaches Nova Scotia." Published in May 1927, $50-75.

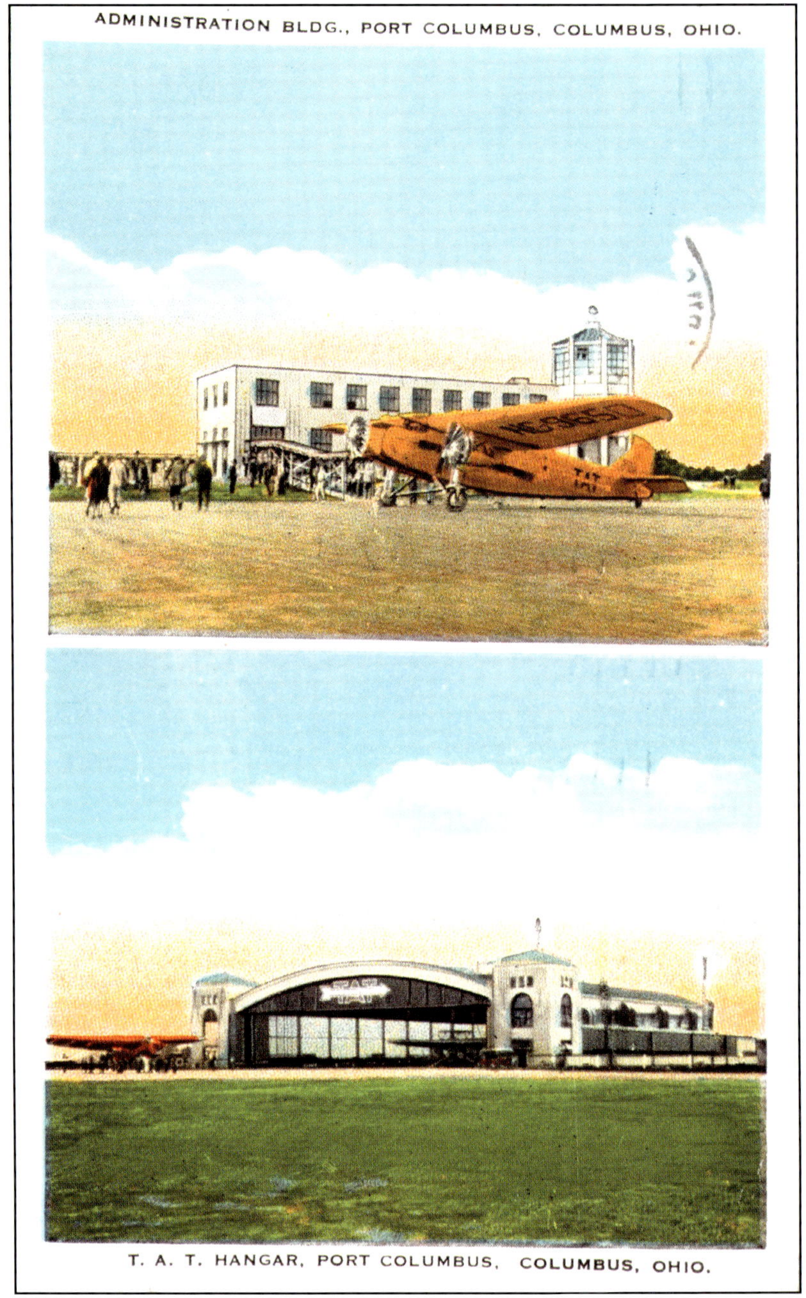

Administration building, Port Columbus. Postmarked 1931, $5-6.
The back reads: ***"America's greatest air-harbor can be reached within 15 minutes from the center of Columbus...It is fully equipped for all night operations."***

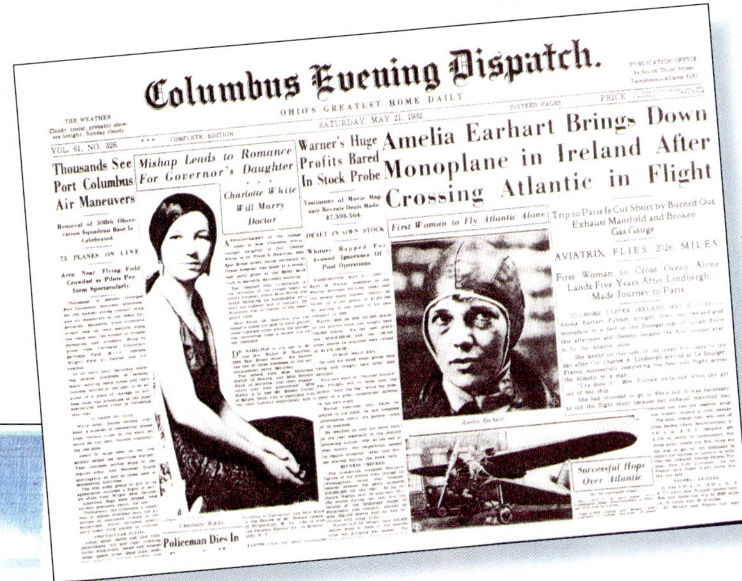
Columbus Evening Dispatch.

OHIO'S GREATEST HOME DAILY

SATURDAY, MAY 21, 1932

VOL. 61, NO. 326

Thousands See Port Columbus Air Maneuvers

Mishap Leads to Romance For Governor's Daughter

Charlotte White Will Marry Doctor

Warner's Huge Profits Bared In Stock Probe

Amelia Earhart Brings Down Monoplane in Ireland After Crossing Atlantic in Flight

First Woman to Fly Atlantic Alone

Trip to Paris Is Cut Short by Burned Out Exhaust Manifold and Broken Gas Gauge

AVIATRIX FLIES 2026 MILES

First Woman to Cross Ocean Alone Lands Five Years After Lindbergh Made Journey to Paris

Successful Hops Over Atlantic

Policeman Dies In

Columbus Evening Dispatch. "Amelia Earhart Brings Down Monoplane." Published in May 1932, $50-75.

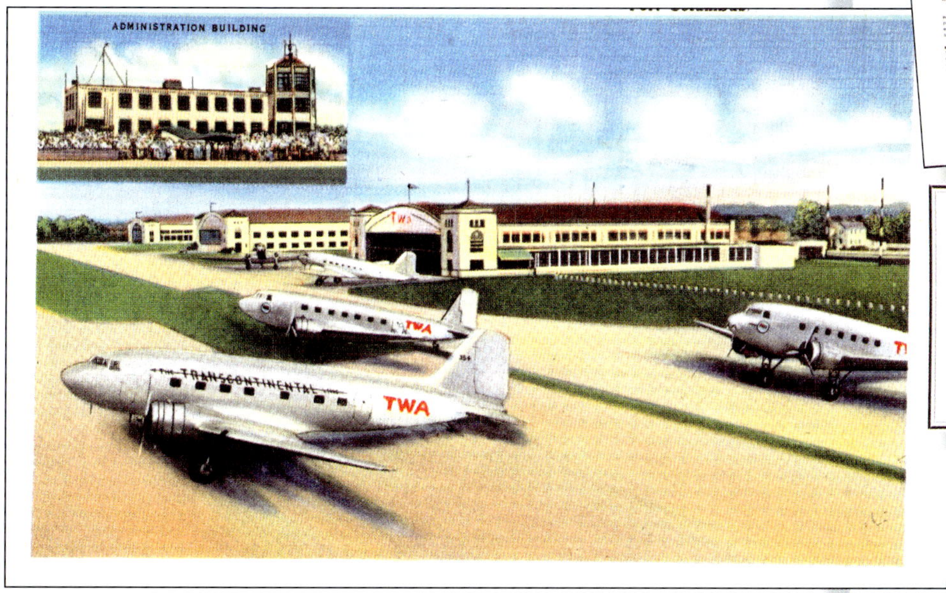

Port Columbus airport. Copyright 1938, $6-7.

ARCODEL SYSTEM
for
DEPENDABLE BUS SERVICE
to
Marion, Lima, Toledo, Newark, Zanesville, Marietta

Charter Coach Service
Room 210

ADams 6310 Interurban Terminal Bldg.

Arcodel Bus Service advertisement. At Columbus Interurban Terminal building. Published 1935, $2-3.

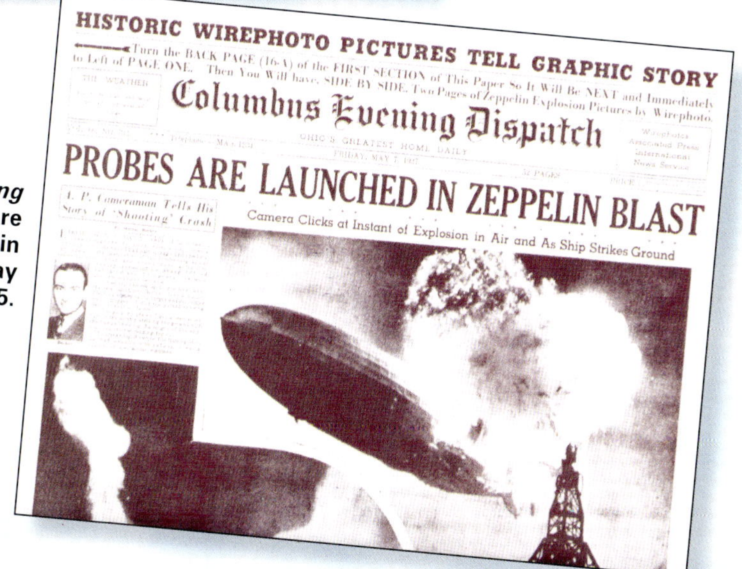
HISTORIC WIREPHOTO PICTURES TELL GRAPHIC STORY

Turn the BACK PAGE (16-A) of the FIRST SECTION of This Paper So It Will Be NEXT and Immediately to Left of PAGE ONE. Then You Will have SIDE BY SIDE Two Pages of Zeppelin Explosion Pictures by Wirephoto.

Columbus Evening Dispatch

OHIO'S GREATEST HOME DAILY

PROBES ARE LAUNCHED IN ZEPPELIN BLAST

Camera Clicks at Instant of Explosion in Air and As Ship Strikes Ground

Columbus Evening Dispatch. "Probes Are Launched in Zeppelin Blast." Published in May 1937, $50-75.

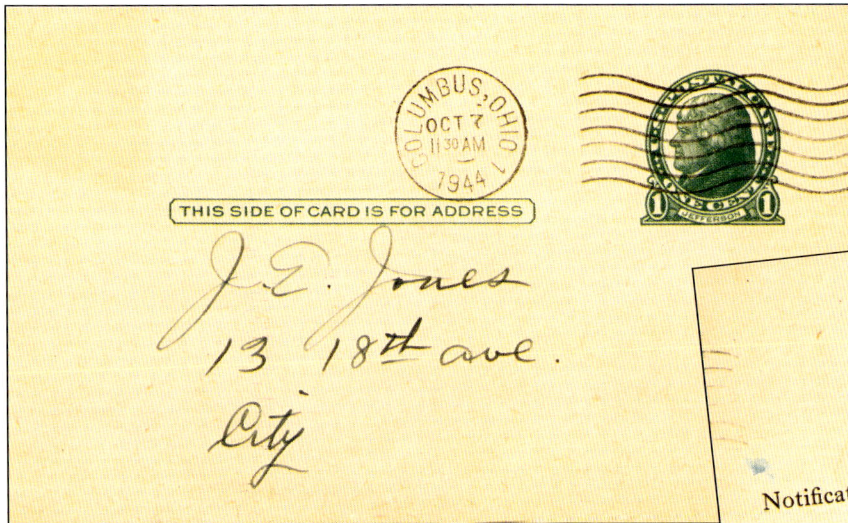

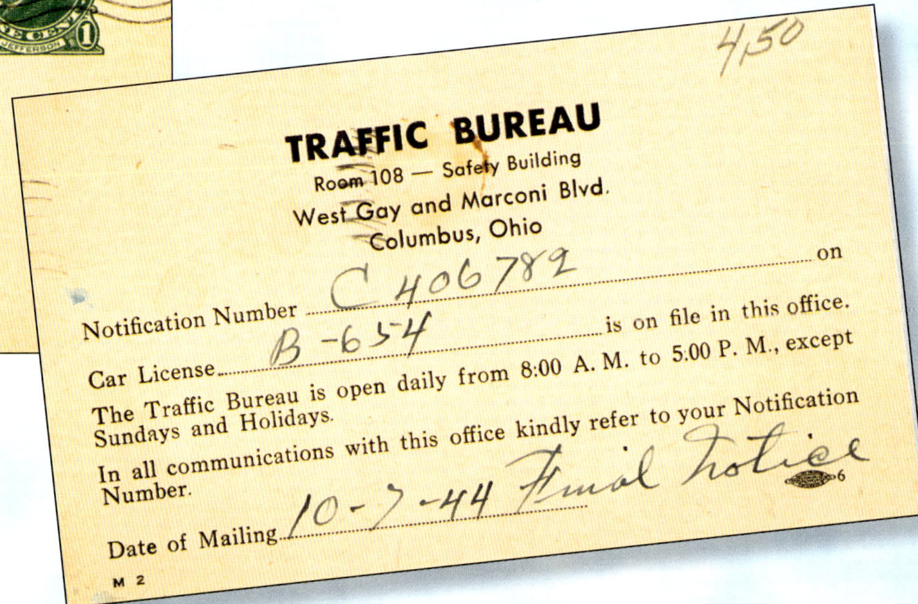

Traffic Bureau postcard. Final notice to city resident. Postmarked 1944, $2-3.

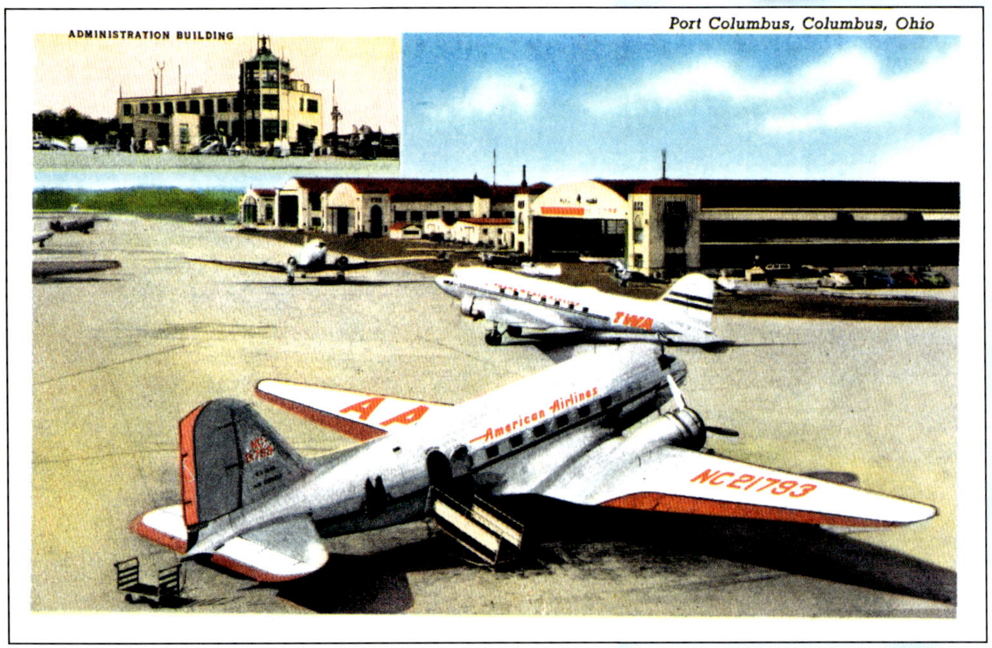

Port Columbus Airport. American Airlines and TWA planes. Circa 1950s, $4-6.

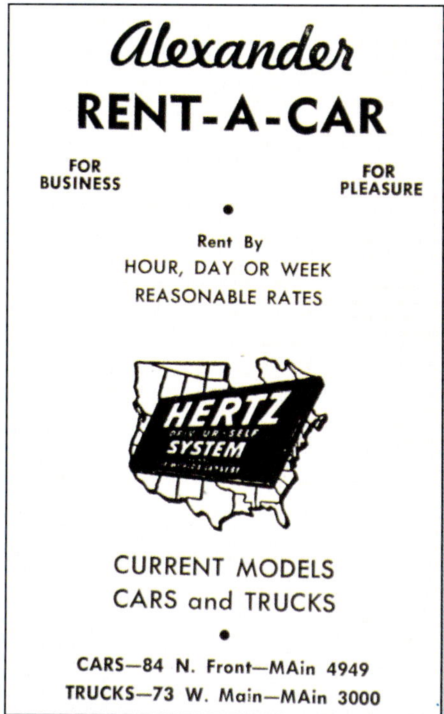

Alexander Rent-A-Car advertisement. Cars and Trucks. Published 1954, $2-3.

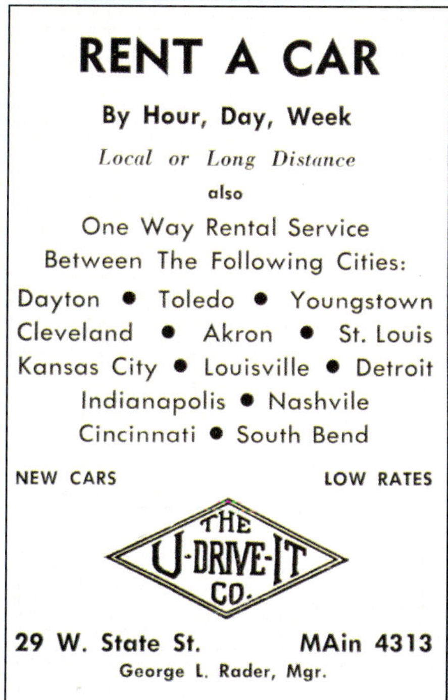

U-Drive-It advertisement. New cars, low rates. Published 1954, $2-3.

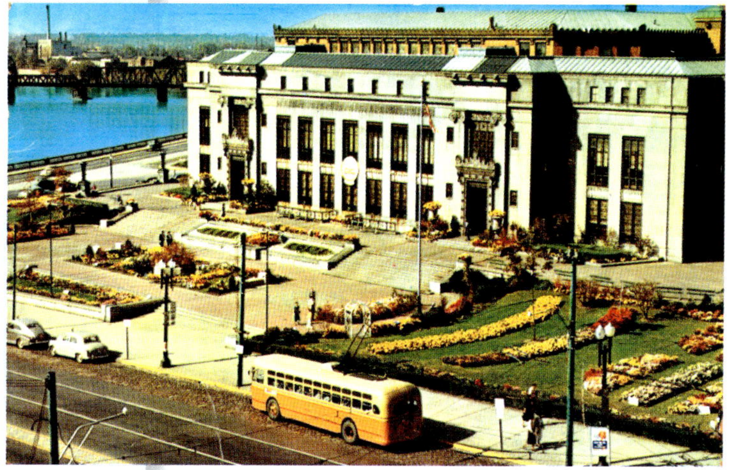

City bus passes Columbus Civic Center. Postmarked 1955, $3-5.

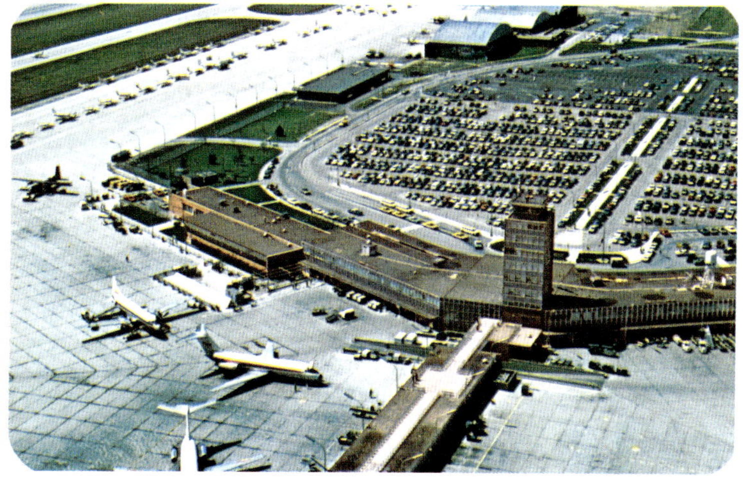

Columbus International Airport Terminal. Circa 1960s, $3-4.

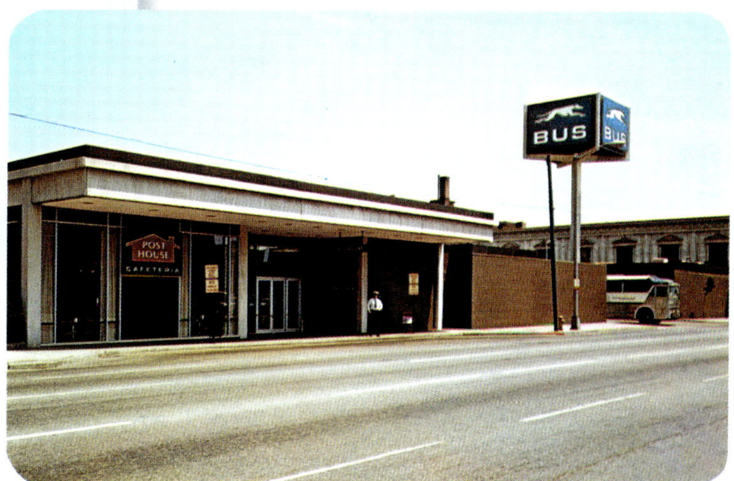

Greyhound Bus Terminal. Circa 1960s, $3-4.

Chapter Six: The Great Ohio State

> Ohio State is a colossus....one of the greatest universities of the country.
> — *Inside U.S.A. by John Gunther, 1947*

It wasn't always Ohio State. But in the opinion of many it was always great.

Back in the 1870s the place was originally the Ohio Agricultural and Mechanical College.

Sources at Ohio State University itself say the founders were deeply divided on the school's initial curriculum. Some held out for an array of strictly agriculture and mechanical arts classes while others favored a broader approach that would include English, foreign languages, and other subjects. The liberal arts education plan narrowly prevailed.

When author John Gunther visited in the latter 1940s, diversity was the hallmark of Ohio State. He noted the course list then included the following:

> *Ice Cream Manufacturing; Elementary Russian; Introduction to Clothing and Textiles; Factors in Successful Marriage; Motor Carrier Organizations; the Social Work Approach to Life Adjustments; Pliny and Catullus; Driers, Klins, and Theory of Firing; Education of Exceptional Children; Epidemic Diseases in Warfare; Principles of Taxonomy: Moncots and Dicots; Intermediate Japanese; Anatomy of the Horse; Old Provencal; and Woodlot Management*

"The variety of curriculum," observed author Gunther of the Ohio State campus, "though commonplace to Americans and typical of all middle western state universities with a strong vocational slant, will astonish any European."

Gunther concluded Ohio State "teaches liberal arts and agriculture first, and then anything that makes for a good living or extension of the wealth of Ohio."

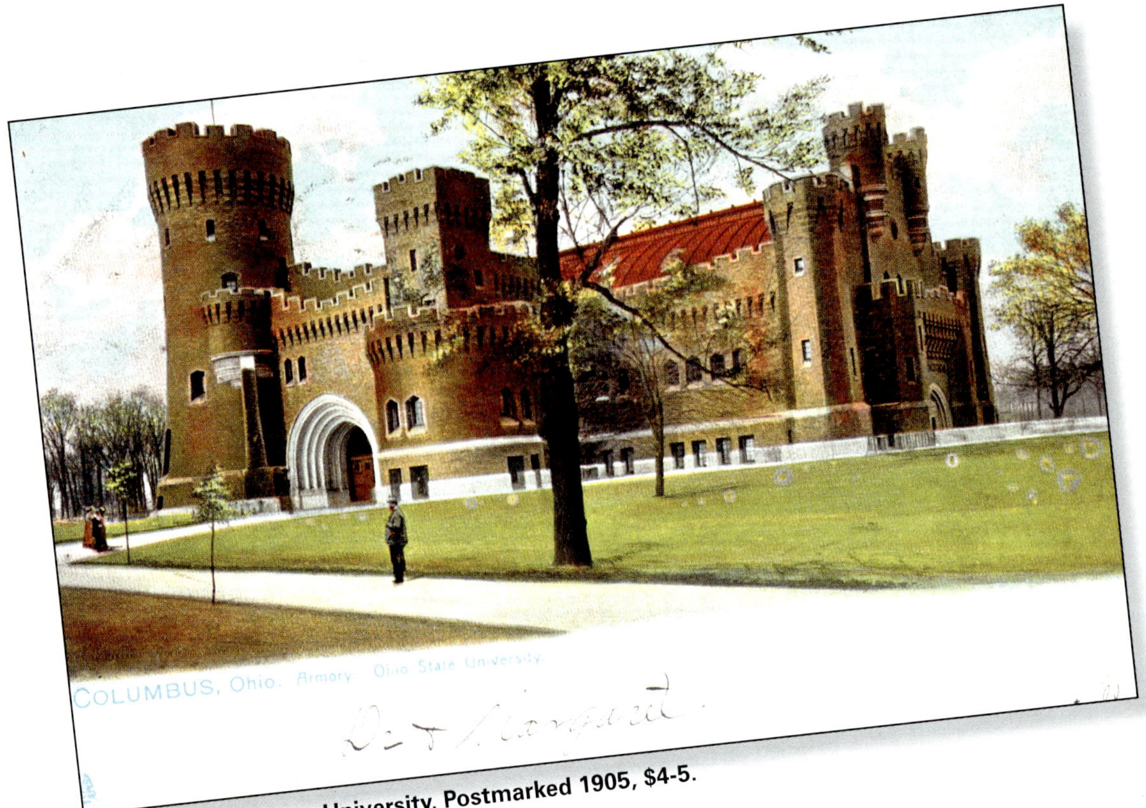

Armory at Ohio State University. Postmarked 1905, $4-5.

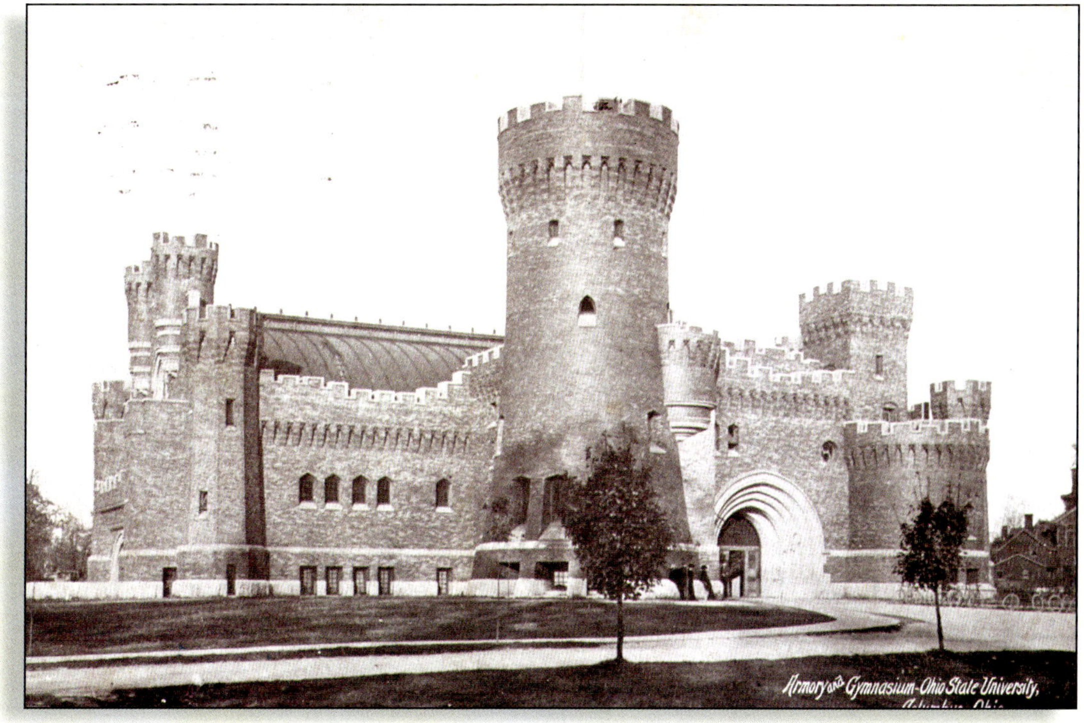

Armory and gymnasium, Ohio State. Postmarked 1911, $3-4.

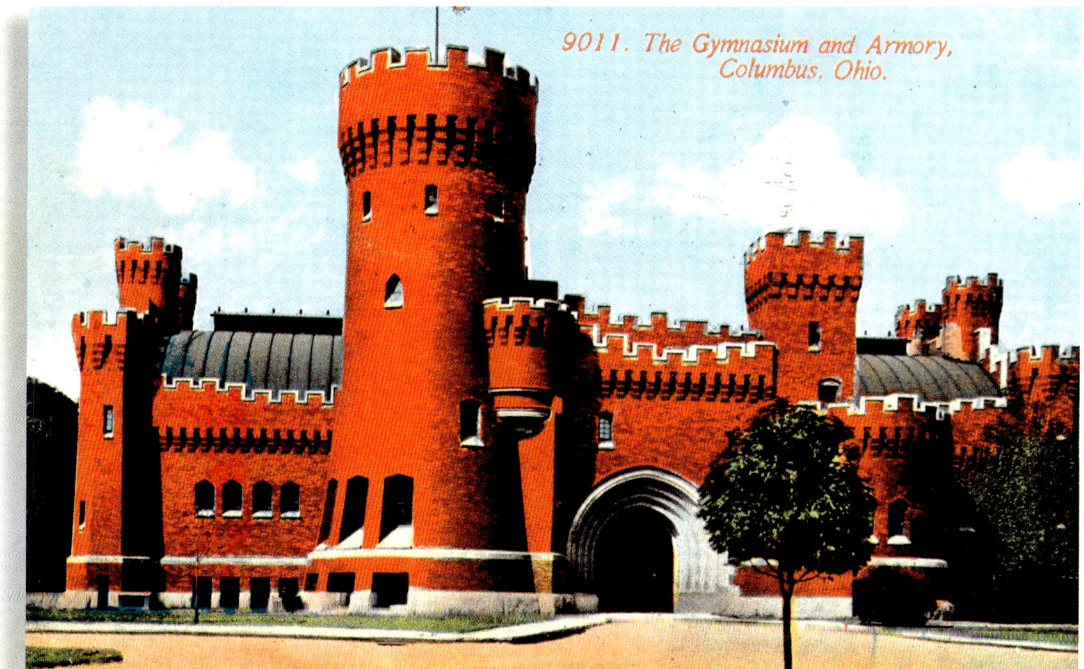

The Gymnasium and Armory. Postmarked 1912, $4-5. Hand-written message on the back reads: *"This is one of the few buildings where we have military. I like it very much so far. Expect to go home Dec. 20 and stay until Jan. 3."*

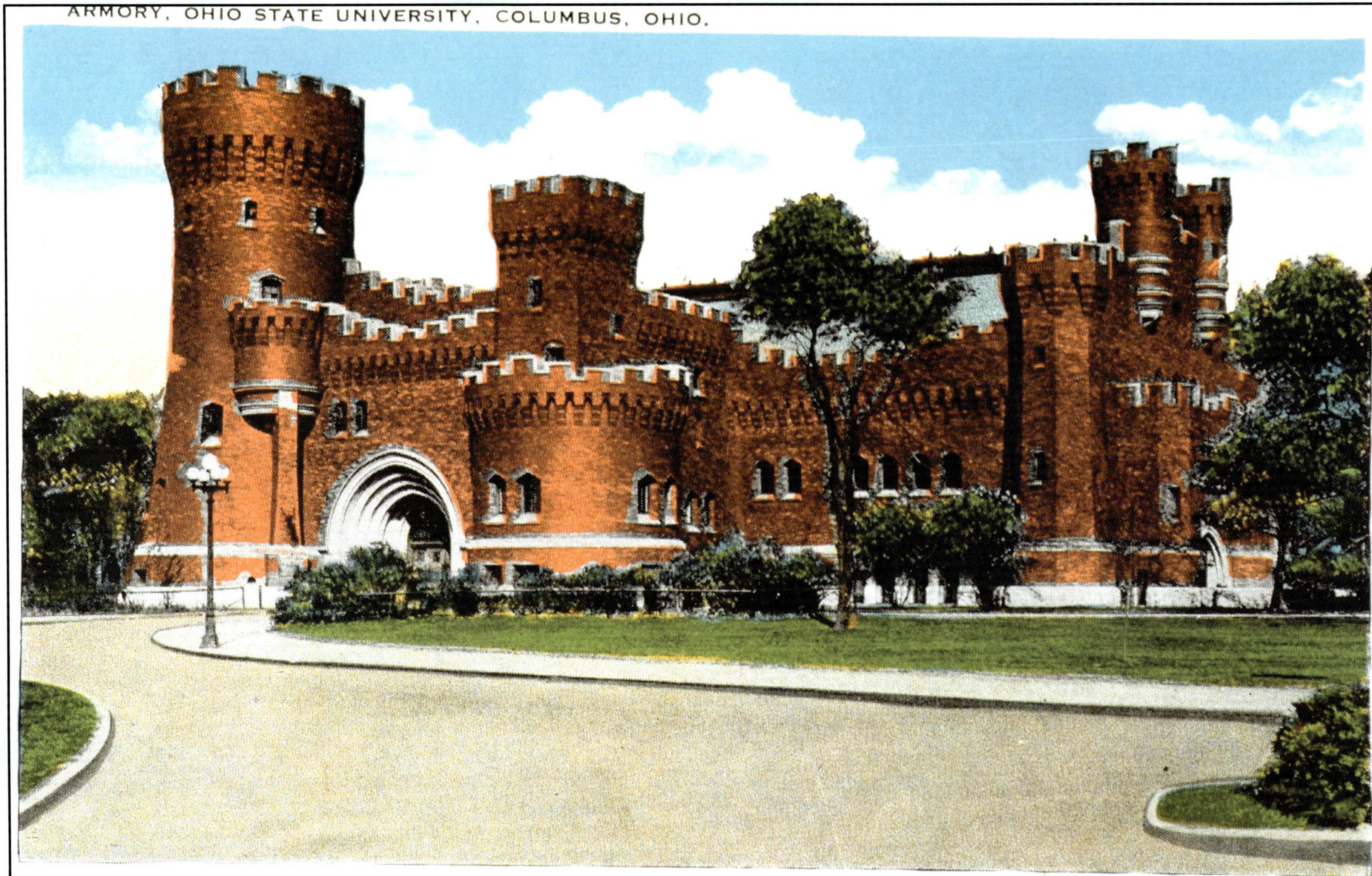

Ohio State University Armory. Circa 1920, $3-4.

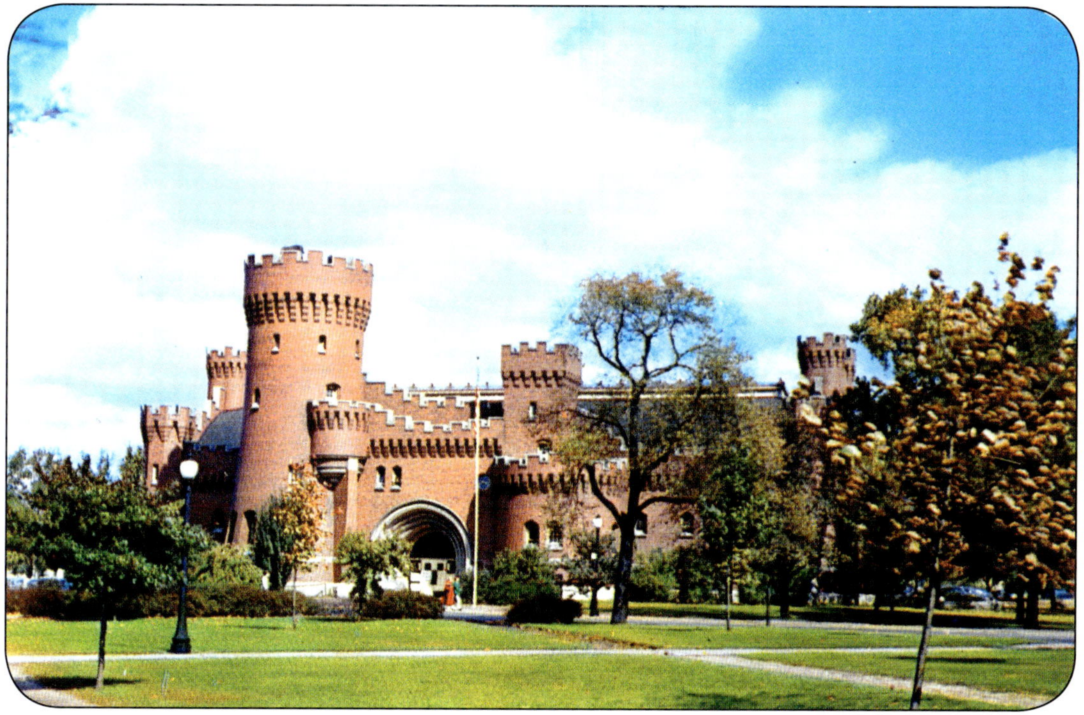

Armory at Ohio State. Circa 1950s, $2-3.
The back reads: *"Well-known spot on the Ohio State University campus is the Armory, now seat of the Department of Naval Services."*

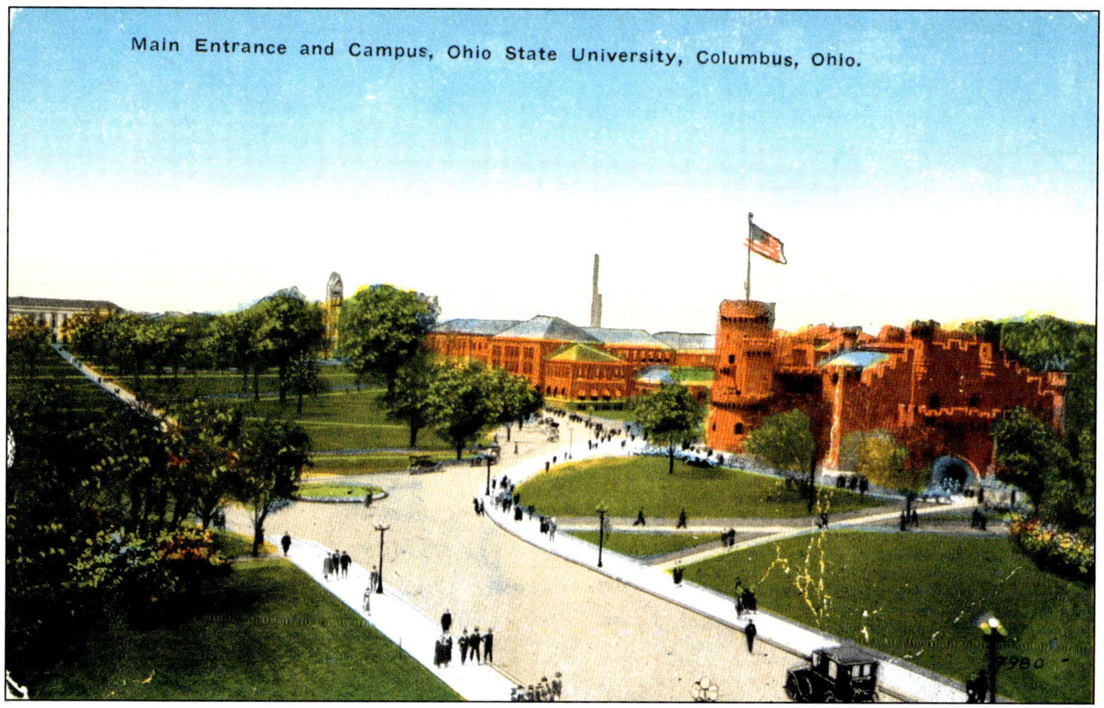

Main Entrance and Campus, Ohio State University.
Circa early 1900s, $4-5.

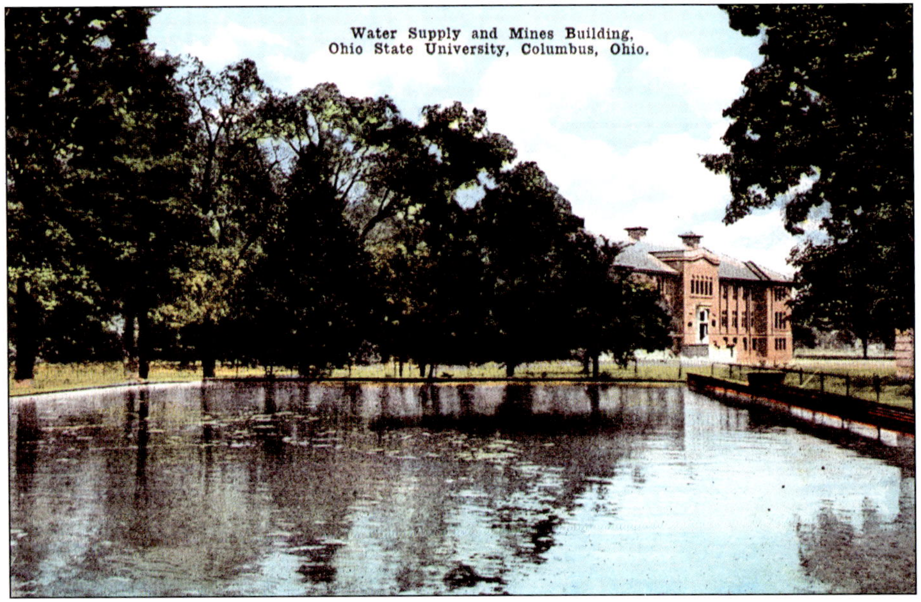

Water Supply and Mines Building, Ohio State University. Circa early 1900s, $4-5.

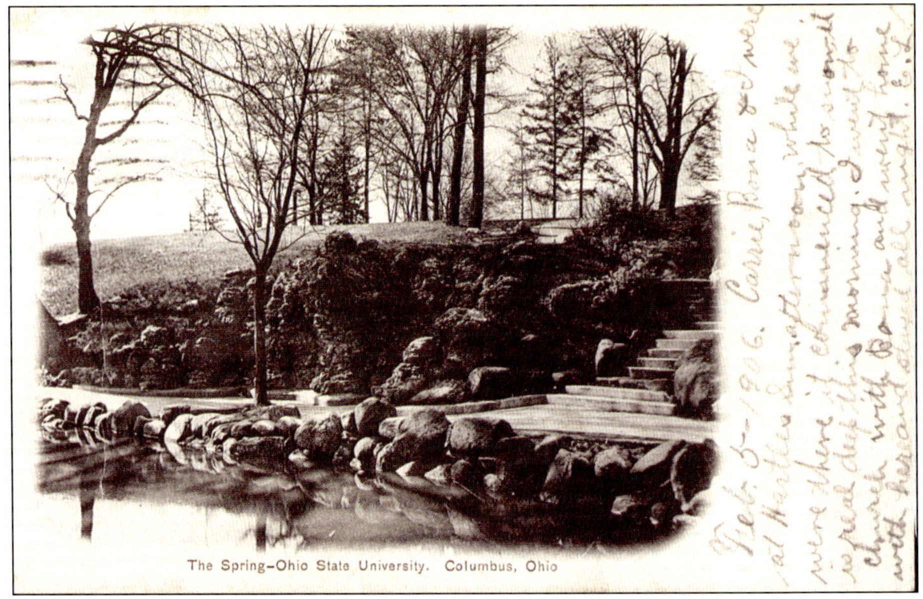

The Spring, Ohio State University. Postmarked 1906, $2-4.

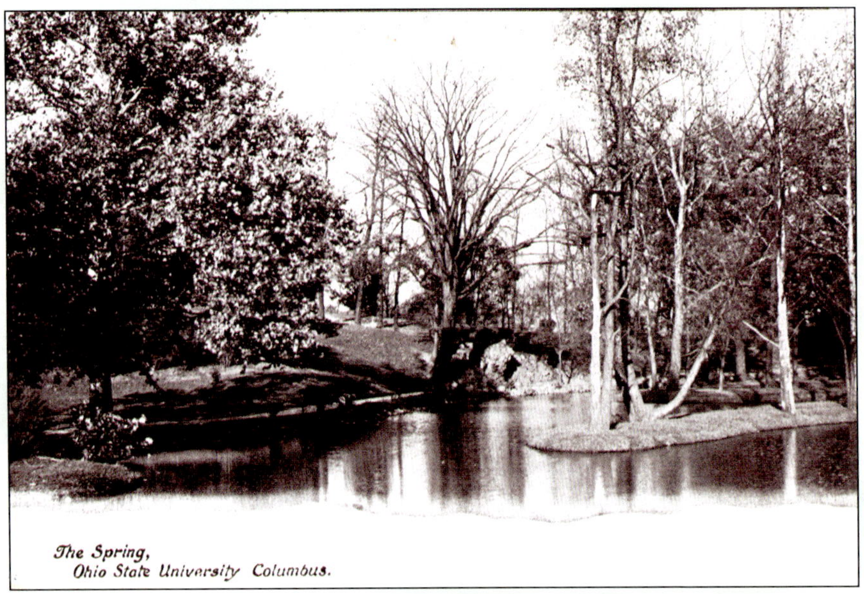

The Spring at Ohio State University. Circa early 1900s, $2-3

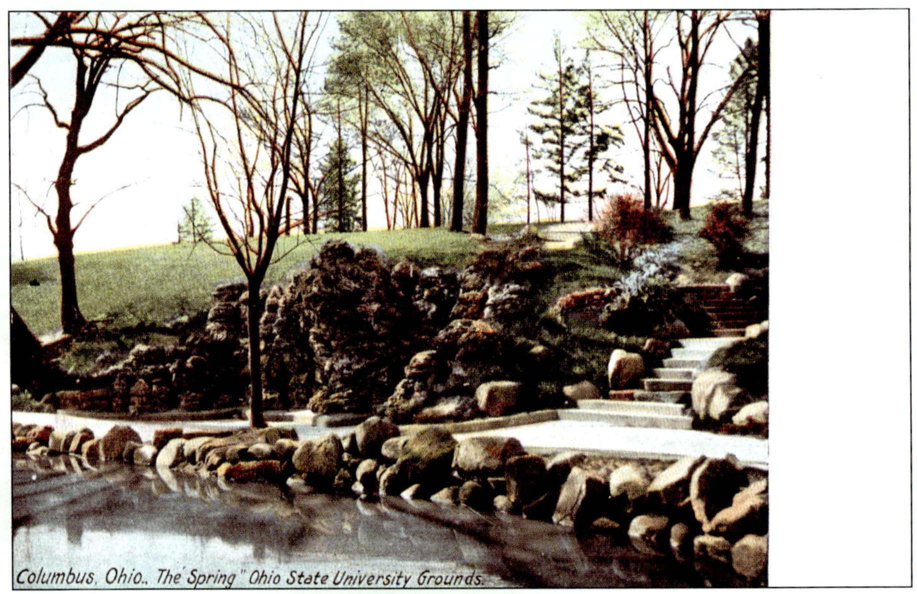

The Spring on Ohio State grounds. Circa early 1900s, $2-3.

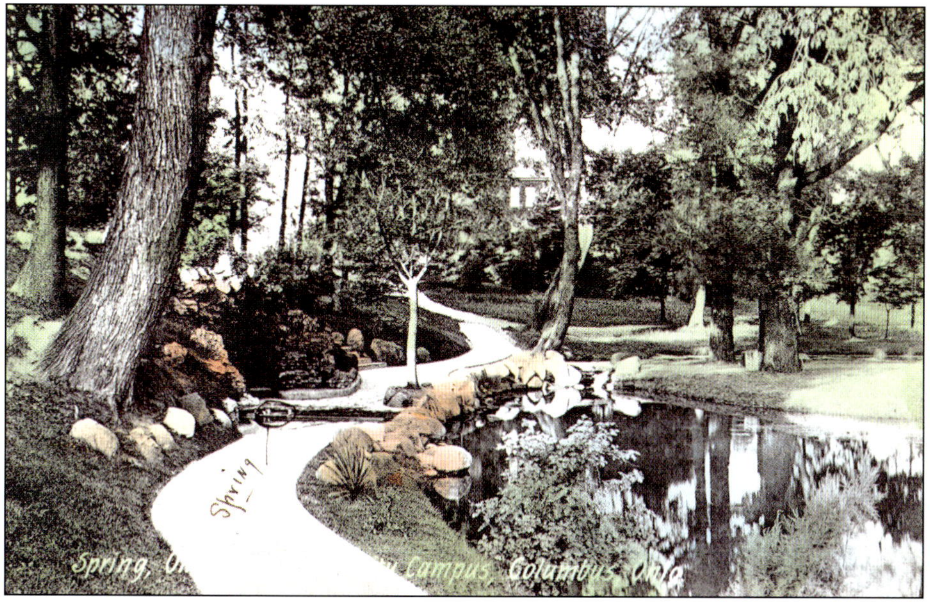

Ohio State campus spring. Postmarked 1908, $3-4. Hand-written message on the back reads: *"Here is where O.S.U. held three shows-natural amphitheatre. I am not long in this old town anymore, June 15 finds me in Chicago if everything goes nicely."*

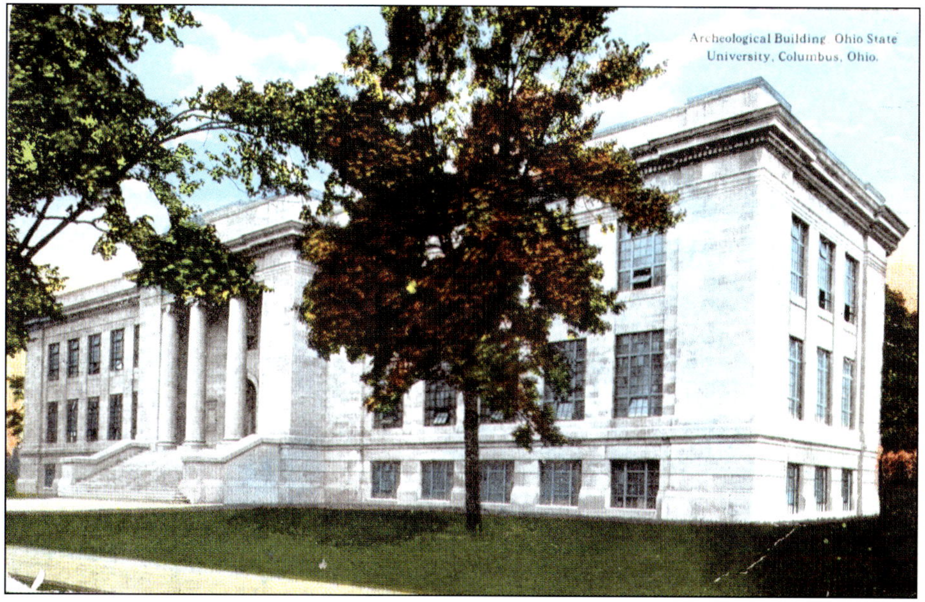

Archeological building, Ohio State. Circa early 1900, $2-3.

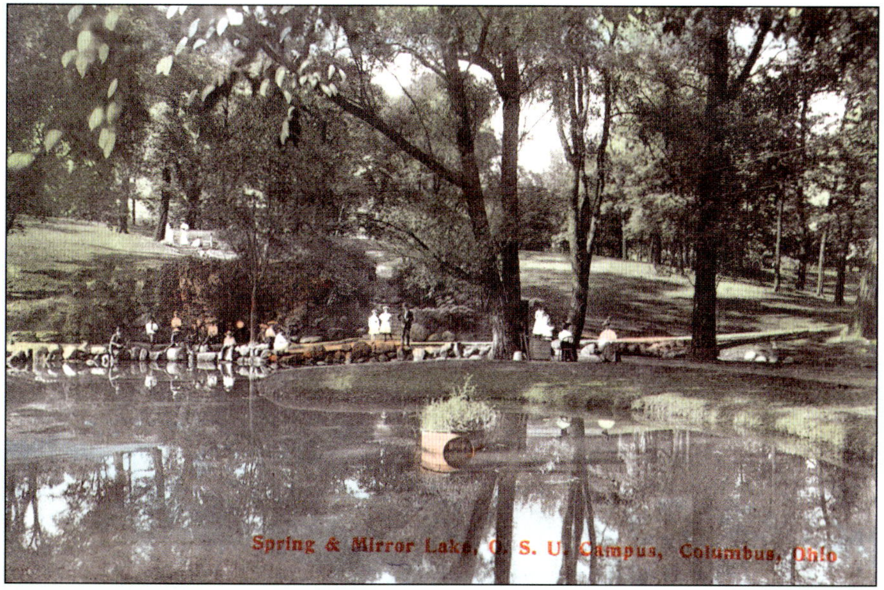

Spring and Mirror Lake, O.S.U. campus. Postmarked 1908, $4-5. Hand-written message on the back reads: *"City express knows nothing of the package. Kindly send blue trousers immediately. Want them for the Senior club formal."*

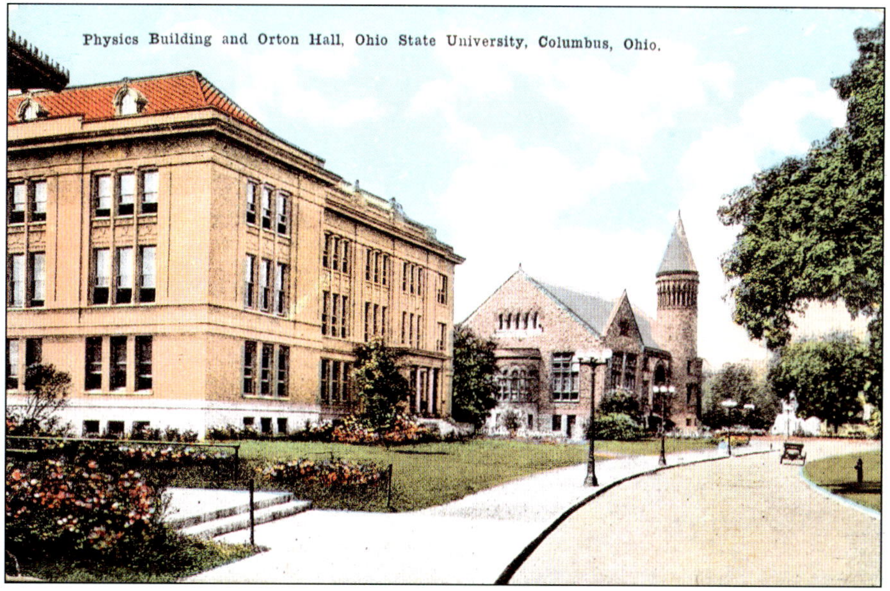

Physics building and Orton Hall. Circa early 1900s, $3-4.

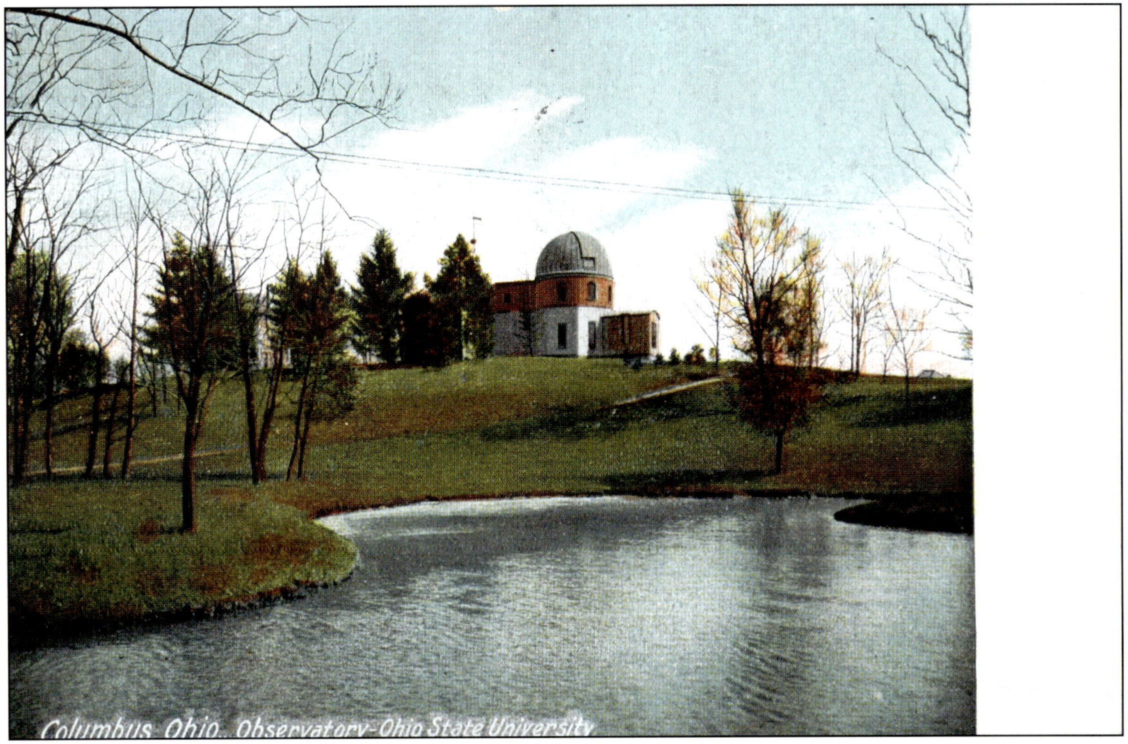

Observatory, Ohio State University. Postmarked 1908, $3-4.

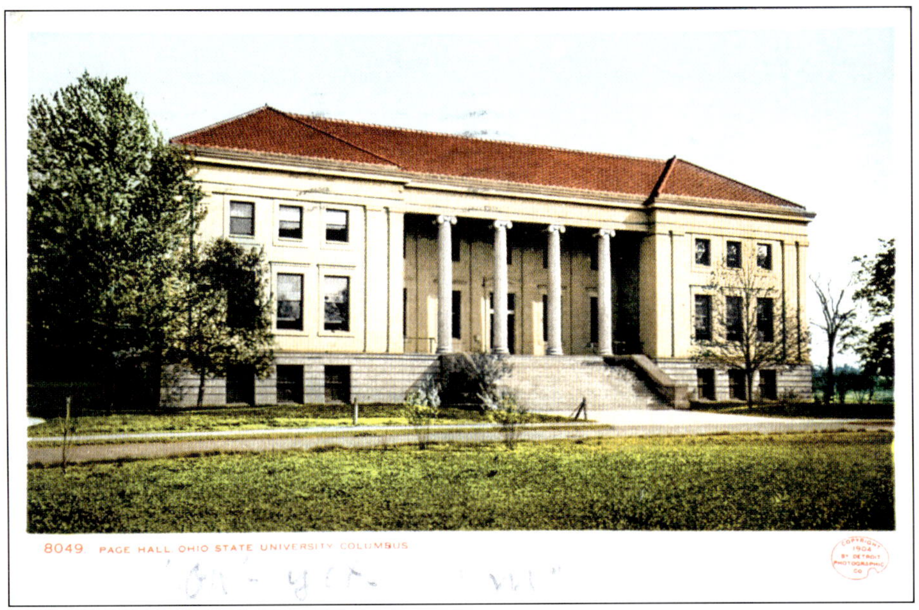

Page Hall, Ohio State University. Postmarked 1910, $4-5.

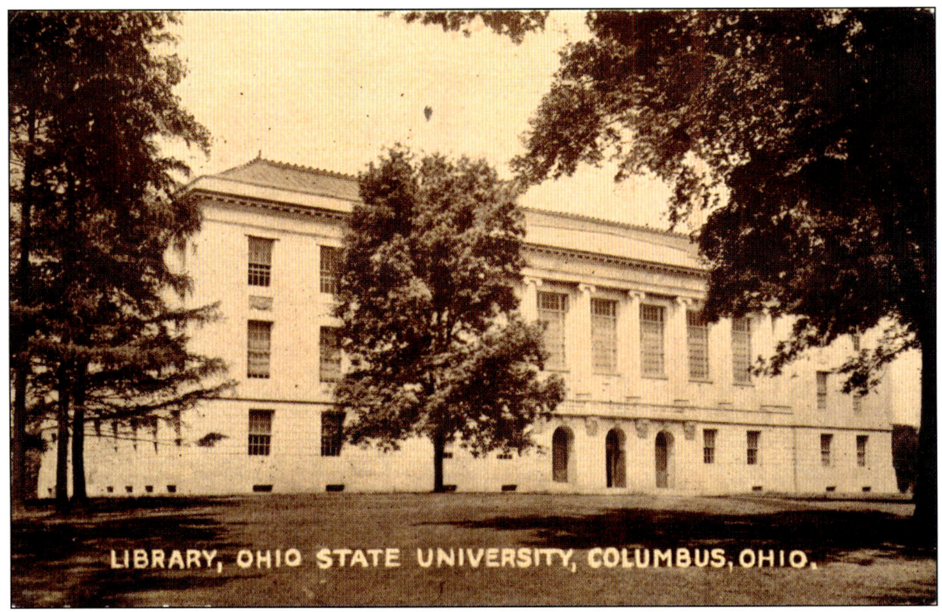

Library, Ohio State University. Postmarked 1914, $2-3.

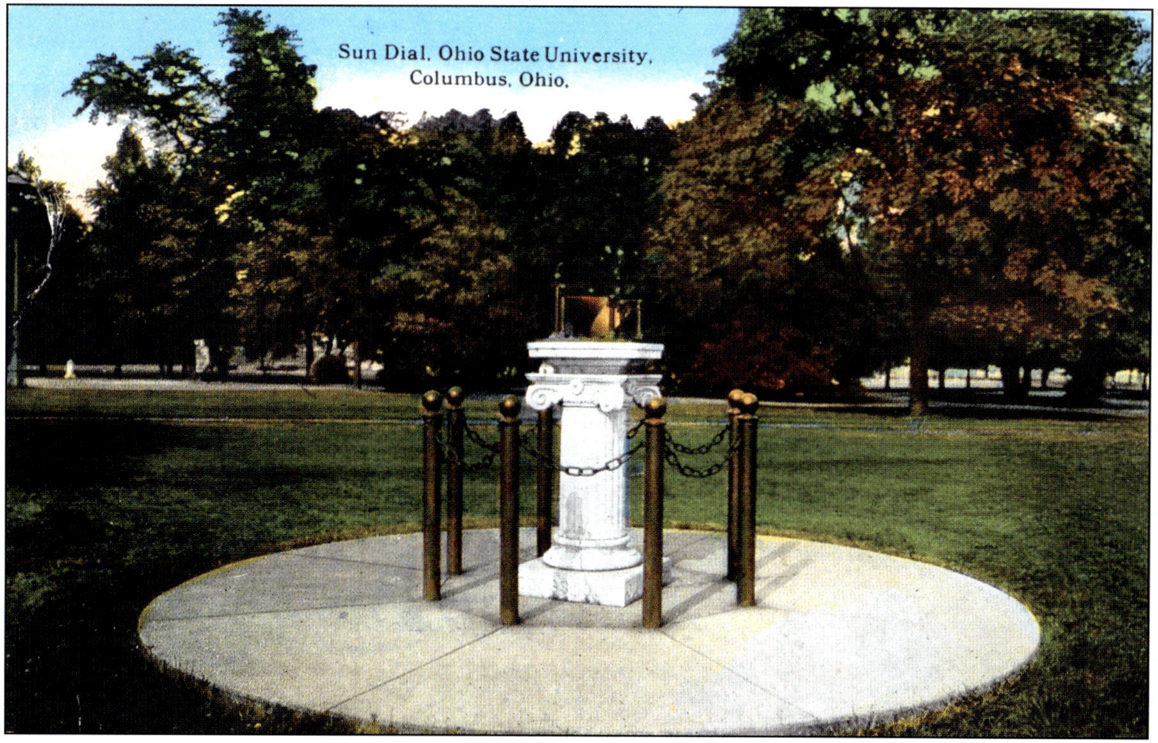

Sun Dial, Ohio State University. Postmarked 1918, $3-4.

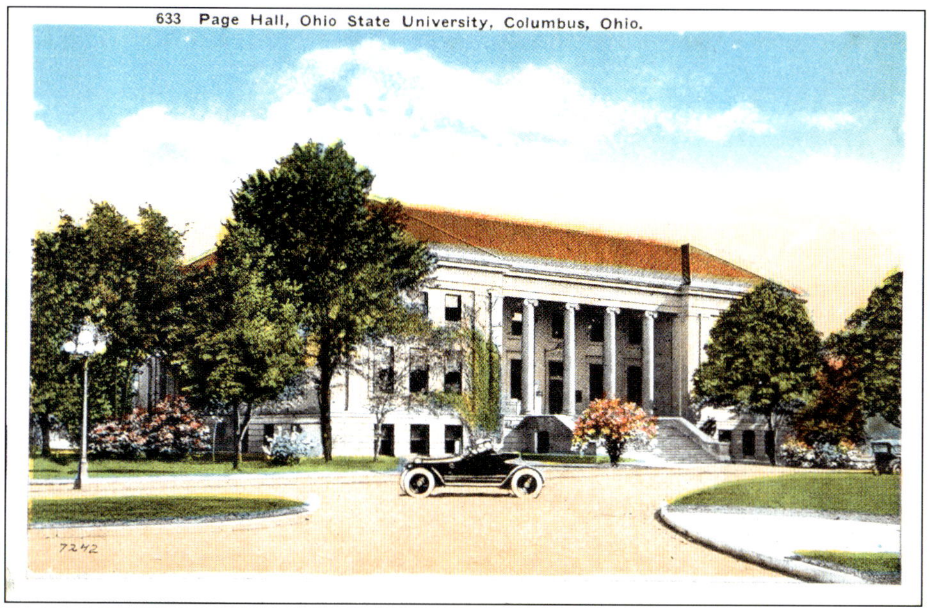

Brown Hall, O.S.U. Circa early 1900s, $3-4.

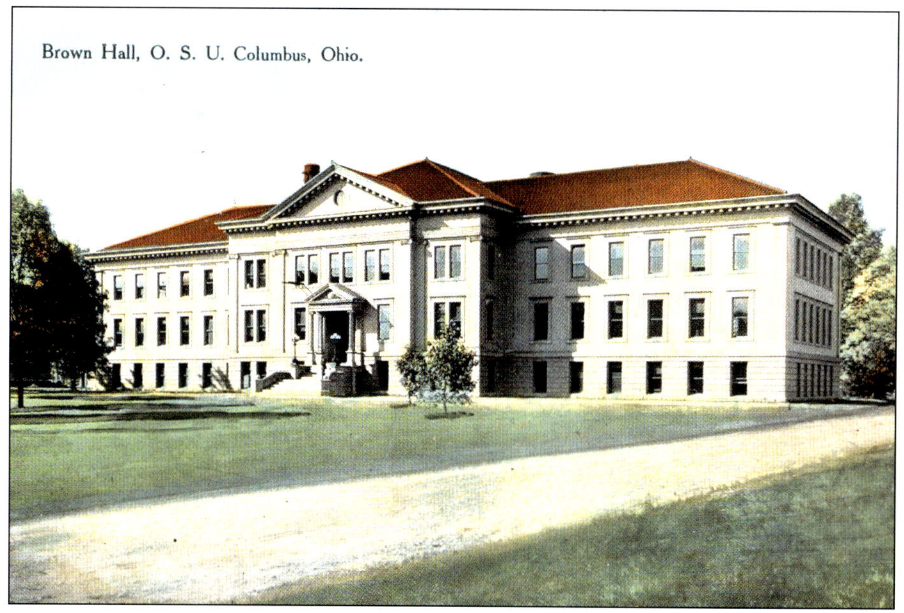

Page Hall at Ohio State. Circa 1920s, $4-5.

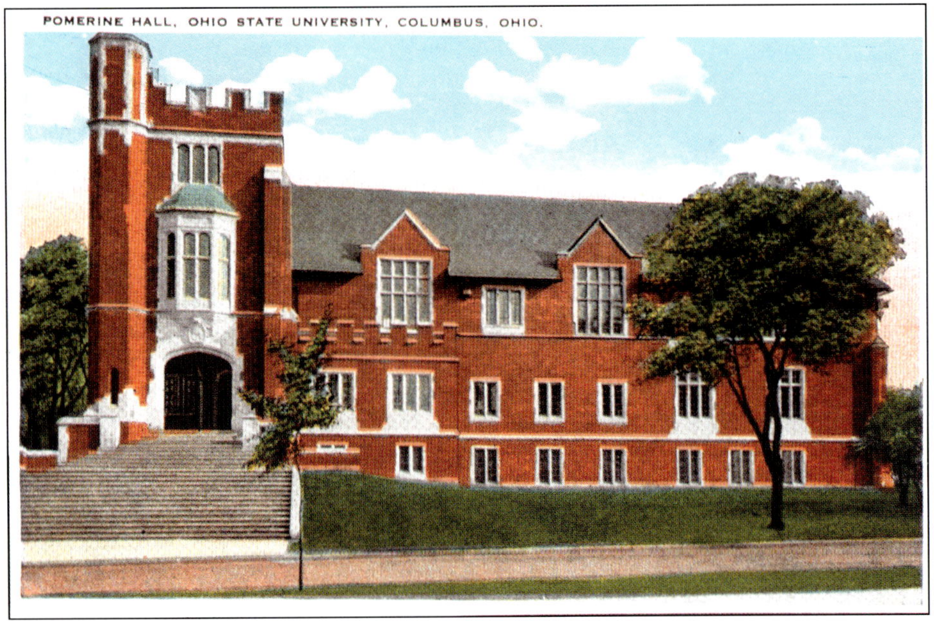

Pomerine Hall, Ohio State University. Circa 1920s, $3-4.

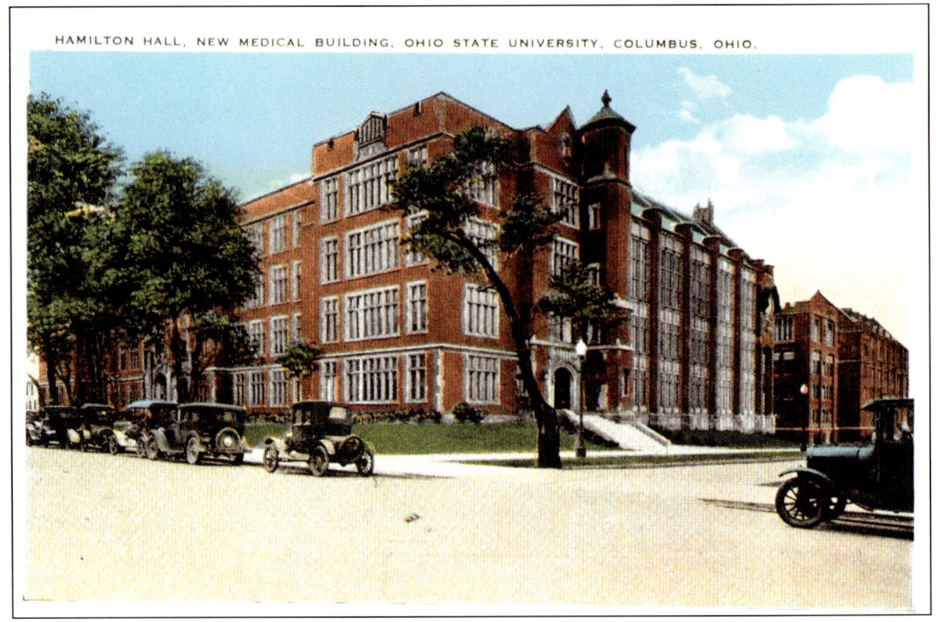

Hamilton Hall, New Medical Building. Circa 1920s, $4-5.

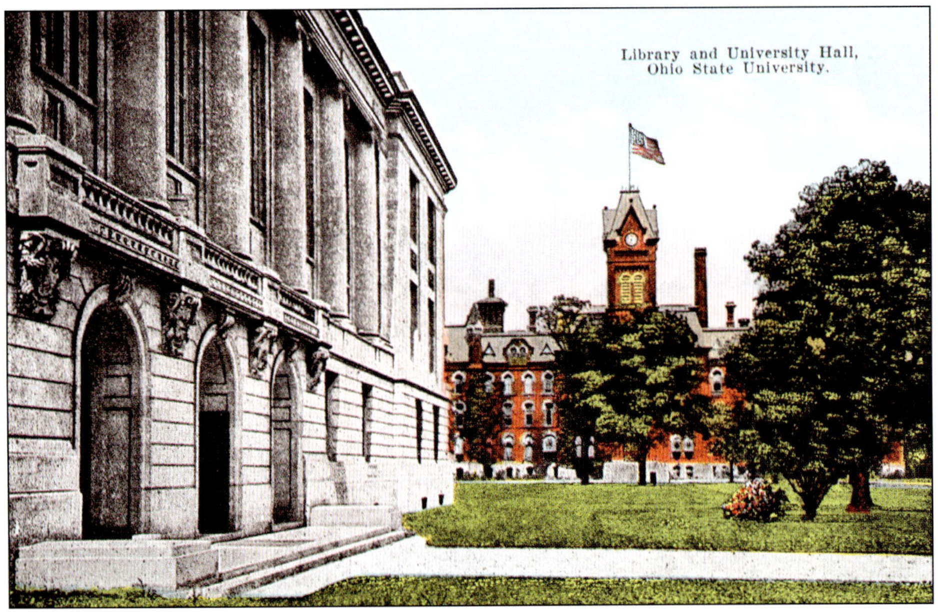

Library and University Hall. Circa 1920s, $3-4.

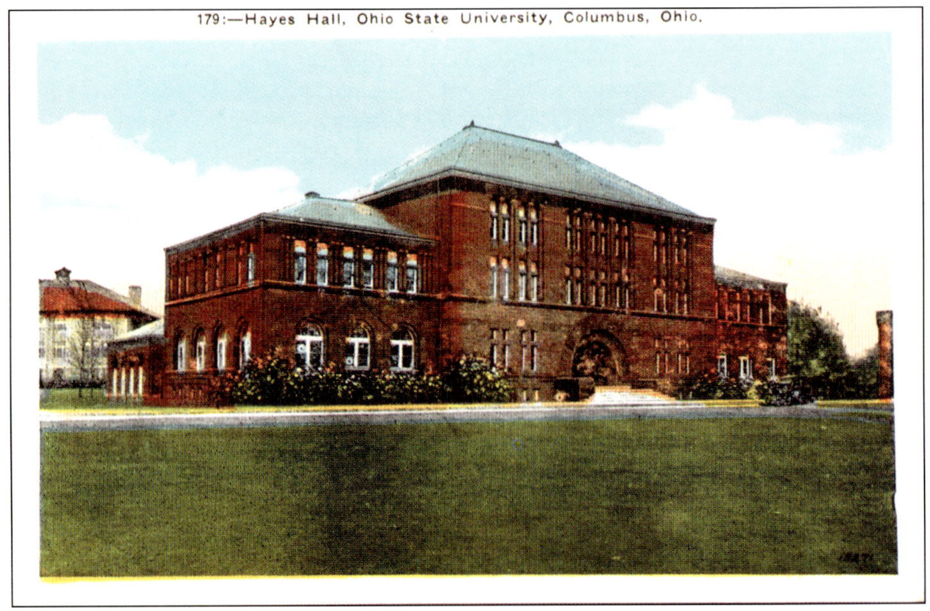

Hayes Hall, Ohio State University. Postmarked 1928, $3-4.

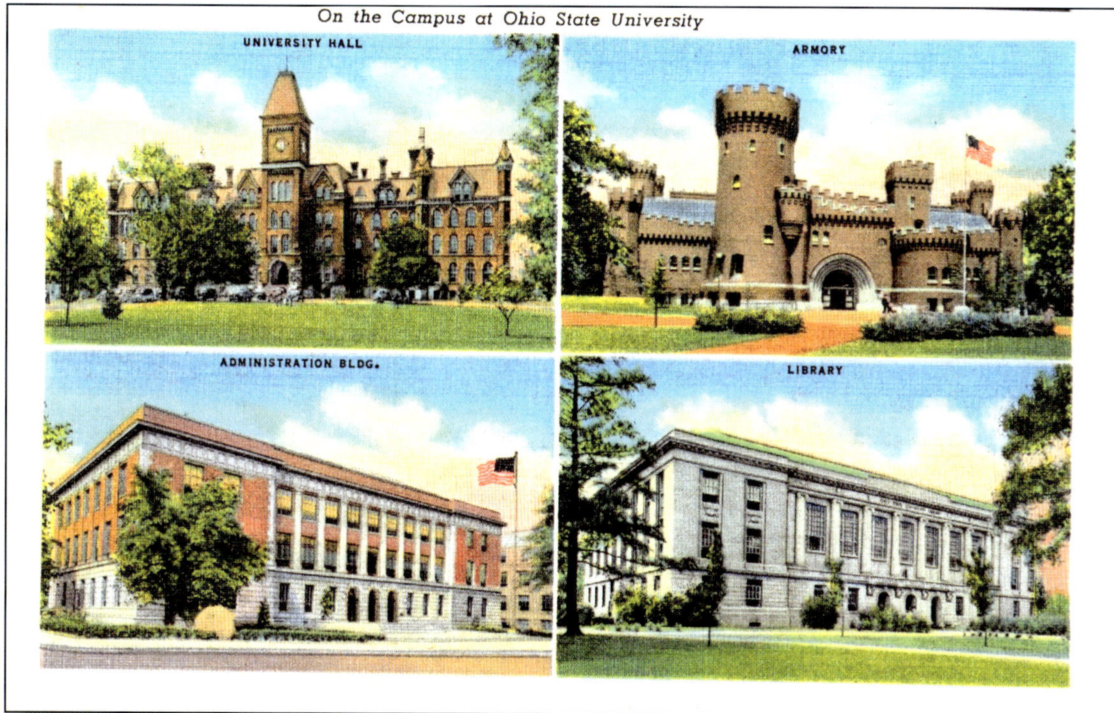

On the Campus at Ohio State. Circa 1930s, $2-3.

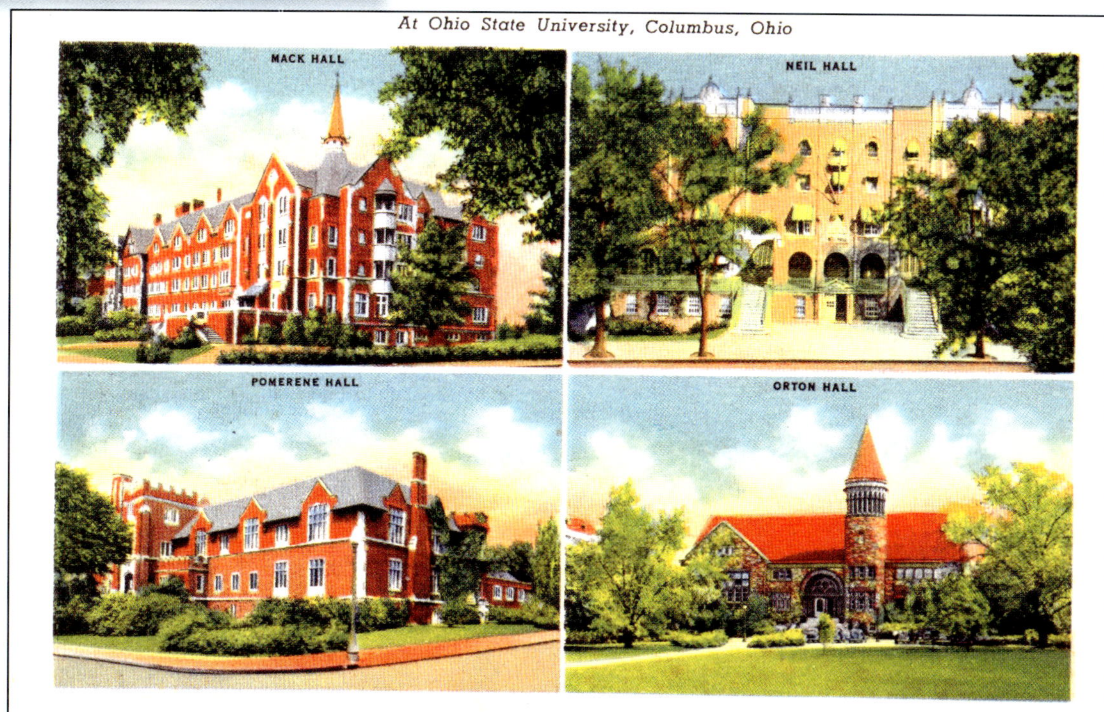

At Ohio State University. Circa 1930s, $2-3.

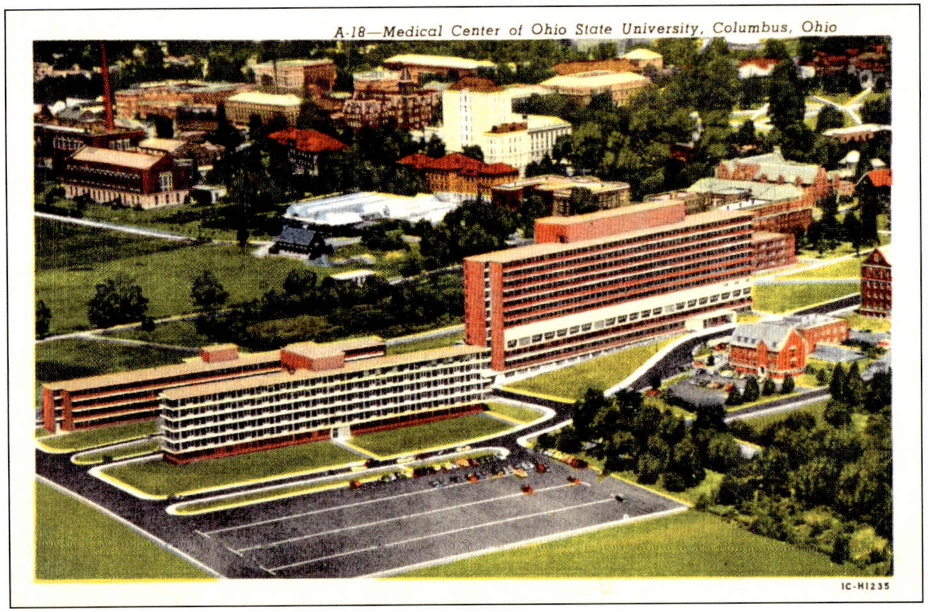

Medical Center at Ohio State. Postmarked 1957, $2-3. The back reads: *"In the background is the rest of O.S.U. Campus."*

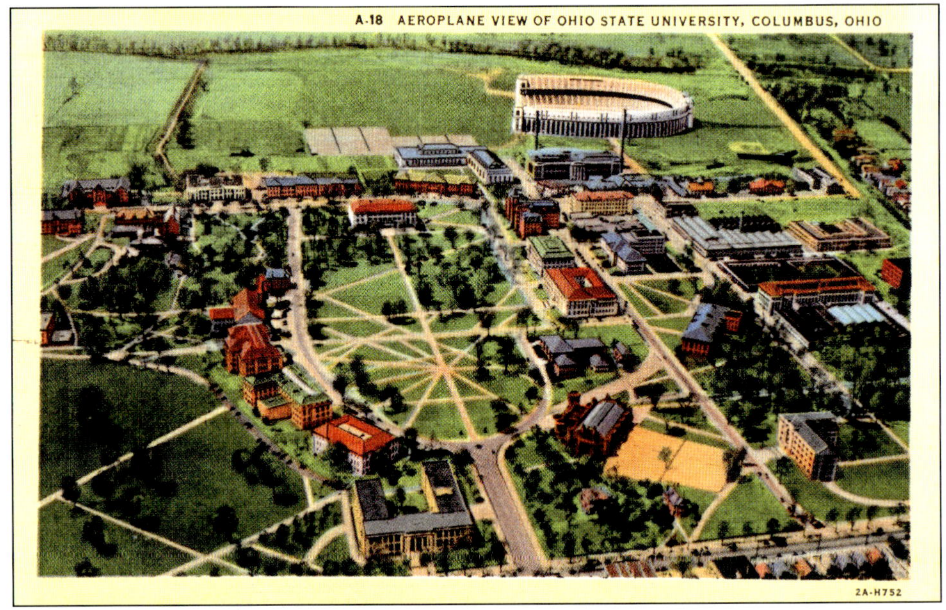

Aeroplane View of Ohio State University. Postmarked 1948, $2-3.

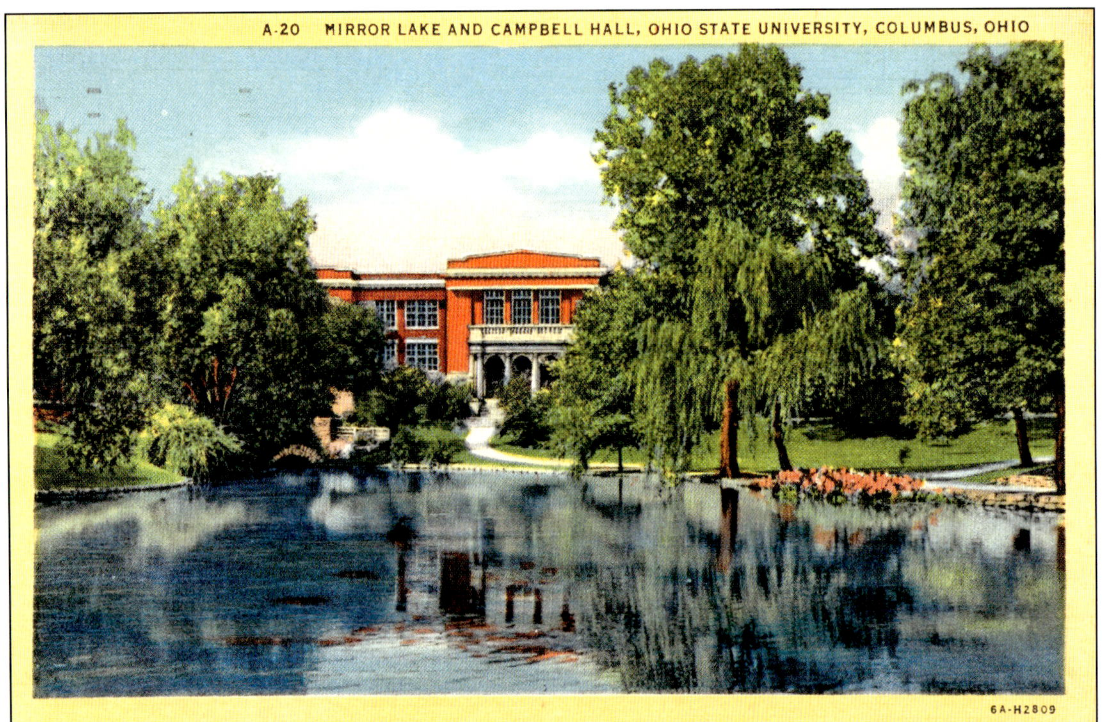

Mirror Lake and Campbell Hall. Postmarked 1951, $2-3.

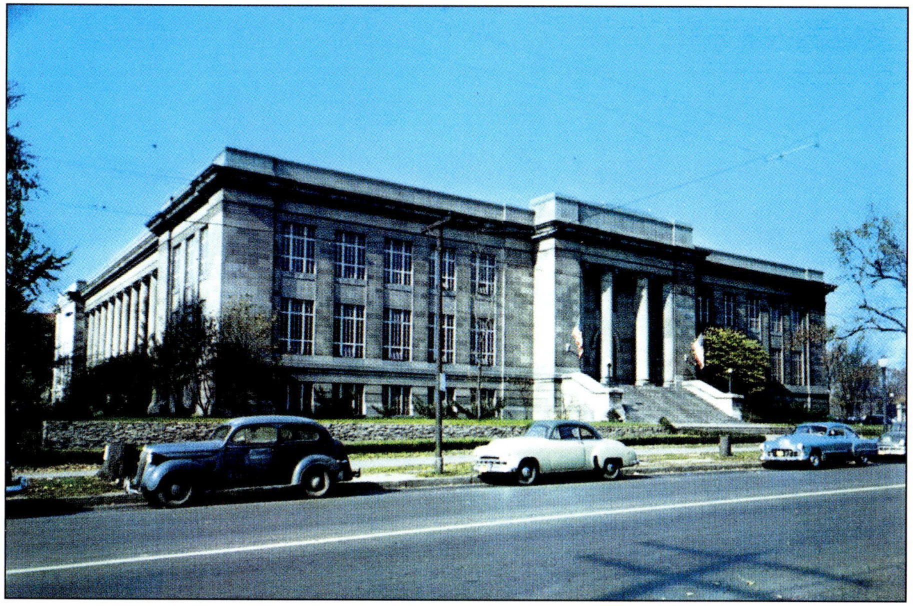

Ohio State Archaeological and Historical Museum. Circa 1950s,

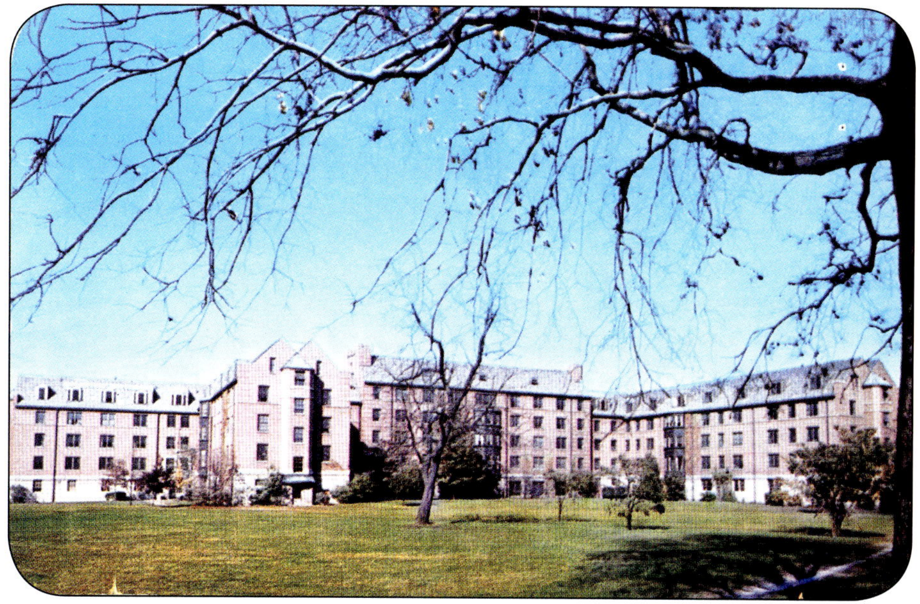

Baker Hall. Circa 1950s, $3-4. The back reads: *"Baker Hall is the largest women's residence hall on the Ohio State University campus. It houses over 600 co-eds."*

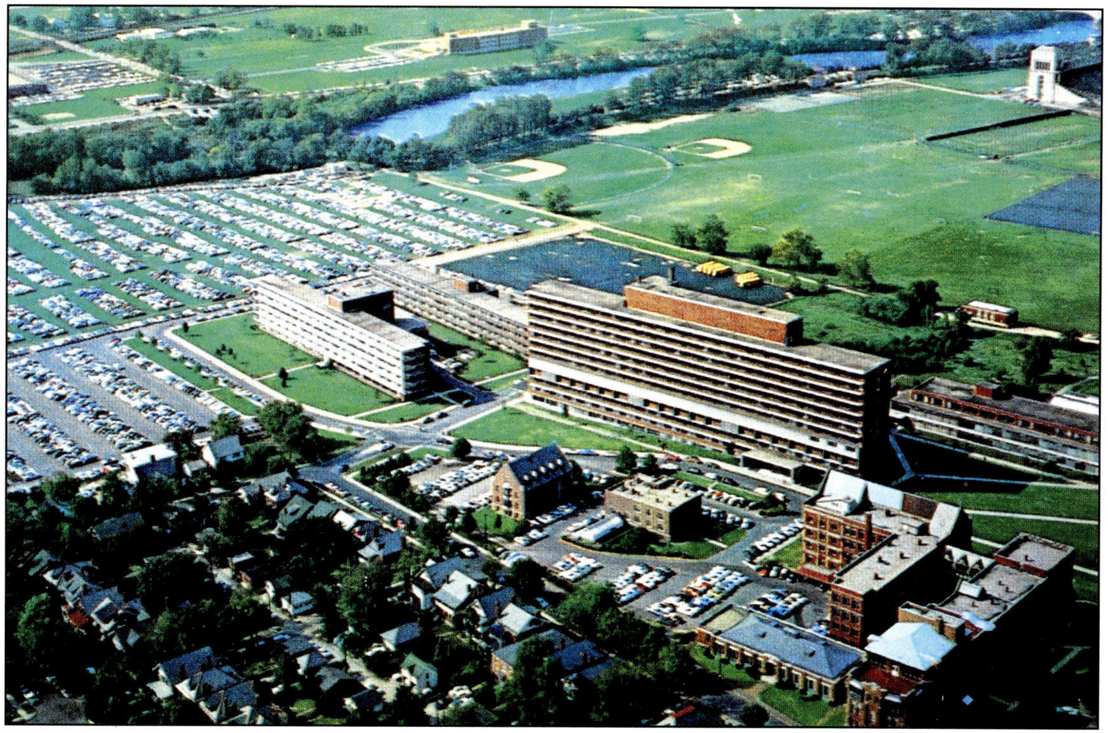

Medical Center of Ohio State University. Postmarked 1959, $2-3.

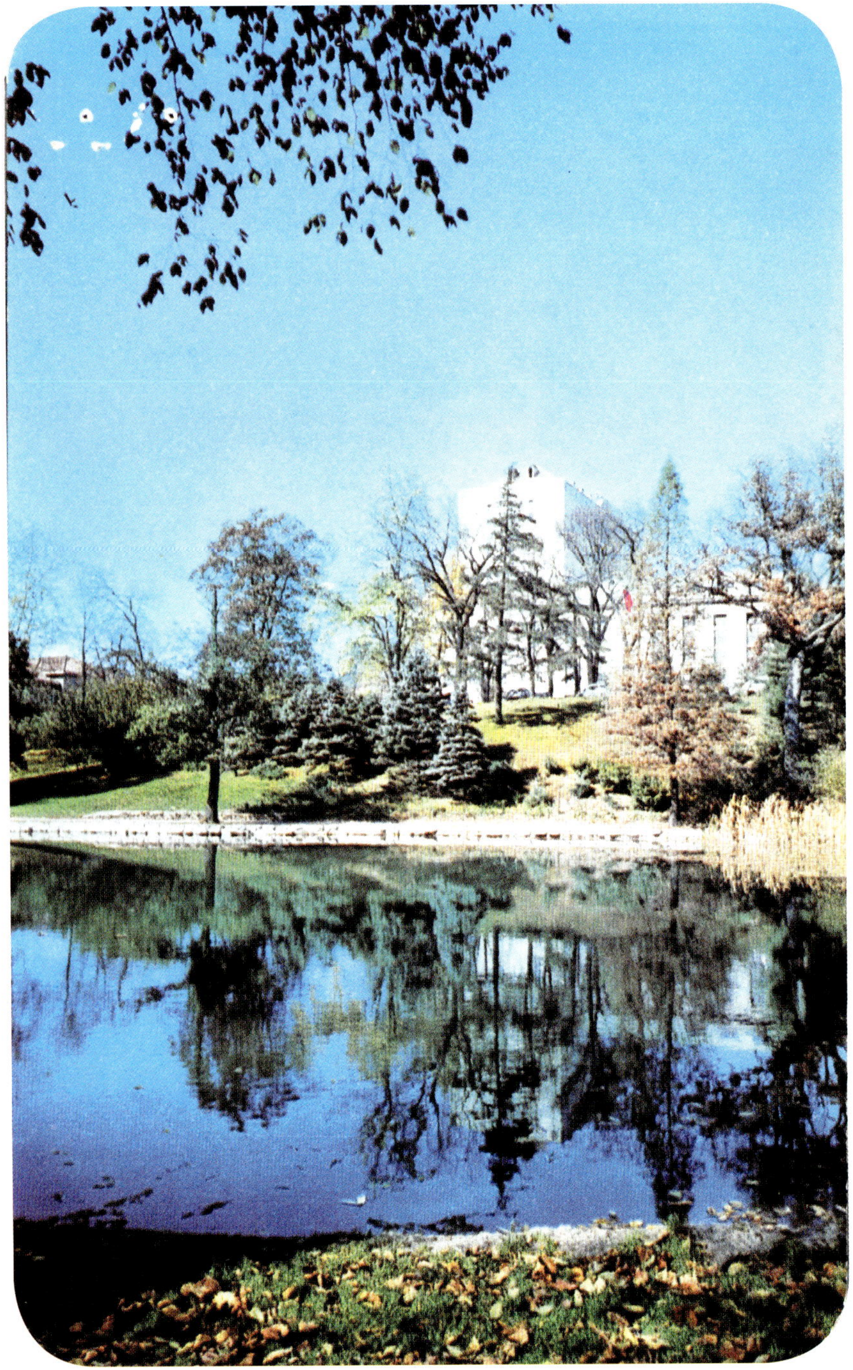

Mirror Lake reflection. Circa 1950s, $2-3. The back reads: *"Reflected in Mirror Lake is Ohio State University's William Oxley Thompson Memorial Library."*

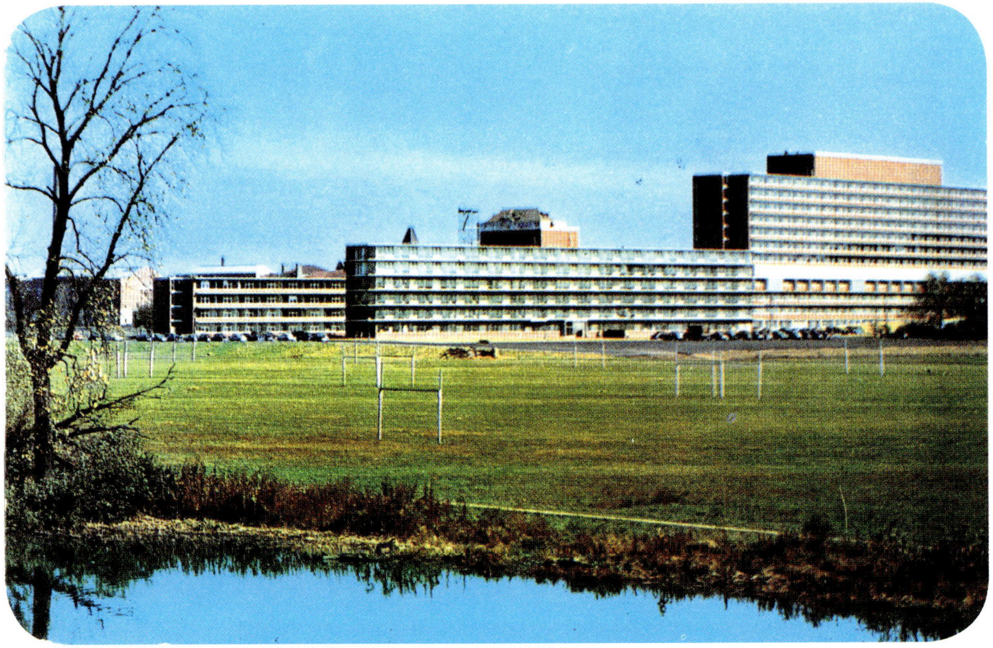

Newly completed Medical Center. Postmarked 1952, $3-4.

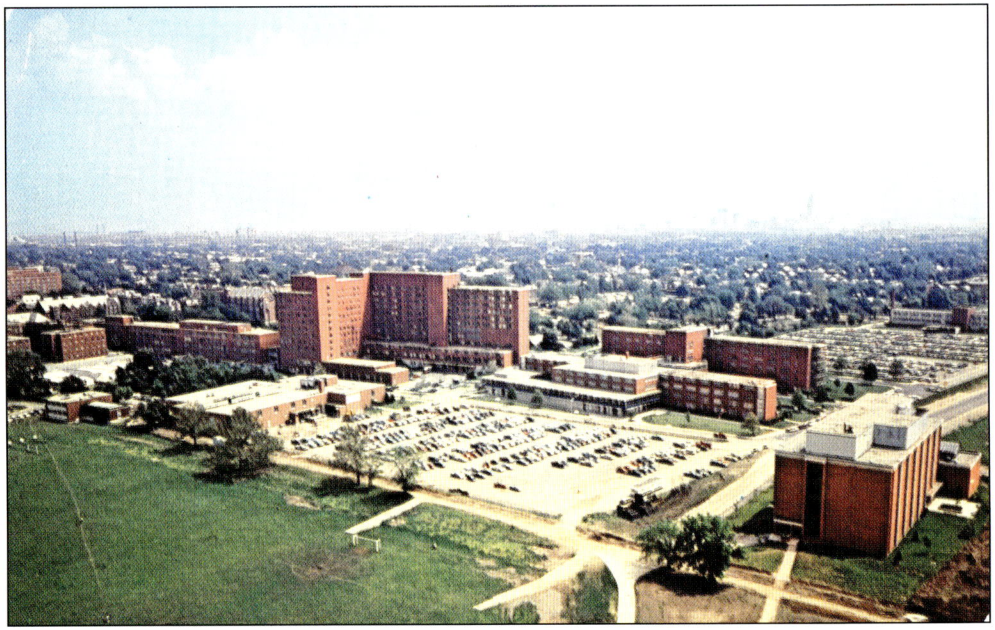

View from Lincoln Student Residential Tower. Circa 1960s, $3-4.

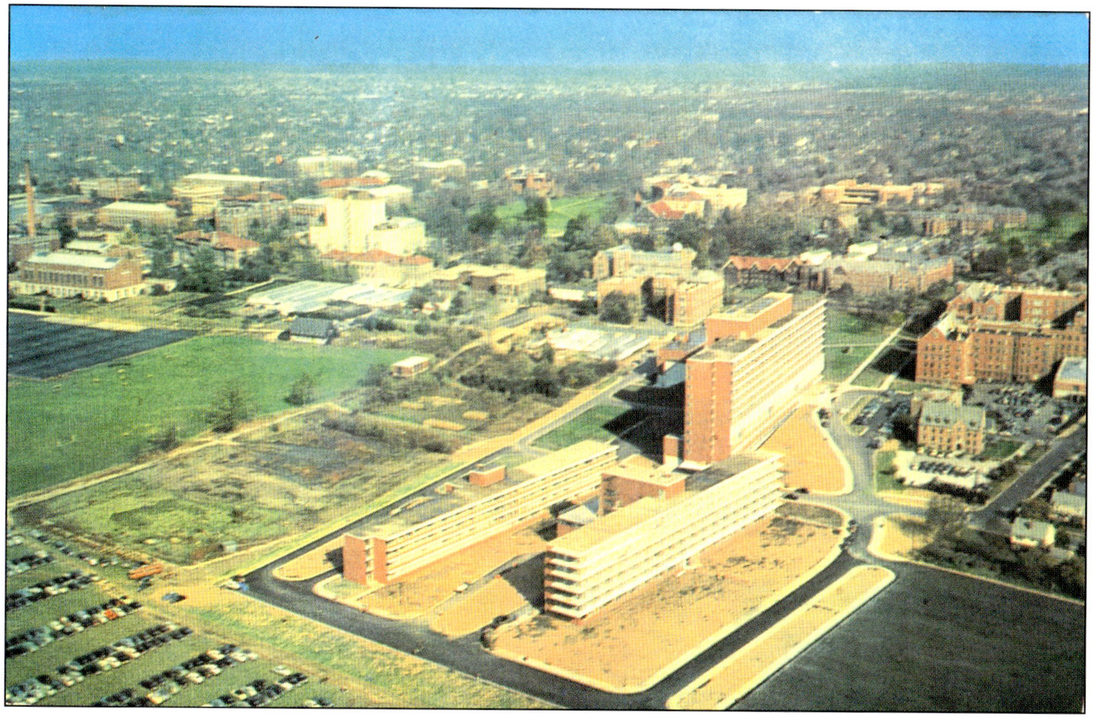

Panorama from the Air. Postmarked 1965, $3-4. Hand-written message on the back reads: *"This is a picture of the campus. It is really huge. The dorms are 10 stories high and I'm on the top floor. The kids are real nice and friendly. I'd tell you more about it but can't get much on a postcard."*

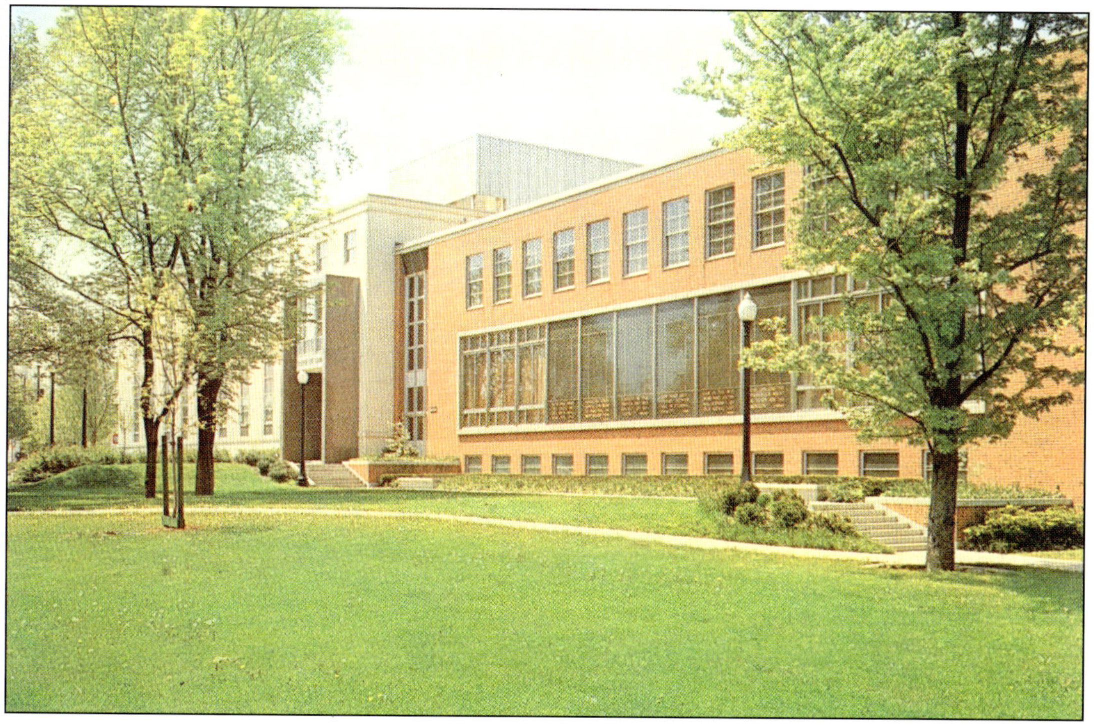

College of Law Building. Circa 1960s, $4-5. The back reads: *"Dedicated April 19-23, 1960."*

Chapter Seven:

Being a Good Sport

Statistics always remind me of the fellow who drowned in the river whose average depth was only three feet.
— Woody Hayes, Ohio State football coach

The one statistic that gets the blood pumping among the sports fans in the city of Columbus is 101,000 plus. That is the capacity of the Ohio State University stadium.

America's landmark horseshoe-shaped stadium has been described as the heart of college football on any given Saturday.

Columbus "is a fanatic and frenzied football town," wrote best-selling author John Gunther back in the late 1940s. He added:

> *"If you don't go to football games on Saturday, people think you're an odd fish and a pariah."*

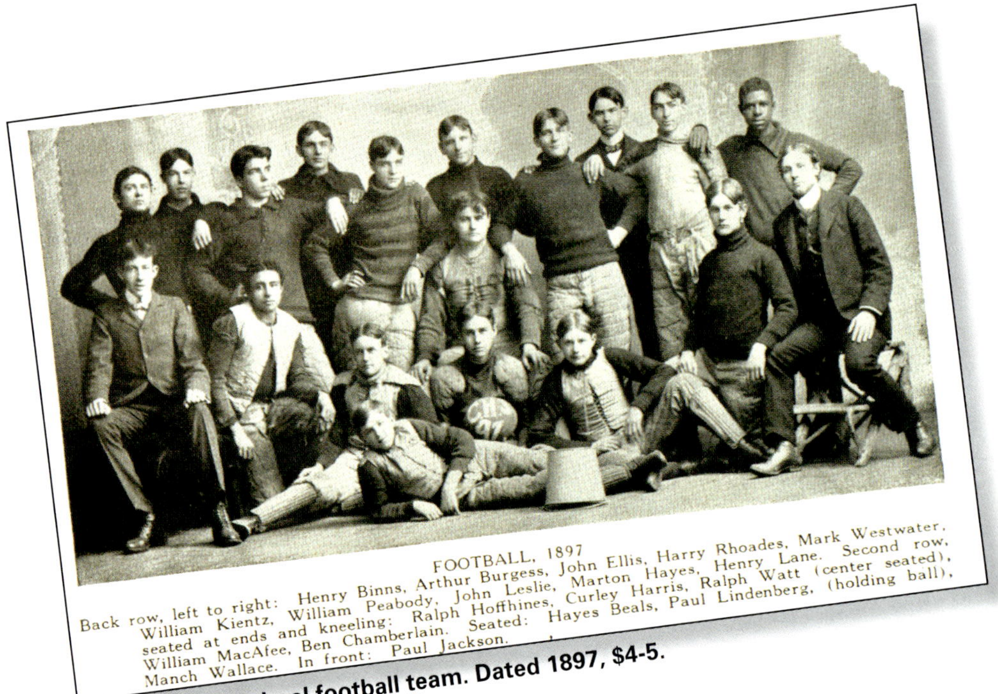

Central High School football team. Dated 1897, $4-5.

The Ohio State stadium has been home to the Buckeyes since 1922. Standing proudly on the banks of the Olentangy River, it is also listed in the National Registry of Historic Places.

Over the years the legendary stadium has undergone many renovations including a $195 million dollar refurbishment and expansion program early in this century. Preserving the famed horseshoe shape has always been paramount, but there still have been subtle changes—often recorded in various postcards.

'Being a good sport' is not just about football, it involves basketball too. Also located on the Ohio State campus is St. John Arena, believed to be the only structure of its kind in the United States. For more than twenty years it was the site of Buckeye basketball games.

The basketball facility, named after former coach and athletic director Lynn St. John, first opened in 1956. Ultimately it made room for more than 13,000 fans. In 1998 the Buckeye basketball teams were moved to Schottenstein Center's Value City Area. However, the St. John Arena has remained a multi-purpose facility hosting various activities and events.

From the early 1930s through 1954 the Columbus Red Birds brought professional baseball to Columbus via the Red Bird stadium.

The Red Birds were a product of the St. Louis Cardinals farm system; prior to that time the minor league team had been independently owned and known locally as the Columbus Senators. Under new management the Red Birds became increasingly popular and attendance at the ballpark tripled between 1930 and 1932.

After decades of both good years and lean years, the Red Birds relocated at the end of the 1954 season to Omaha, Nebraska. But, Columbus baseball was later served by the Columbus Jets and finally the Columbus Clippers.

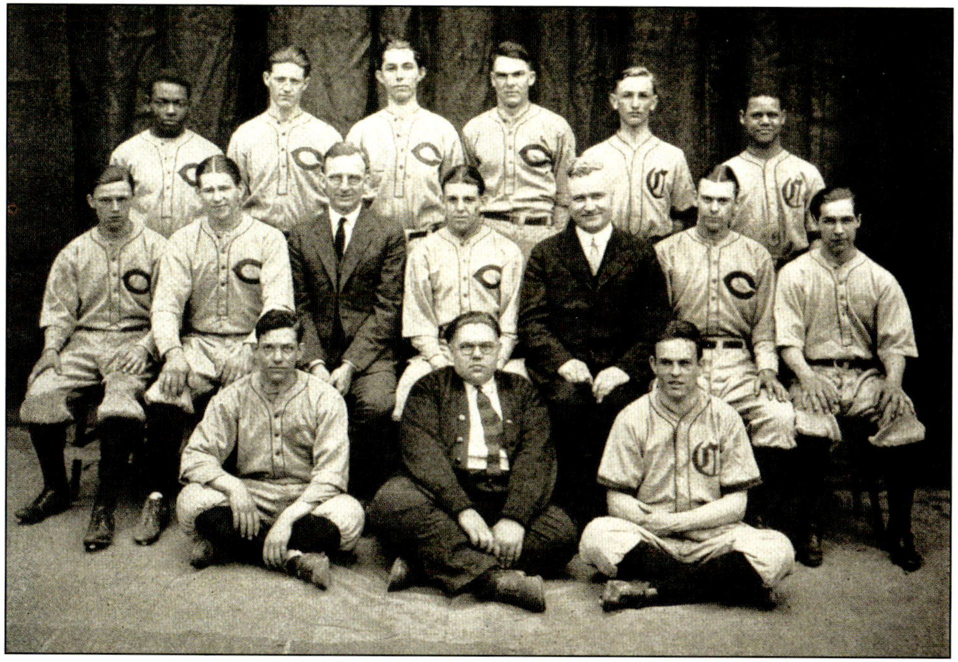

Commerce High School baseball team. Dated 1924, $4-5.

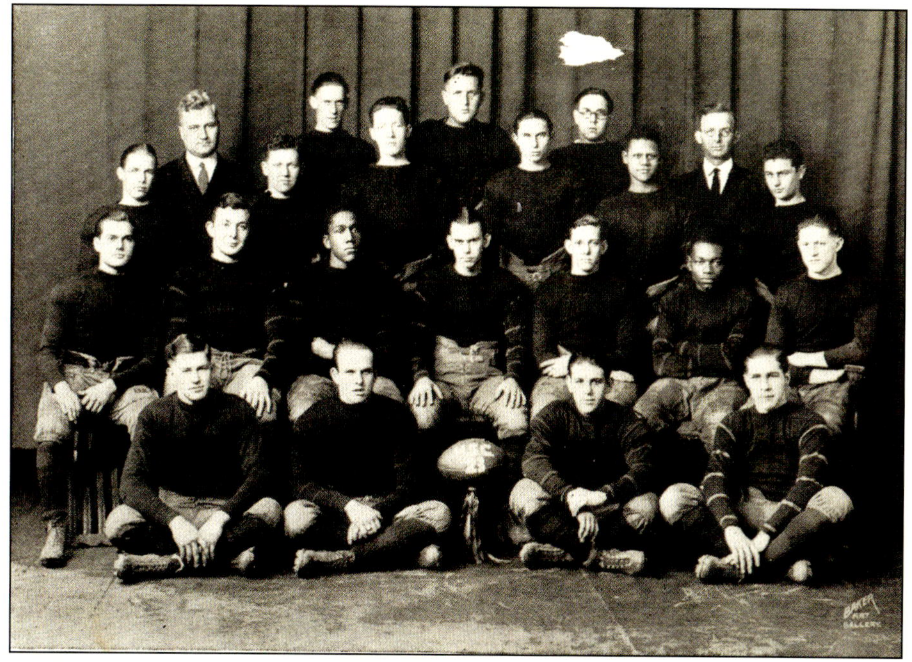

Commerce High School football team. Dated 1924, $4-5.

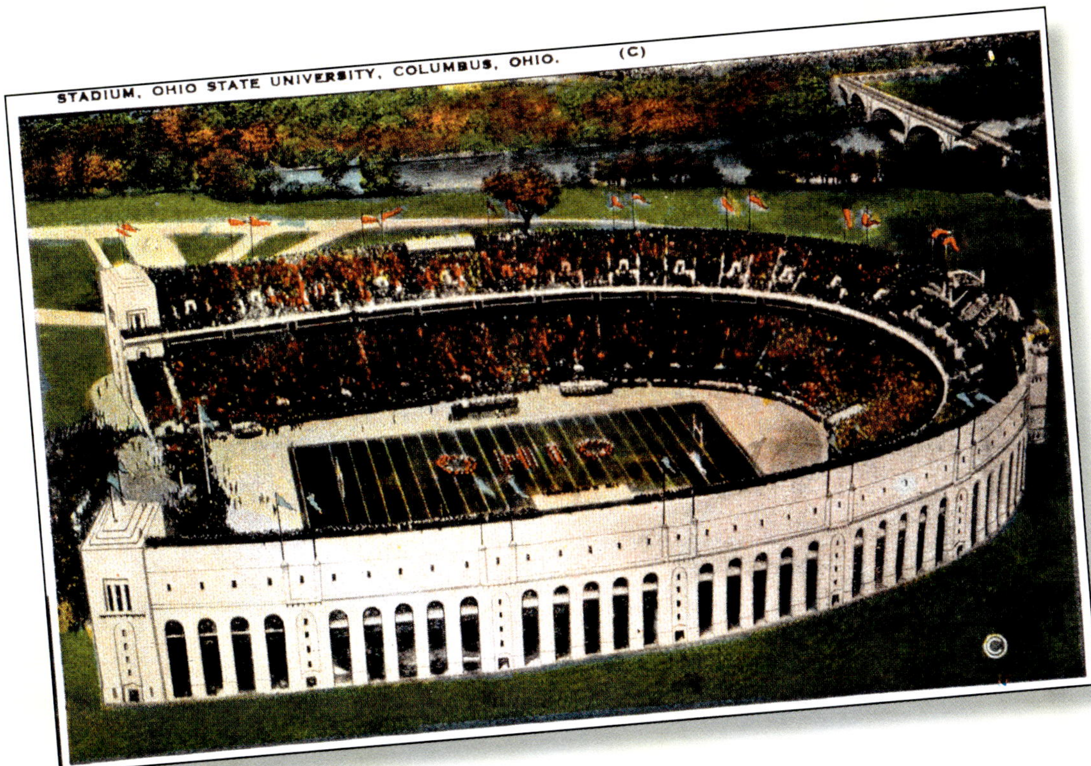

Stadium, Ohio State University. Circa 1920s, $3-4.

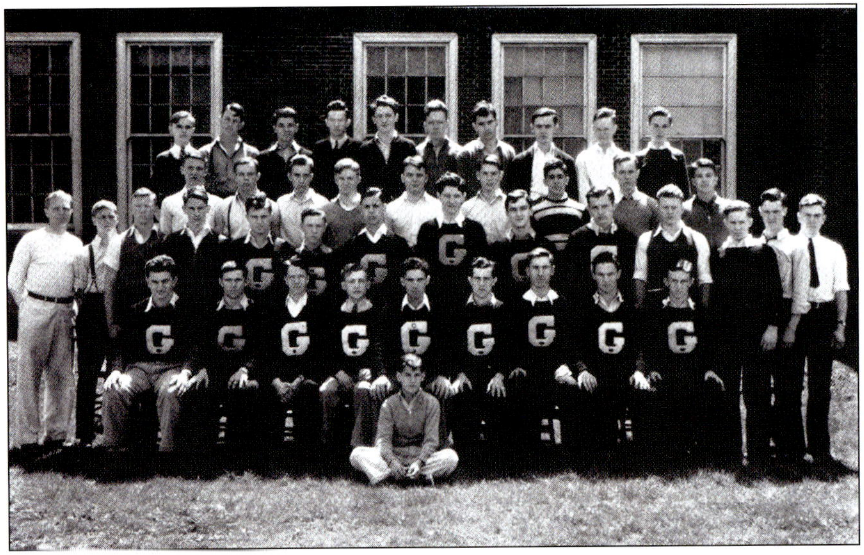

Grandview Heights High School football team. Dated 1935, $4-5.

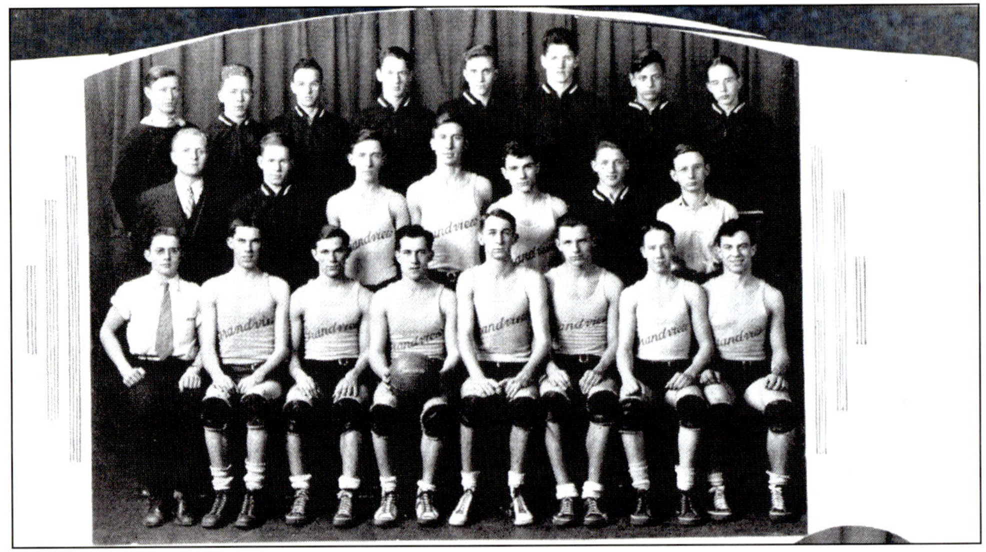

Grandview Heights High School basketball team. Dated 1935, $4-5.

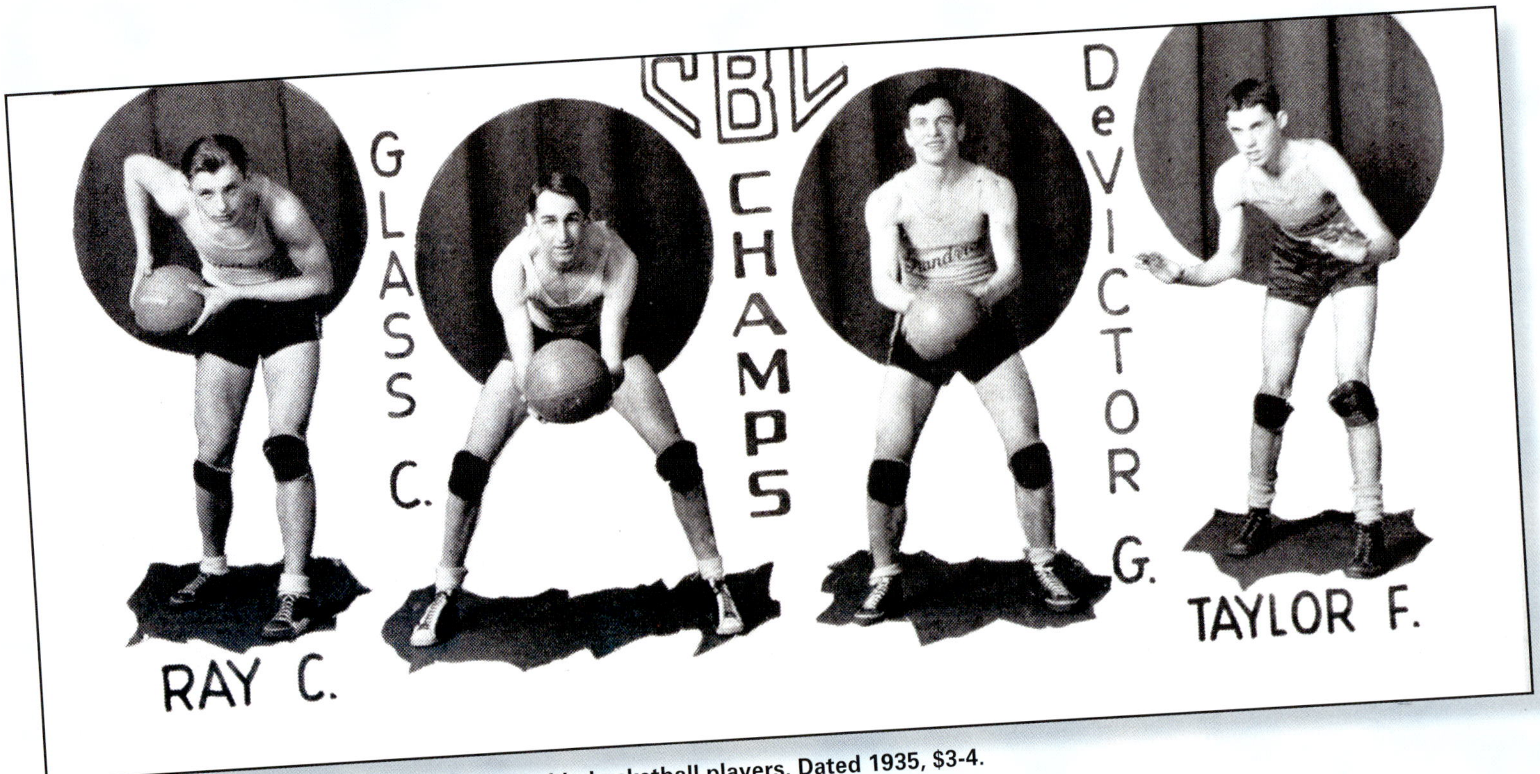

Grandview Heights High School championship basketball players. Dated 1935, $3-4.

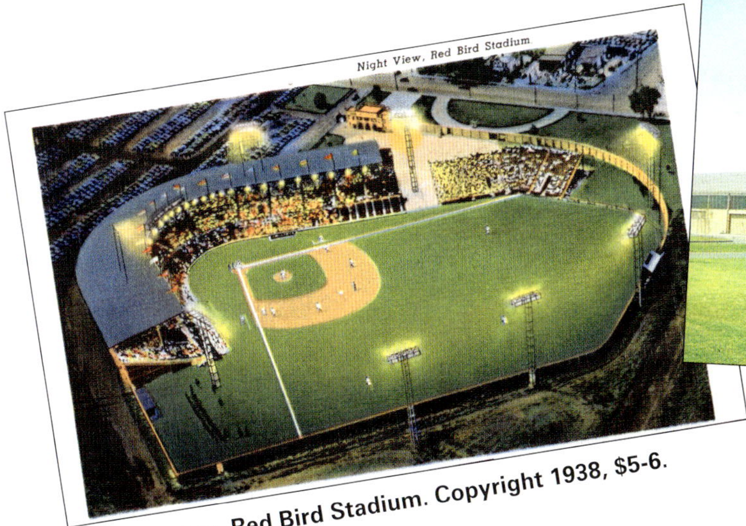

Night view, Red Bird Stadium. Copyright 1938, $5-6.

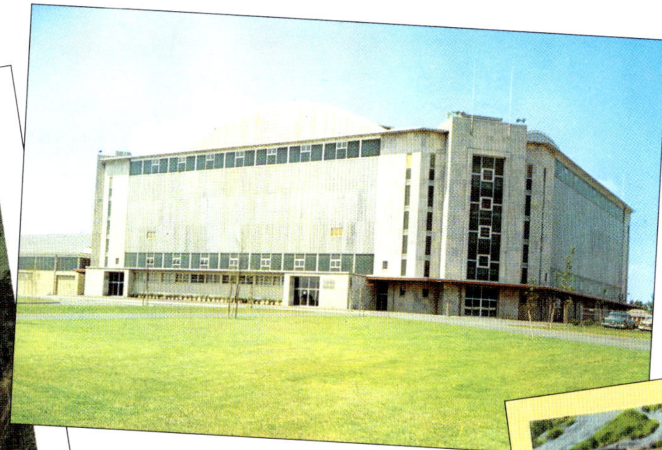

St. John Arena. Circa 1960s, $4-5.
The back reads: *"....believed to be the only structure of its kind in the United States, located on the O.S.U. Campus, is 120 feet high at the peak and contains 6,400,000 cubic feet. The capacity is 13,392 with all seats built around the basketball floor. Construction is in a double-decked arrangement with 9,400 seats downstairs and 4,000 in the balcony."*

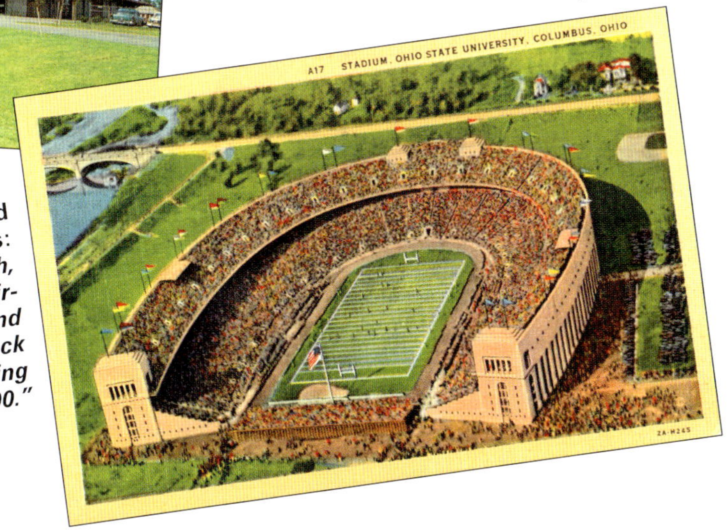

Ohio State Stadium. Postmarked 1943, $5-6. The back reads: *"Covers 10 acres, 109 feet high, 750 feet long, 597 feet wide. Circumference one third mile and a one fourth mile cinder track is between stands and playing field. Capacity 80,000."*

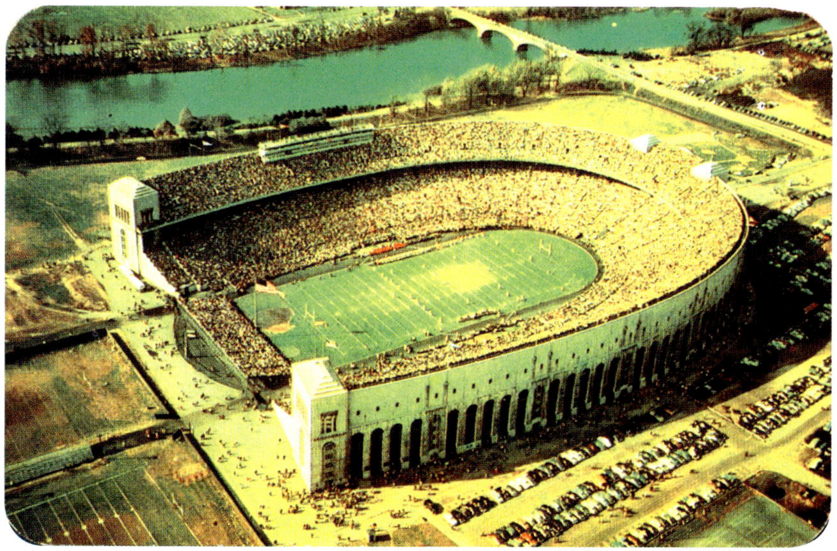

Aerial view of Ohio State University stadium. Circa 1950s, $4-5.
The back reads: *"Ohio Stadium is the gridiron home of the famed Buckeyes of Ohio State University. Each autumnal football classic is a vivid scene of color and spectacle."*

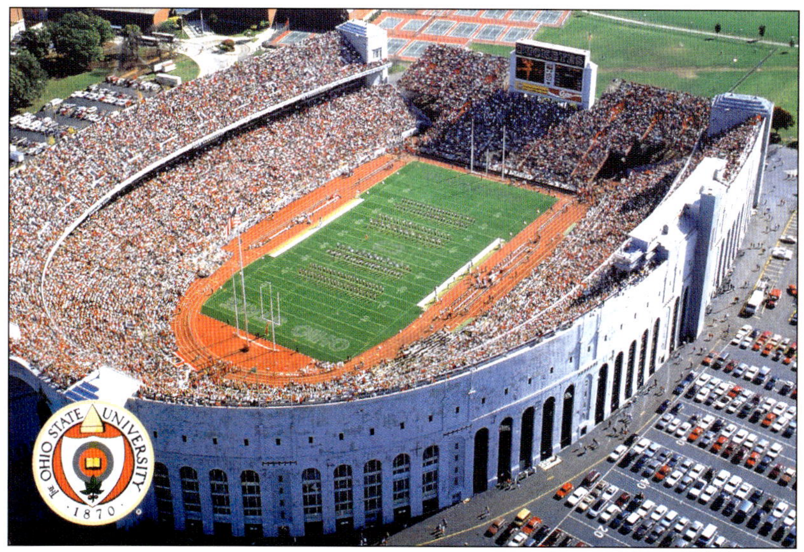

Home of the Bucks. Circa 1990s, $1-3.

Chapter Eight: The Great Flood

> They were absolutely helpless. So were we.
> — *a Reporter's eyewitness account of the 1913 Columbus flood*

The Great Ohio Flood struck the city of Columbus — and the heartland of America — in the spring of 1913. In its wake were hundreds of deaths, millions of dollars in damage, and many memorable scenes captured on postcards.

Like so many other weather-related disasters of that era, the Great Flood brought out many established photographers as well as would-be photographers. The overall result was an astonishing collection of history-in-the-making images.

It was truly an awesome event to behold.

First, the rains came. Excessive rains, six to eleven inches of continuing downpour, spilled over the state of Ohio. Tens of thousands of homes were flooded.

In Columbus itself, nearly one hundred people died when the Scioto River reached record levels and poured nine to seventeen feet of flood waters through otherwise calm neighborhoods. Terrified residents fled to the safety of rooftops and trees. Thirteen people were reportedly rescued from a single tree.

One journalist's account read:

> *"With our field glasses we could see thousands of people on roofs and in windows as effectively cut off from the world as they would have been on the moon."*

Glen Marston, a correspondent for the Chicago Journal, wrote:

> *"They were absolutely helpless...So were we. No boat could live a moment in the rushing current, which took houses, bridges, railway tracks, telegraph poles—everything—in its overwhelming sweep."*

Of the thousands of citizens living in the city of Columbus at that time some, 1,500 became refuges reporting to city hall. Another 5,000 was said to be stuck on a hilltop on the west edge of the city. The rest were "clinging to rooftops, trees and poles in isolated areas," according to the eyewitness reporter.

Then...came the fires.

"To add to the horrors of the flood, fire broke out in a half dozen places," according to the journalist's narrative later repeated in the book, *The Story of the Great Flood and Cyclone Disasters* edited by Thomas.

It continued:

> *"Nothing but the water-soaked roofs saved the district. Some of the burning houses were in water to the second story, and so the flames, while destructive enough where they started, could not spread far. The fire department was helpless. There were billions of gallons of water and not a drop which could be used. Many of the fires could not be approached closely enough to determine their exact location."*

The bleak account of the Columbus disaster continued:

> *"Boats which had carried these same people on jaunts last summer had been turned into funeral craft...a ghastly work for picnic boats."*

In Columbus, the gray view from Broad Street was one of total desolation. In the midst of the flood stood a streetcar half submerged in the floodwaters. Its crew had abandoned it when the levee broke. In some places the street was completely filled with floating houses and wreckage.

Observed the reporter at the scene in the city:

> *"I have seen fires, floods and avalanches before, but nothing compared with this. There is nothing in one's imagination to compare to such a disaster. One must go through it. There was a hotel full of people without any conveniences what ever—back to the primitive—and yet there was never a murmur of discontent—the sights and sounds across the river so dwarfed our petty inconveniences that we forgot them. We considered ourselves lucky to be alive."*

But Columbus and much of the Buckeye state was anything but lucky.

The statewide devastation, preserved in a multitude of graphic postcards, took years if not a full decade to recover from. It remains one of the most singular tragic natural disasters of the twentieth century.

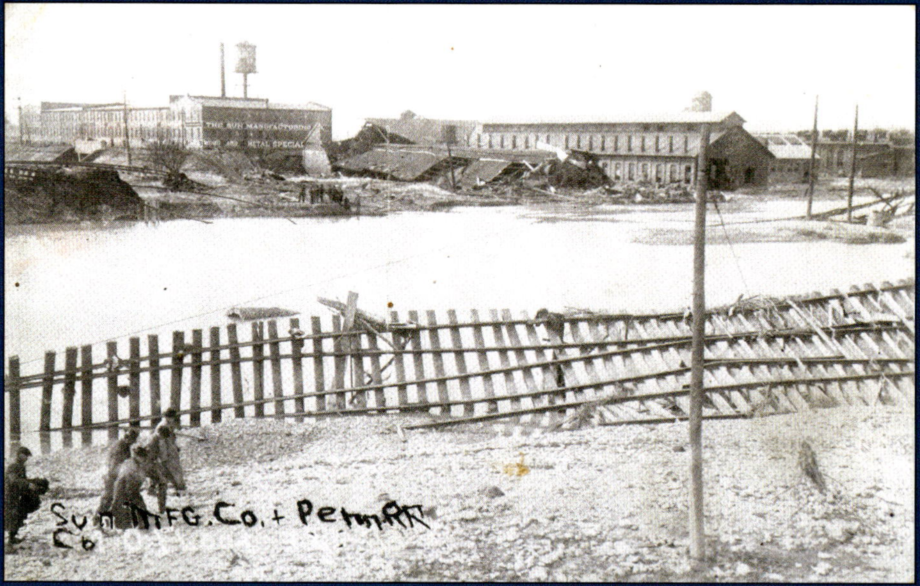

Sun Manufacturing Company and Pennsylvania Railroad. Postmarked 1913, $4-5.

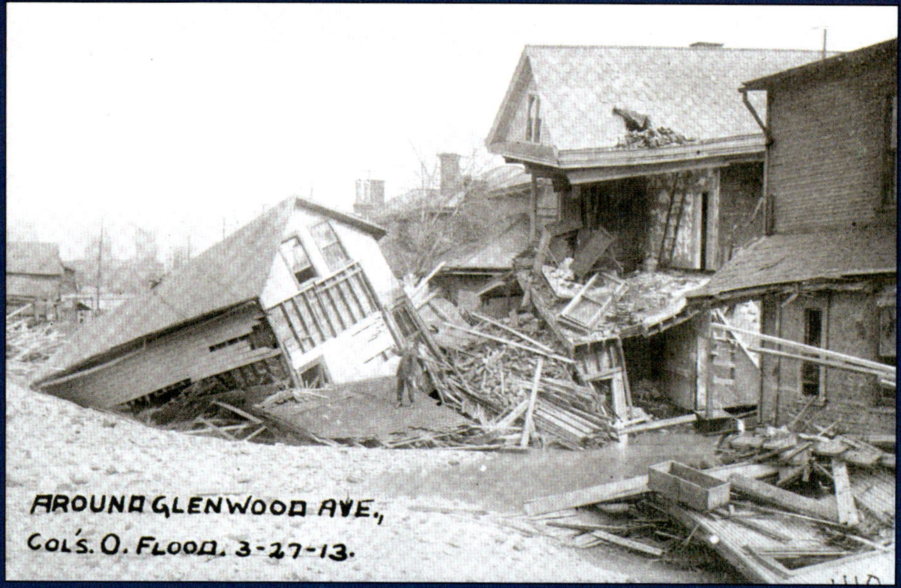

Around Glenwood Avenue. Dated 1913, $5-6.

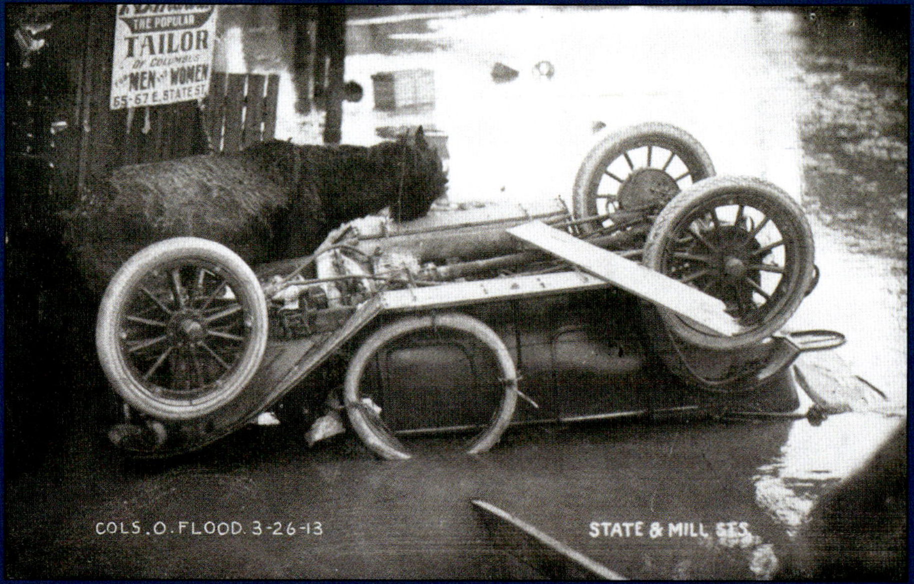

State and Mill Streets. Dated 1913, $5-6.

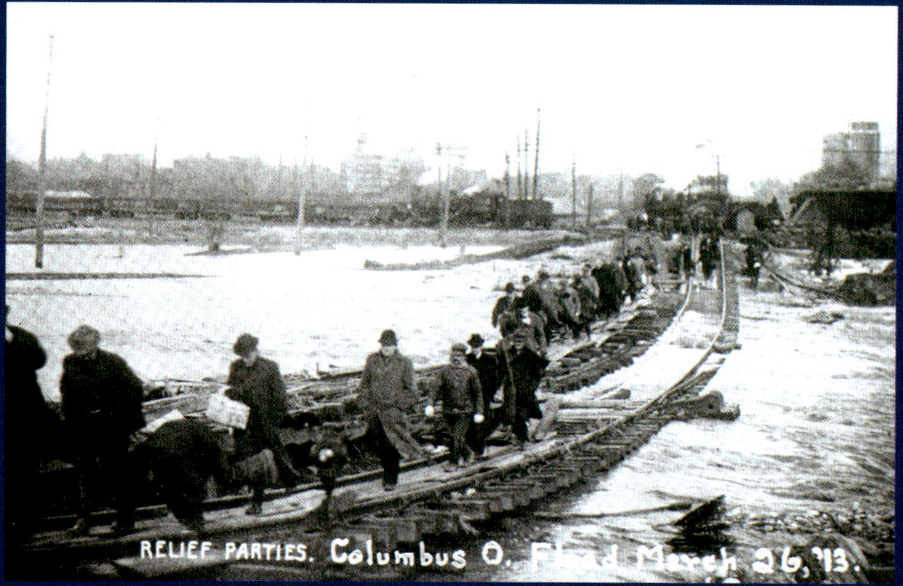

Relief Parties. Dated 1913, $5-6.

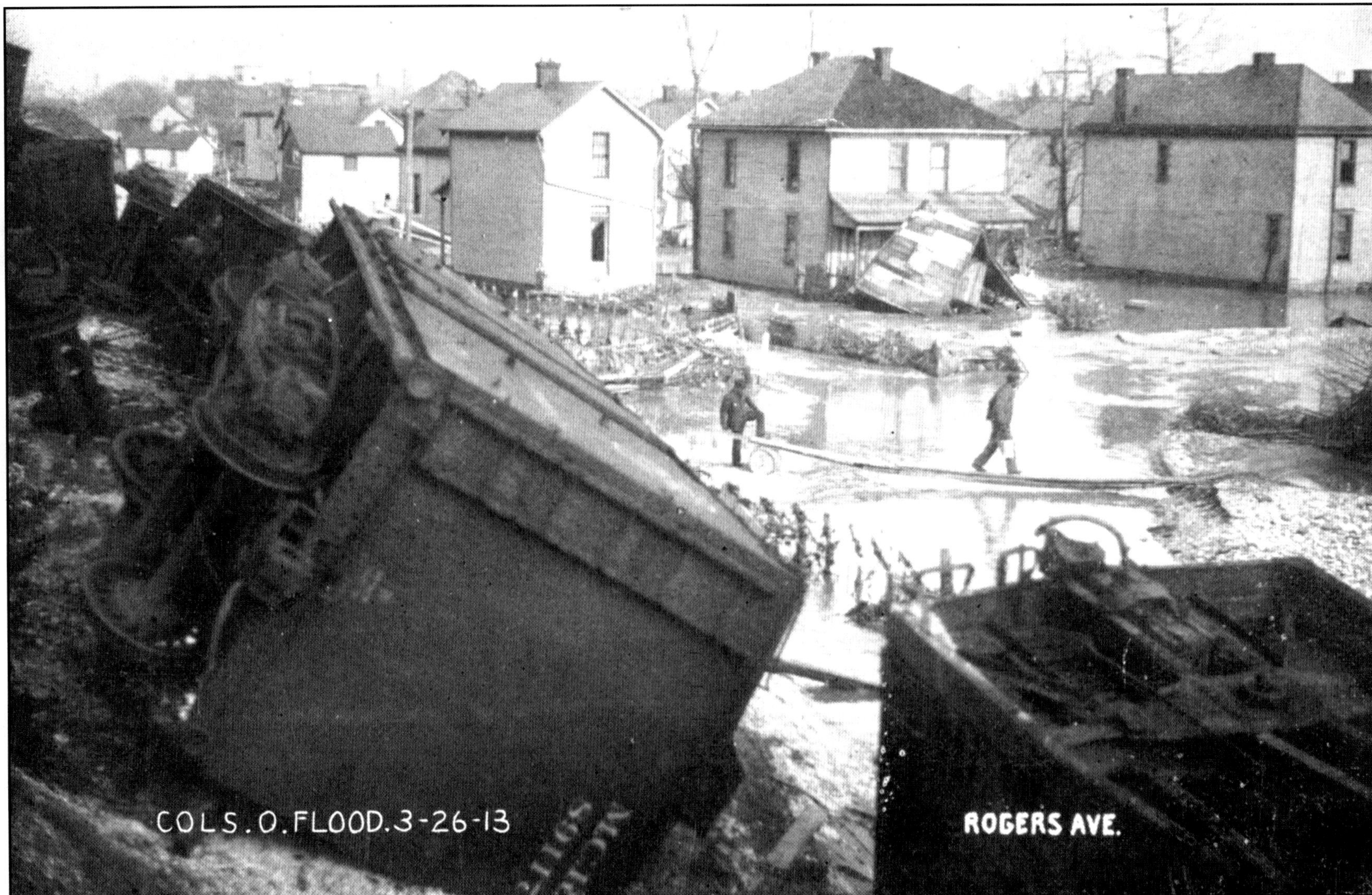

Rogers Avenue. Dated 1913, $4-5.

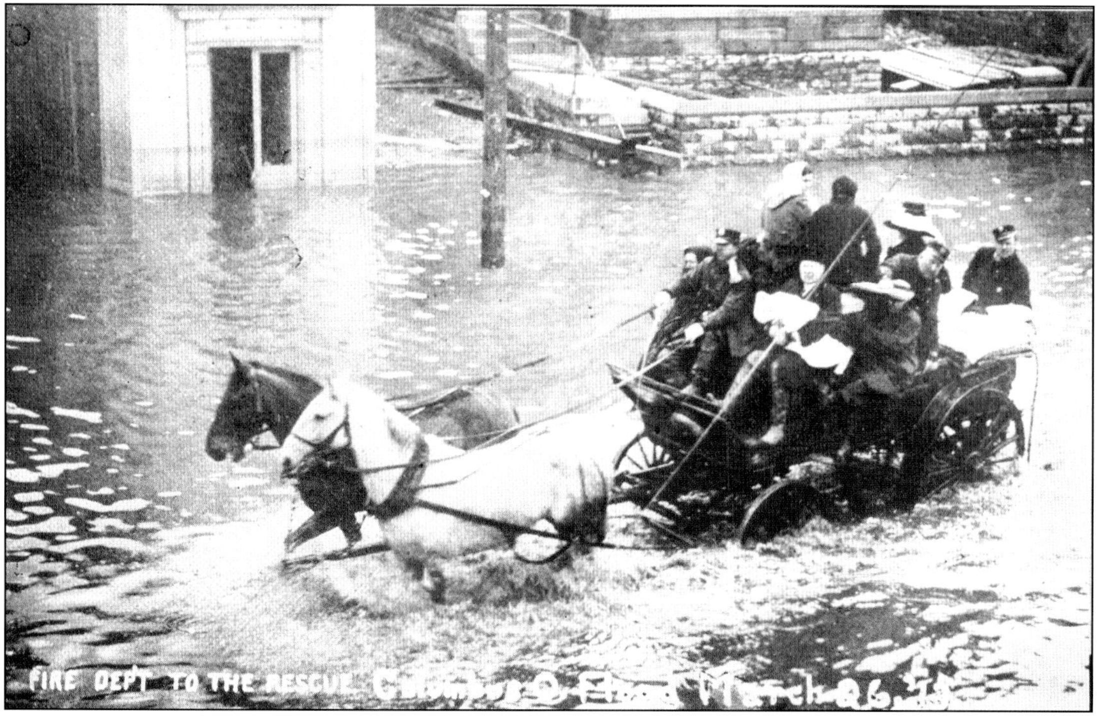

Fire Department to the Rescue. Dated 1913, $8-10.

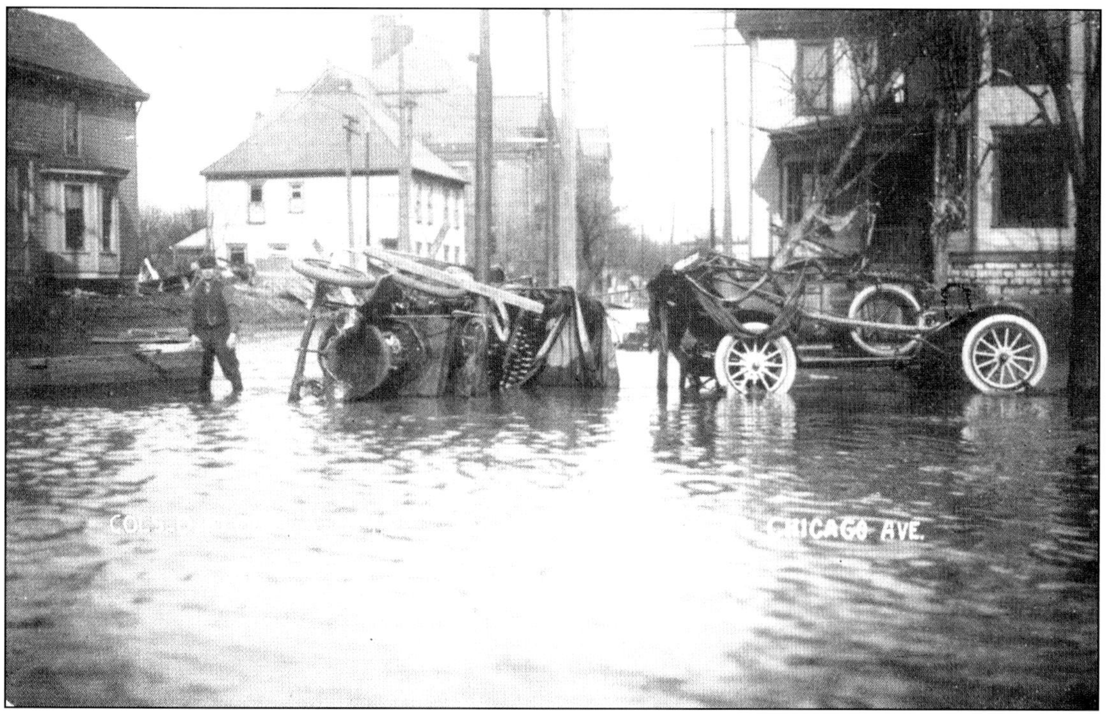

Chicago Avenue. Dated 1912, $5-6.

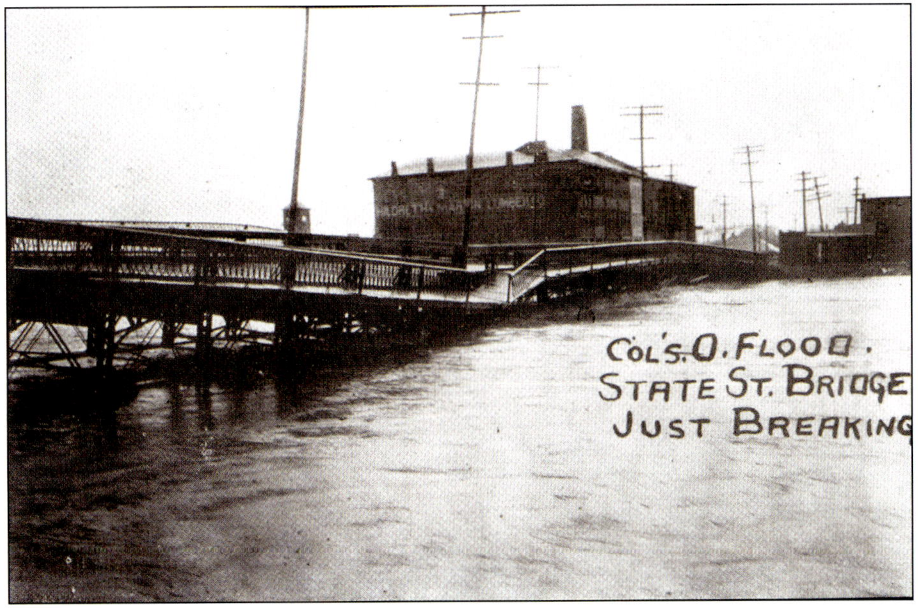

State Street Bridge Just Breaking. Dated 1912, $5-6.

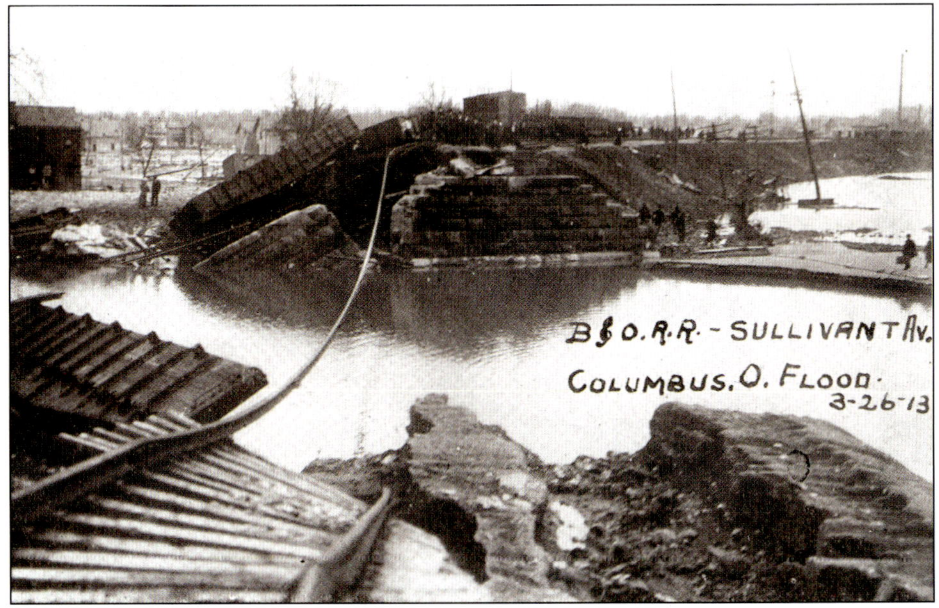

Baltimore and Ohio Railroad at Sullivant Avenue. Dated 1913, $5-6.

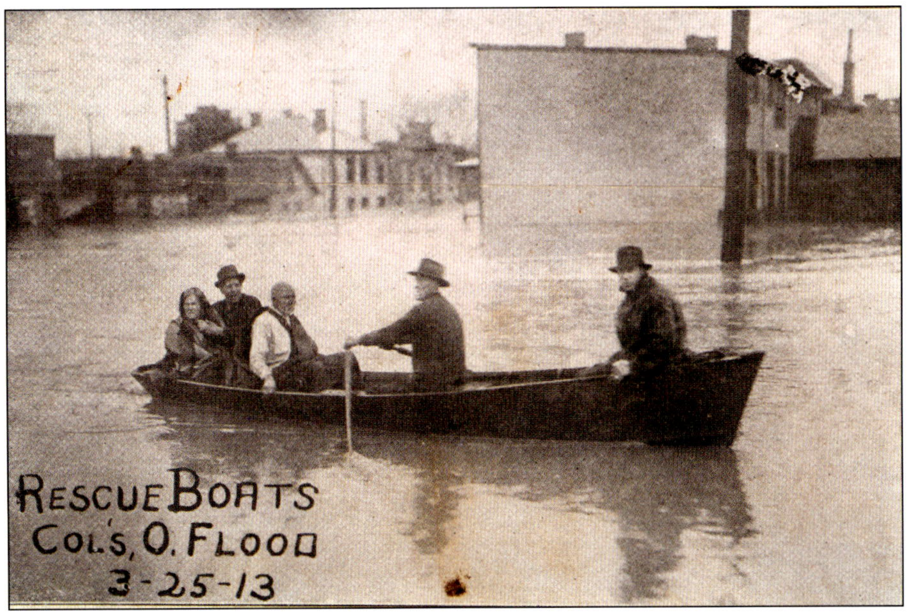

Rescue Boats. Dated 1913, $7-8.

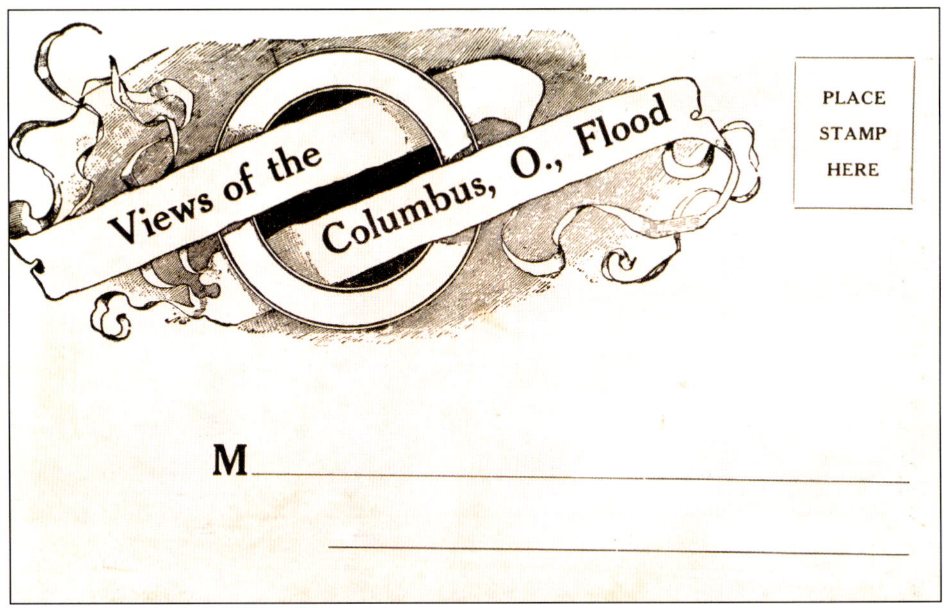

Souvenir folder of Columbus Flood. Dated 1913, $4-5.

Chapter Nine: The Learning Curve

> The free man cannot long be an ignorant man.
> — *Former Ohio Governor and U.S. President, William McKinley*

In historical terms the learning curve in the city of greater Columbus has been a broad one.

From public schools to private colleges the academic environment was ever changing here in the twentieth century.

Early in the 1890s there was but one Columbus High School. By the 1890s North High School was added and the original name of the Columbus High was briefly changed to Asa Lord High School. Within a few years, though, the geographical location became more favored and Central High School was coined. In 1910 the name of the building was changed again, to the regal sounding High School of Commerce.

The Indianola Junior High School began operations in 1904. It was considered the first junior high school in the United States. The first building was located at 140 East 16th Avenue in Columbus. Many decades later it became the Indianola Informal School, featuring non-traditional approaches to classroom situations.

The Ohio State School for the Blind was established in Columbus in 1837, thus becoming one of the nation's first public schools for the visually impaired. Early in the 1900s the school was moved from Parsons Avenue to a location at 5330 North High Street.

Saint Mary of the Springs was formally opened in 1924 as a Catholic women's college. The college enjoyed rapid growth initially, but underwent challenging financial times over the decades. In 1964 men were allowed for the first time to enroll. The College of Saint Mary of the Springs became the Ohio Dominican College in 1968. By the end of the twentieth century its enrollment reached 1,900 students—and would double in the decade that followed.

Bliss College opened in 1899, but after nearly a century of offering many legal, medical, and business-related courses, it closed in 1993. During the fall of that year enrollment had reached 370 students.

In the 1970s, there were 118 elementary schools, twenty-nine junior high schools, and seventeen senior high schools operating in Columbus. There were also sixty-six private schools then active.

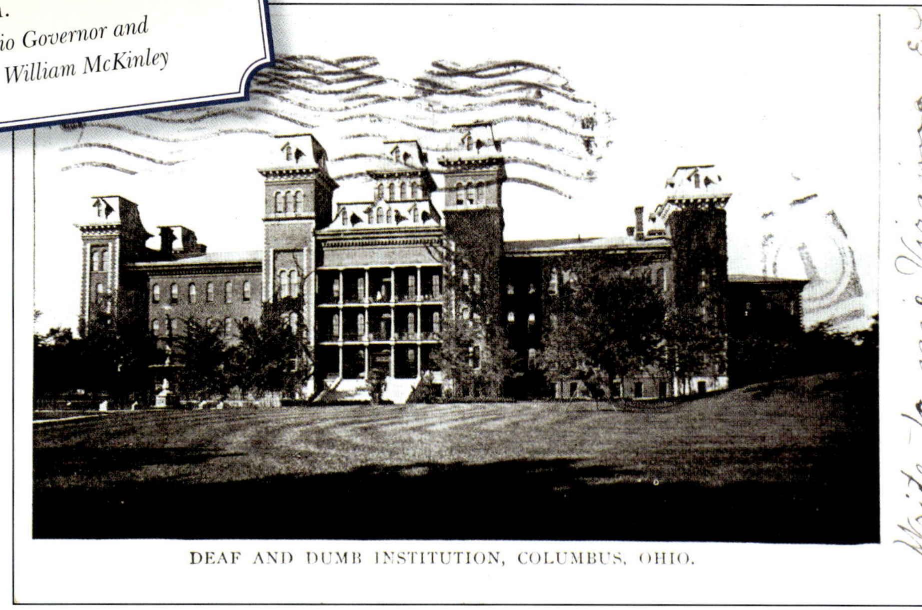

Deaf and Dumb Institution. Postmarked 1906, $6-8.

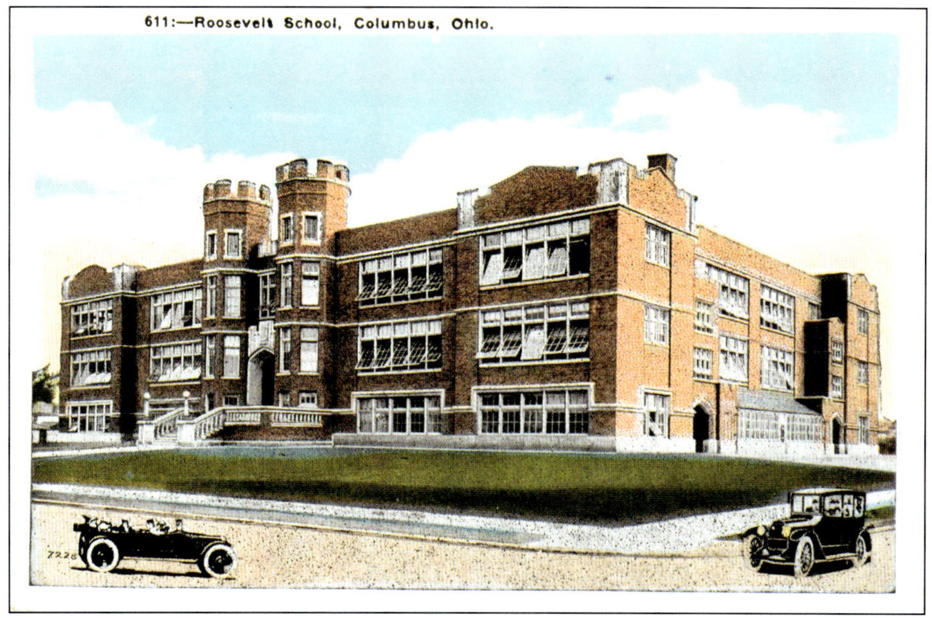

Roosevelt School, Columbus, Ohio. Circa early 1920s, $3-5.

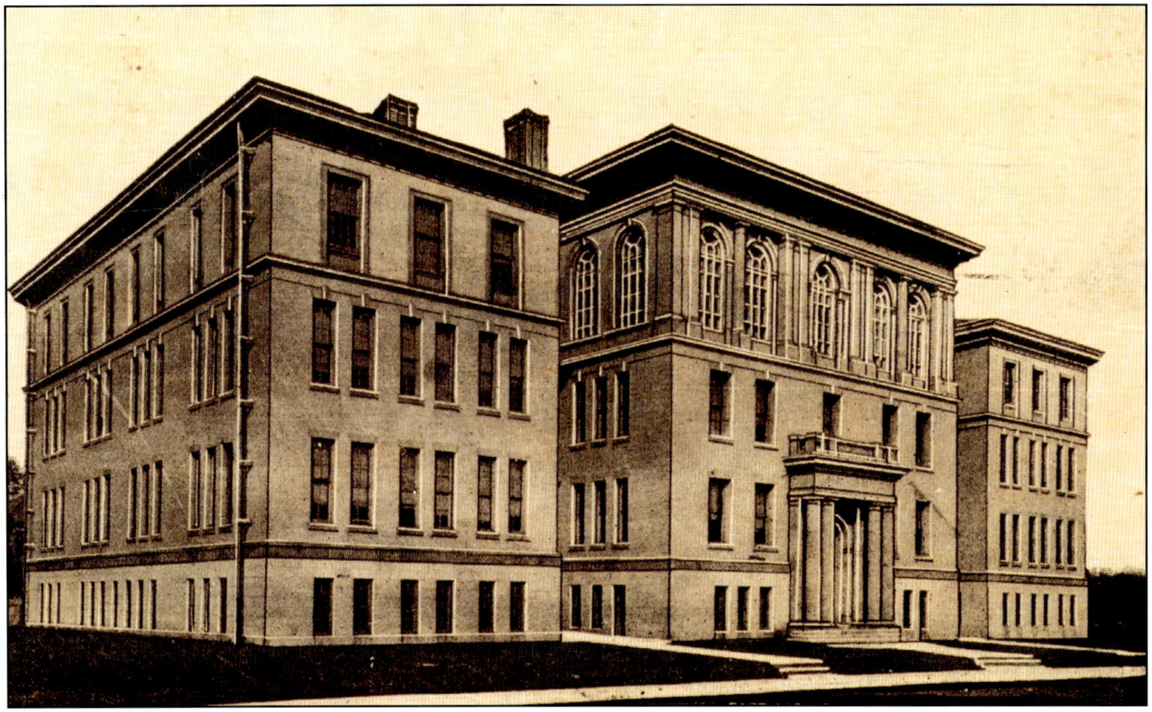

Central High School, Columbus. Circa 1920s, $2-4.

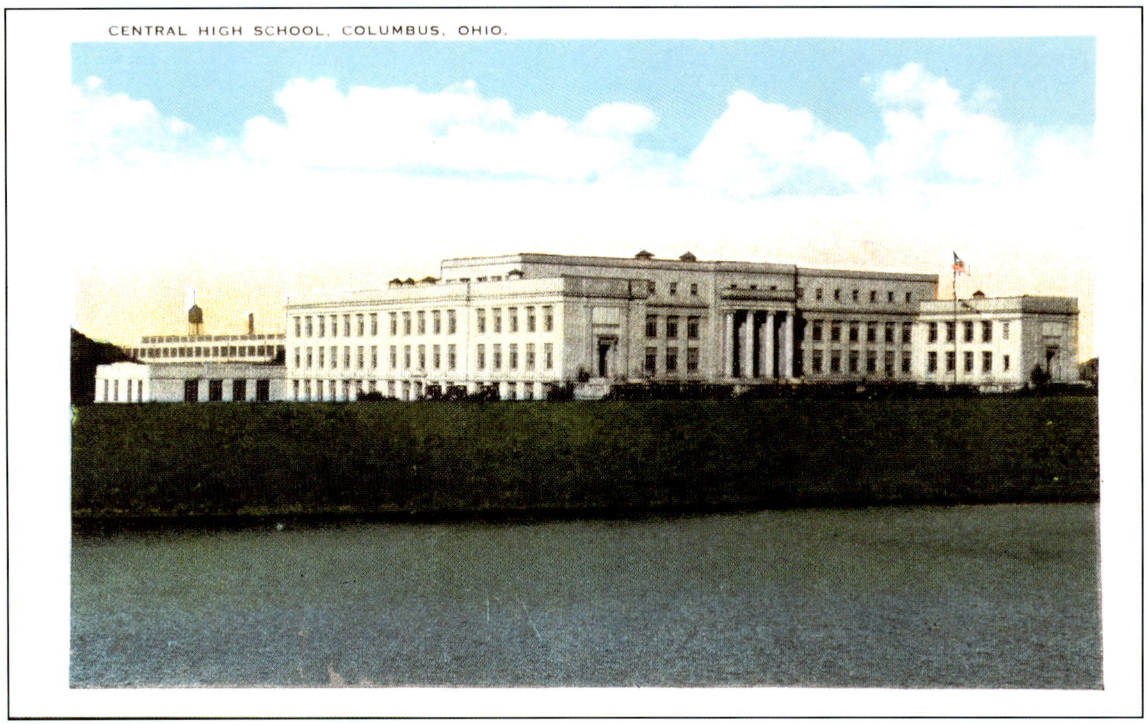

East High School, Columbus. Postmarked 1910, $5-6. Hand-written message on the back reads: *"Dear Friend, Am well and hope this will find you the same. It's fine for sleighing here and hope it is when I come home Xmas."*

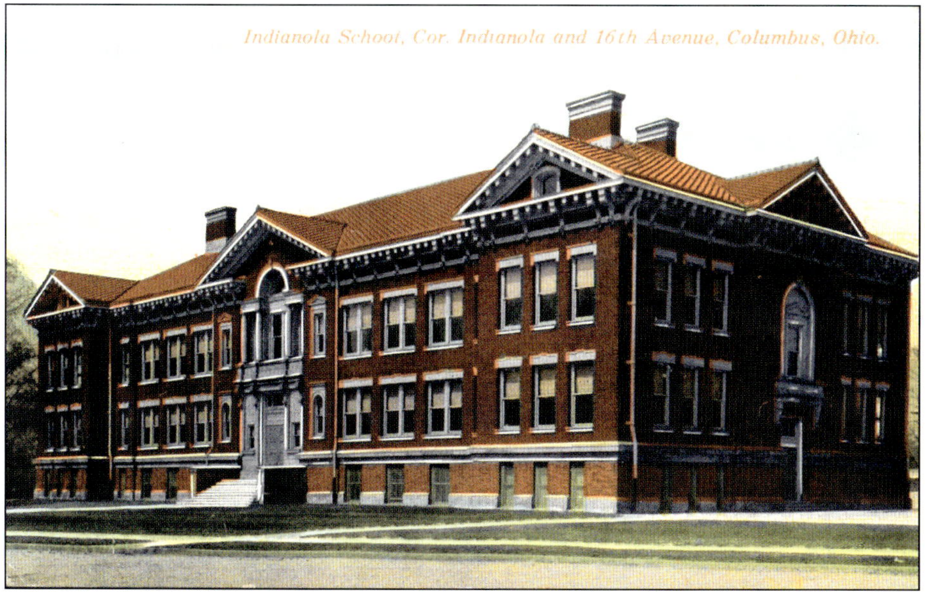

Indianola School, Indianola and 16th Avenue. Circa early 1900s, $3-4.

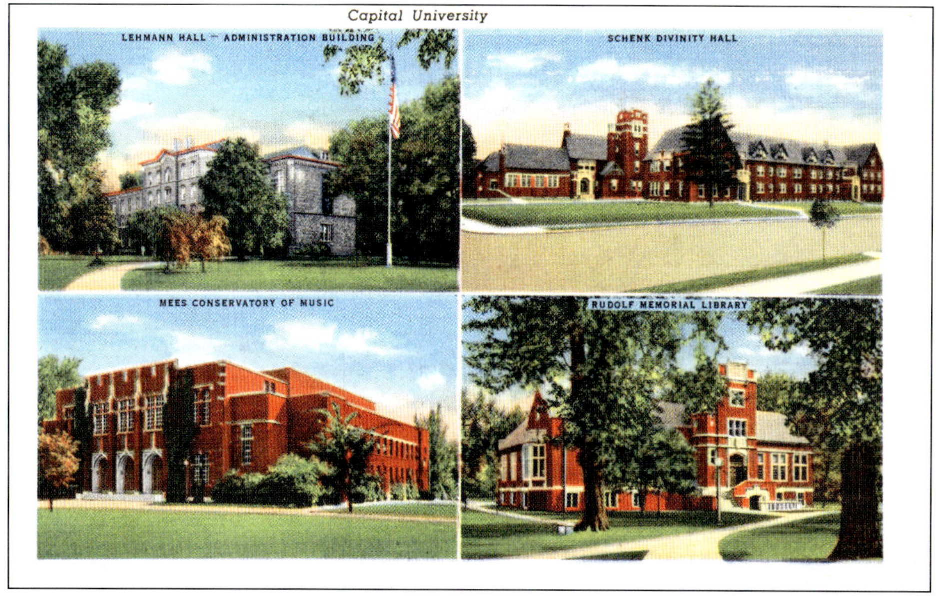

Capital University. Copyright 1938, $3-4.

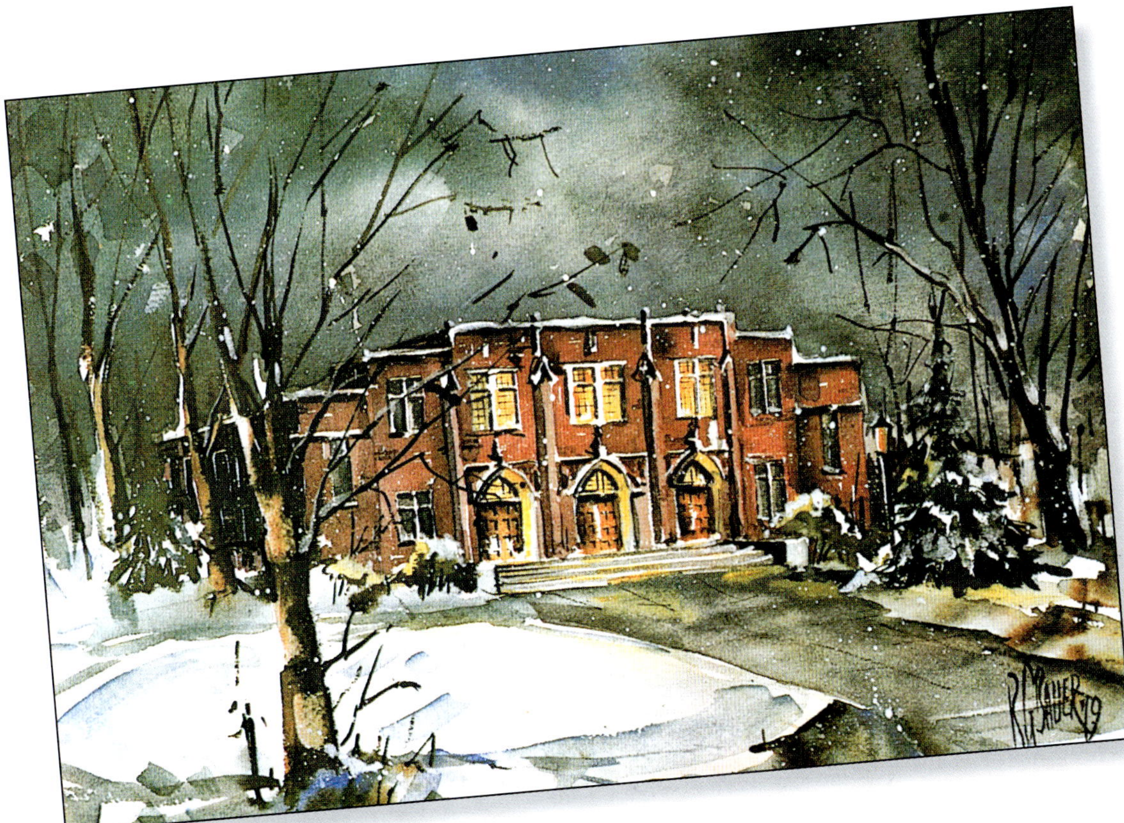

Capital University, 2199 East Main Street. Circa 1960s, $2-3.

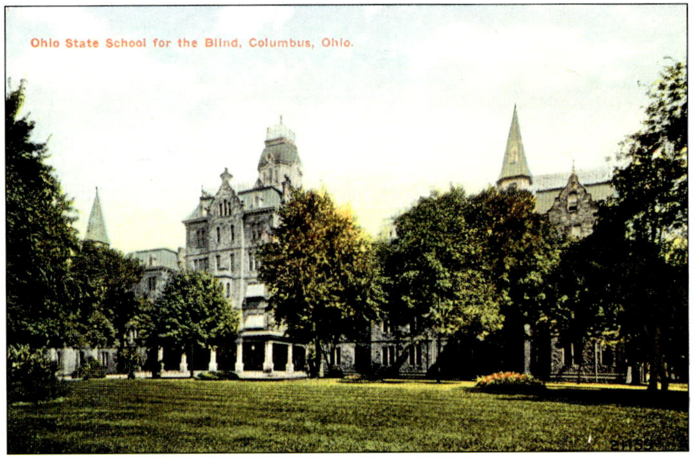

Ohio State School for the Blind, Columbus. Circa early 1900s, $4-5.

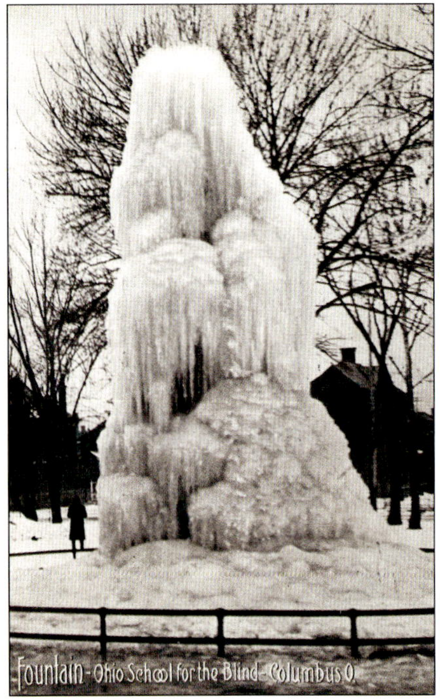

Fountain at the Ohio School for the Blind. Postmarked 1911, $2-3.

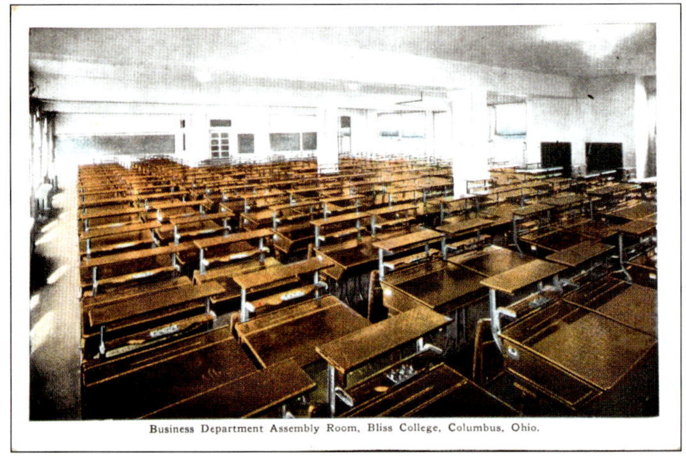

Business Department Assembly Room, Bliss College. Circa 1930s, $5-6. The back reads: ***"Every Bliss student receives actual business experience in our model office. Businessmen know that when they employ Bliss graduates they are securing the services of young people who know the work thoroughly – that is why there is such a demand for Bliss trained help."***

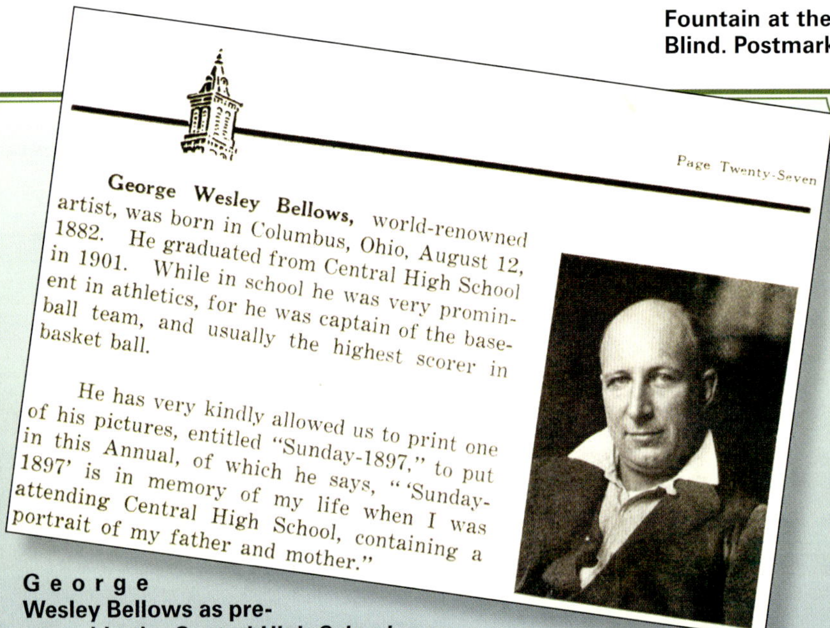

Page Twenty-Seven

George Wesley Bellows, world-renowned artist, was born in Columbus, Ohio, August 12, 1882. He graduated from Central High School in 1901. While in school he was very prominent in athletics, for he was captain of the baseball team, and usually the highest scorer in basket ball.

He has very kindly allowed us to print one of his pictures, entitled "Sunday-1897," to put in this Annual, of which he says, "'Sunday-1897' is in memory of my life when I was attending Central High School, containing a portrait of my father and mother."

George Wesley Bellows as presented in the Central High School yearbook of 1924. Bellows was mainly famous for boxing scenes rendered in the early 1900s. Later Bellows became noted for lithography prints. He graduated from Central High School in 1901. Yearbook dated 1924.

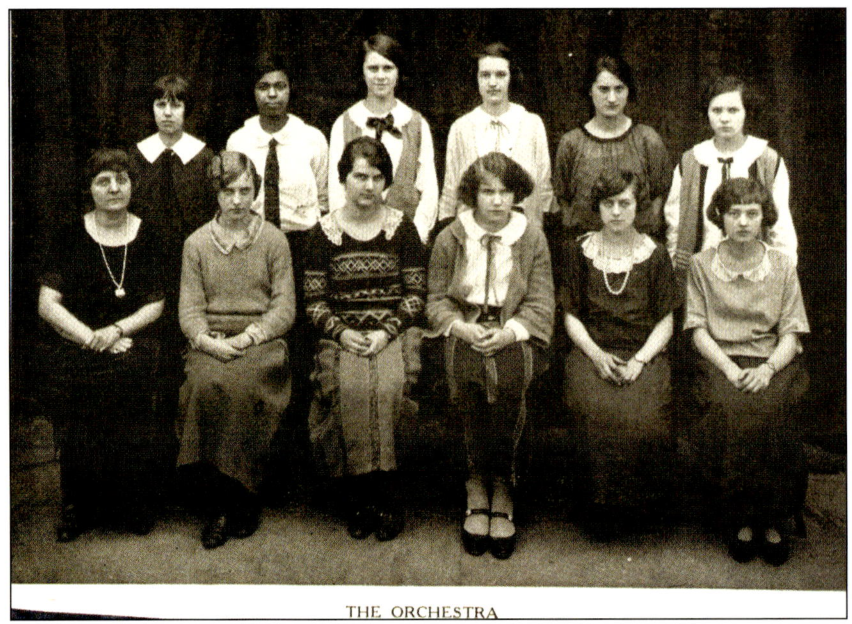

The Orchestra, Central High School, Columbus. Dated 1924, $3-4.

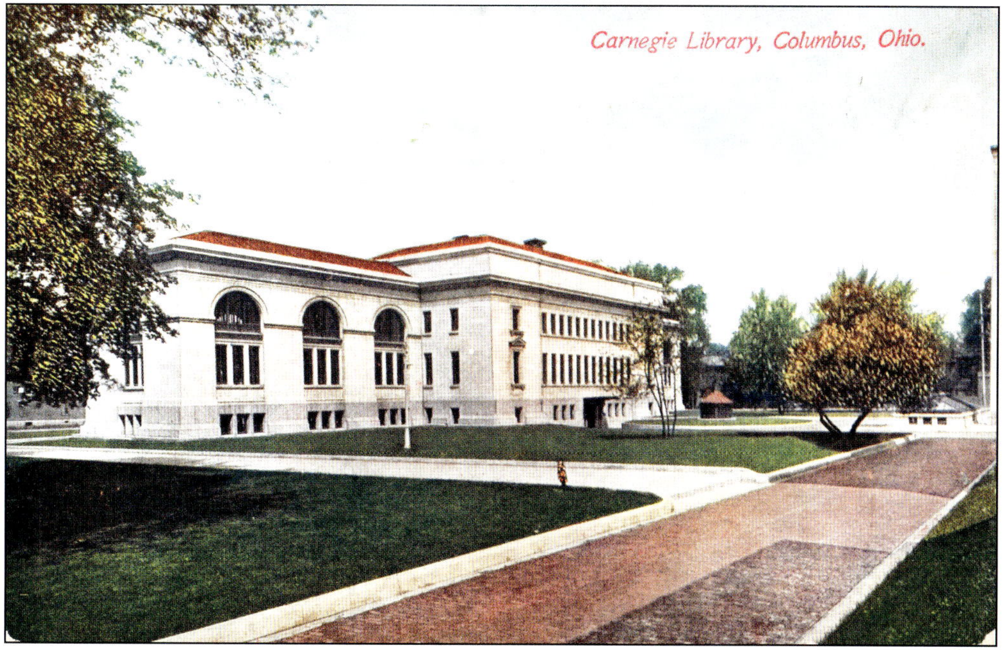

Carnegie Library, Columbus. Circa 1900s, $3-4.

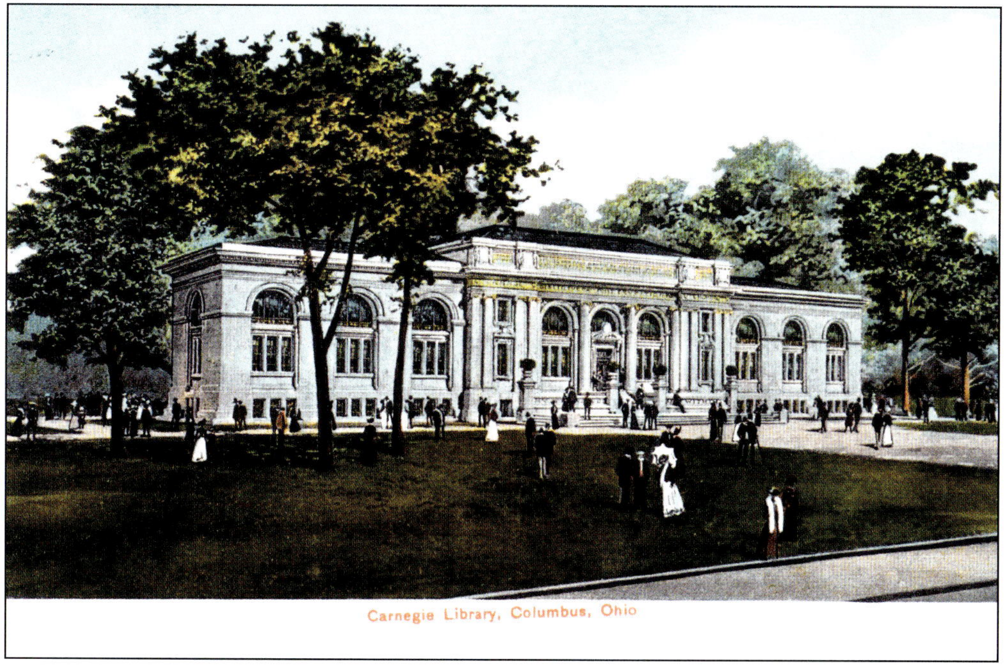

Visitors outside Carnegie Library, Columbus. Circa 1900s, $3-4.

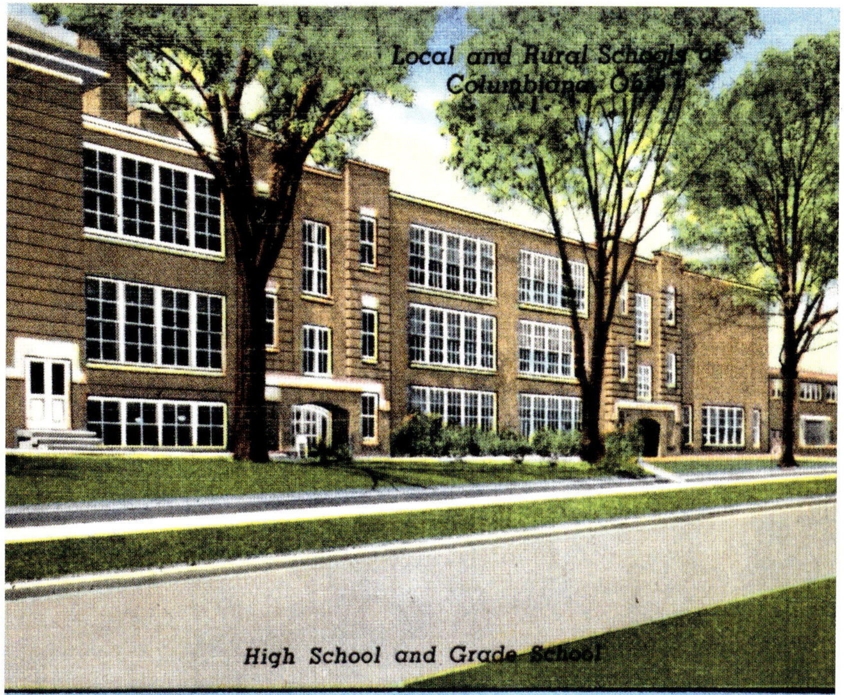

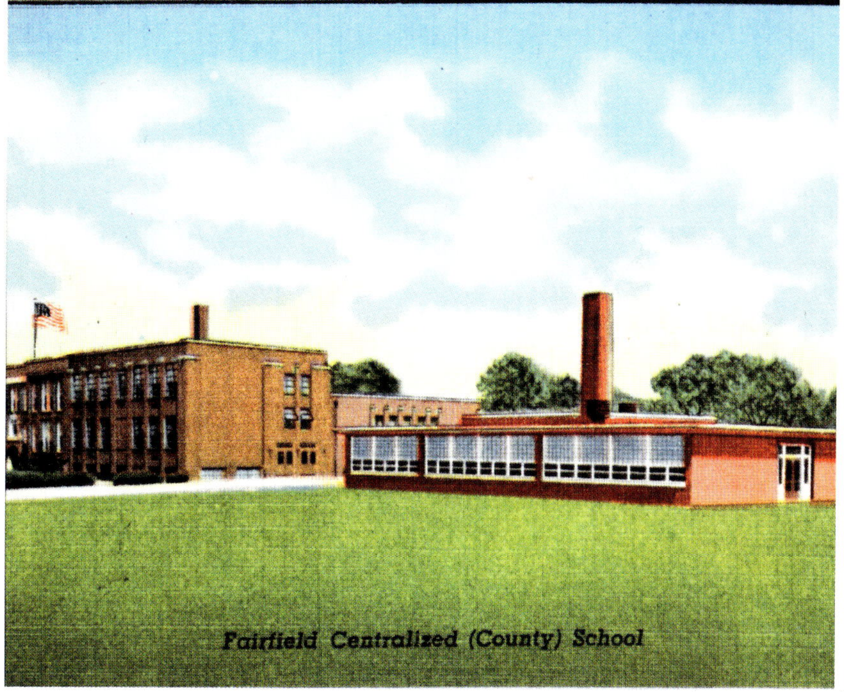

Local and rural schools of Columbus, Ohio. View of high school and grade school, and Fairfield Centralized (County) School. Circa 1930s, $3-4.

COMMENCEMENT PROGRAM

High School Auditorium

June 6

Eight O'clock

Concert		High School Orchestra
Processional, "God of Our Fathers"		Class of '35
	High School Orchestra	
Invocation		Dr. Roy Burkhart
	Pastor, First Community Church	
Songs—{Salutation / Morning		Samuel R. Gaines / Speaks-Baldwin
	Senior Chorus	
The Tercentenary Celebration		W. C. Rohleder
	Superintendent	
The Secondary School of 1635		Robert Dabe
The Development of Secondary Education in Our Community		Norma Goss
Songs—{The White Road Westward / Thank God for a Garden		Raymond Mitchell / Teresa Del Riego
	Senior Octette	
Our School Today		Jane Harmount
Presentation of Class		L. K. Replogle
	Principal	
Awarding of Diplomas		Robert W. Laylin
	President of the Board of Education	
Acceptance of Diplomas		Moreton Hughes
	President of Senior Class	
Farewell Song		Class of '35
Benediction		Dr. Roy Burkhart
	Pastor, First Community Church	
Recessional, "Priests' March"		Class of '35
	High School Orchestra	

Commencement Program, Grandview Heights High School. Dated 1935, $4-5.

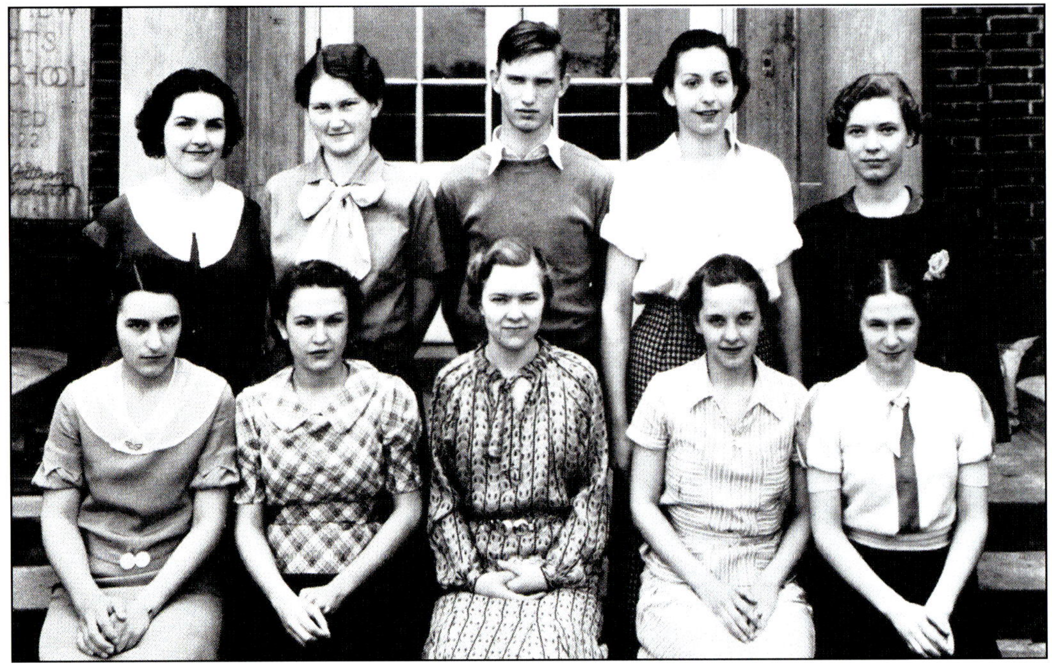

Honor roll seniors at Grandview Heights High School. Dated 1935, $4-5.

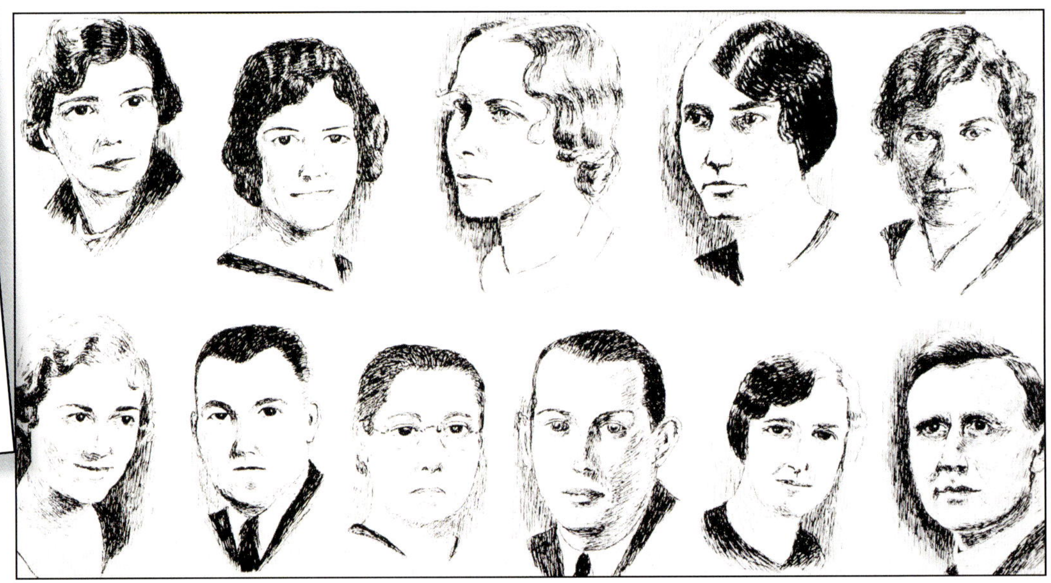

School faculty, Grandview Heights High School. Dated 1935, $3-4.

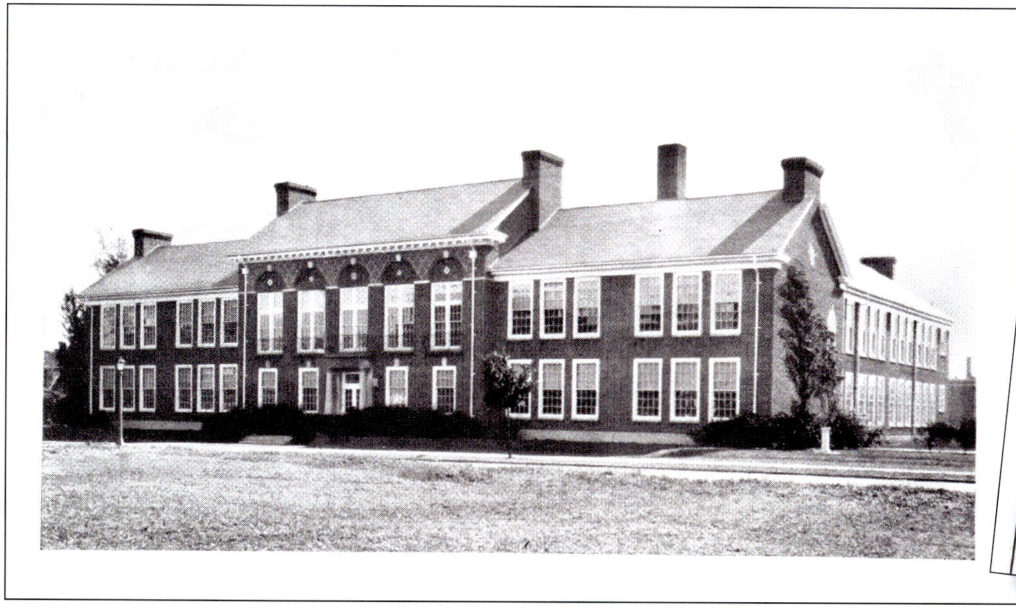

Grandview Heights High School, Columbus, Ohio. Circa 1930s, $4-5.

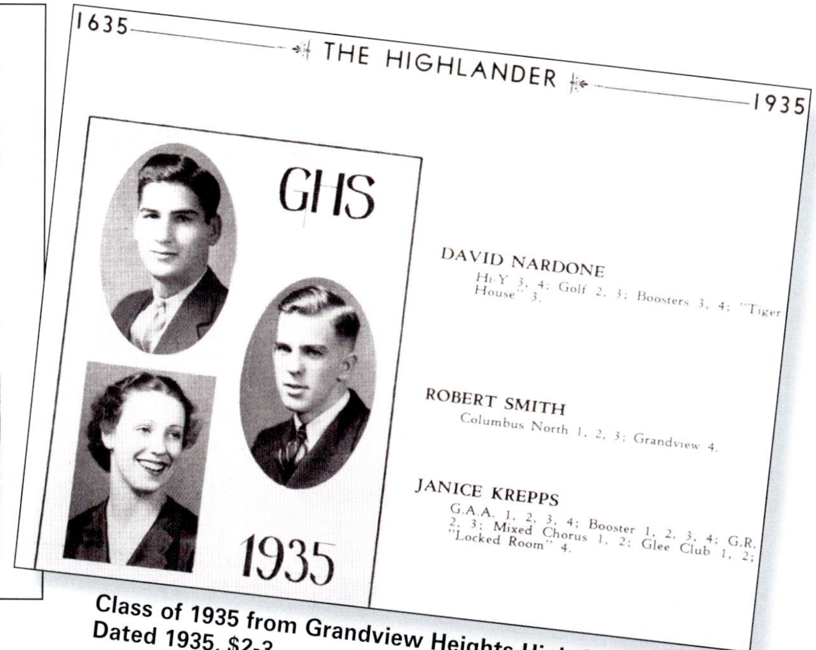

1635 THE HIGHLANDER 1935

GHS

1935

DAVID NARDONE
Hi-Y 3, 4; Golf 2, 3; Boosters 3, 4; "Tiger House" 3.

ROBERT SMITH
Columbus North 1, 2, 3; Grandview 4.

JANICE KREPPS
G.A.A. 1, 2, 3, 4; Booster 1, 2, 3, 4; G.R. 2, 3; Mixed Chorus 1, 2; Glee Club 1, 2; "Locked Room" 4.

Class of 1935 from Grandview Heights High School. Dated 1935, $2-3.

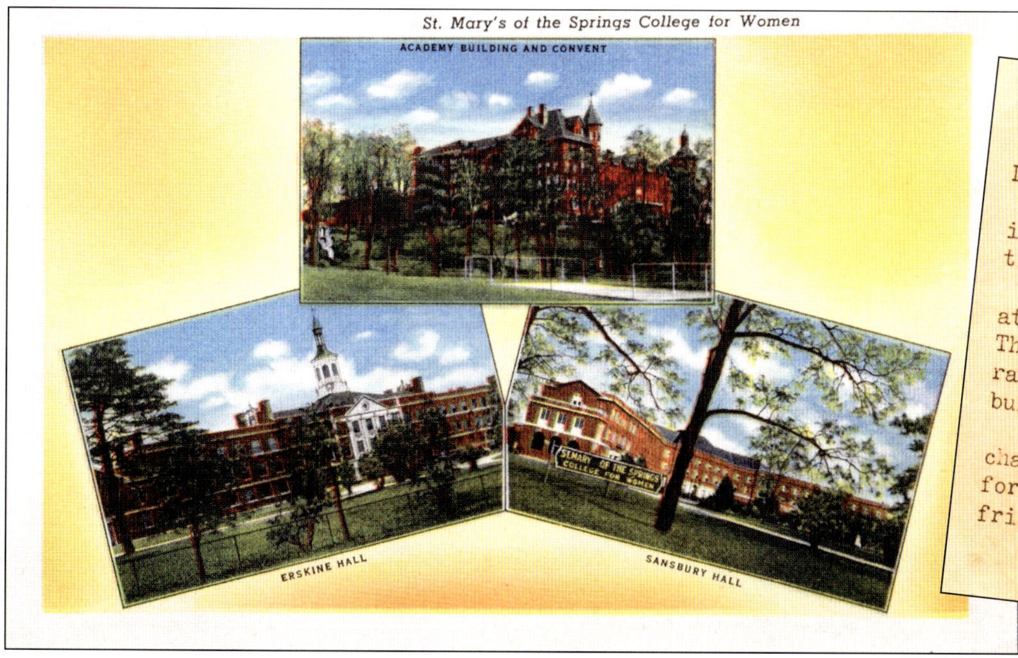

St. Mary's of the Springs College for Women. Copyright 1938, $3-4.

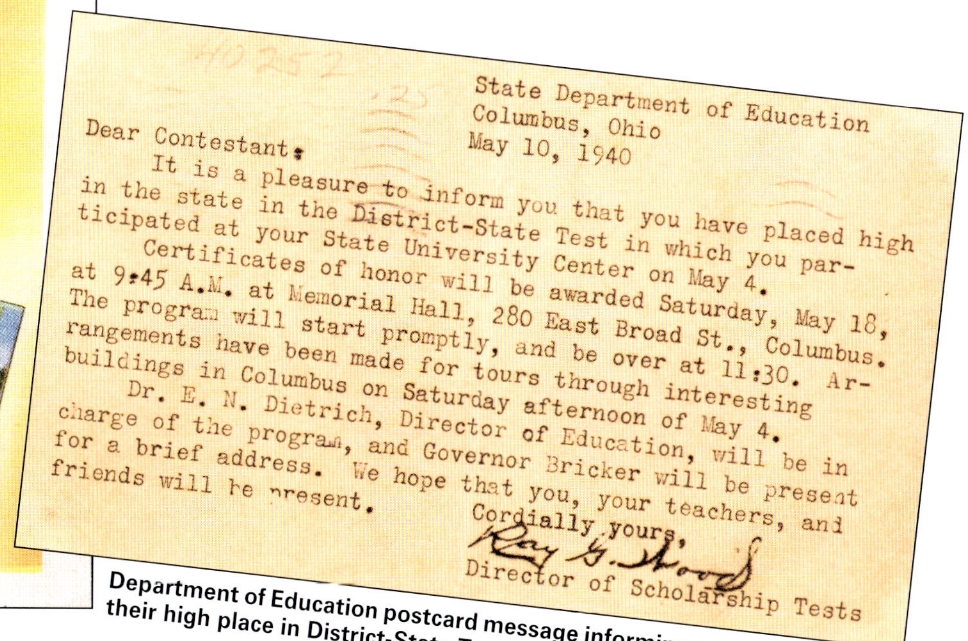

State Department of Education
Columbus, Ohio
May 10, 1940

Dear Contestant:

It is a pleasure to inform you that you have placed high in the state in the District-State Test in which you participated at your State University Center on May 4.

Certificates of honor will be awarded Saturday, May 18, at 9:45 A.M. at Memorial Hall, 280 East Broad St., Columbus. The program will start promptly, and be over at 11:30. Arrangements have been made for tours through interesting buildings in Columbus on Saturday afternoon of May 4.

Dr. E. N. Dietrich, Director of Education, will be in charge of the program, and Governor Bricker will be present for a brief address. We hope that you, your teachers, and friends will be present.

Cordially yours,

Ray G. Wood

Director of Scholarship Tests

Department of Education postcard message informing contestants of their high place in District-State Test. Dated 1940, $2-3.

Chapter Ten: In Memorial

> We have to create something here that enshrines this forever and that allows people to build on it and grow.
>
> — *Rudy Giuliani, former Mayor of New York City*

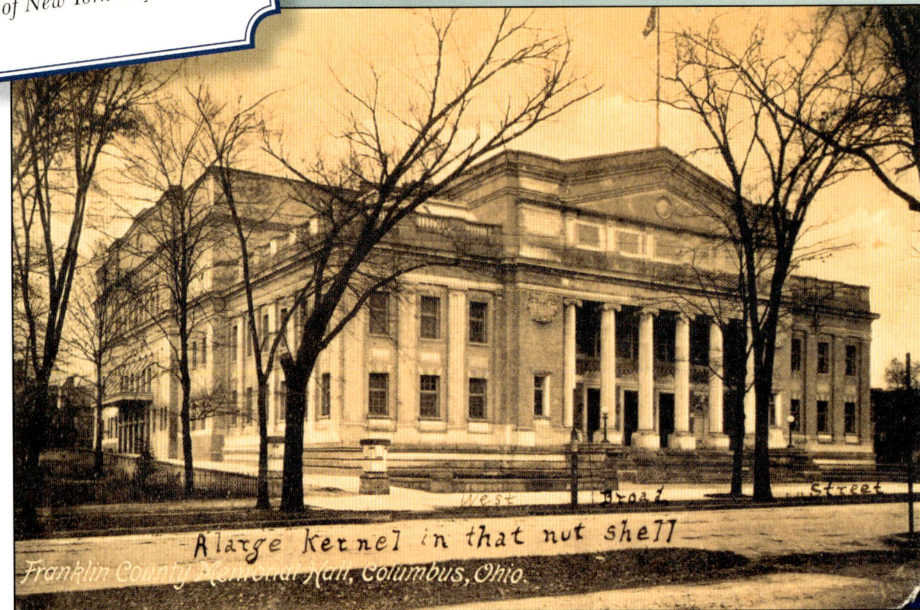

Franklin County Memorial Hall. Postmarked 1906, $3-4.

Many people and events in the city of Columbus have been further enshrined with noble memorials—from slain President William McKinley to the graves of Confederate soldiers in historic Camp Chase.

President McKinley was tragically assassinated early in the twentieth century just as the era of the postcard was dawning. The timing of the national tragedy and the production of curious postcards were grimly in tune.

Twice elected to the presidency, Ohio born McKinley had endeared himself to the public during the campaign of 1896. After receiving the Republican Party's nomination McKinley more or less retired to his residence in Canton, Ohio. While Democrat challenger William Jennings Bryan toured the country and spoke to millions, McKinley conducted what historians now call his 'front porch campaign.'

McKinley used the relatively new device called the telephone in a decisive way. Reportedly he constantly stayed in contact with thirty or forty campaign managers in various states through his home telephone. The strategy worked and McKinley won election by an overwhelming margin.

In 1900 McKinley won re-election by defeating Bryan again, and Prohibition candidate John Wooley.

On September 6, 1901 the ill-fated President was attending a public reception at the Pan-American Exposition in Buffalo, New York. McKinley greeted guests at a private residence in that city. Shortly after 4 p.m. Leon Czolgosz, a disgruntled factory worker and self-proclaimed anarchist, approached the President. Using a revolver hidden in his handkerchief, the assassin shot McKinley twice.

President McKinley lingered for many days before his condition worsened. He died September 14 still at the home where he was wounded. Justice was swift. The assassin, Czolgosz, was convicted of the crime of murder after a trial that lasted little more than eight hours. Czolgosz was electrocuted at Auburn State Prison on October 29, 1901. The execution had taken place just fifty-four days after the shooting of the President, and just forty-five days following McKinley's actual death.

By 1903 a memorial statue of the late President was commissioned for the state capital in Columbus. Funding came from $25,000 in public subscriptions and $25,000 from Ohio state funds. That same year McKinley was also memorialized with his image appearing on the official postcard of the U.S. government.

As work continued on the statue in Columbus, numerous postcards were published related to the life and subsequent death of President McKinley. In 1906, on the fifth anniversary of McKinley's assassination, the impressive memorial statue was dedicated. It too became a very popular subject for postcards.

The group statue, "These Are My Jewels," is equally impressive. The work of Levi T. Scofield, it honors Ohio soldiers and statesmen. Included are Presidents Grant, Hayes, Garfield, Generals Sherman and Sheridan, Salmon Chase, and Secretary of War Edwin Stanton.

On King Avenue is the memorial to Confederate soldiers who died at Camp Chase during the Civil War. The site contains the graves of some 2,260 soldiers.

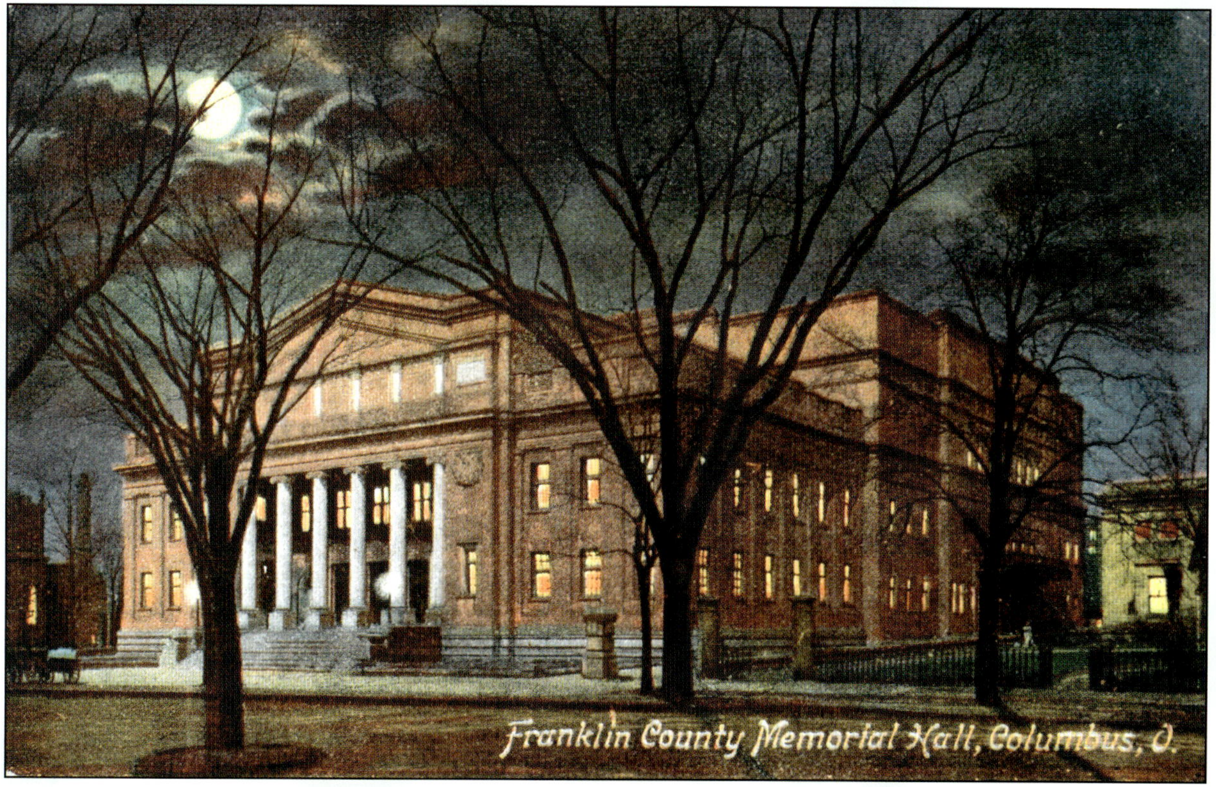

Night view of Memorial Hall. Postmarked 1909, $2-4. Hand-written message on the back reads, *"Did you notice the young man opposite us on the train that Sunday evening? He carried our suitcases to the street car. Bonna."*

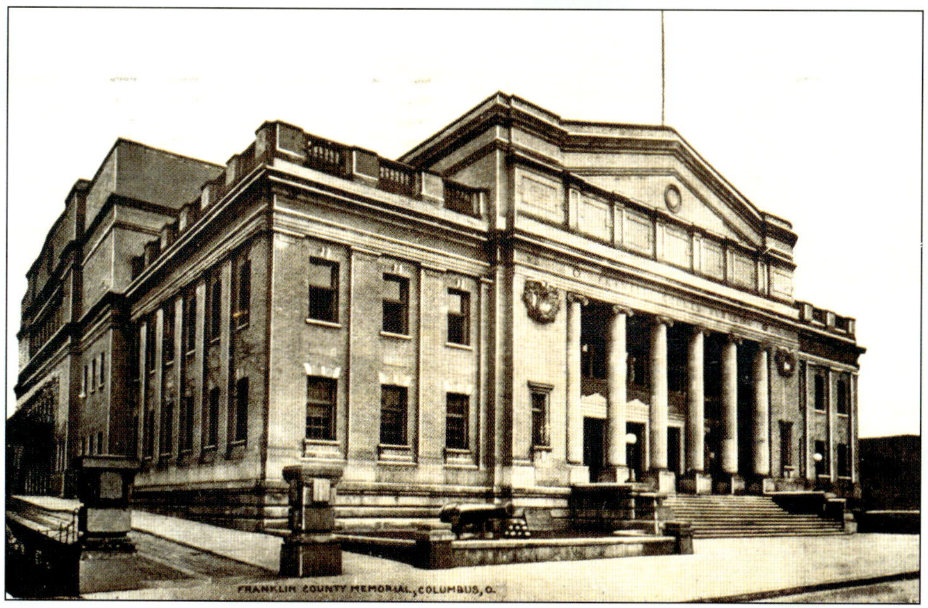

Franklin County Memorial. Postmarked 1910, $2-3.

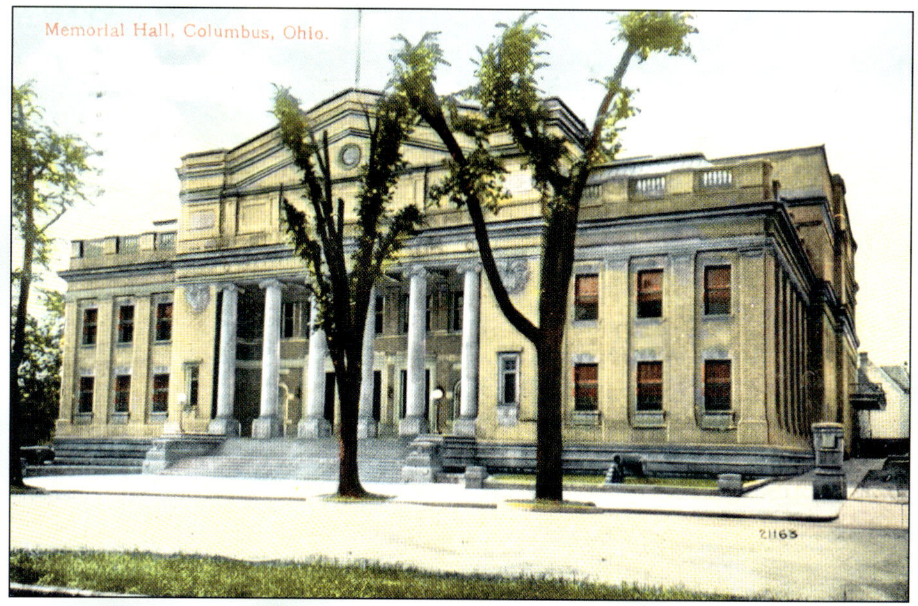

Memorial Hall, Columbus. Postmarked 1911, $2-4.

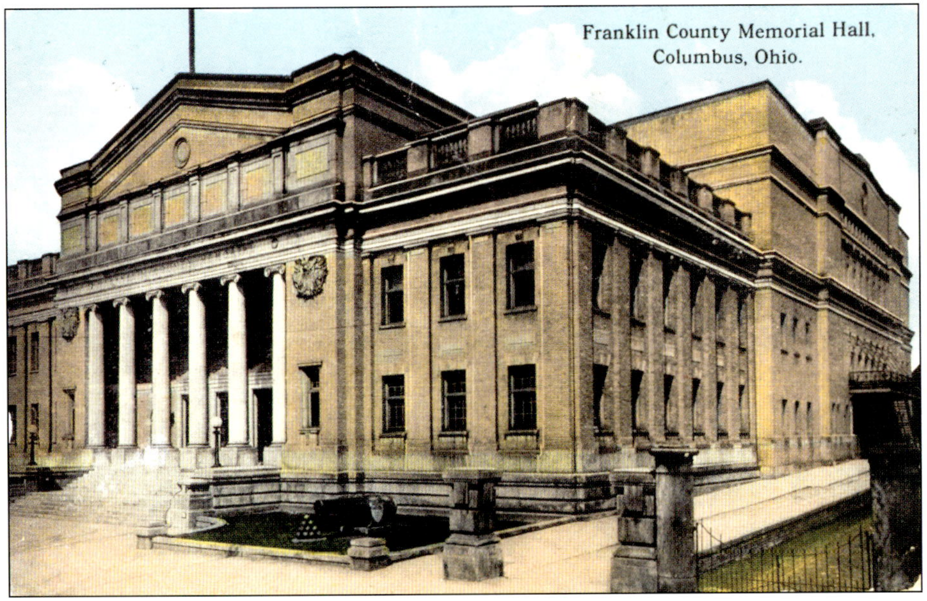

Franklin County Memorial Hall. Postmarked 1912, $2-3.

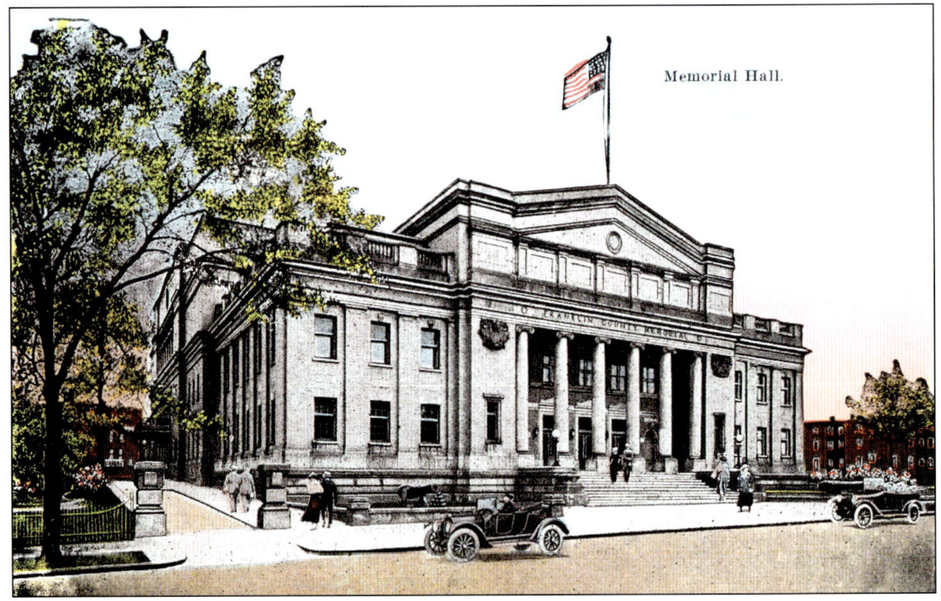

U.S. Flag atop Memorial Hall. Postmarked 1925, $3-4.

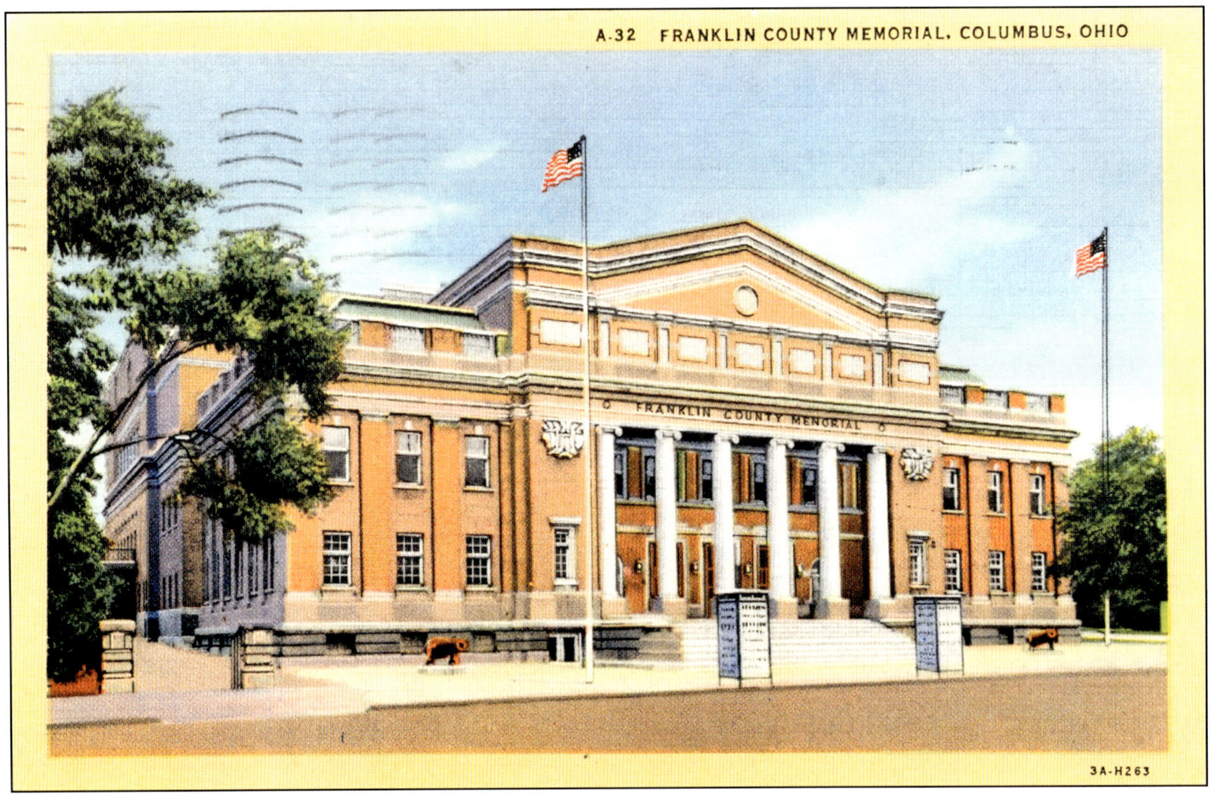

Franklin County Memorial.
Postmarked 1945, $2-3.

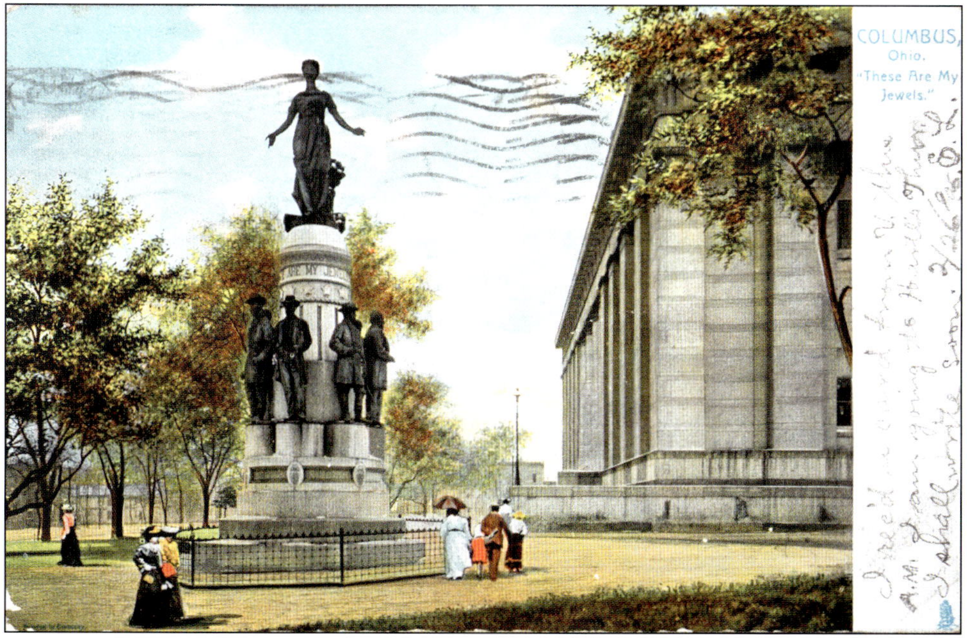

These Are My Jewels, Columbus, Ohio. Raphael Tuck & Sons. Postmarked 1906, $3-4.

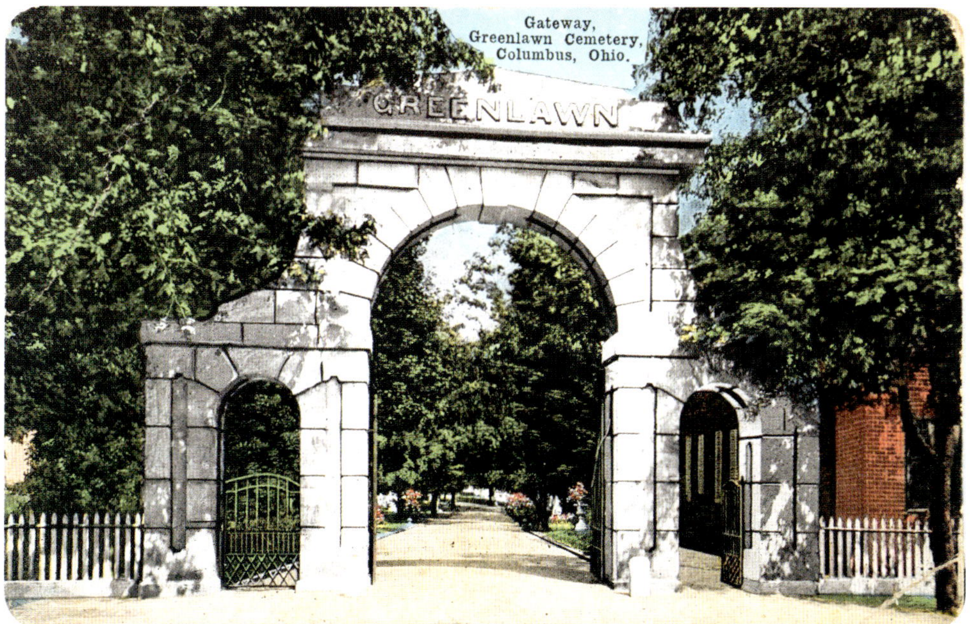

Gateway, Greenlawn Cemetery. Postmarked 1910, $3-5.

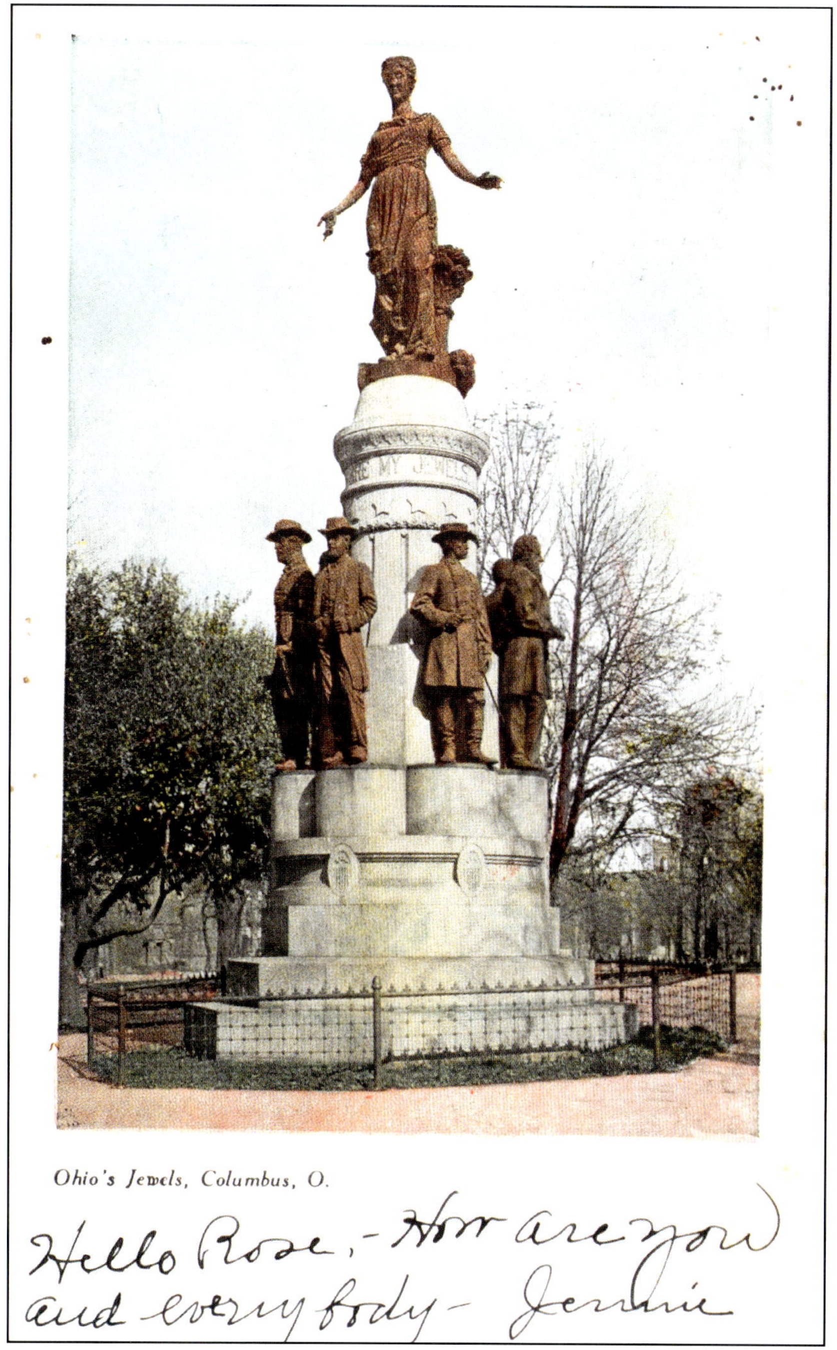

Ohio's Jewel. J. Murray Jordan, Publisher. Postmarked 1907, $4-5.

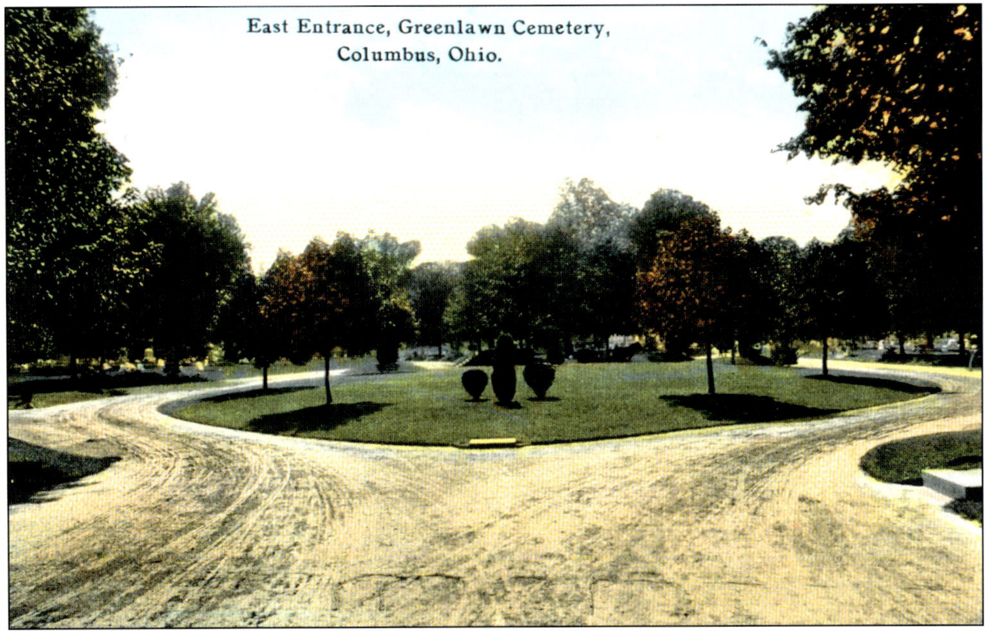

East Entrance, Greenlawn Cemetery. Circa 1900s, $2-3.

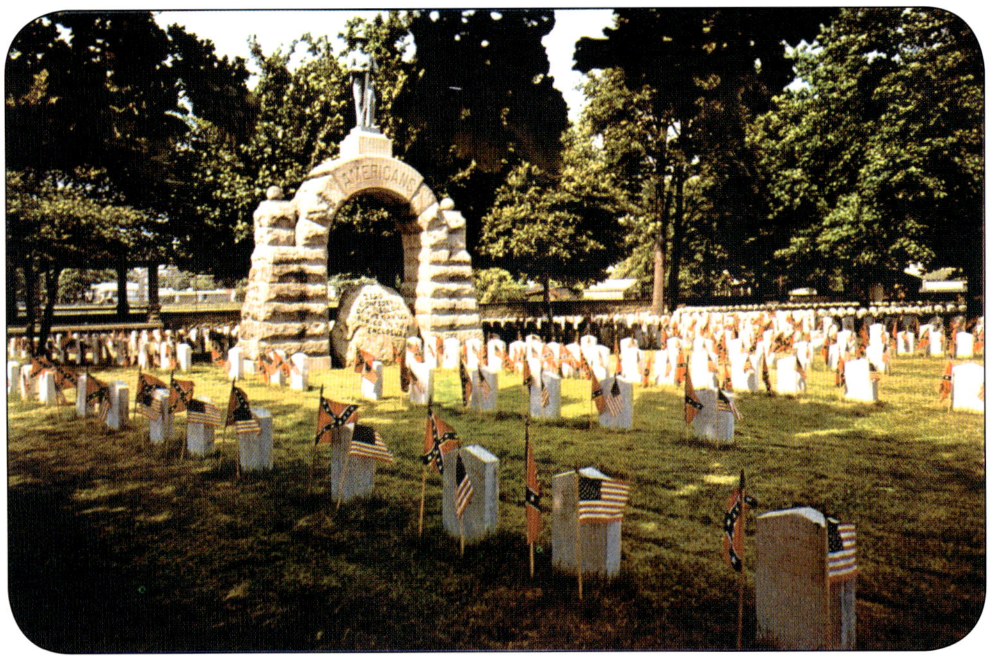

Camp Chase. Circa 1960s, $2-3.

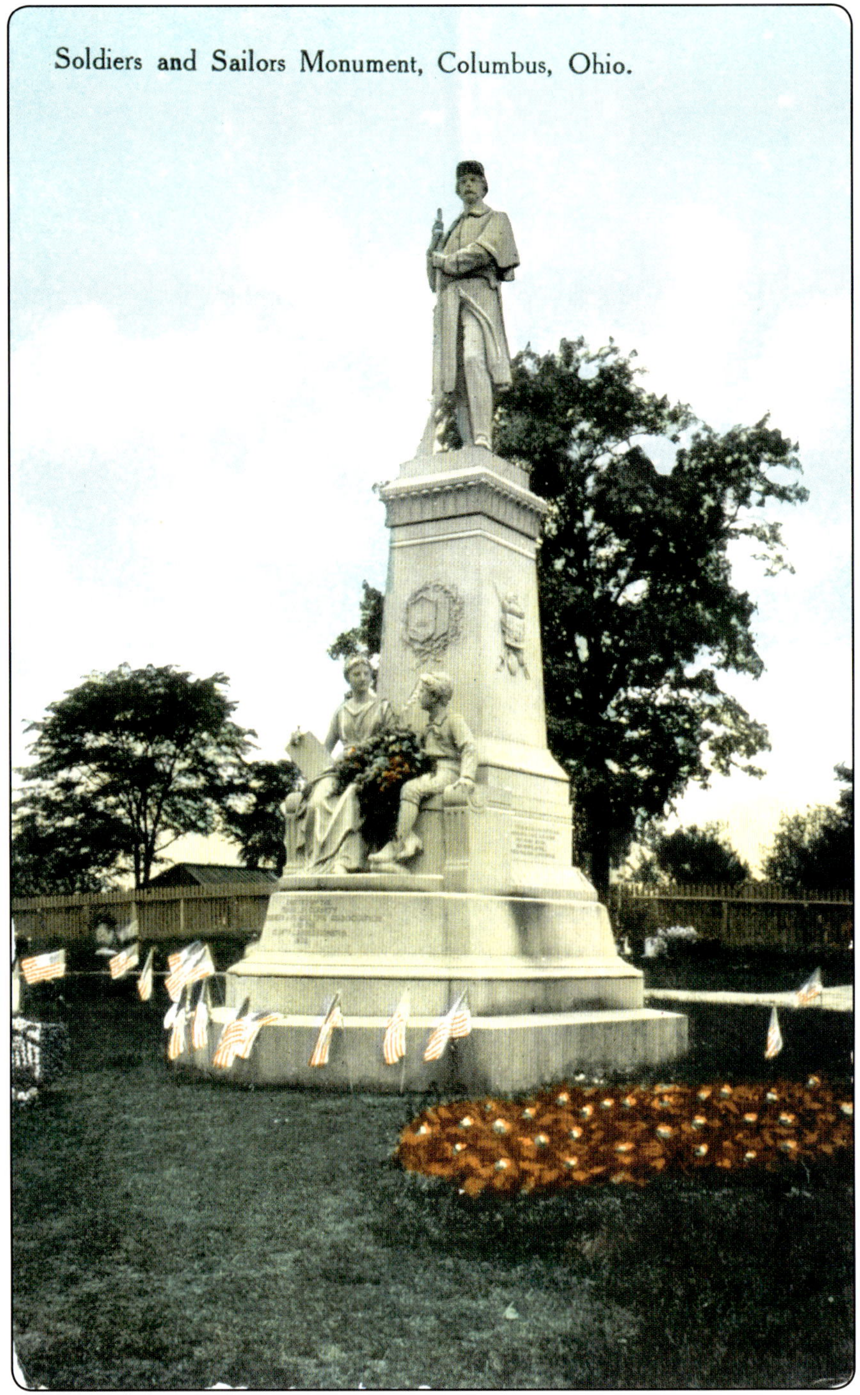

Soldiers and Sailors Monument, Columbus. Circa early 1900s, $3-4.

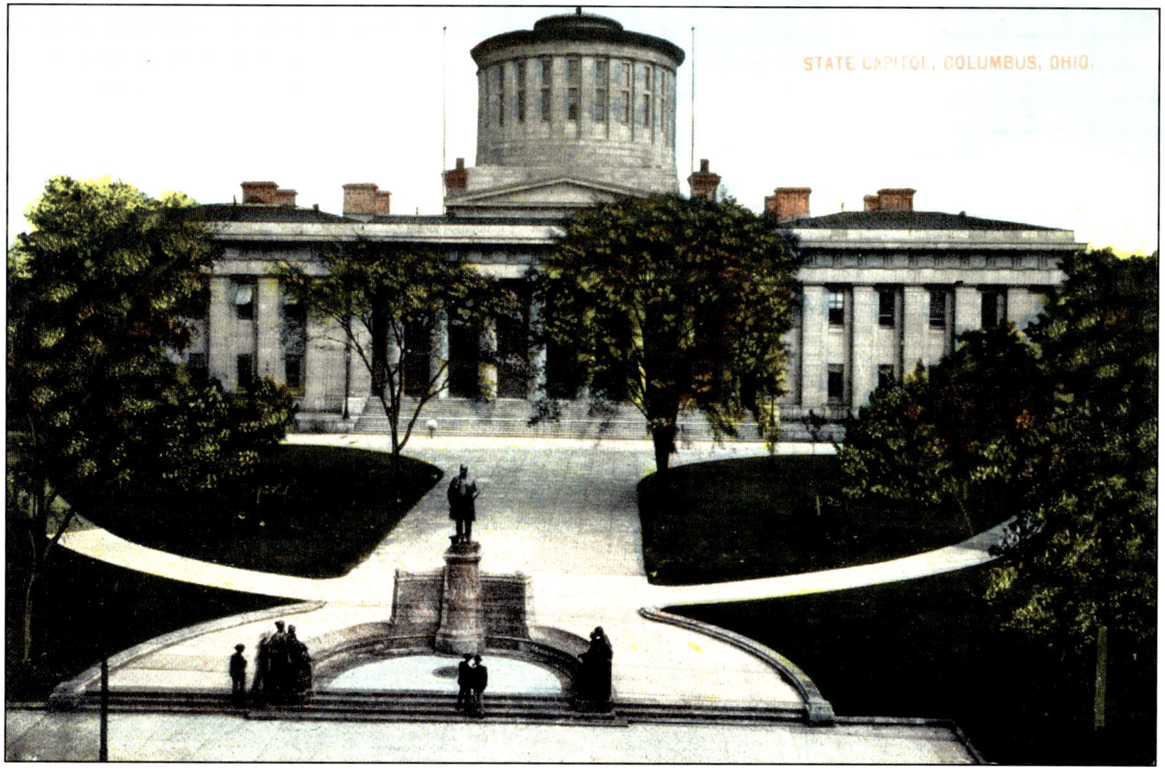

State Capitol with McKinley statue in the foreground. Circa early 1900s, $2-3.

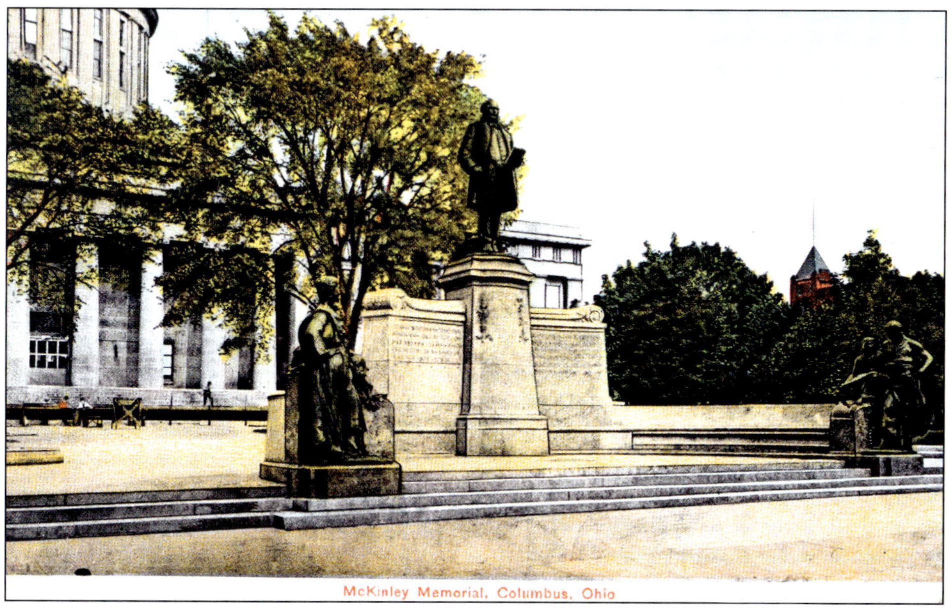

McKinley Memorial, Columbus. Circa early 1900s, $3-4.

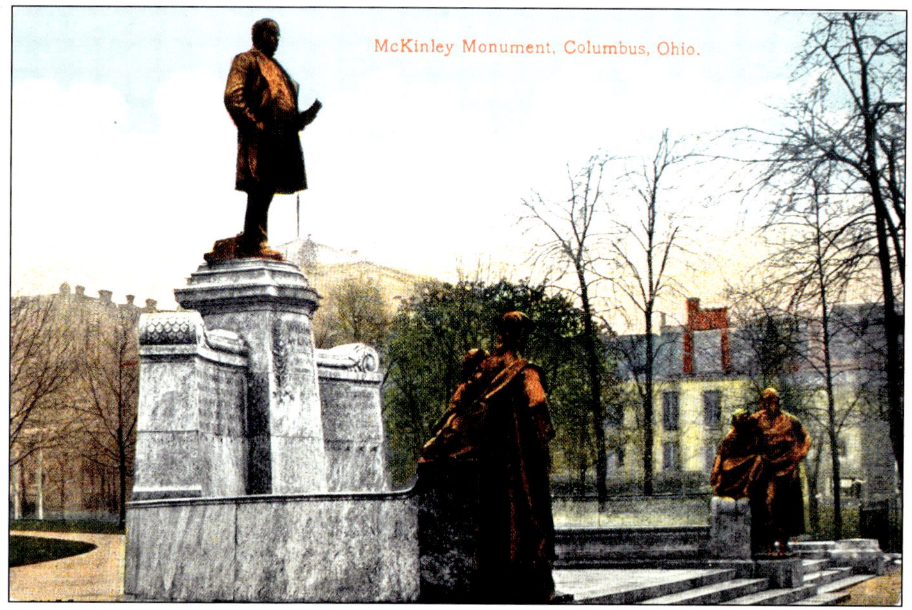

McKinley Monument, Valentine-Souvenir Co. Circa early 1900s, $3-4.

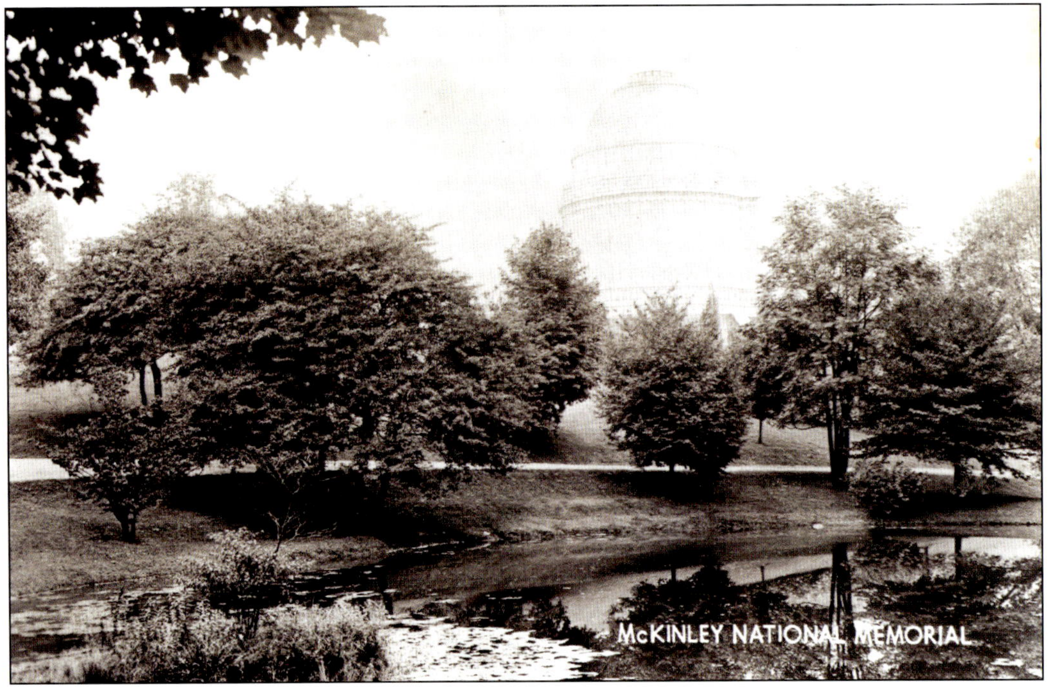

McKinley National Memorial. Circa early 1900s, $3-4.
The back reads: *"This memorial to William McKinley, 25th President of the United States, was erected by contributions from more than a million men, women and children in the U.S. and foreign lands. The McKinley National Memorial is administered by the Ohio State Archaeological and Historical Society, Columbus."*

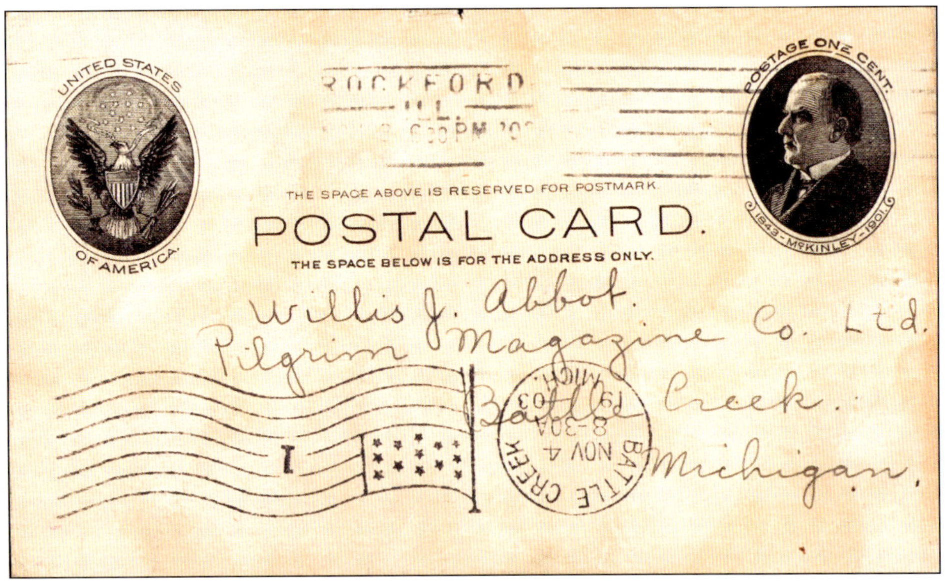

McKinley Postal Card. Postmarked 1903, $3-5.

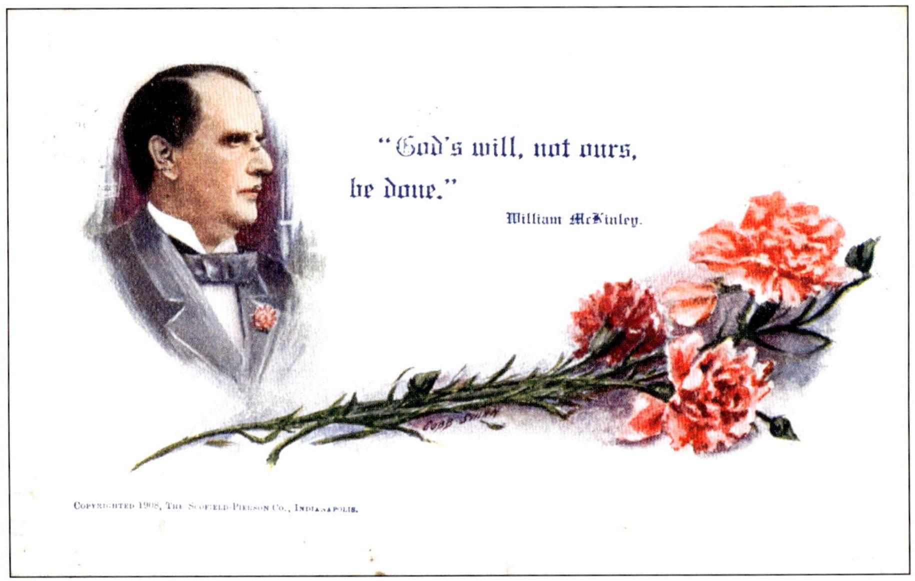

McKinley Memorial postcard. Postmarked 1911, $5-7.
The back reads: *"As the birthday of our beloved martyred President William McKinley, January 29, occurs this year on Sunday, the McKinley Club will observe said anniversary on Monday evening, January 30, as a tribute to him whose public services and kindly disposition ever remains as one of sweetest memory. The Hon. A.M. Hall will make the address. Wear a pink carnation."*

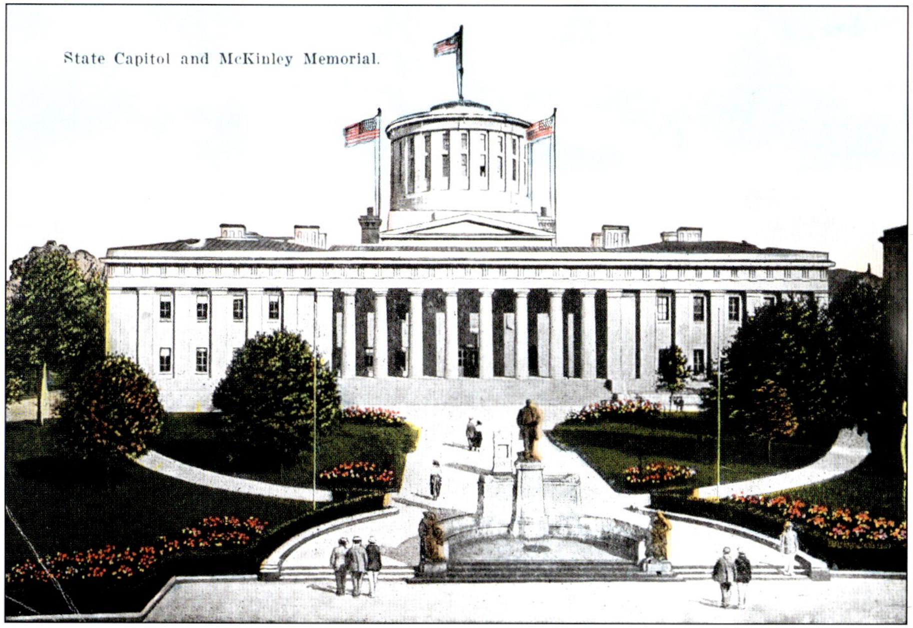

State Capitol and McKinley Memorial. Postmarked 1925, $3-4.

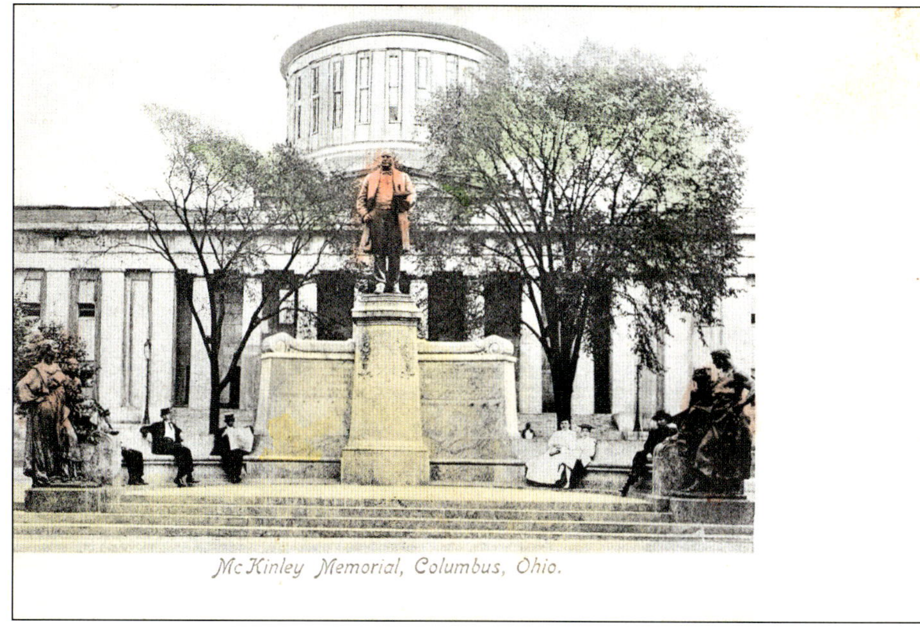

McKinley Memorial, Columbus, Ohio. Postmarked 1909, $3-4. Hand-written message on the back reads, *"Dear Folks, Grandma is getting better... We had an awful storm hear (sic) last night, the lightning struck a tree in our yard but nobody was hurt."*

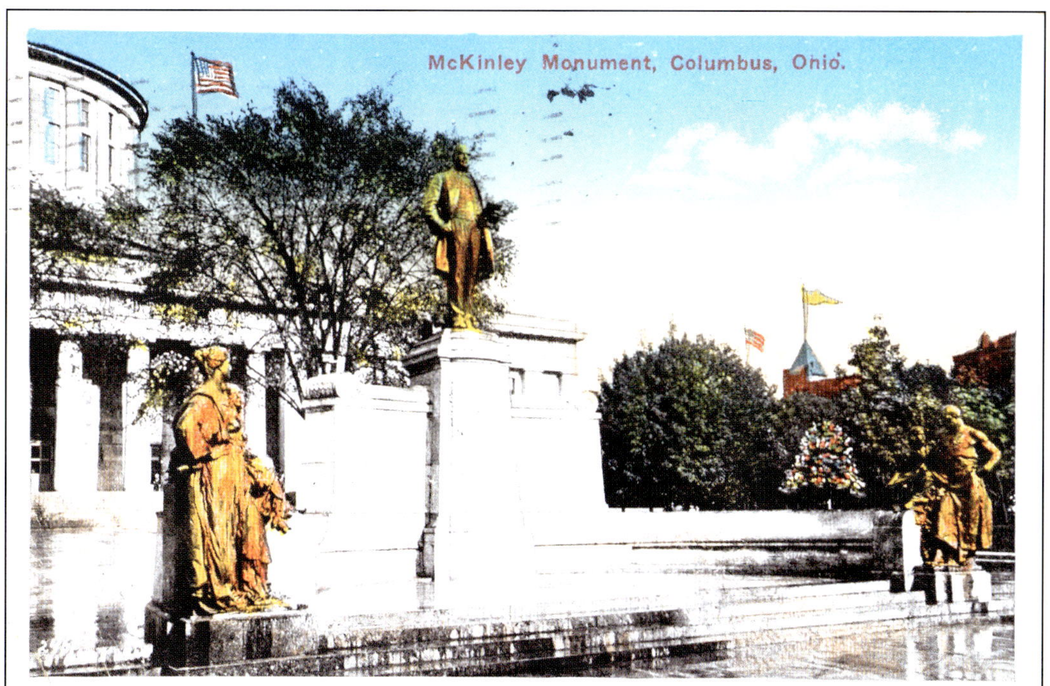

McKinley Monument, Columbus, Ohio. Postmarked 1917, $3-5.

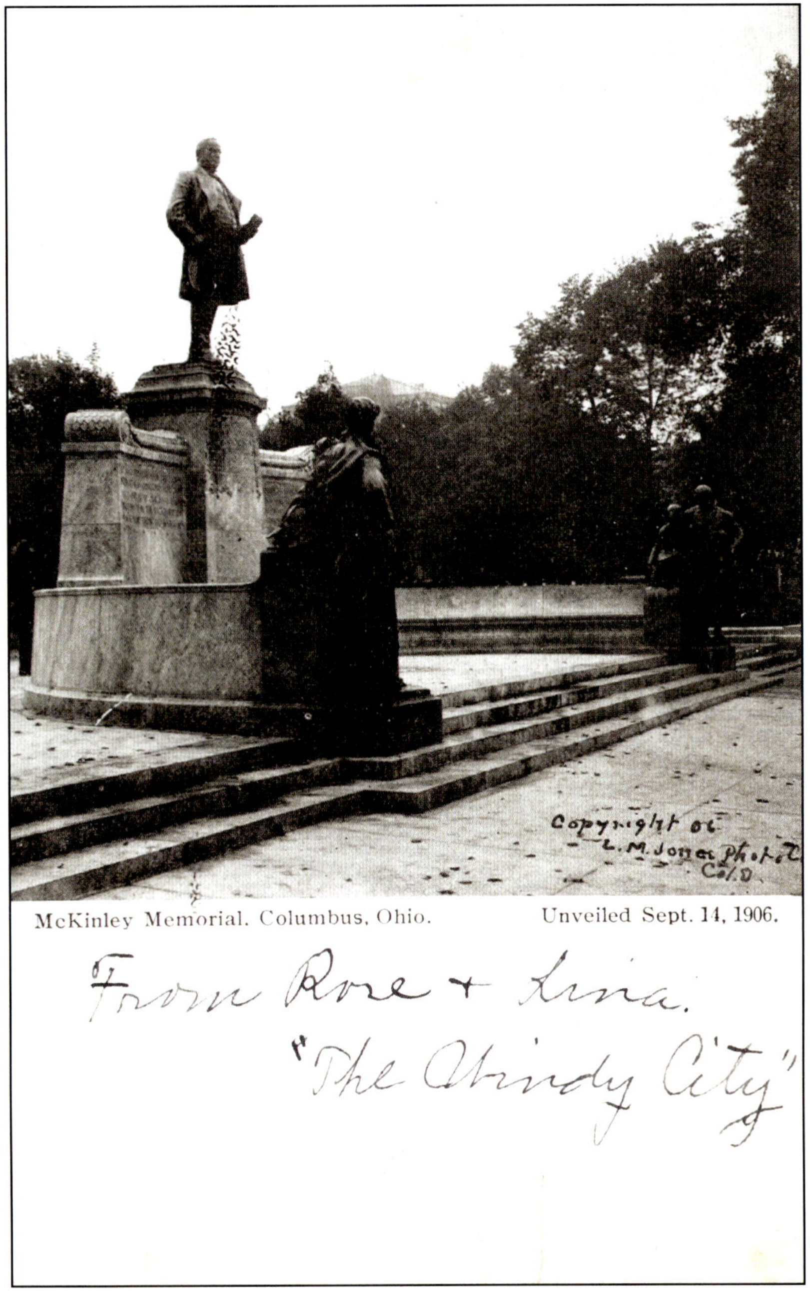

Memorial unveiled September 11, 1906. Postmarked 1906, $5-6.

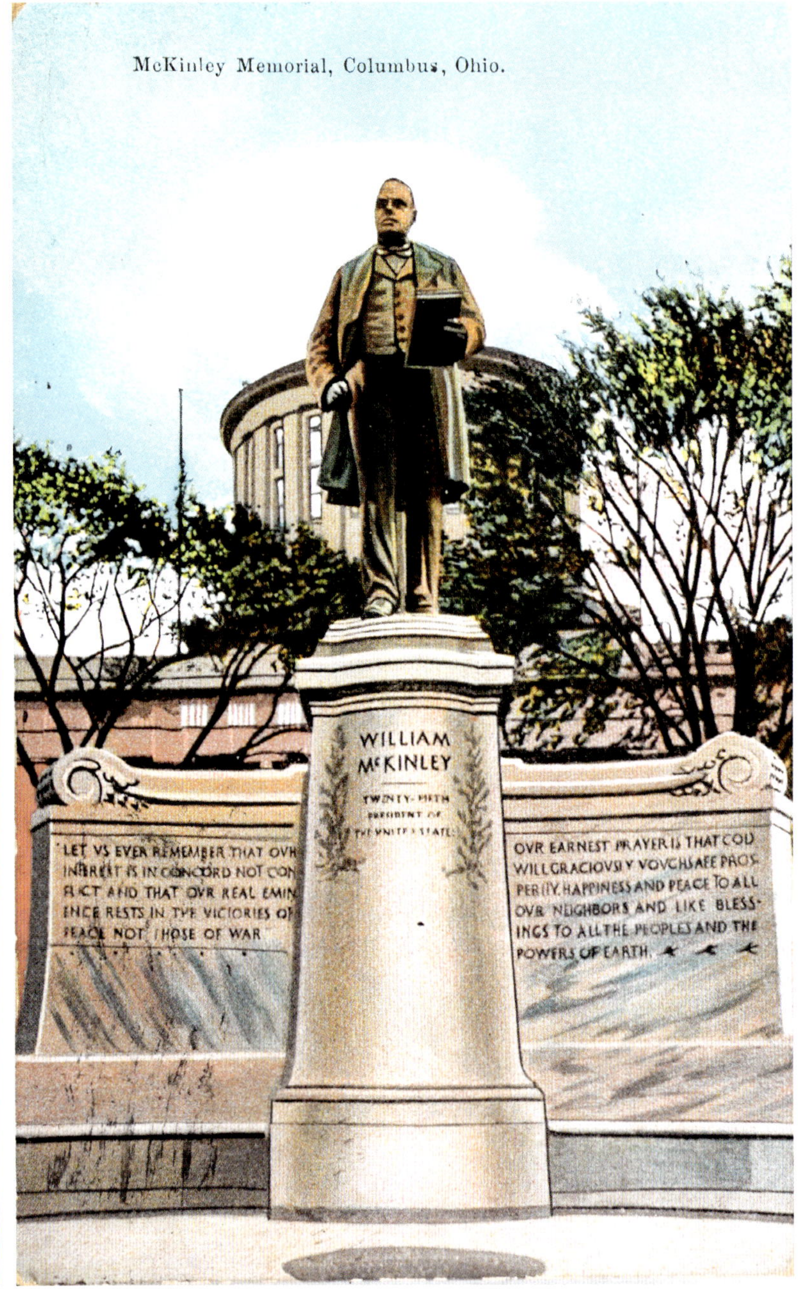

President McKinley Memorial. Postmarked 1908, $3-4.

Chapter Eleven: Out for a Good Time

Rock, music, dining, dancing—wow!
It's time to write the Nitecap.
— Nita Hutch, columnist for This Week in Columbus, 1954

Clearly there were a lot of opportunities for a good time back in the Columbus of the 1950s.

There was the Columbus Town Meeting, which celebrated its 50th anniversary in 1954, and the Seafood Bay, which offered all the lobster "you can eat" for $4.75. At The Tremont someone named Lorette preformed at the Hammond organ, a woman named Charmaine sang at the Coral Reef, and dinner was elegantly served at Margetti's on East Broad.

From cafeteria to show bar the city offered a wealth of entertainment and dining selections during that era.

Even earlier the country club had been very much in vogue along with the Athletic Club. During the 1920s, The Ohioans offered their dance orchestra talents aaround the city, and crowds filled the Ohio Theatre.

A meal at Palumbo's Grandview Restaurant might have been a good idea in the 1930s. They promised moderate prices, and "David Davies baby beef served exclusively." Not far away was Wolgamot's Drug Store with Whitman's and Littleton's Candies along with all Rexall Remidies too.

In the 1940s there were more stylish restaurants and there was even roller-skating at Rollerland.

By the 1950s there were still entertaining places to visit between any meetings or just for a good time. At The Tremont, also on High Street, the meal came with "soft candlelight and restful charm" plus Lorette at the Hammond Organ. At the other end of High Street was a combination of original Dixieland music and charcoal broiled steaks at The Frolics. Elsewhere Charmaine, "the girl with the Parisian air," sang nightly at the Coral Reef and Jimmy Bowman entertained "King Cole style" at the Latin Lounge. Further north the Kitty Show Bar featured the comedy combo of the Noveliers and dancing each evening.

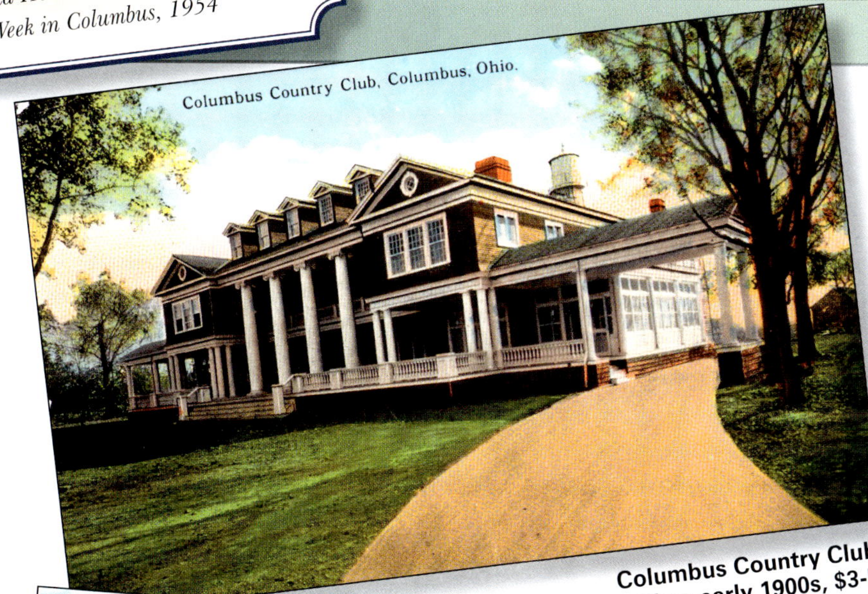

Columbus Country Club. Circa early 1900s, $3-5.

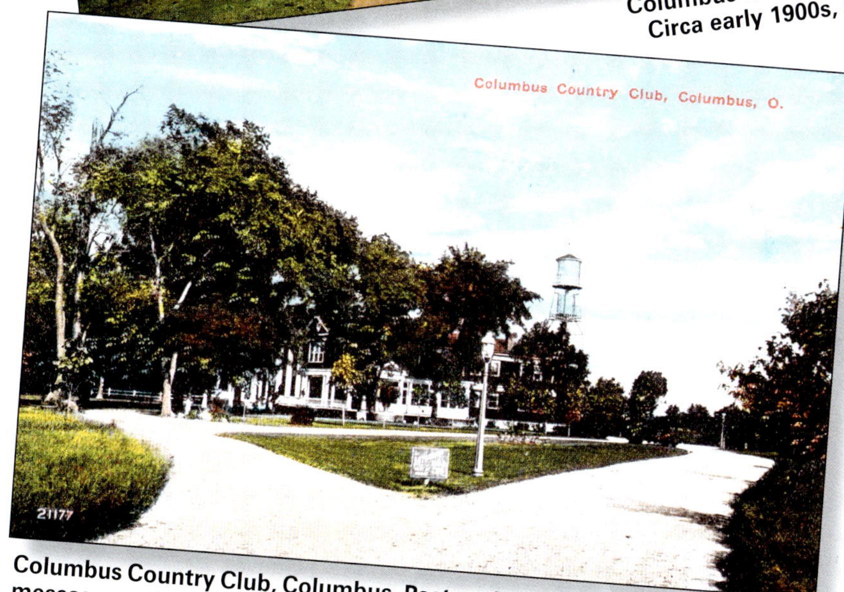

Columbus Country Club, Columbus. Postmarked 1912, $2-3. Hand-written message on the back reads: *"At last we reached home but tired out. I did the washing then cried all night with my arms. A two weeks washing was a plenty. Last night we had a family picnic at Olentangy Park. I went canoeing and danced some. I think I need a vacation now more than when I left."*

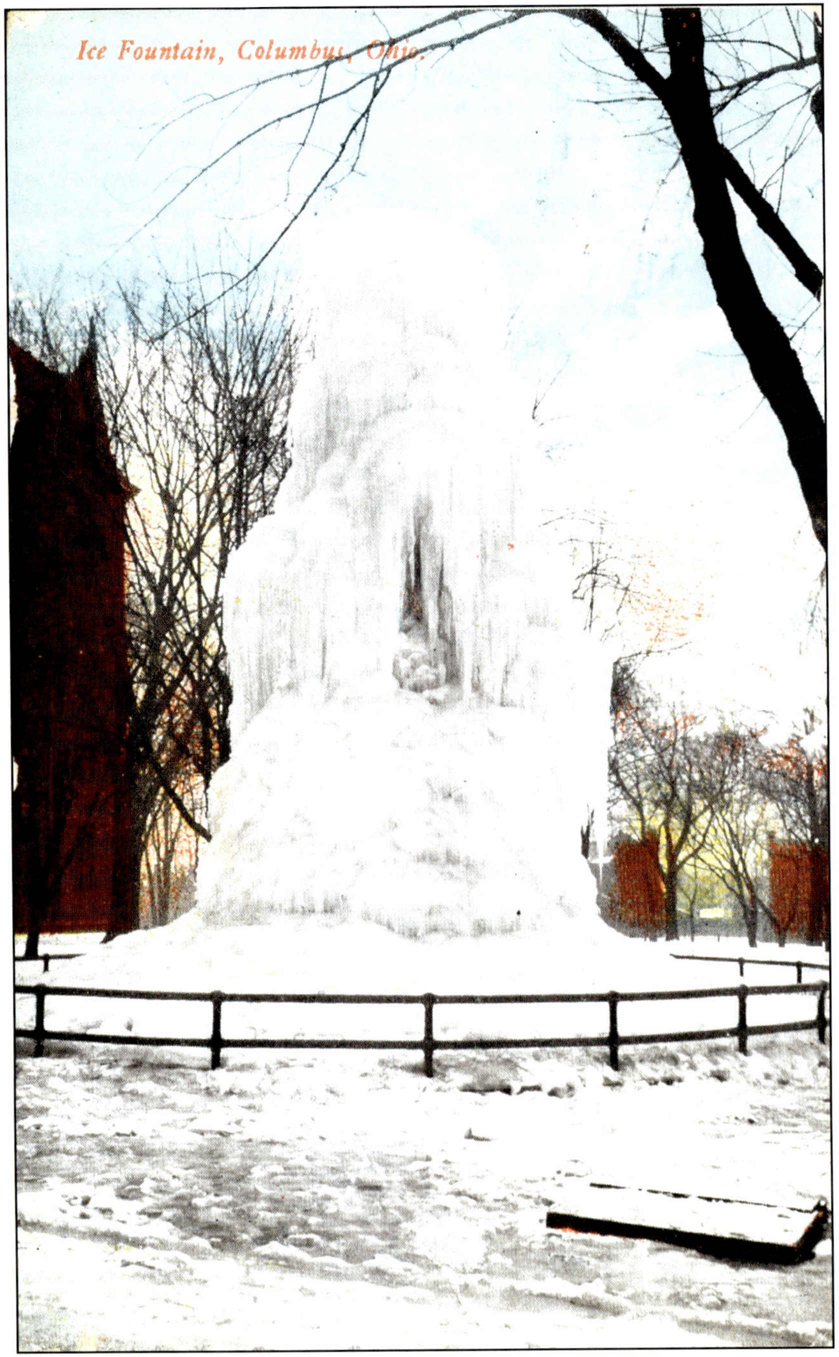

Ice Fountain, Columbus, Ohio. Postmarked 1914, $2-3.
Hand-written message on the back reads: *"Excuse the delay – have been to Buckeye Lake and just got back."*

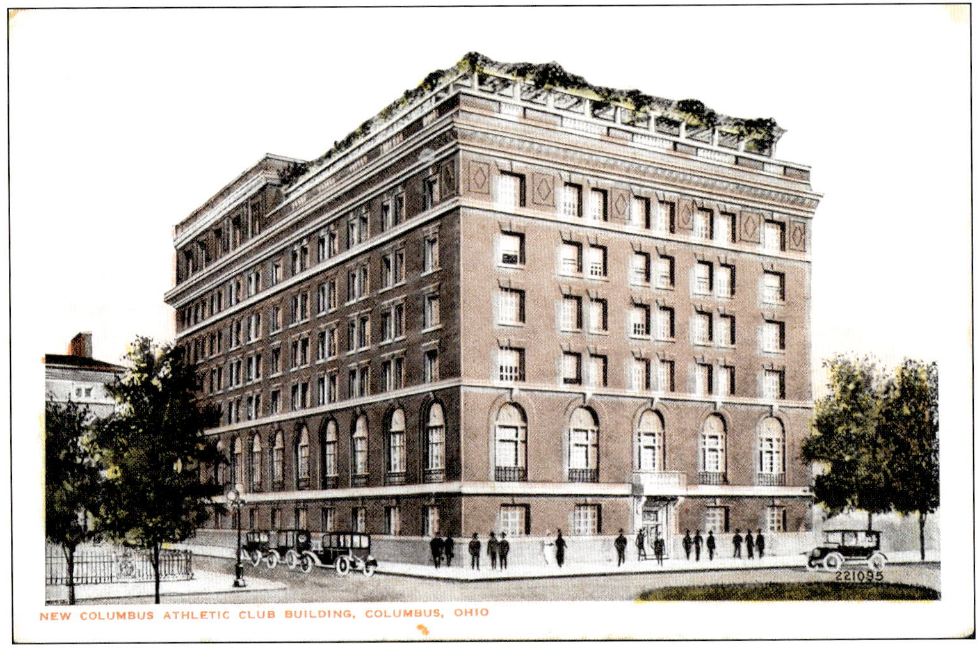

New Columbus Athletic Club Building. Circa early 1900s, $3-5.

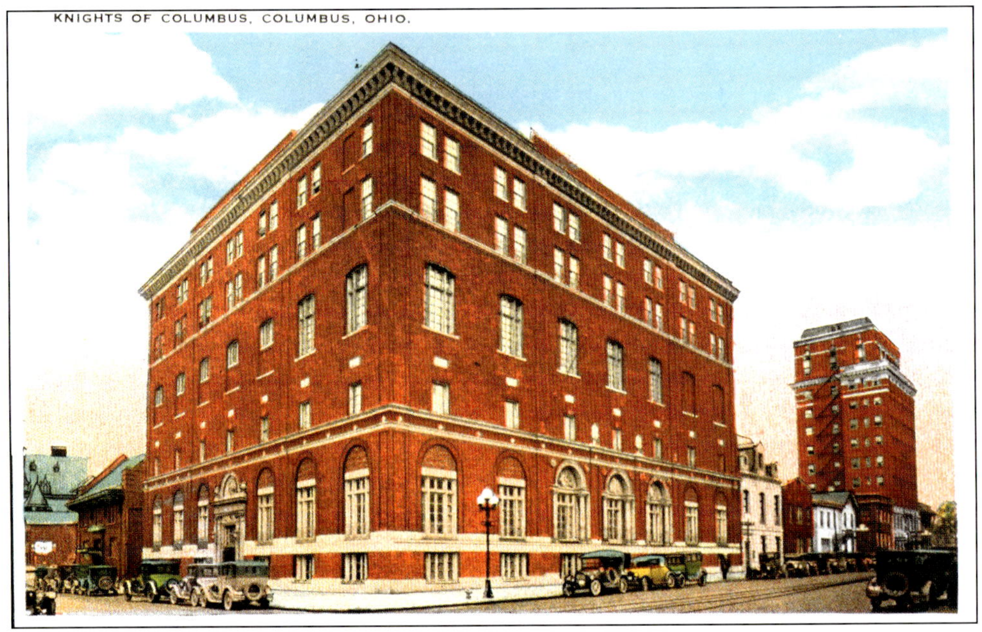

Knights of Columbus, Columbus, Ohio. Circa 1920s, $3-4.

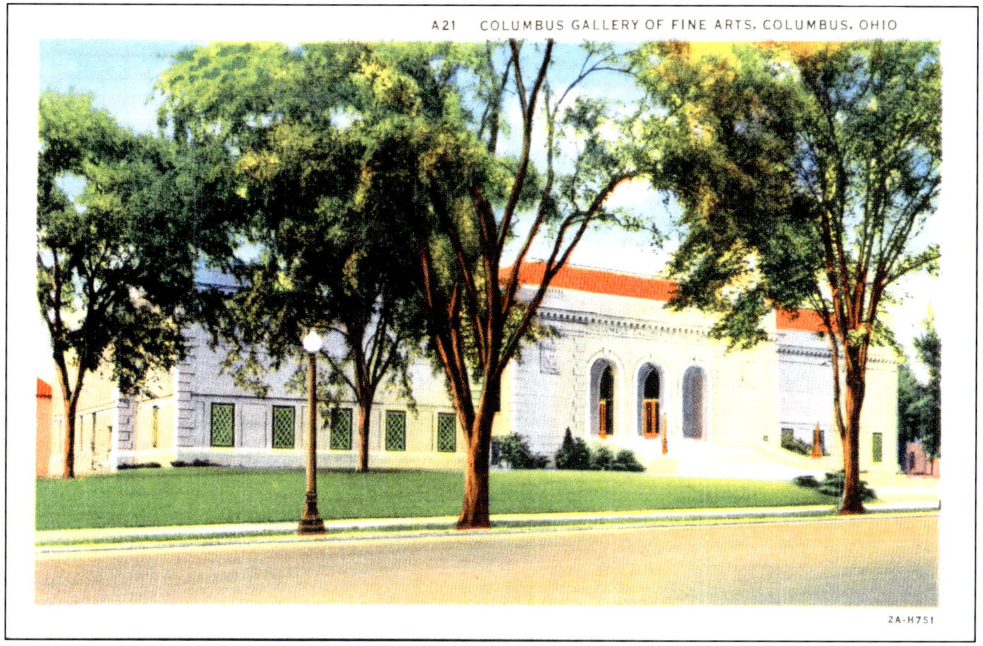

Columbus Gallery of Fine Arts. Circa 1920s, $3-4.

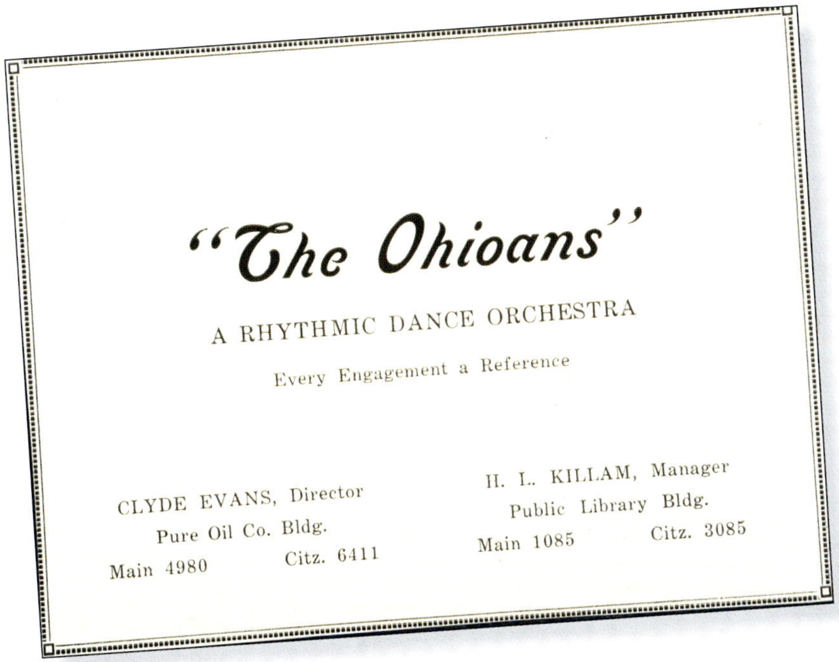

The Ohioans orchestra advertisement. Dated 1924, $2-3.

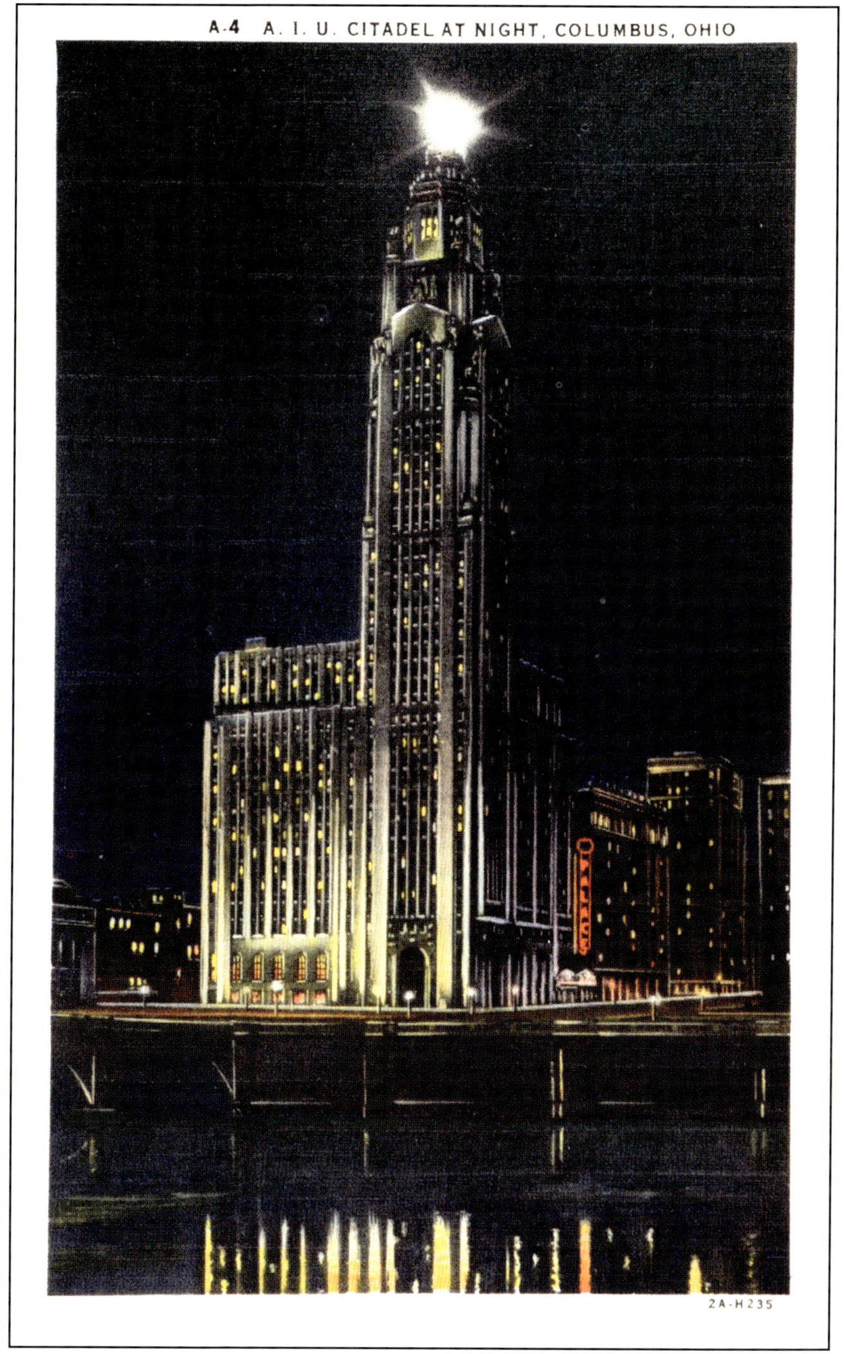

A.I.U. Citadel. Undated, $2-3. The back reads: *"One of the most beautiful buildings in the world. The R.K.O. Palace Theatre and Deshler Wallick Hotel occupy space in the Citadel."*

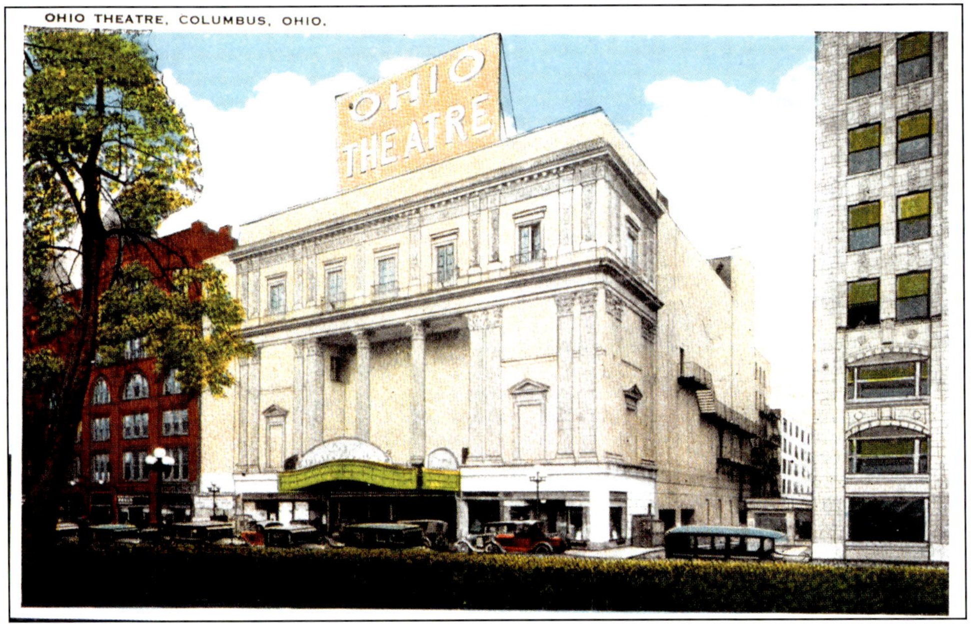

Ohio Theatre, Columbus, Ohio. Circa 1920s, $3-4.

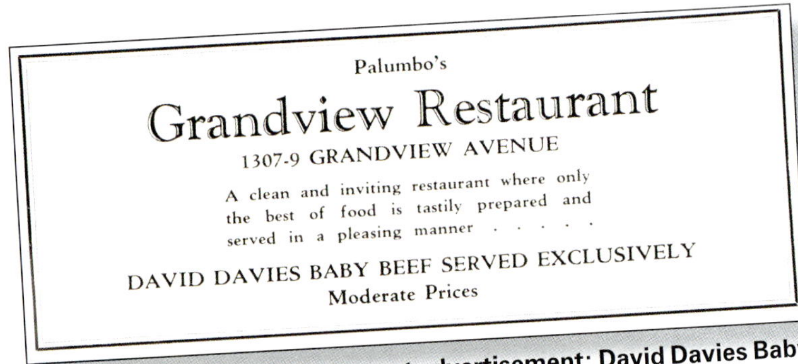

Palumbo's Grandview Restaurant advertisement: David Davies Baby Beef served exclusively. Published 1935, $2-3.

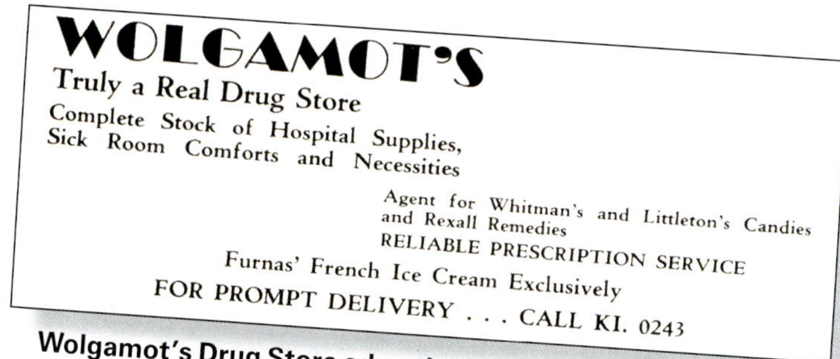

Wolgamot's Drug Store advertisement: Furnas' French Ice Cream exclusively. Published 1935, $2-3.

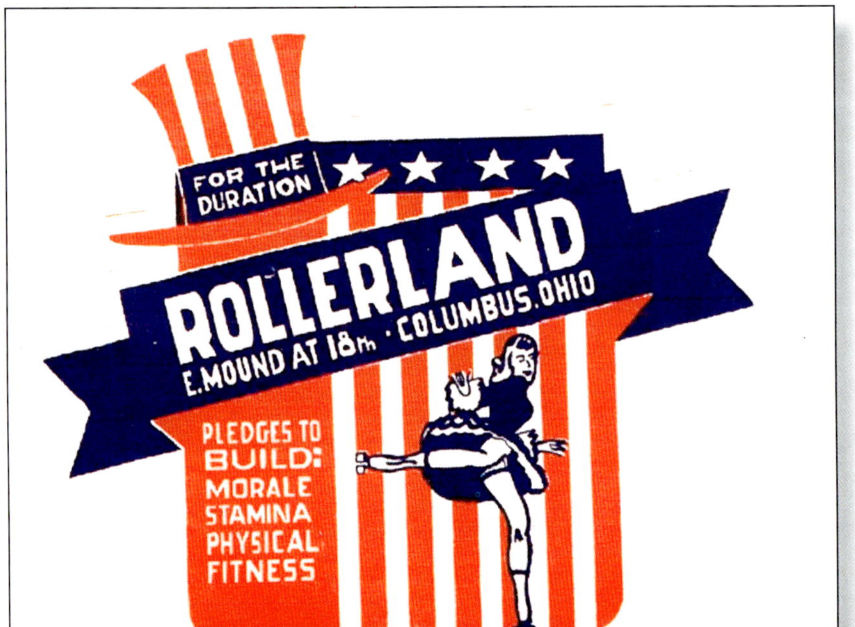

Rollerland Skating Rink label. Circa early 1940s, $5-7.

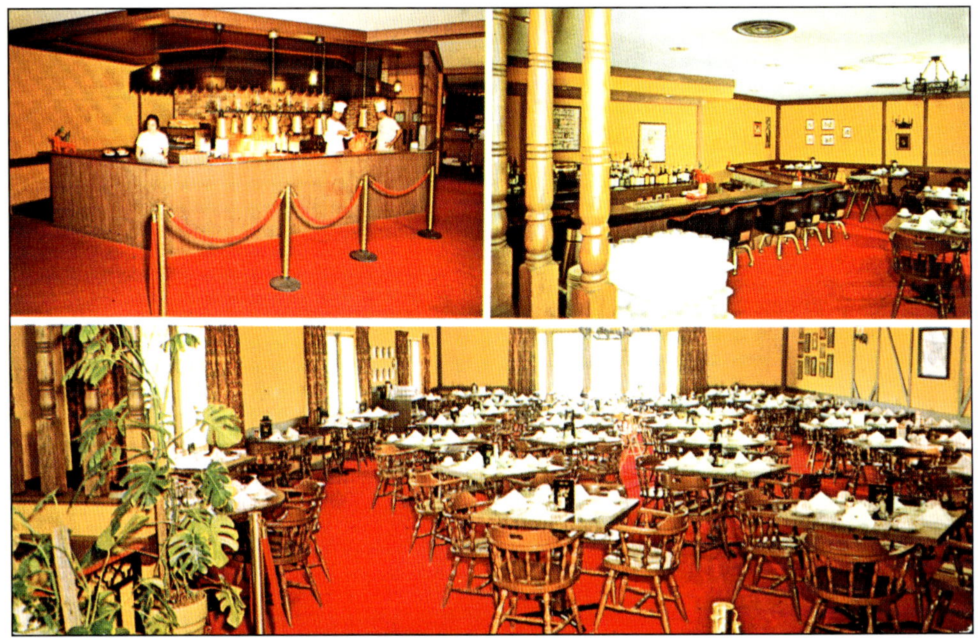

The Red Ox Steak House, 3330 East Broad Street. Circa 1950s, $3-4.

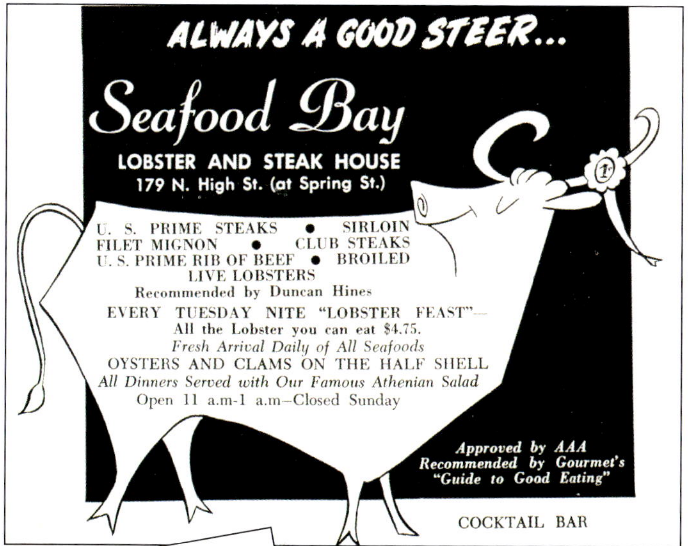

Seafood Bay advertisement: "All the lobster you can eat $4.75." Published 1954, $2-3.

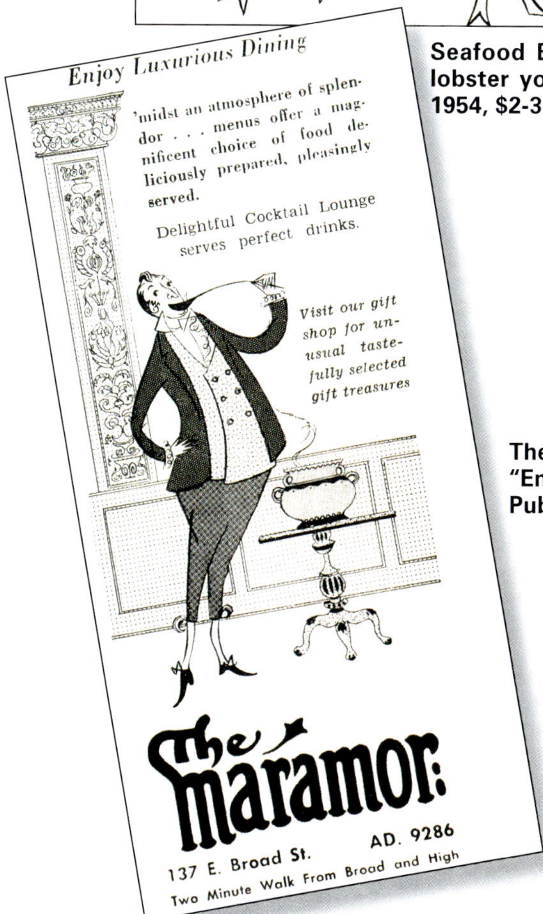

The Maramor advertisement: "Enjoy luxurious dining." Published 1954, $2-3.

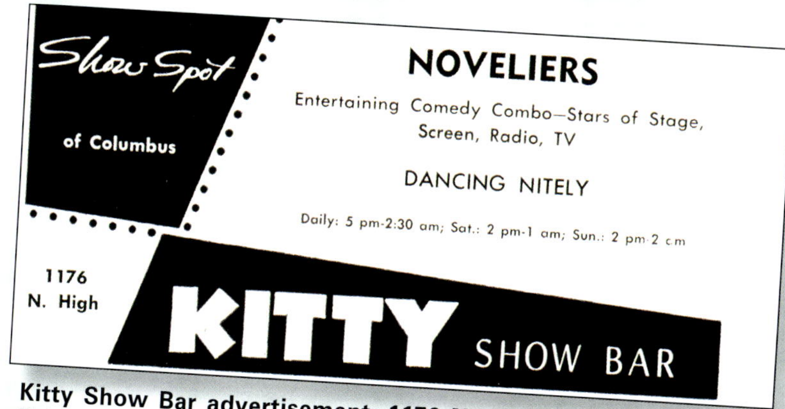

Kitty Show Bar advertisement, 1176 North High Street. Published 1954, $2-3.

Latin Lounge advertisement. "Columbus' Smartest Theatre-Cocktail Lounge." Published 1950s, $2-3.

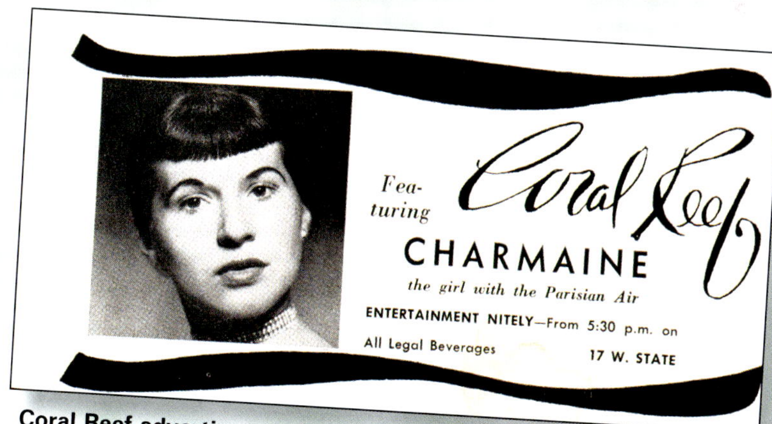

Coral Reef advertisement, featuring Charmaine: "The girl with the Parisian Air." Published 1950s, $2-3.

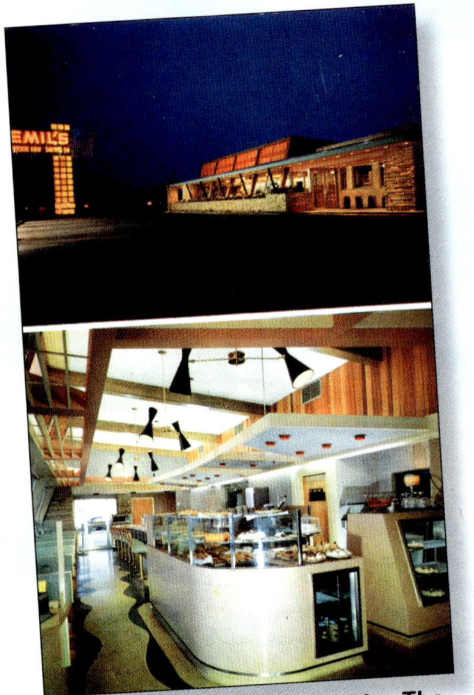

Emil's Steer Inn. Circa 1950s. The back reads: *"Nationally known Drive In, sandwich shop and restaurant. The nation's newest and most ultra-modern eating place. Dedicated to the serving of delicious food, fine pastries and rich French ice cream."*

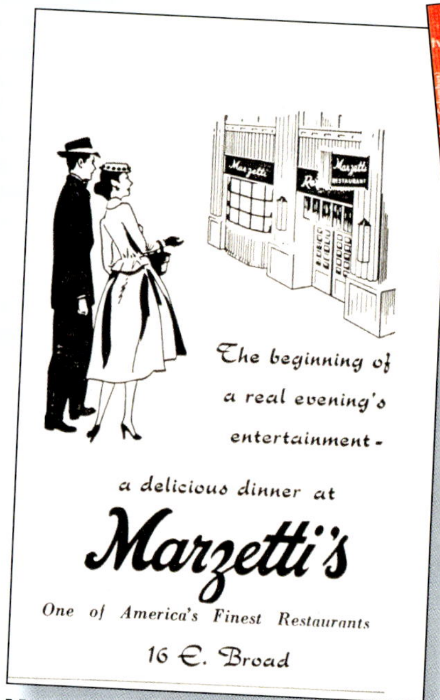

Marzetti's advertisement: "One of America's finest restaurants." Circa 1950s, $2-3.

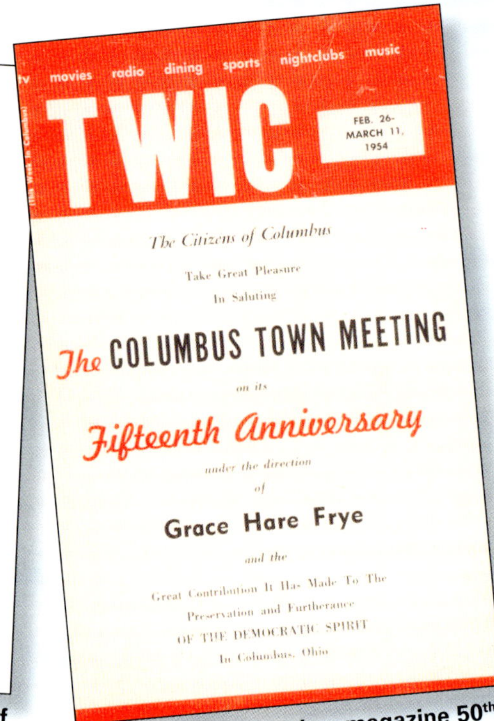

This Week In Columbus magazine 50th anniversary of The Columbus Town Meeting. Feb.-March 1954 issue. $6-7.

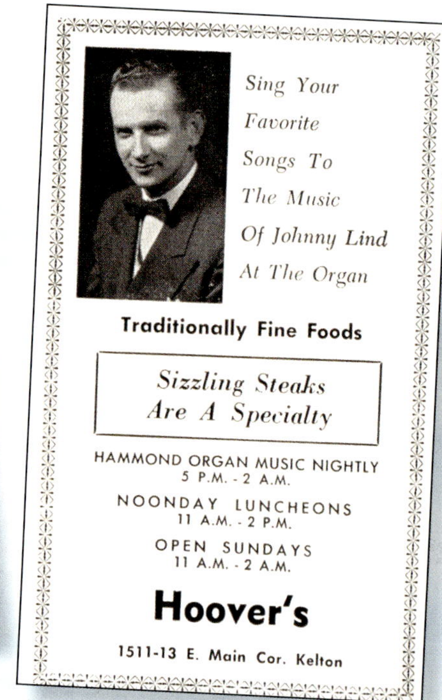

Hoover's advertisement featuring Johnny Lind at the organ. Published 1954, $2-3.

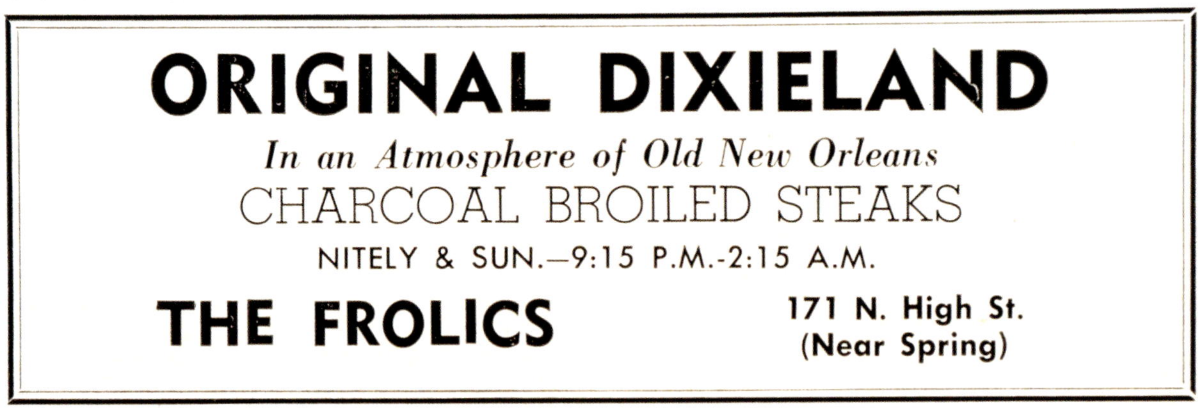

The Frolics advertisement: "In an atmosphere of Old New Orleans." Circa 1950s, $2-3.

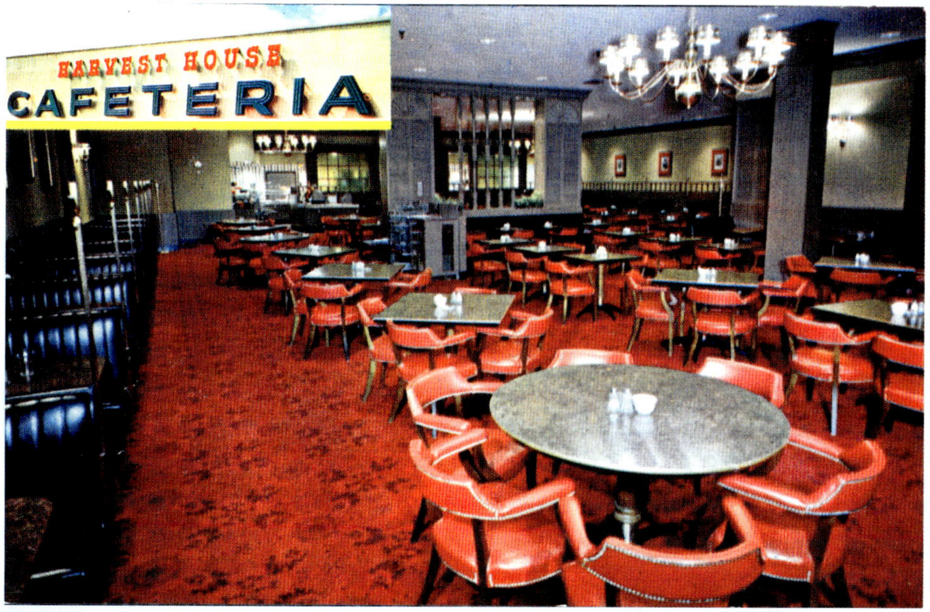

Harvest House Cafeteria, Westland Shopping Center. Circa 1960s, $4-5.

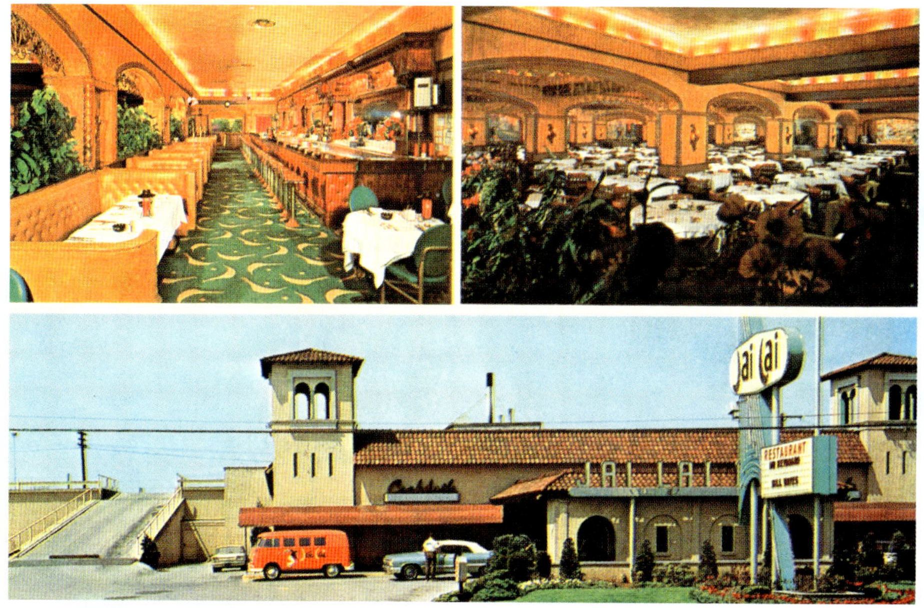

The Jai Lai restaurant. Circa 1960s, $4-5. The back reads: *"...the metropolitan restaurant of the Midwest, with a seating capacity of 500 and featuring a 60 foot hand-carved oak bar."*

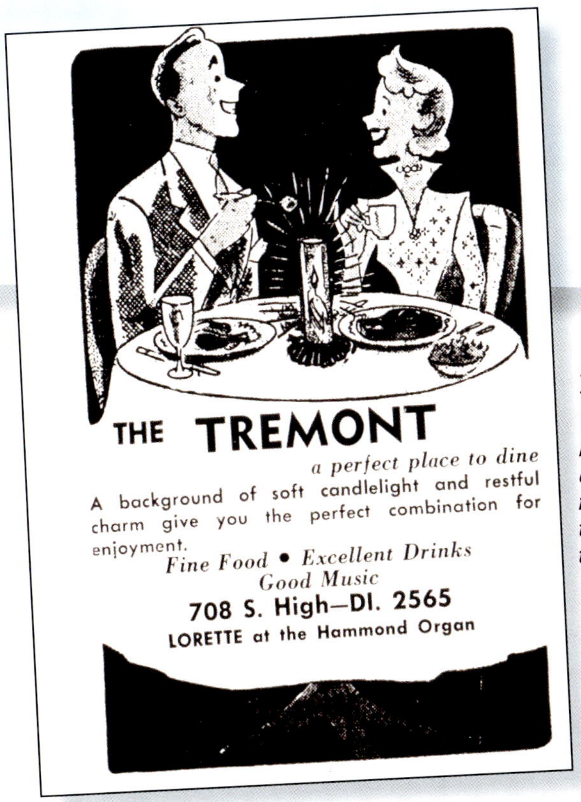

Advertisement for the Tremont. Published 1954, $2-3. *"A background of soft candlelight and restful charm give you the perfect combination for enjoyment."*

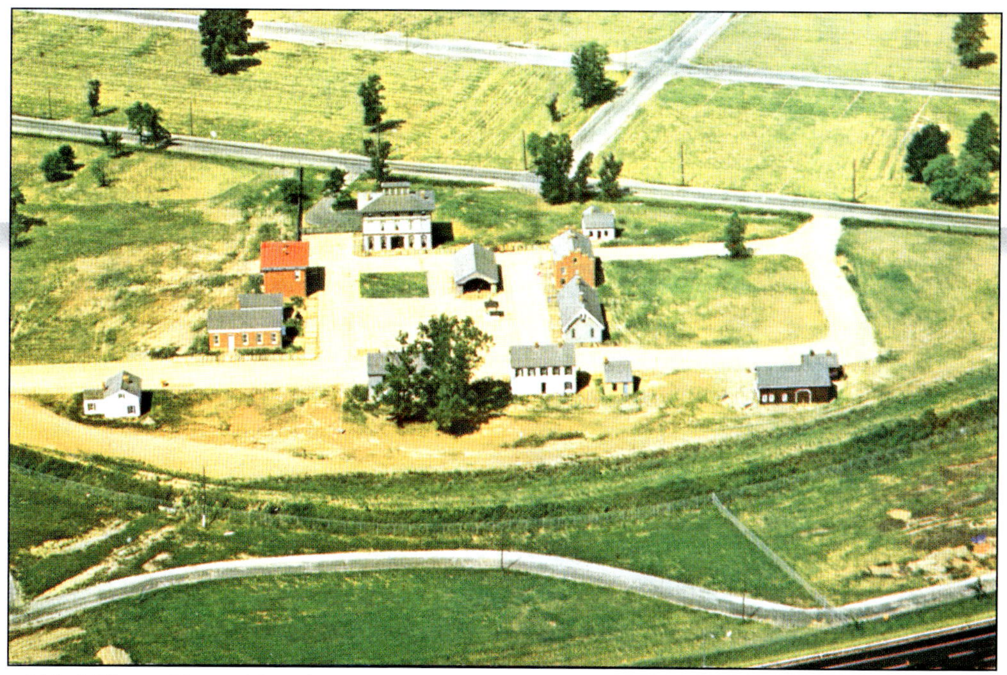

Ohio Village. Circa 1960s, $3-4.

Chapter Twelve: Commerce and Government

Transportation, equipment, machinery, fabricated and primary metals, food, printing and publishing are among the principal industries, but education and government are Columbus' most important functions.
— *Mobile Travel Guide, 1995*

One day in 1926 the big news in Columbus was the unveiling of plans for the new city hall.

A front-page story in the *Columbus Sunday Dispatch* put it this way:

> *"Mayor Thomas is presenting to the voters of Columbus an opportunity of civic advancement which will bring unmeasured beauty and pride to the city at almost unbelievable cost."*

The Dispatch added further:

> *"The civic center idea, born in the minds of those Columbus citizens of vision has a chance for life. The mayor calls upon the voters of Columbus to give it a chance of life. Former Mayor George Karb has taken upon his shoulders the task of doing the heavy work of presenting the city hall bond issue before the citizenry in its proper light. Their aim is a Greater Columbus."*

Greater Columbus was heralded elsewhere as well.

A 1920s travel folder featuring scenes of a bustling Columbus could have hardly been more ecstatic:

> *"Columbus is a community of thrifty, home-owning and home-living citizens, who love their city and love their state; where children are happy; where human relations are closely knit; where business is honorable; and where toil is respected."*

The lofty praise was concluded with the firm assertion that the capital city of Columbus "rises high in the scale of industry and commerce, with superior establishments, widely diversified in character."

Notably first on the list was the state capitol building itself. Standing in the heart of the city its Doric style was called "severe but dignified" by one traveling writer in the 1940s. In *The American Guide* travel book of the same decade, Henry Alsberg suggested that the use of convict and private labor in its construction went well, resulting in a "massive simplicity adorned by fine colonnades."

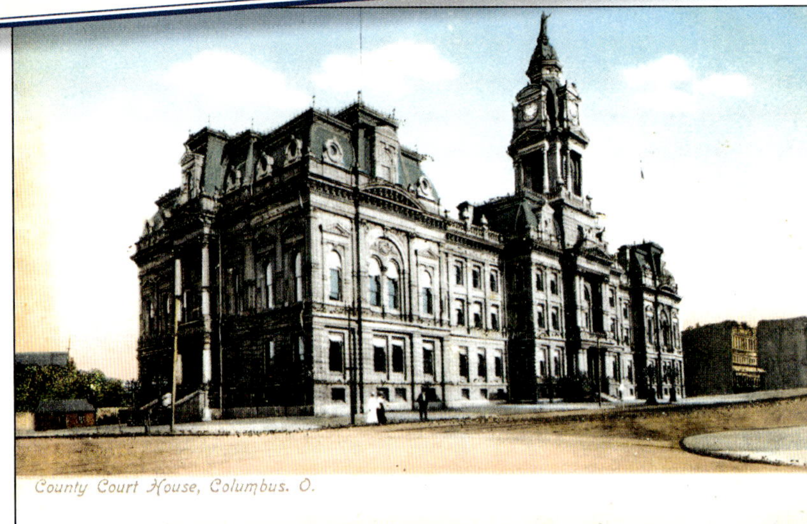

County Court House, Columbus. Circa early 1900s, $3-4.

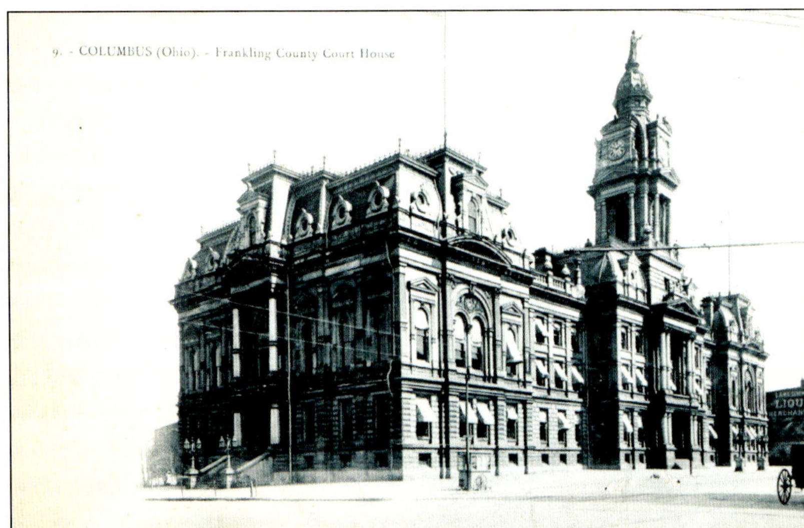

Franklin County Courthouse. Circa early 1900s, $3-4.

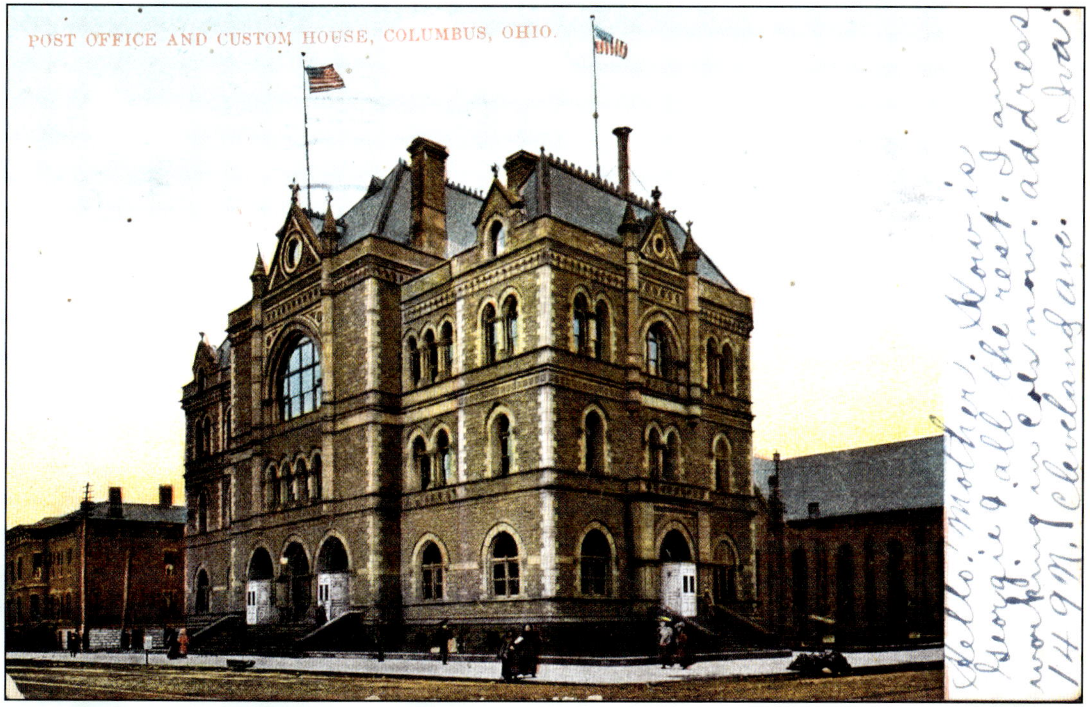

Post Office and custom house, Columbus. Postmarked 1906, $3-5. Hand-written message on front side reads: *"I am working in Columbus now."*

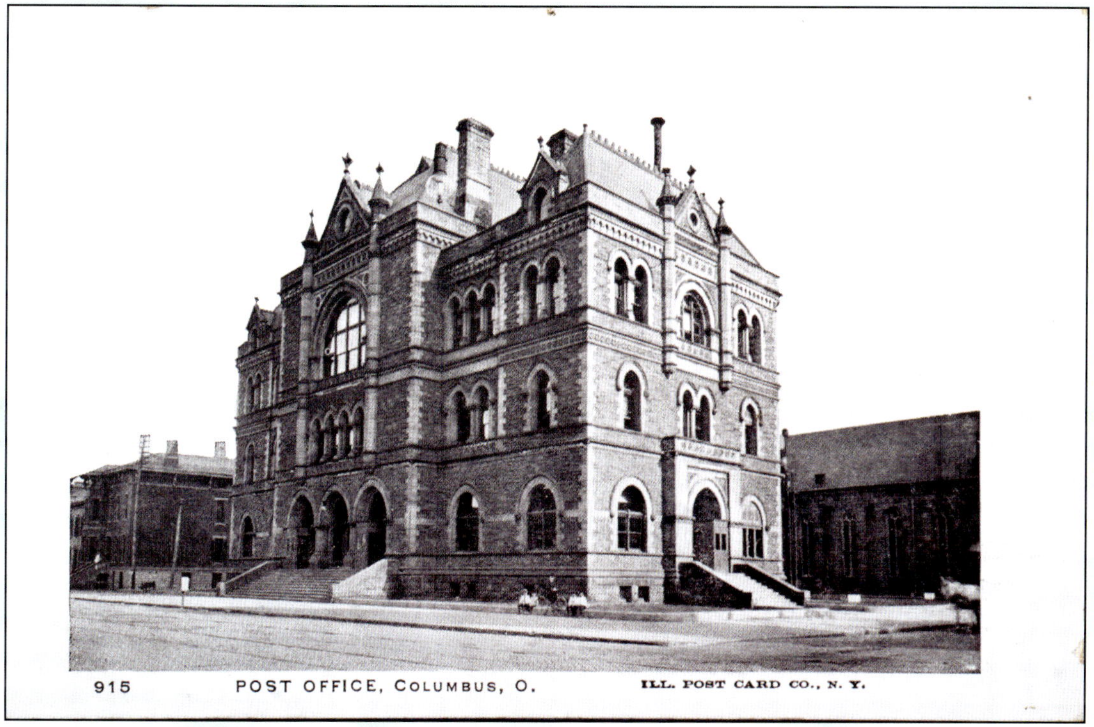

Post Office, Columbus. Circa early 1900s, $3-4.

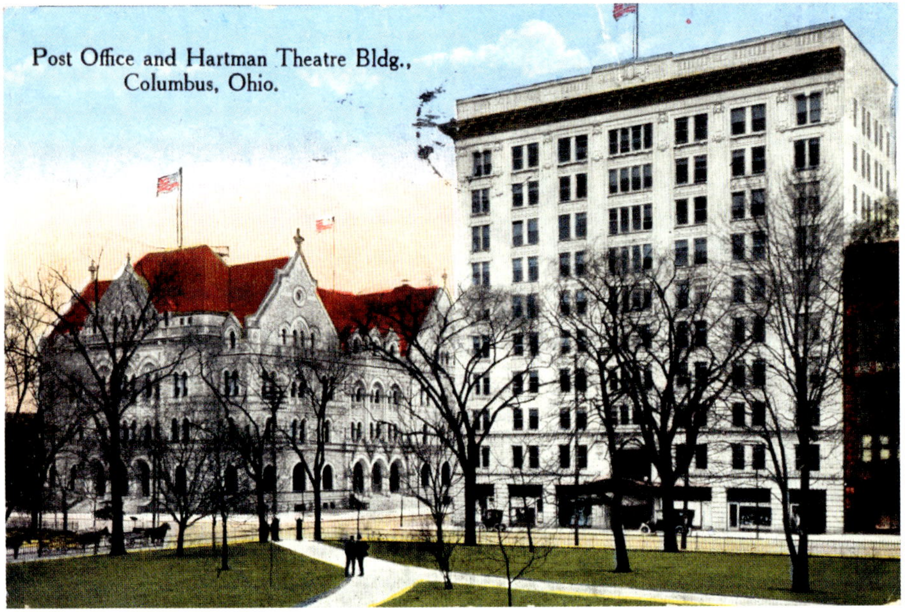

Post Office and Hartman Building. Postmarked 1916, $3-4.

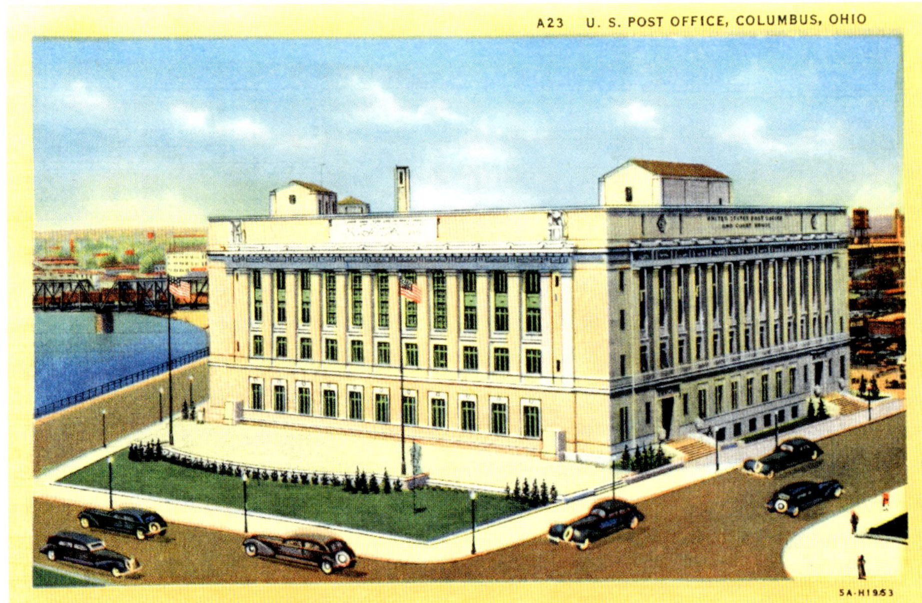

U.S. Post Office, Columbus. Circa 1930s, $2-3.

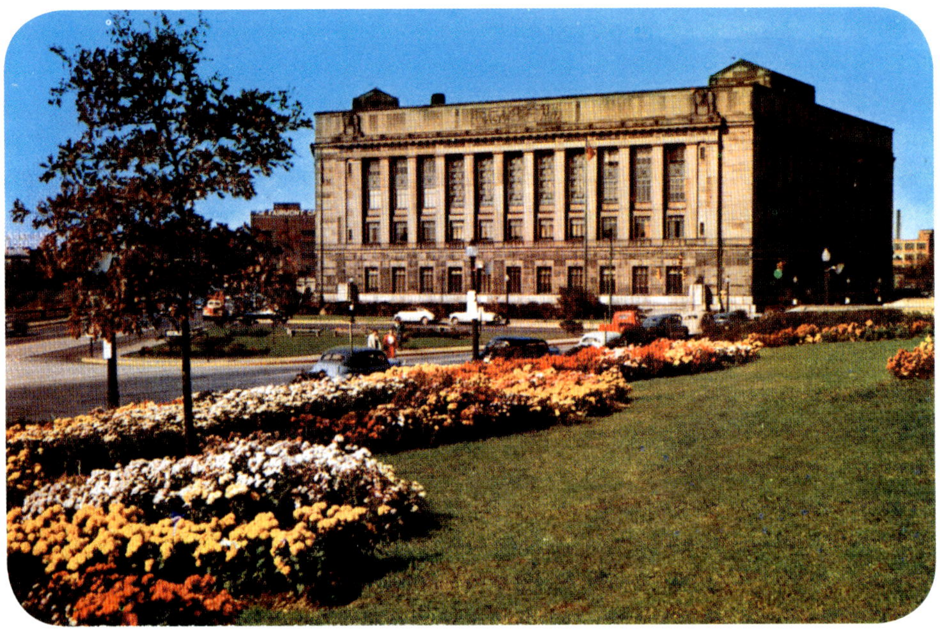

Federal Post Office. Circa 1960s, $2-3. The back reads: *"Center of postal activity in Columbus, Ohio is the Main Federal Post Office. This structure also houses many government offices."*

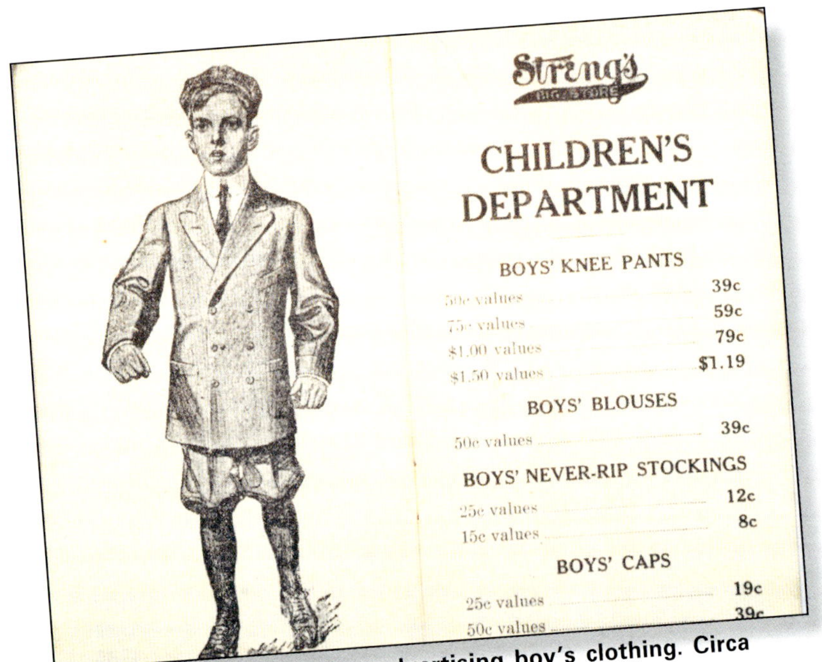

Strong's BIG STORE

CHILDREN'S DEPARTMENT

BOYS' KNEE PANTS

50c values 39c
75c values 59c
$1.00 values 79c
$1.50 values $1.19

BOYS' BLOUSES

50c values 39c

BOYS' NEVER-RIP STOCKINGS

25c values 12c
15c values 8c

BOYS' CAPS

25c values 19c
50c values 39c

String's Big Store booklet advertising boy's clothing. Circa 1909, $5-6.

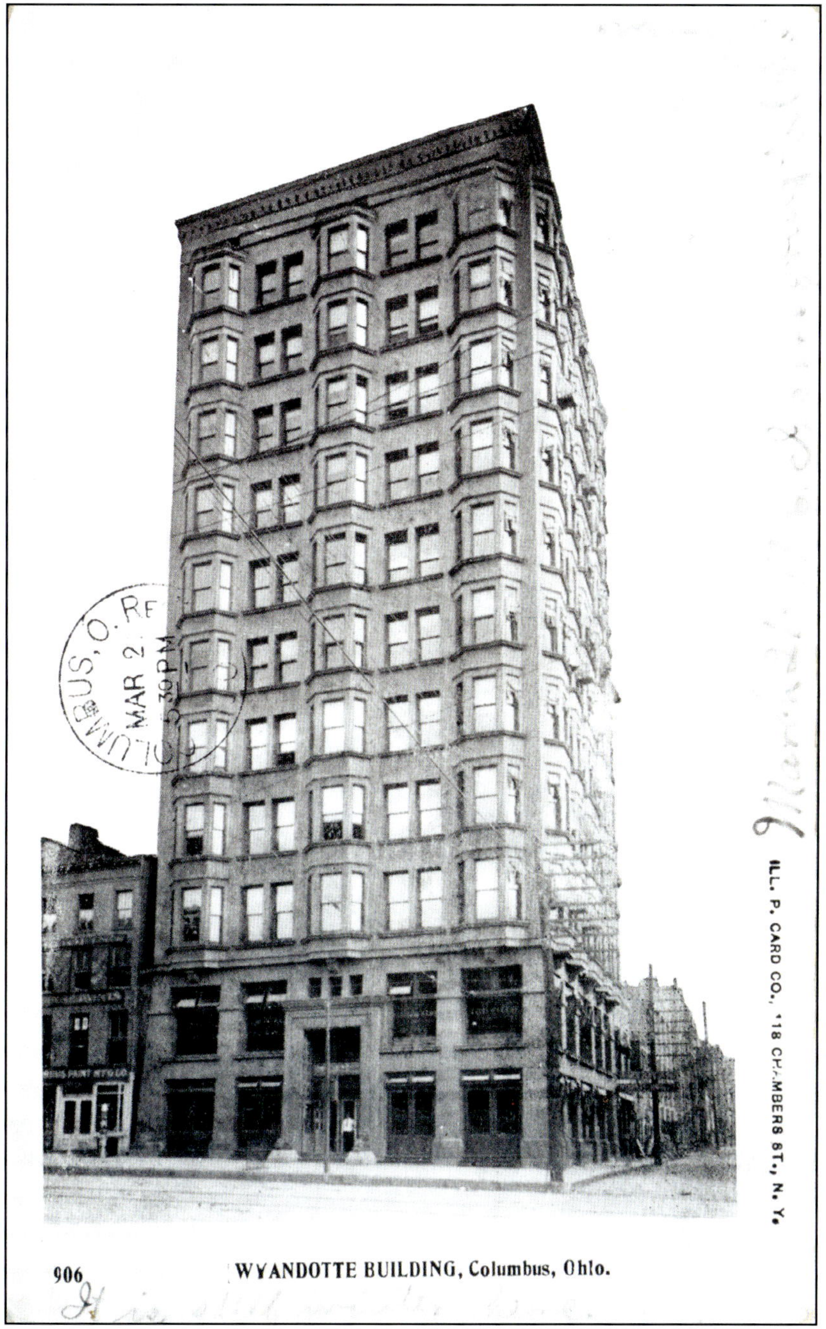

Wyandotte Building, Columbus. Postmarked 1906, $4-6.

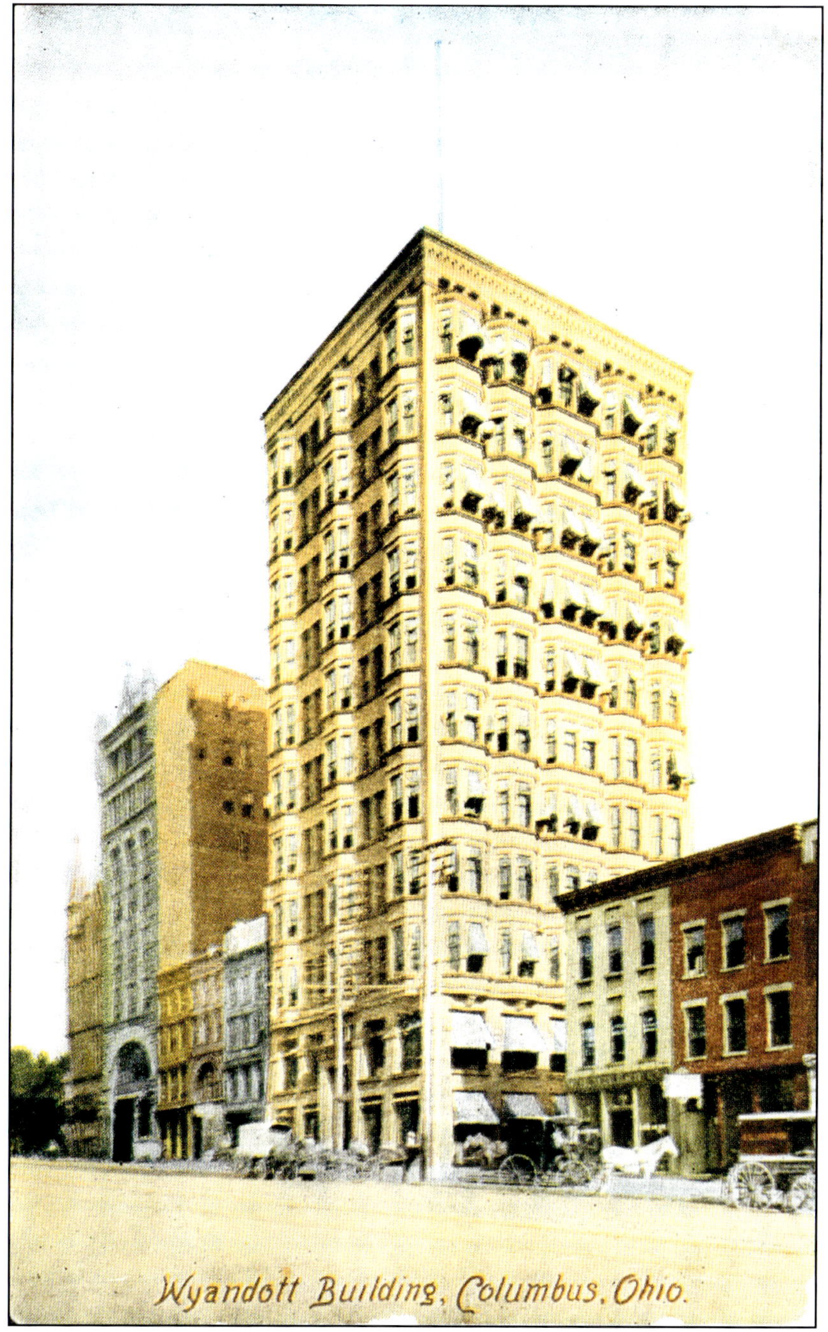

Wyandott(e) Building. Postmarked 1908, $4-5. Hand-written message on the back reads: *"I forgot to tell you I will get off the car on Walnut Street, so if you come to the car you want to wait at that corner."*

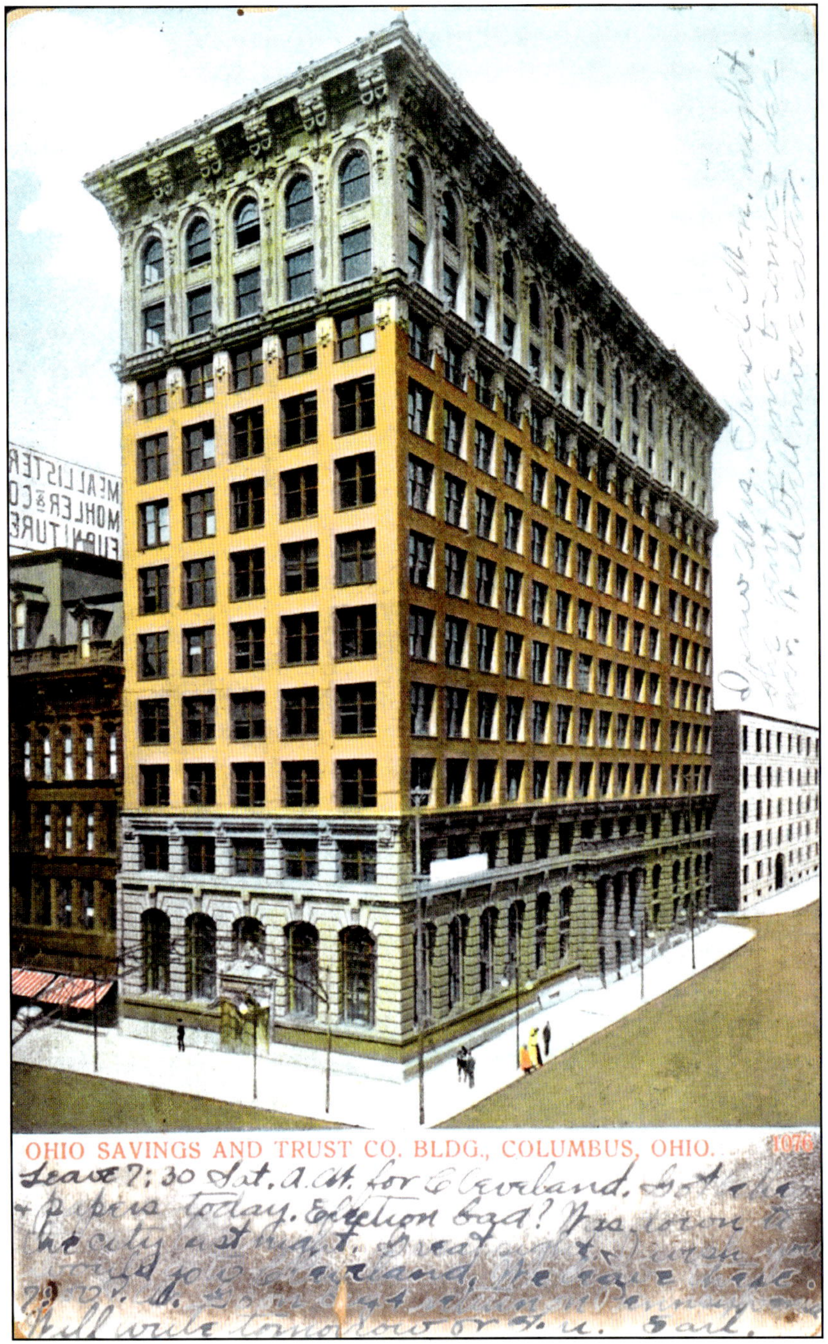

Ohio Savings and Trust Company building. Postmarked 1908, $4-5.

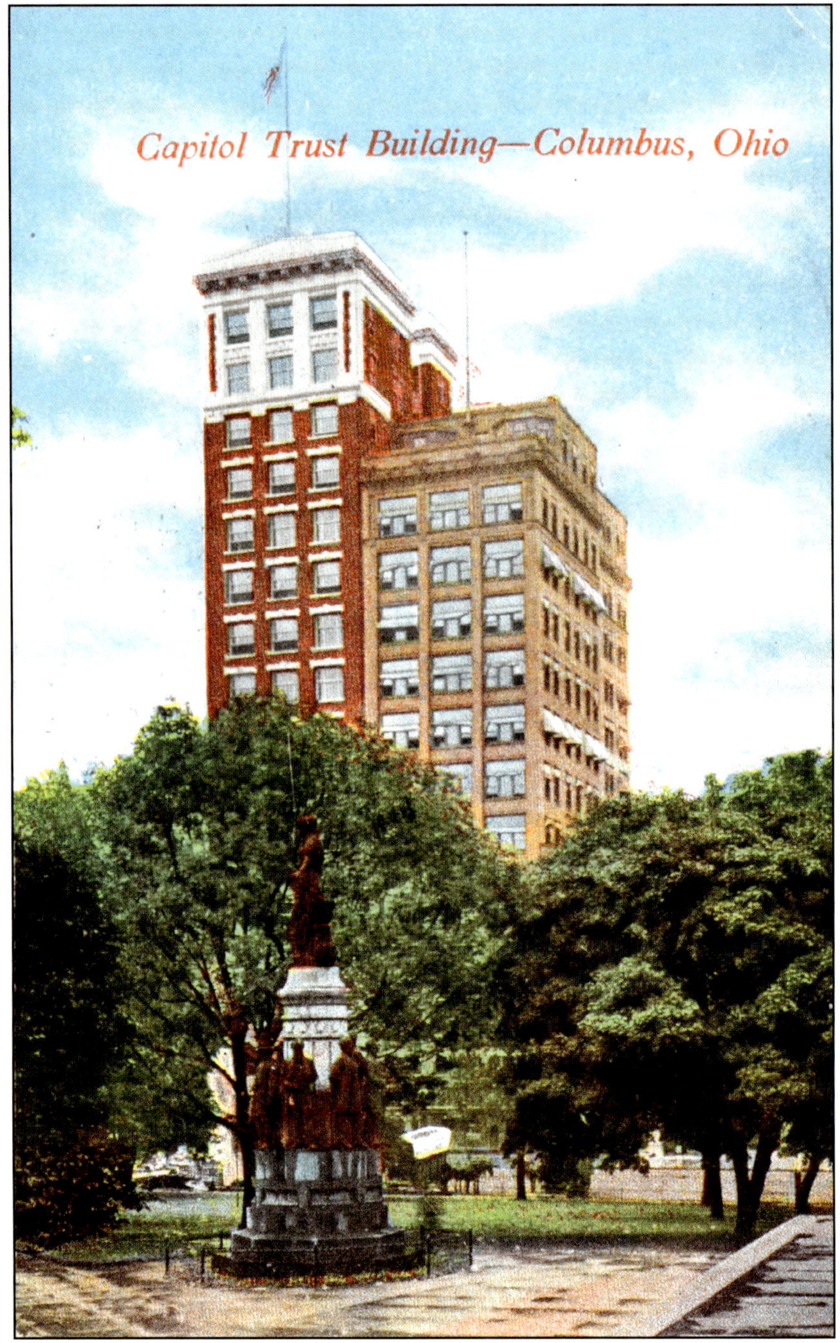

Capitol Trust building, Columbus. Postmarked 1908, $4-5.

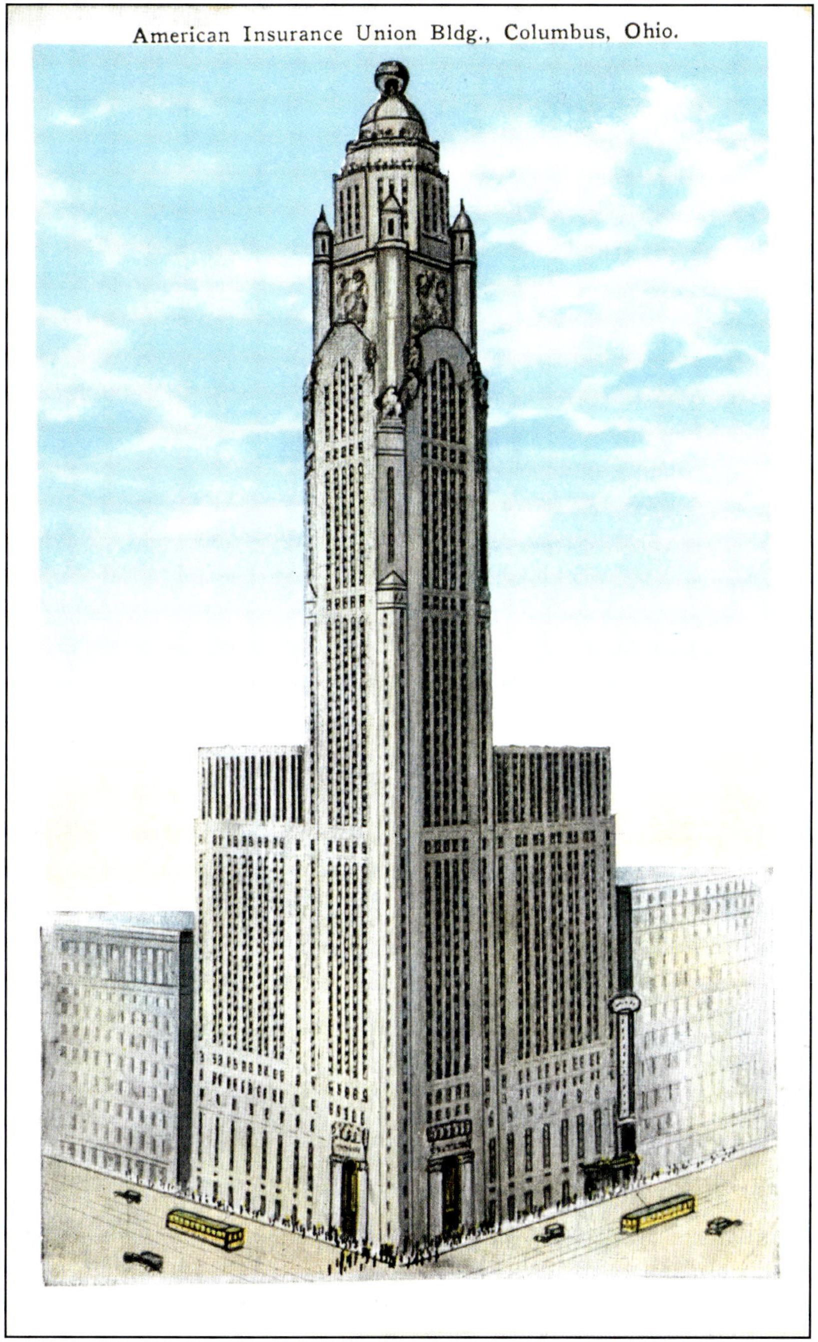

American Insurance Union building. Circa 1920s, $2-3.

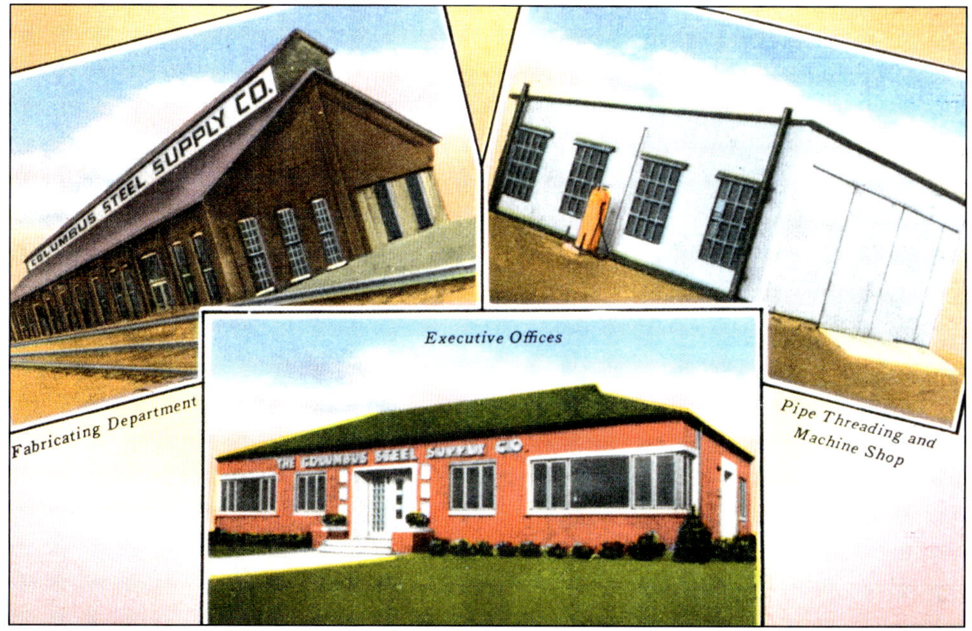

Columbus Steel Supply Company. Undated, $6-7. The back of the card reads: *"Out plant, offices and ware-housing facilities now cover approximately 15 acres of ground, making us the largest suppliers of new and used pipe, steel items, oil, gas, water well casing and tubing in the world."*

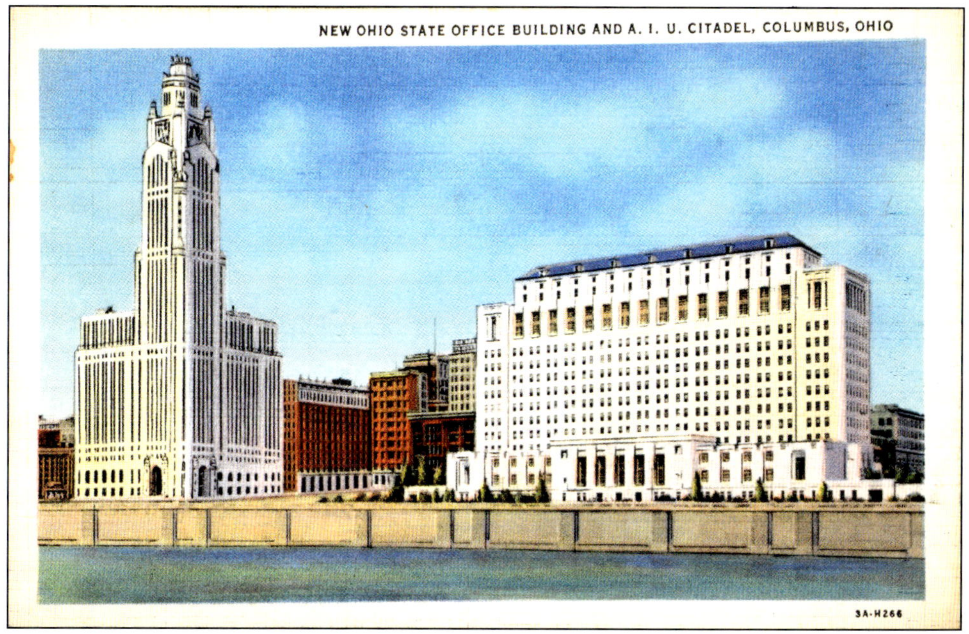

"New" Ohio State Office Building. Striking Art Deco structure was opened in 1933. Circa 1930s, $2-3.

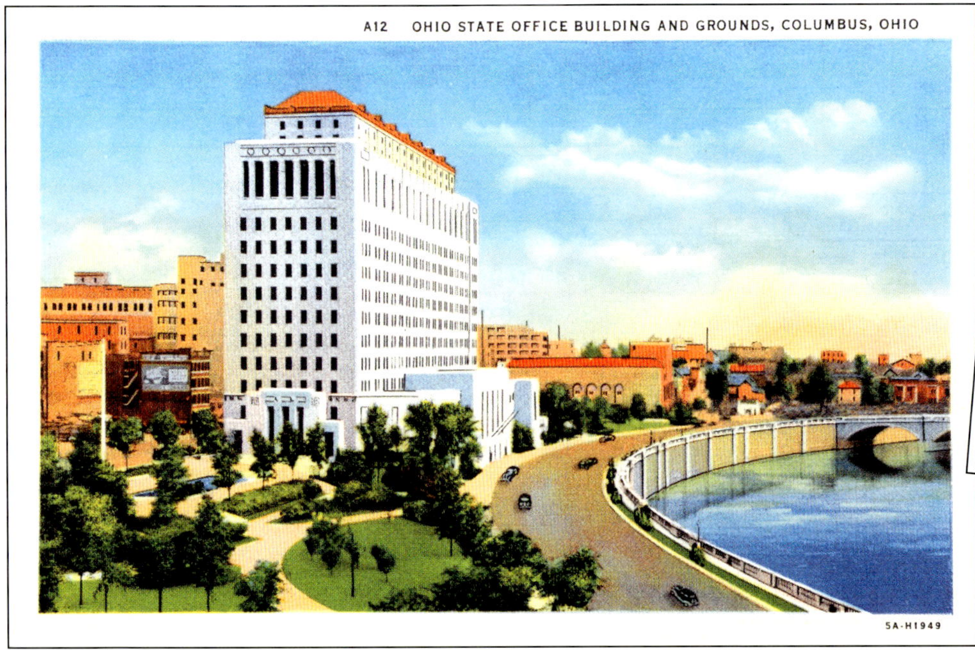

Ohio State Office Building. Circa 1930s, $2-3. The back reads: *"Seventeen different departments of the State Government together with departments of the State Library are located in this building."*

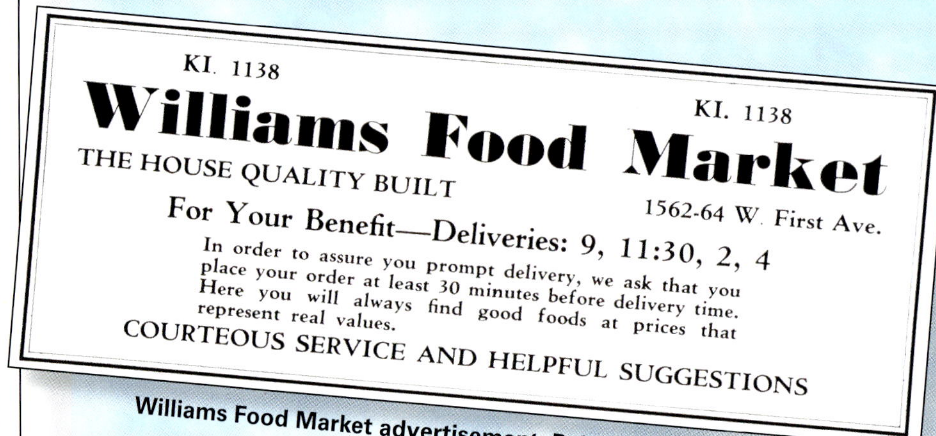

Williams Food Market advertisement. Published 1935, $2-3.

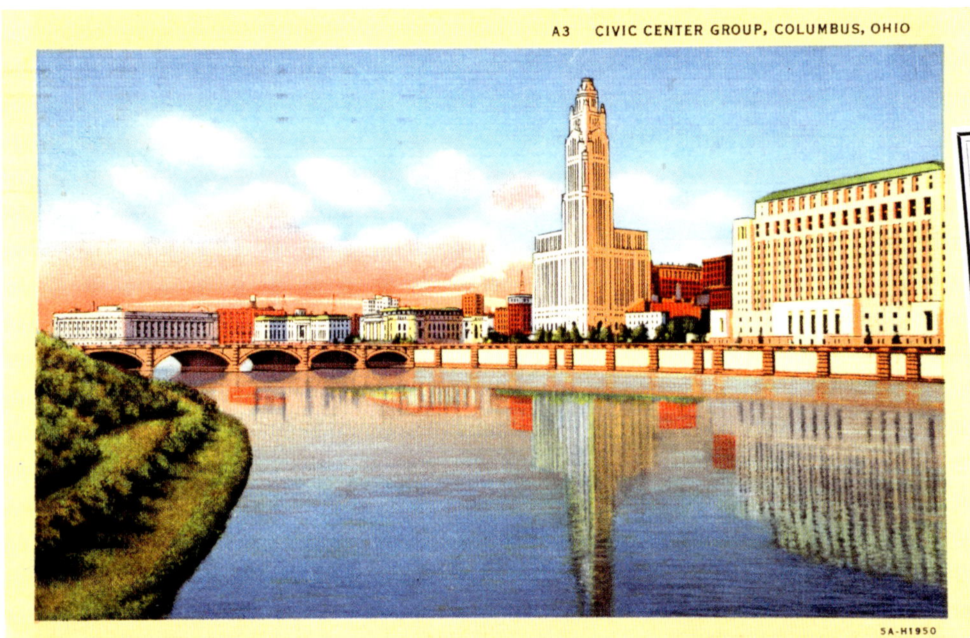

Civic Center Group, Columbus. Circa 1930s, $2-3.

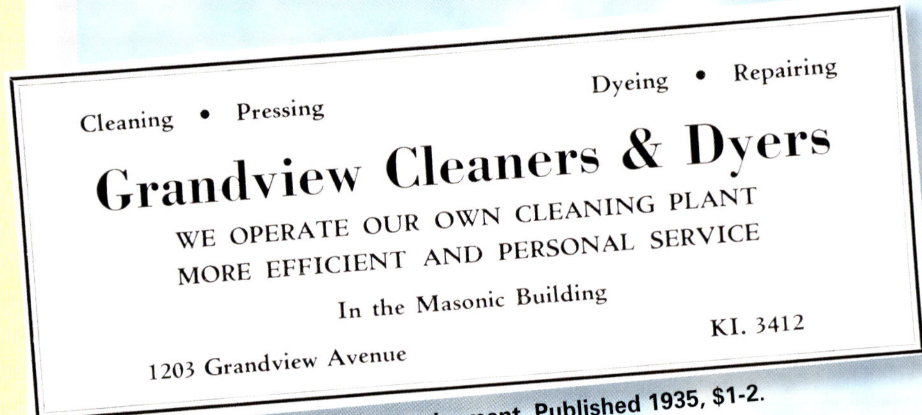

Grandview Cleaners advertisement. Published 1935, $1-2.

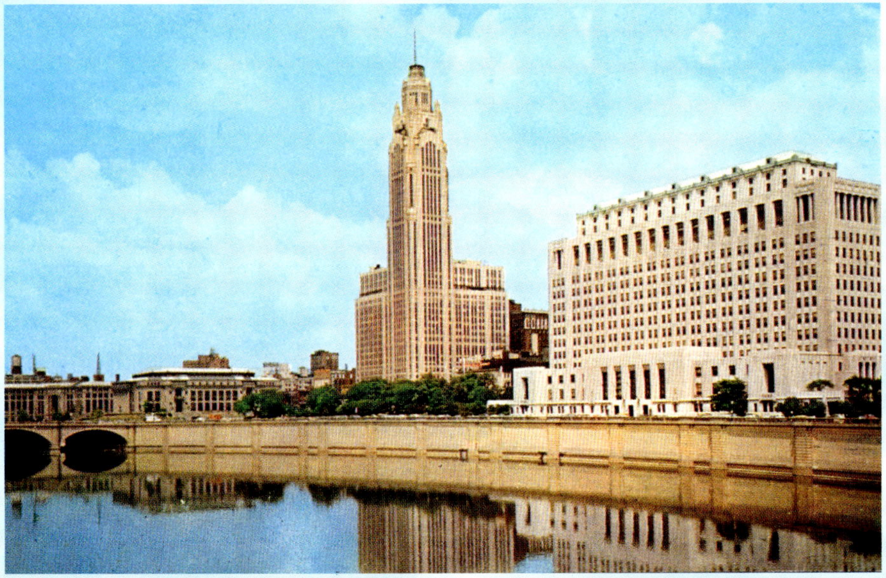

Civic Center Group. Undated, $2-3.

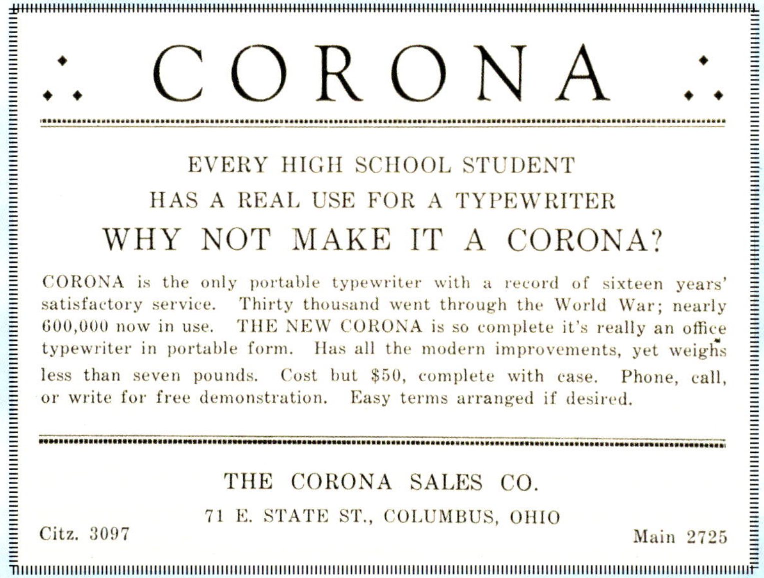

Corona Sales Company advertisement, 71 East State Street, Columbus. Published 1924, $2-3.

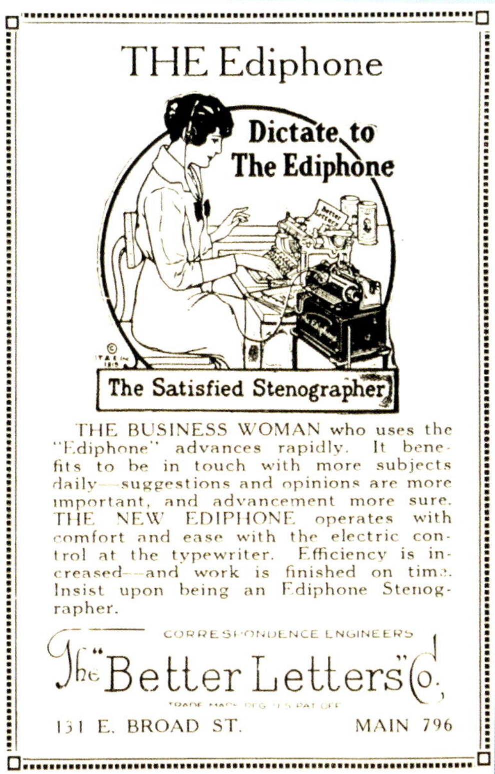

Better Letters Company advertisement, 131 East Broad Street. Published 1924, $2-3.

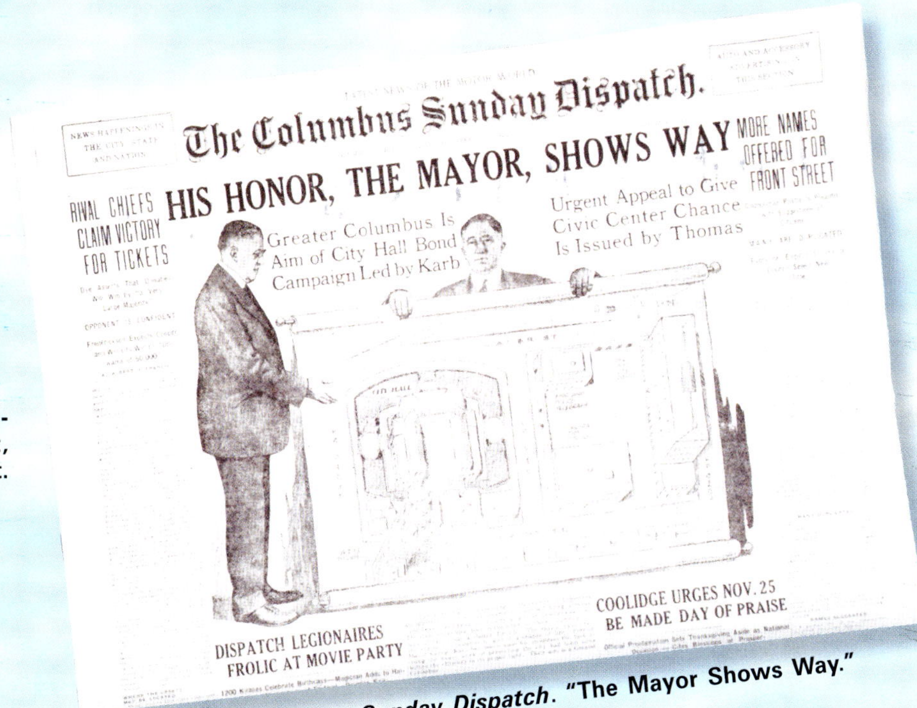

The Columbus Sunday Dispatch.

HIS HONOR, THE MAYOR, SHOWS WAY

RIVAL CHIEFS CLAIM VICTORY FOR TICKETS

Greater Columbus Is Aim of City Hall Bond Campaign Led by Karb

Urgent Appeal to Give Civic Center Chance Is Issued by Thomas

MORE NAMES OFFERED FOR FRONT STREET

DISPATCH LEGIONAIRES FROLIC AT MOVIE PARTY

COOLIDGE URGES NOV. 25 BE MADE DAY OF PRAISE

Columbus Sunday Dispatch. "The Mayor Shows Way." October 31, 1926, $35-45.

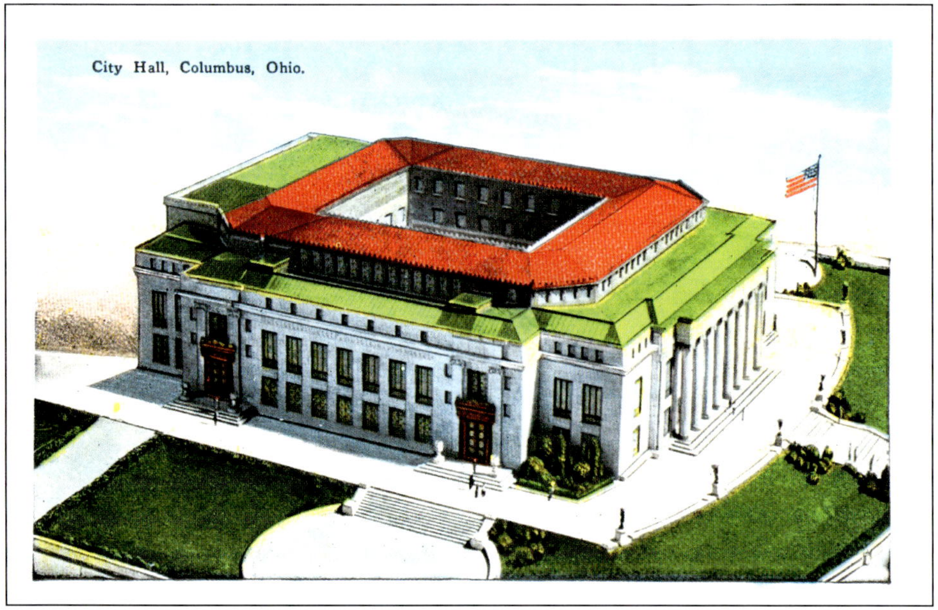

City Hall, Columbus. Circa 1920s, $4-5.

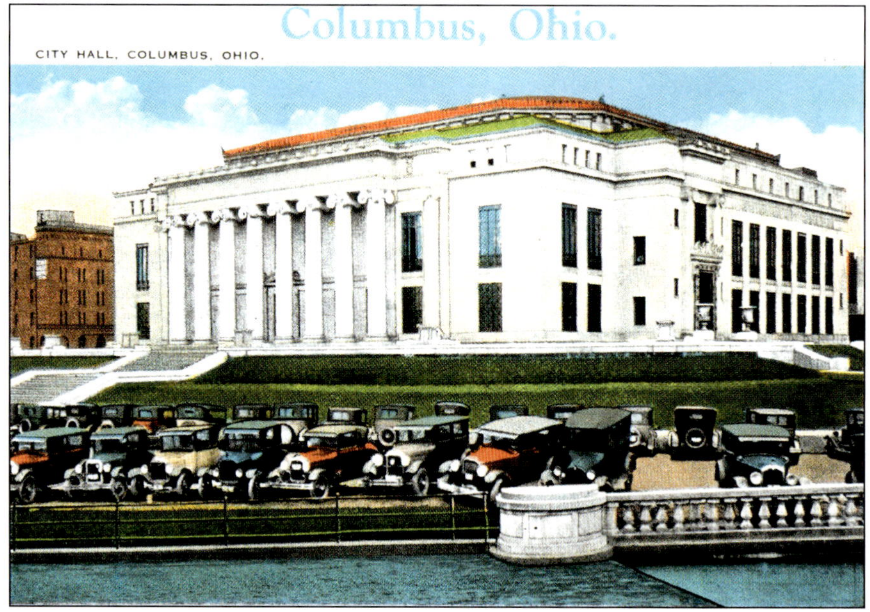

Full parking lot at City Hall. Circa 1920s, $5-6.

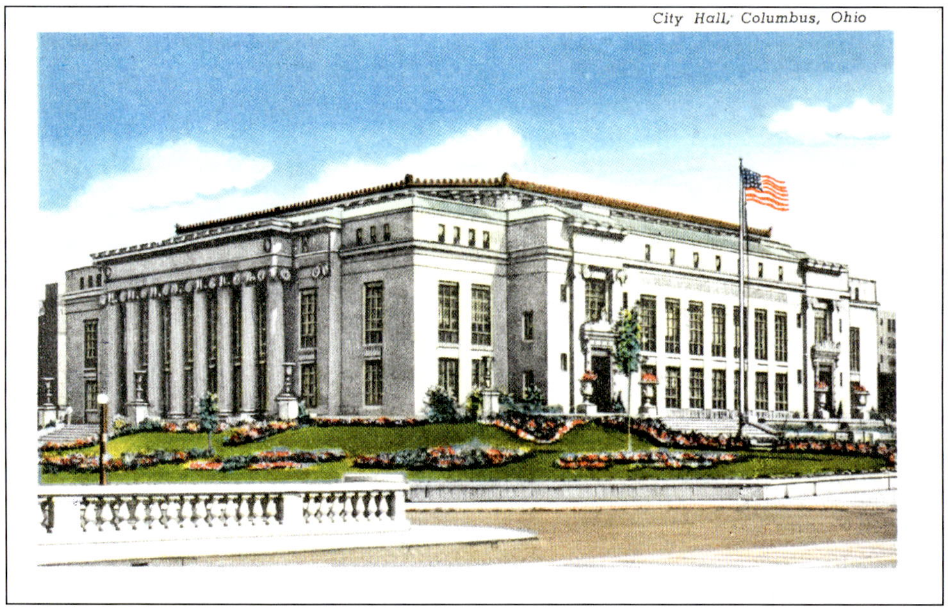

City Hall, Columbus, Ohio. Circa early 1950s, $3-4.

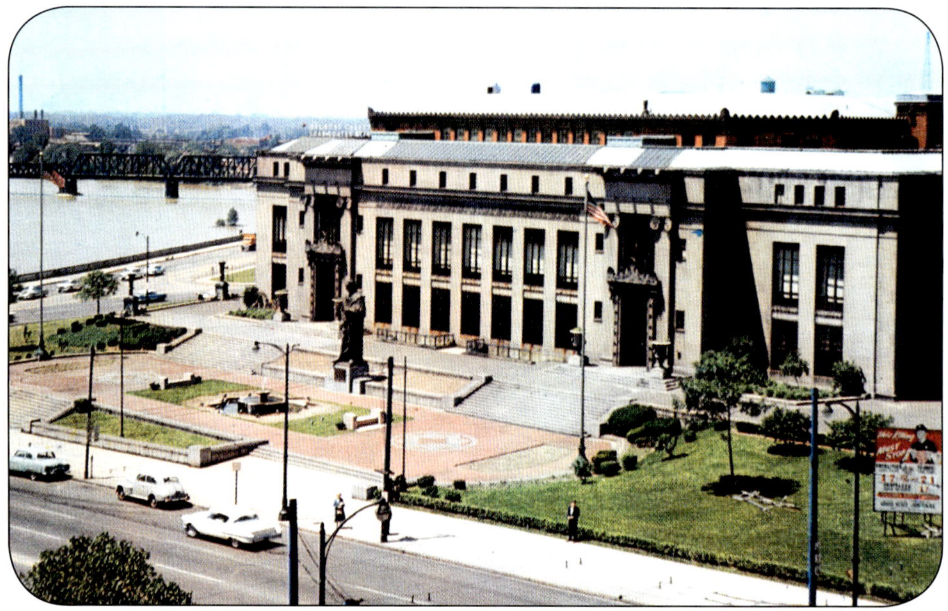

City Hall. Circa early 1960s, $3-4.

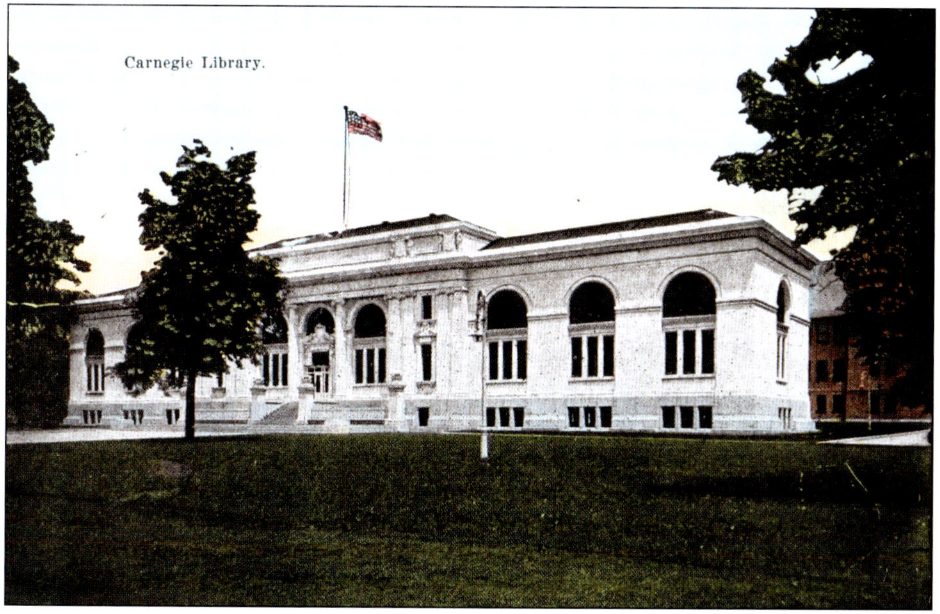

Carnegie Library. Circa 1920s, $2-3.

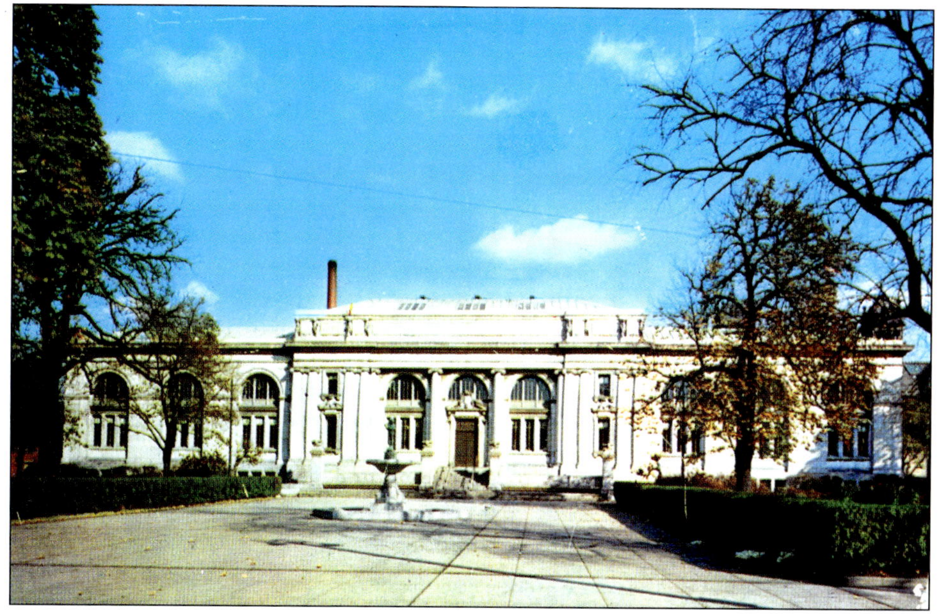

Columbus Public Library. Circa 1950s, $2-4. The back reads: *"..stands on the site of the residence of Rutherford B. Hayes, 19th U.S. President, which he occupied while serving as Governor of Ohio."*

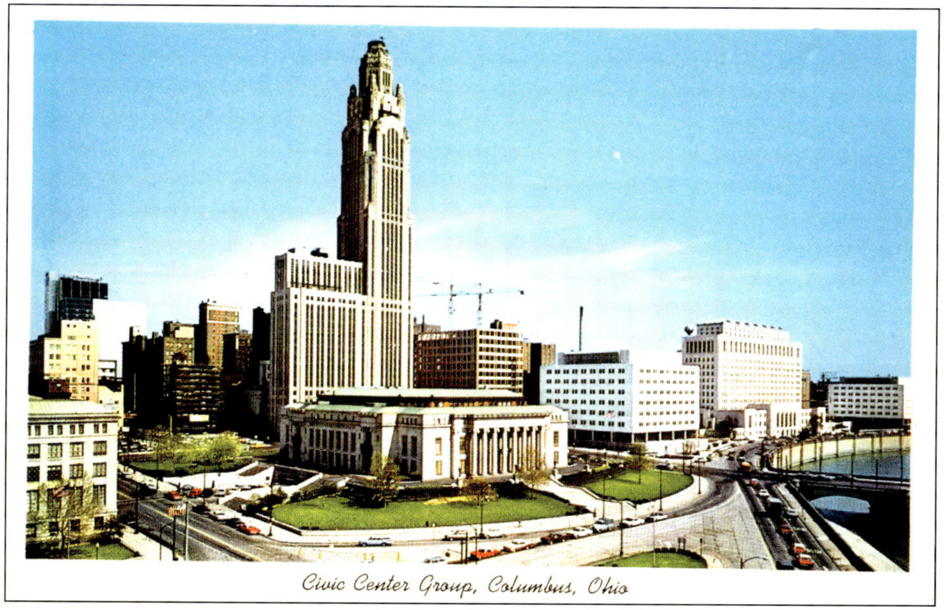

Civic Center Group. Circa 1960s, $3-4. The back reads: *"Showing City Prison left, City Hall with Leveque Lincoln Tower and new Huntington Bank Bldg. in background with State Highway, State Office and Bureau of Unemployment Buildings to extreme right."*

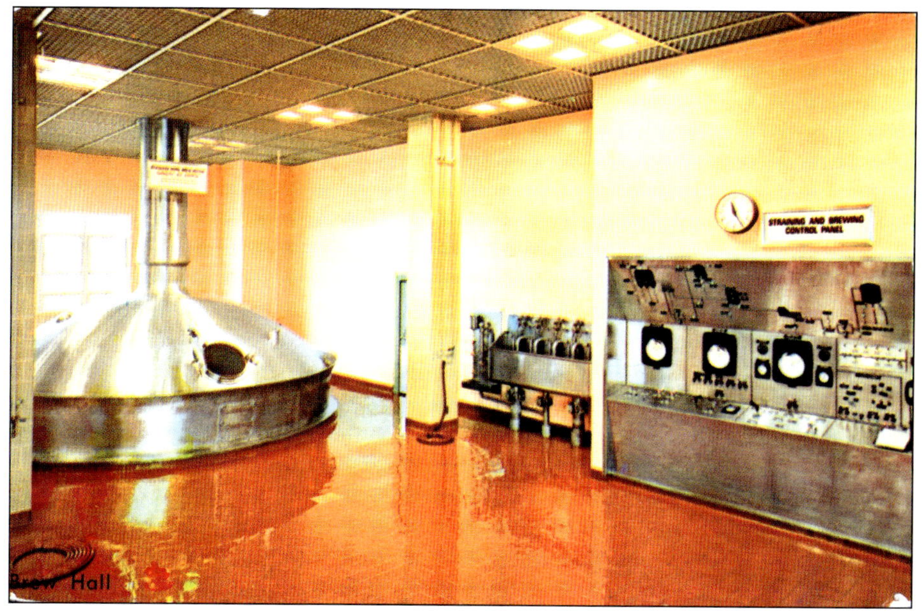

Anheuser-Busch. Circa 1969, $3-4. The back reads: *"Annual capacity 1,770,000 barrels. Brewery tours daily."*

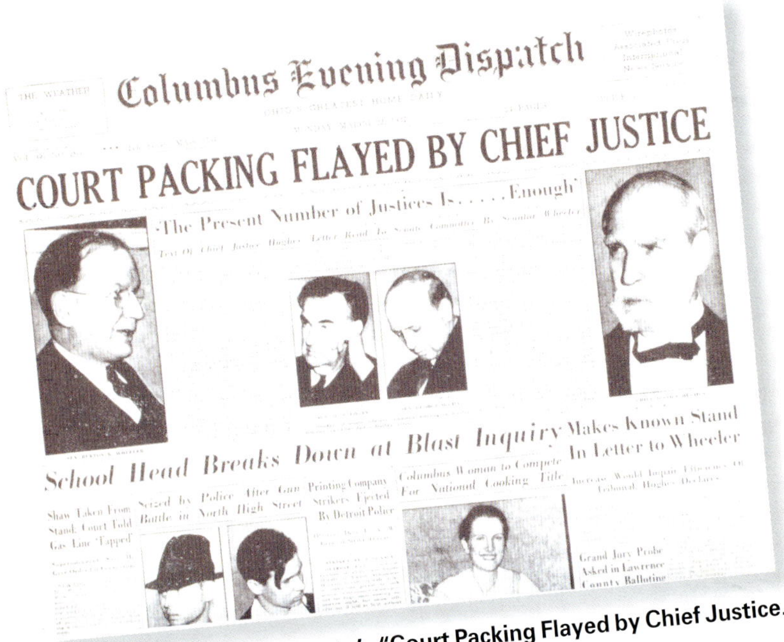
Columbus Evening Dispatch

COURT PACKING FLAYED BY CHIEF JUSTICE

"The Present Number of Justices Is . . . . . Enough"

School Head Breaks Down at Blast Inquiry

Makes Known Stand In Letter to Wheeler

Columbus Woman to Compete For National Cooking Title

Grand Jury Probe Asked in Lawrence County Balloting

Columbus Evening Dispatch. "Court Packing Flayed by Chief Justice." March 22, 1937 edition, $20-25.

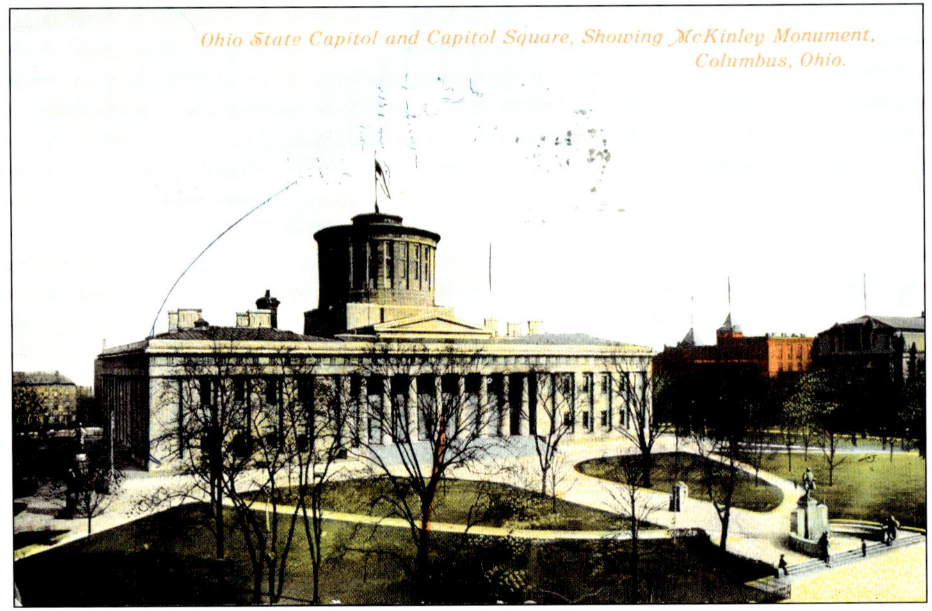

Capitol Square showing McKinley Monument. Postmarked 1910, $3-4.

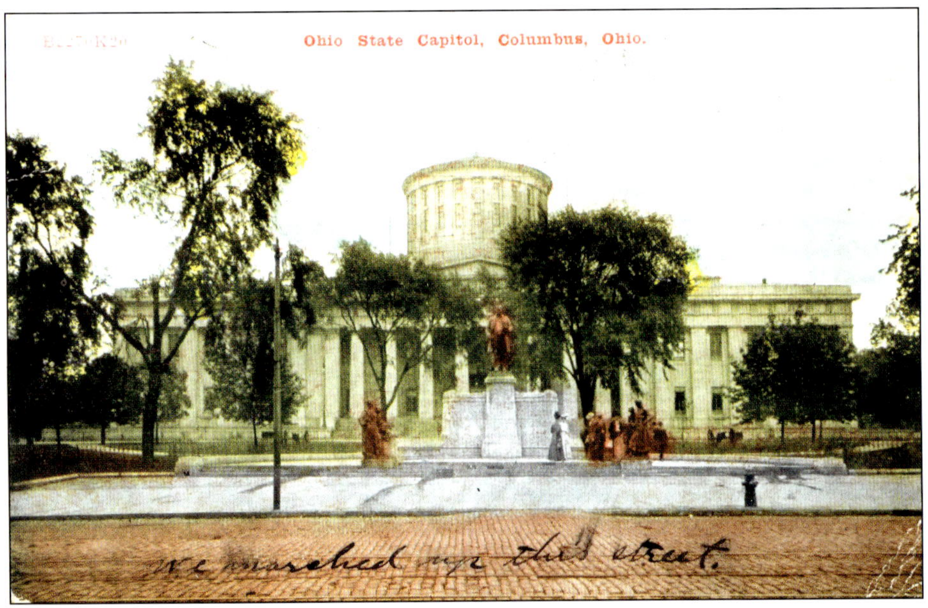

Ohio State Capitol. Postmarked 1912, $2-3.

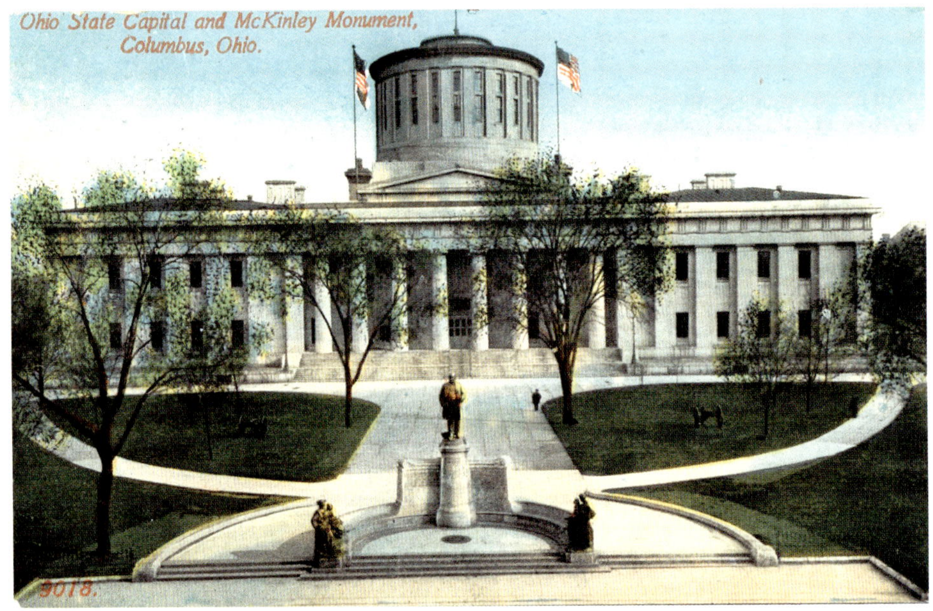

Ohio State Capitol. Postmarked 1914, $2-3.

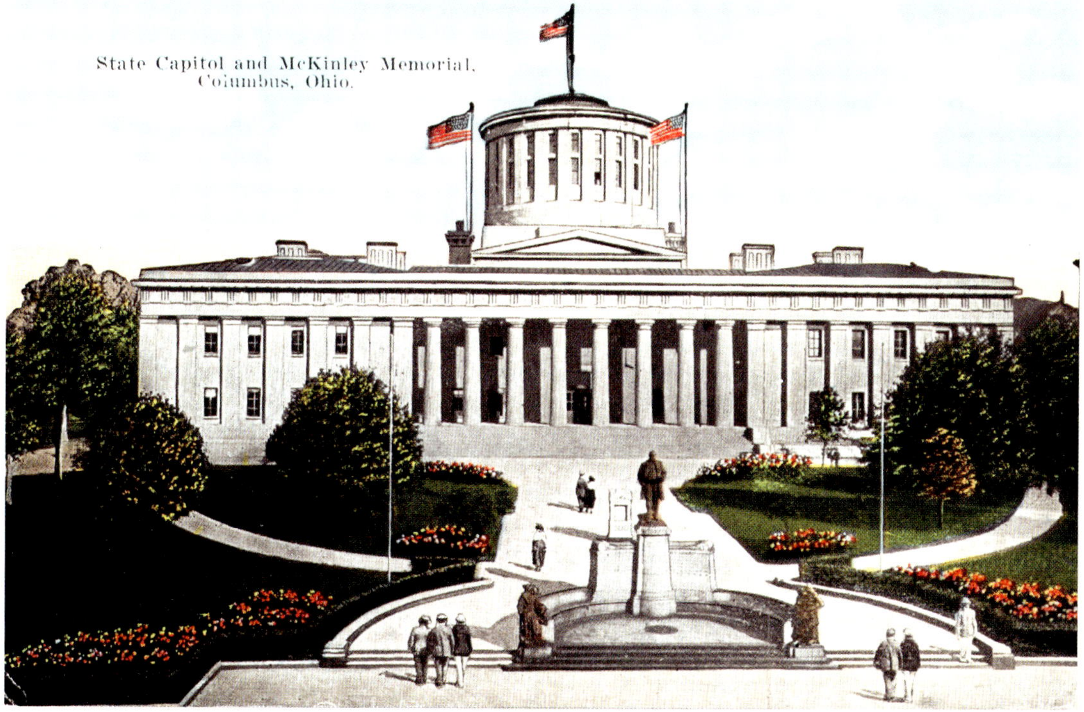

McKinley Memorial and State Capitol.
Circa 1900s, $2-4.

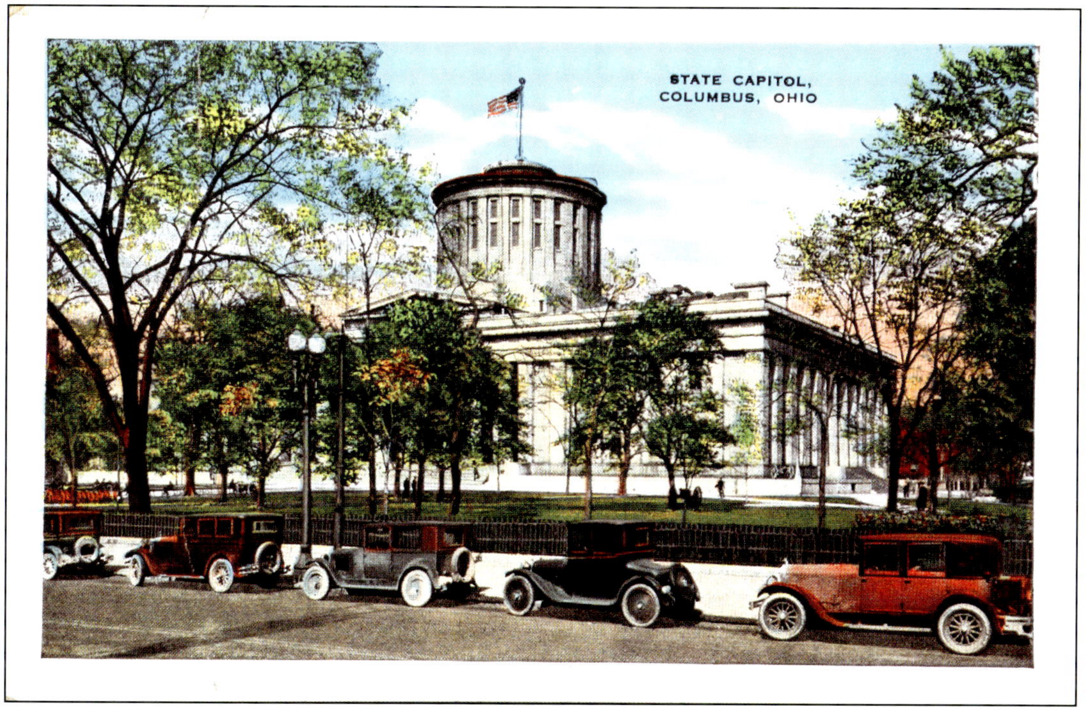

State Capitol parking.
Circa 1920s, $4-5.

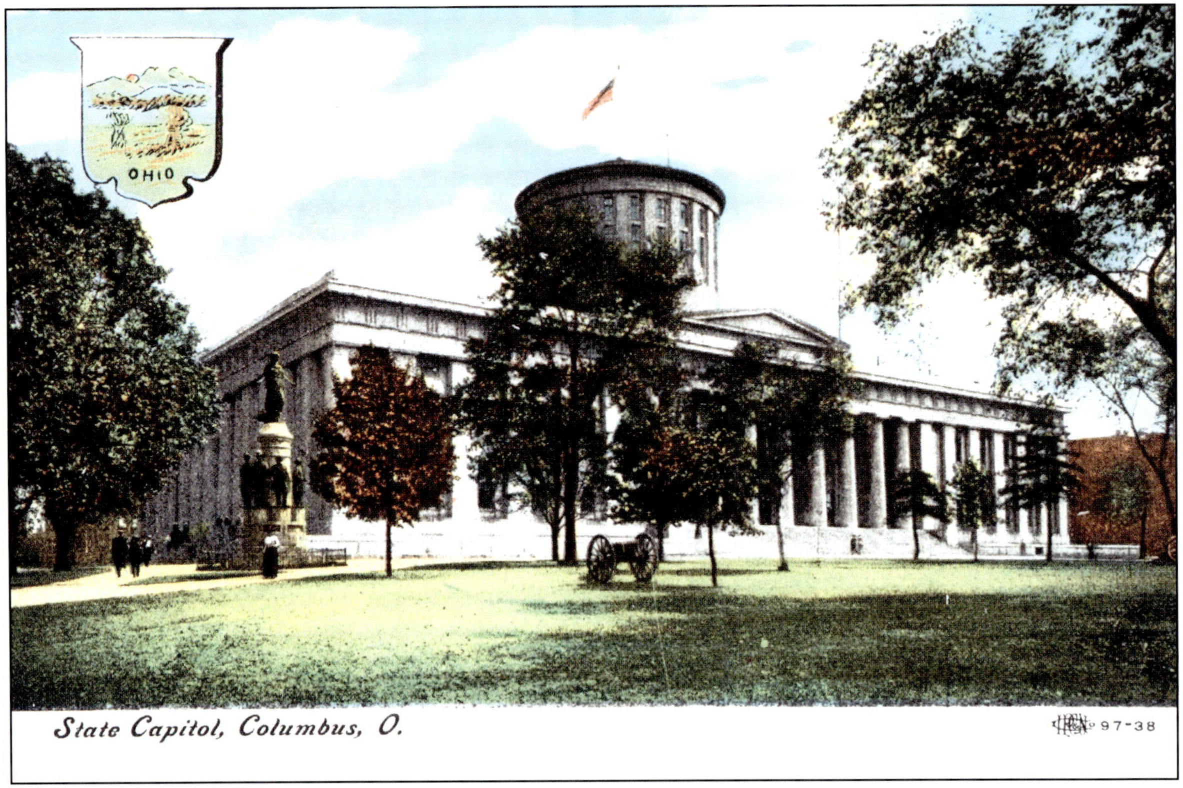

State Capitol, Columbus. Undated, $2-4.

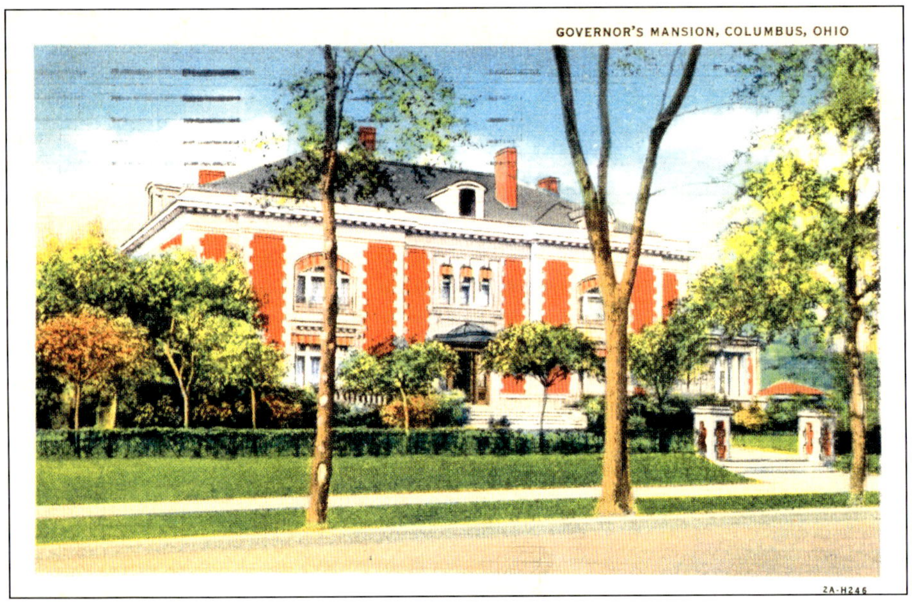

Governor's Mansion. Postmarked 1936, $2-3.

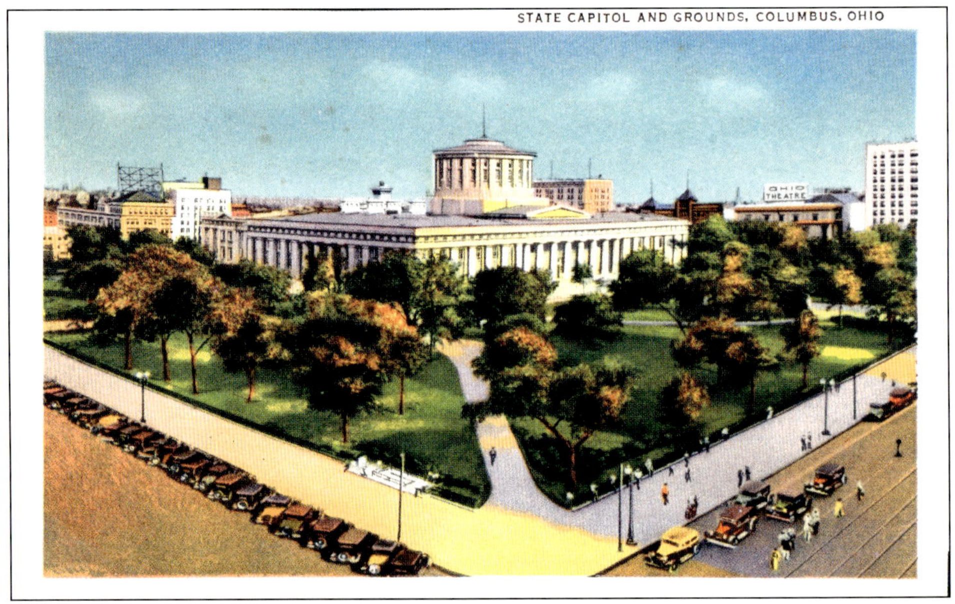

State Capitol and Grounds. Circa 1930s, $2-3.

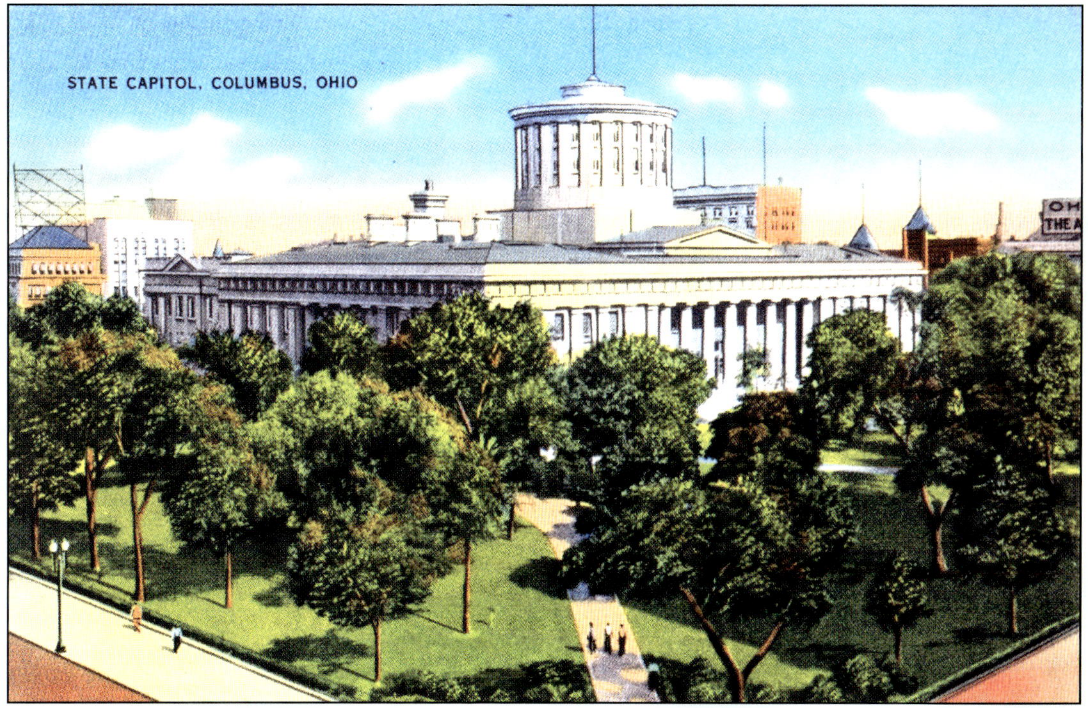

State Capitol, Columbus. Circa 1930s, $2-3. The back reads: *"Its columns are conceded to be the finest examples of Doric architecture in the world."*

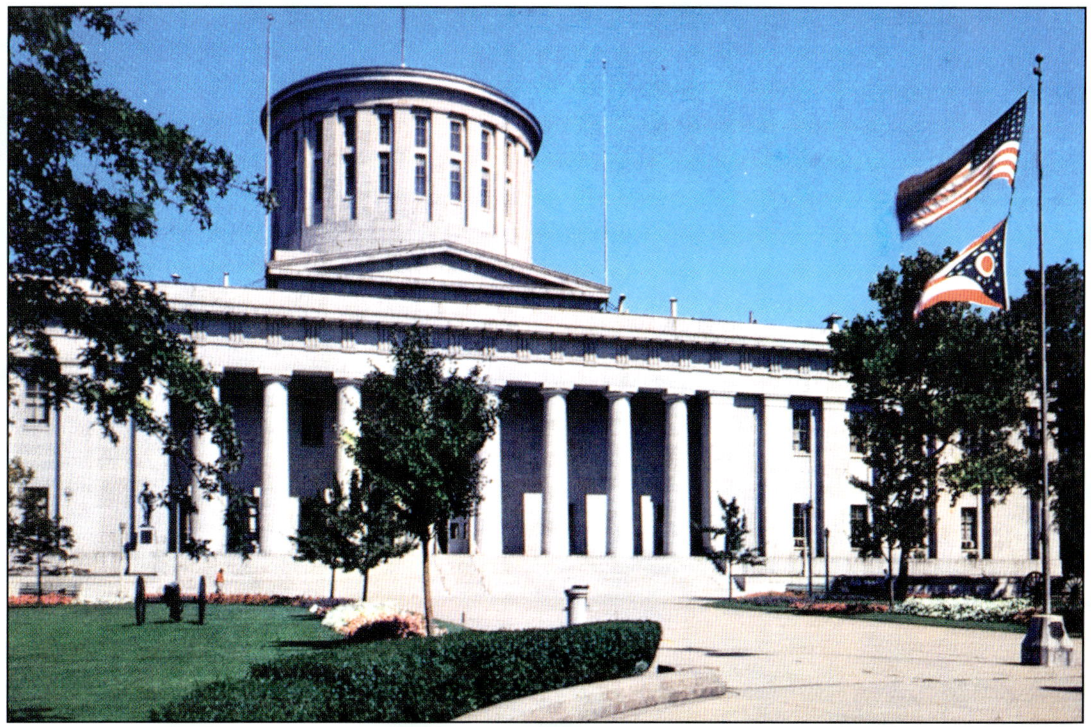

Capitol Building. Postmarked 1961, $2-3.

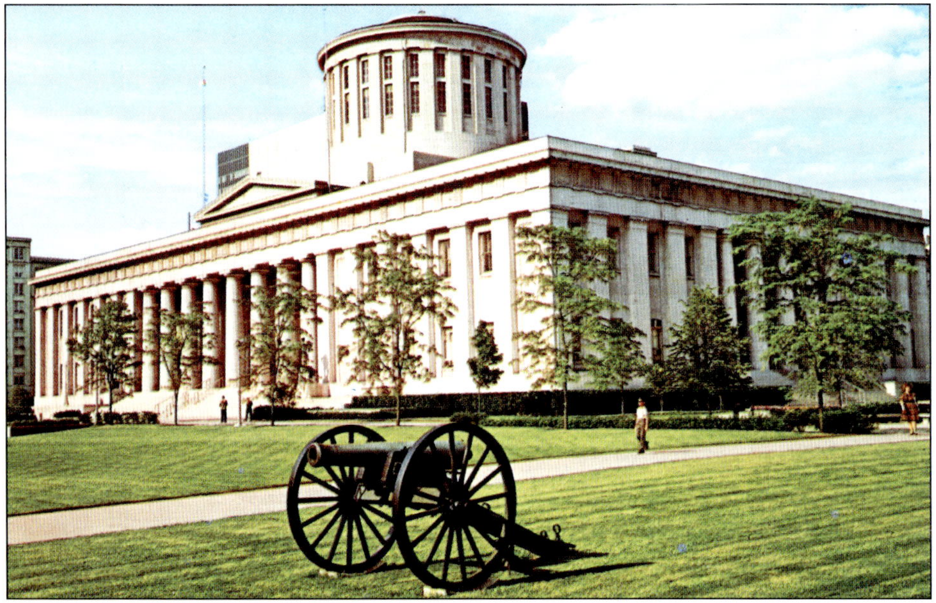

Cannon on Capitol. Circa 1960s, $3-4.

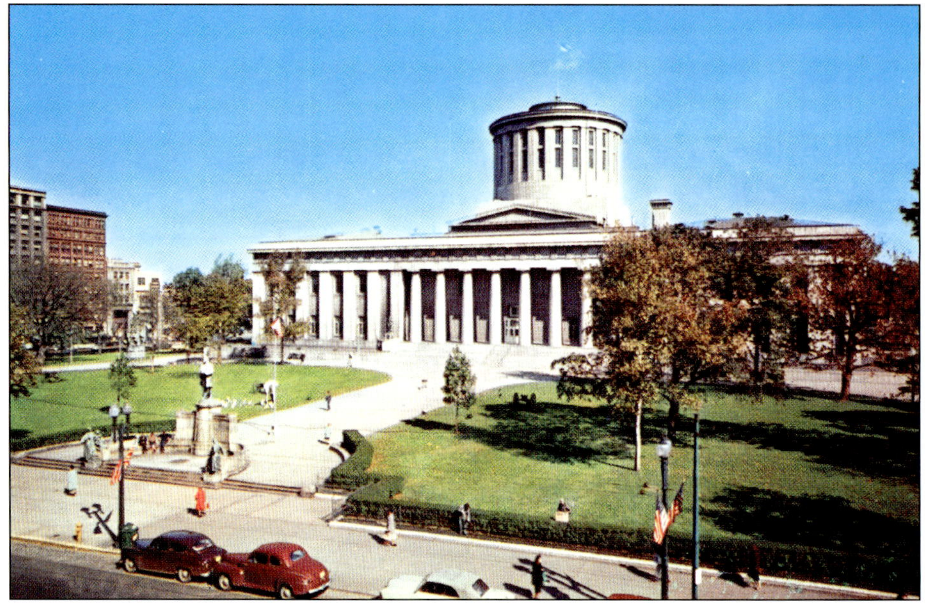

Traffic at Capitol. Circa 1960s, $3-4.

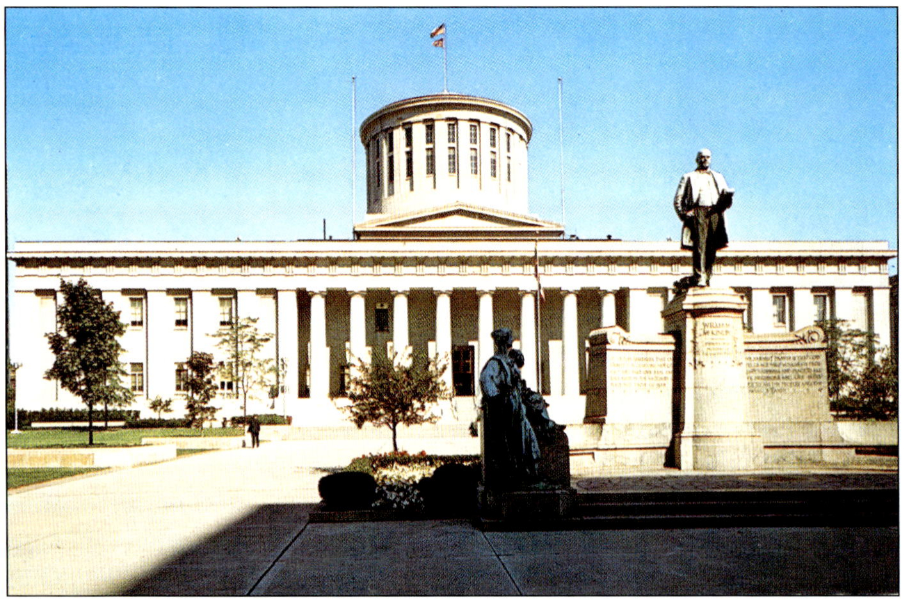

Statehouse Main Entrance. Circa 1970s, $1-3.

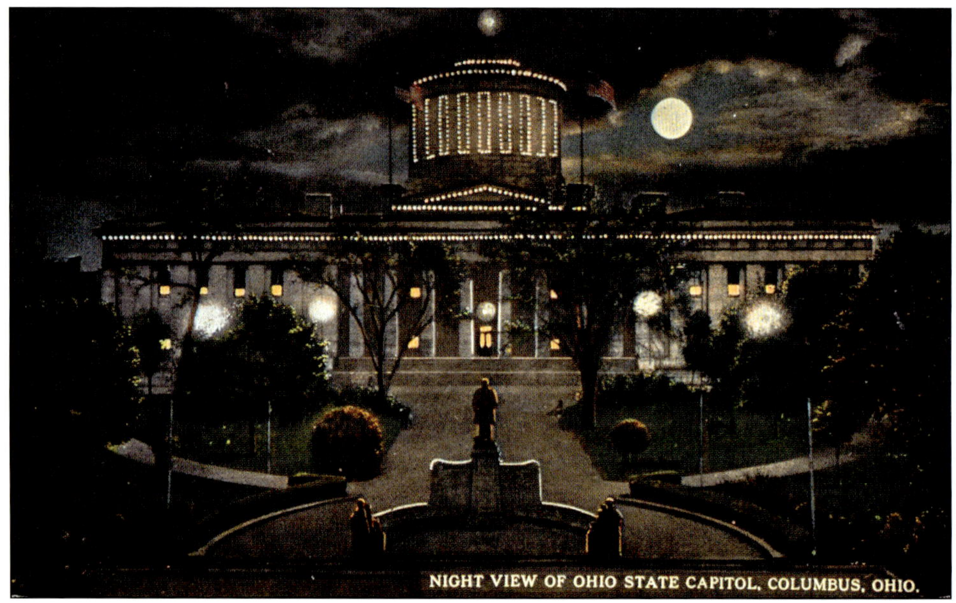

Night view of Ohio State Capitol. Circa early 1900s, $3-4.

Chapter Thirteen: Around Town

> Columbus has developed into an important industrial and commerce center.
> — *Lincoln Library of Essential Information, 1924*

While the whole nation considered the city of Columbus to be important back in the 1920s, there was no consensus on just how that came about.

The scholarly volume *Influences in American History* by Albert Brigham said it certainly wasn't—as it was with many other American cities—a matter of pure geography.

"Columbus has no conspicuous geographic causes lying behind its prosperity," wrote a solemn Brigham in 1903.

He added:

> *"It is indeed on the Scioto, it is in the midst of a rich region, but most of all, it is in the center of a rich state and its capital. It is in part, therefore, due to political causes, and may be briefly dismissed by the geographer."*

When Brigham wrote those words early in the twentieth century, the city of Columbus was indeed prosperous and industry was advancing. Even after the great destructive flood of 1913, the area rebounded with achievements like the ambitious Civic Center. By the latter 1920s, for example, the newly completed O'Shaughnessy Dam was considered "one of the beauty spots of central Ohio" in a nationally published travel guide.

There was a growth of churches too.

In his rather gruff way, author John Gunther wrote of his visit to Columbus in the 1940s: "it is a strong religious town. There are more Methodists, I heard, within a 100 mile radius of Columbus than any other city in the world." Gunther, a best-selling author, never really explained the source of the anecdote. However he added more specifically in the 1947 book *Inside U.S.A.* that Columbus then had over seven hundred separate church organizations.

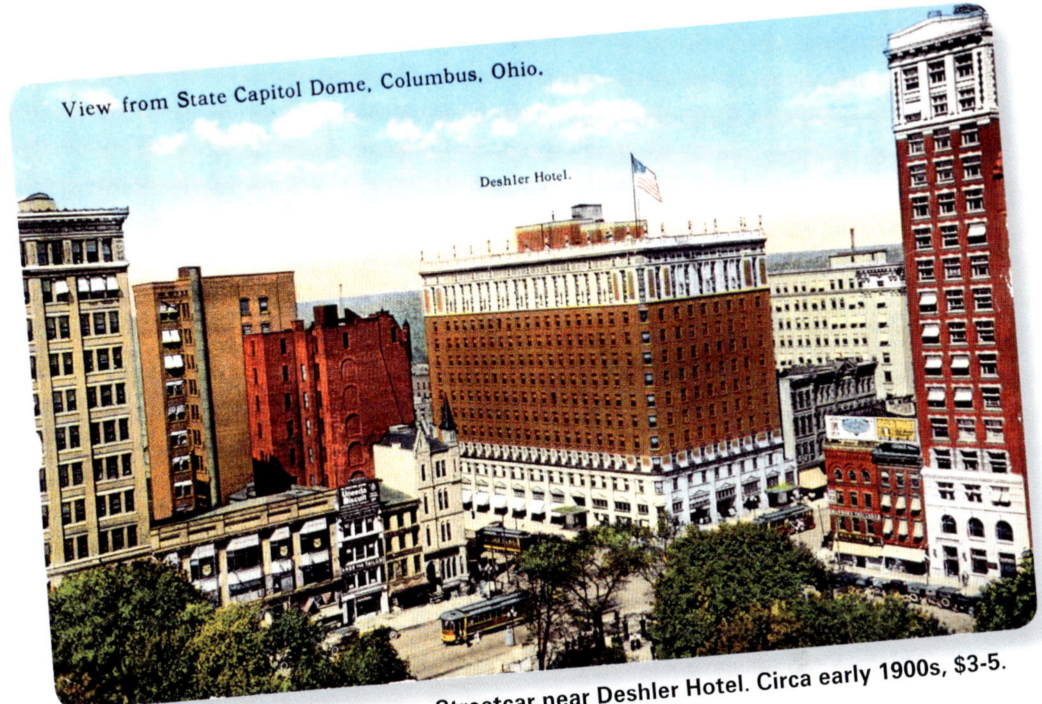

View from State Capitol Dome. Streetcar near Deshler Hotel. Circa early 1900s, $3-5.

Then, apparently stepping back and taking a long-distant, broader view of the city, the visiting writer-journalist said Columbus was "archetypically American and archetypically middle western. It healthily represents a familiar preoccupation with co-operative thinking, a desire to create leadership which is the chief community problem almost everywhere in the United States."

The chief challenge for the city of Columbus as Gunther saw it some six decades ago was "to overcome apathy and develop in citizens a sense of responsibility to the city as a whole."

Civil Center Group. Circa 1930s, $2-3.

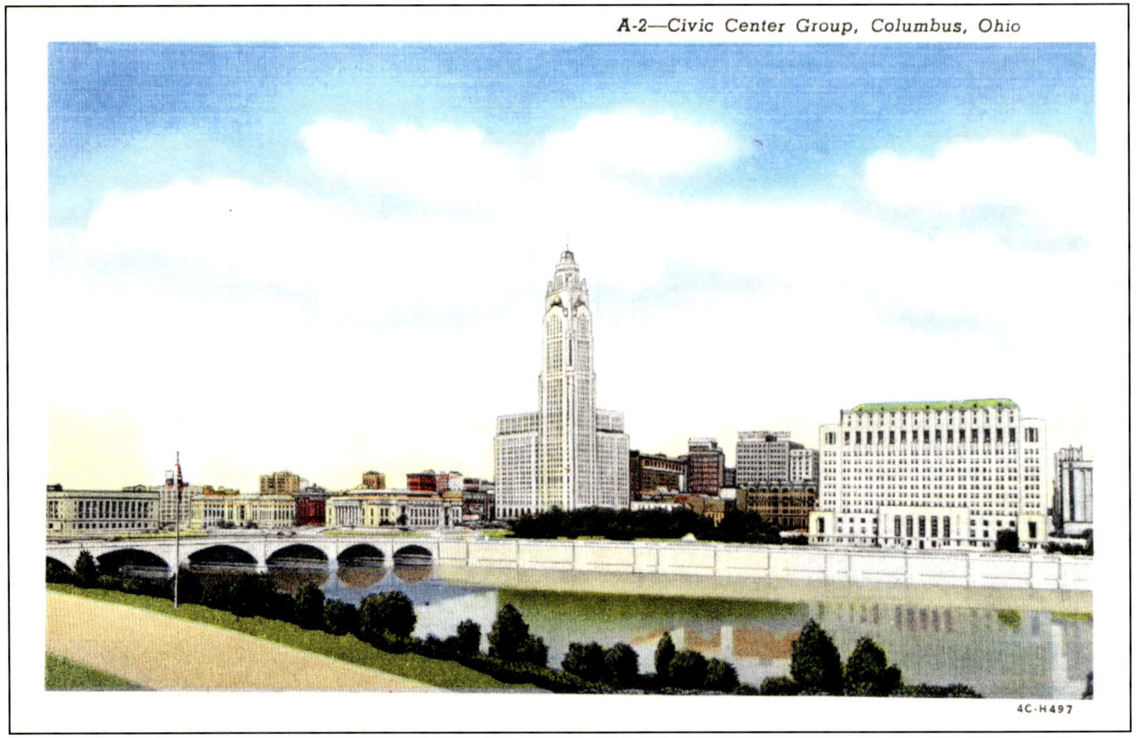

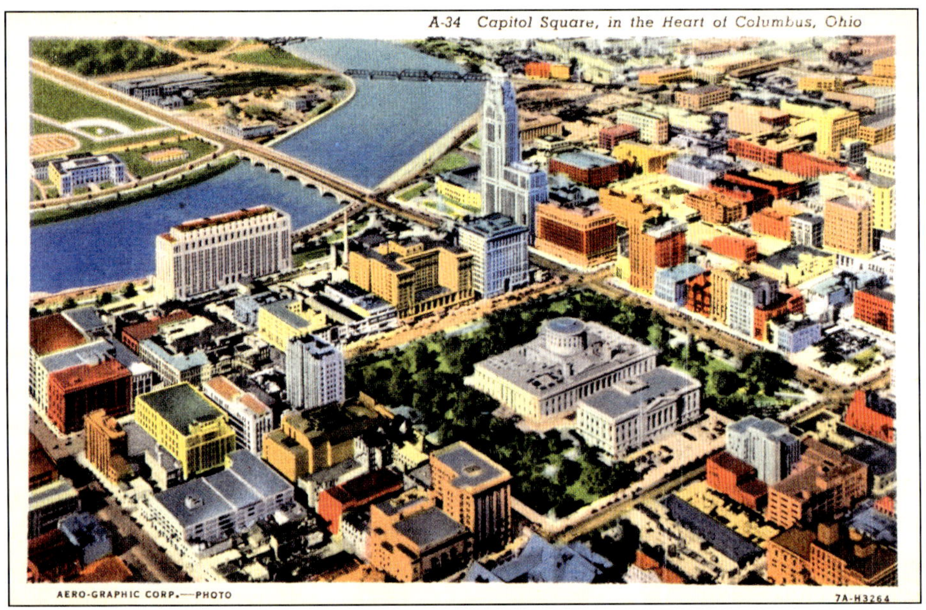

Capitol Square in the heart of Columbus. Postmarked 1954, $2-3. The back reads: *"...Columbus from the air."*

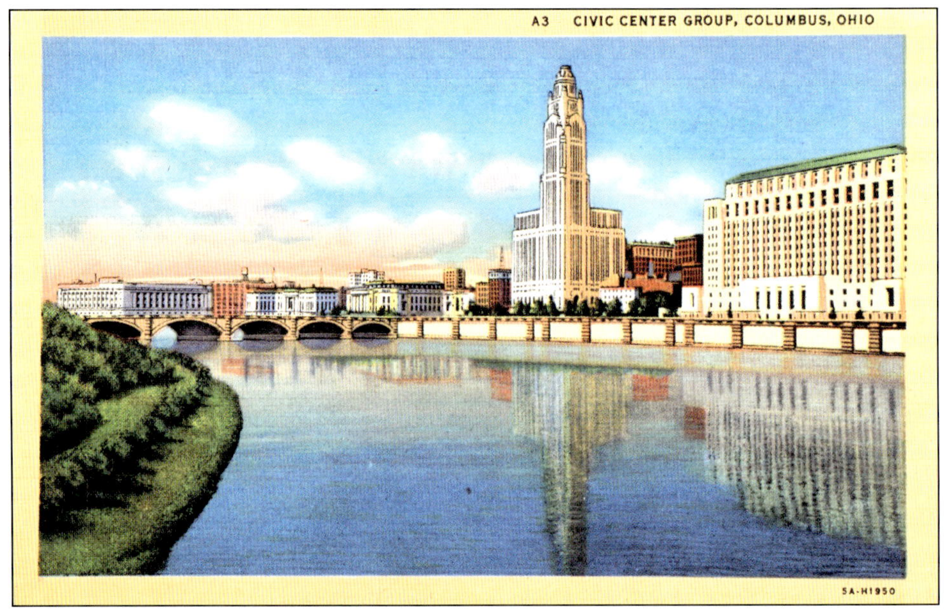

Civil Center Group. Circa 1930s, $2-3.

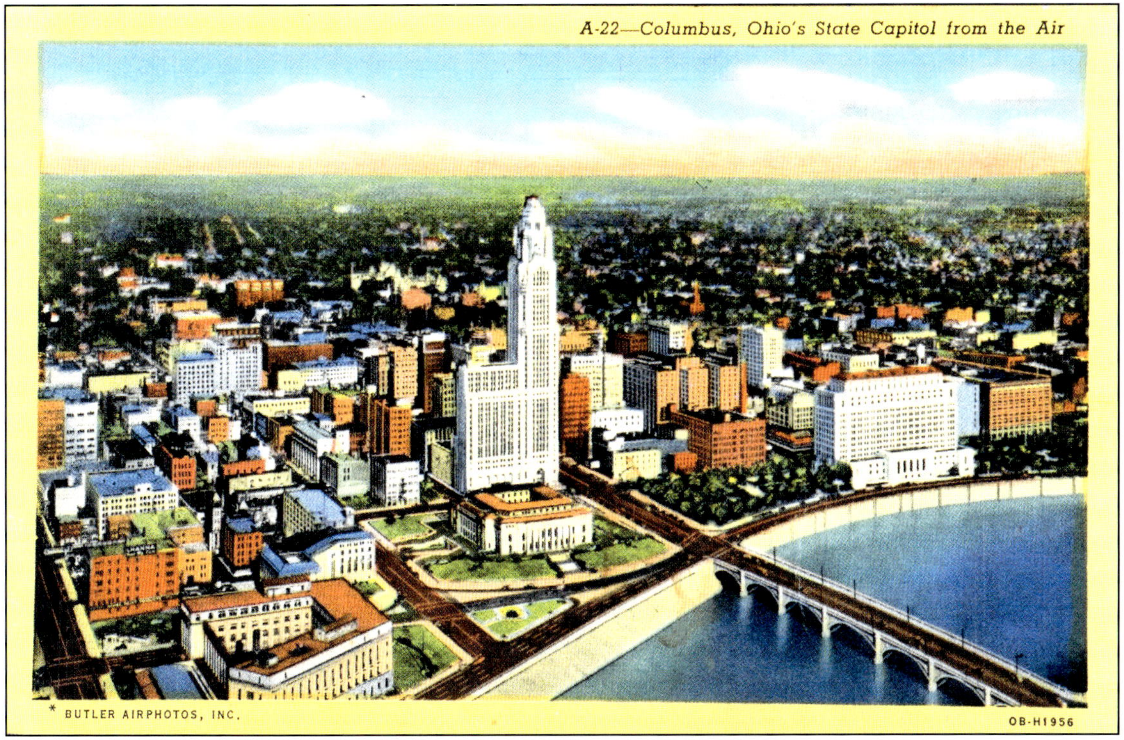

Ohio's State Capitol from the Air Capitol Square in the heart of Columbus. Postmarked 1954, $2-3. The back reads: *"...Columbus from the air."*

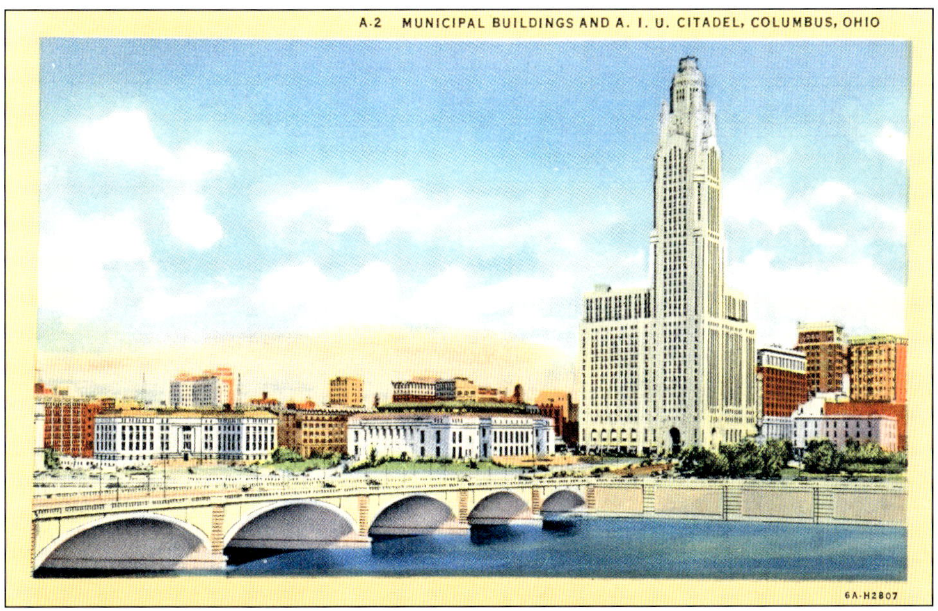

Municipal buildings, Columbus, Ohio. Circa 1930s, $2-3. The back reads: *"Approaching downtown Columbus from the west over the Broad St. Bridge shown on this card."*

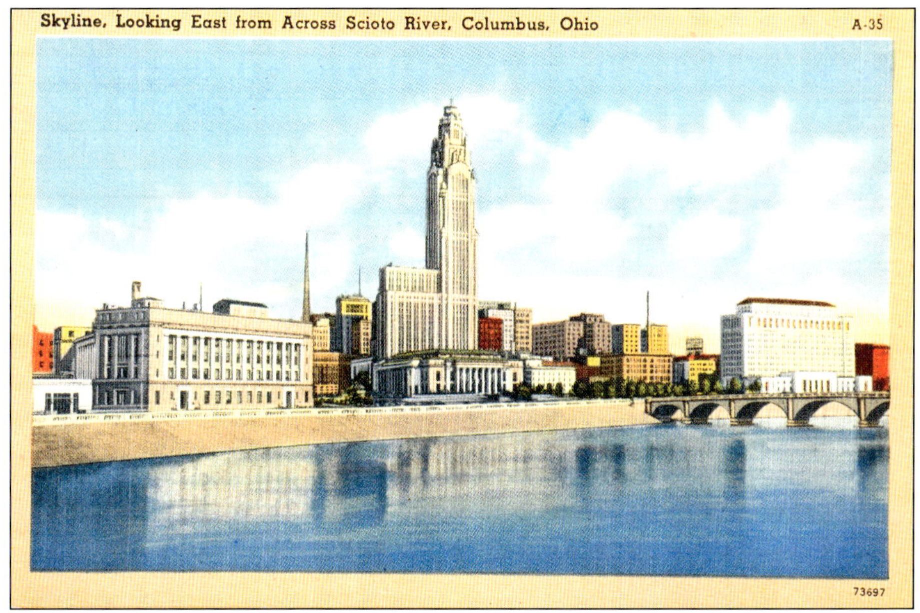

Skyline, looking east from across Scioto River. Circa 1930s, $2-3.

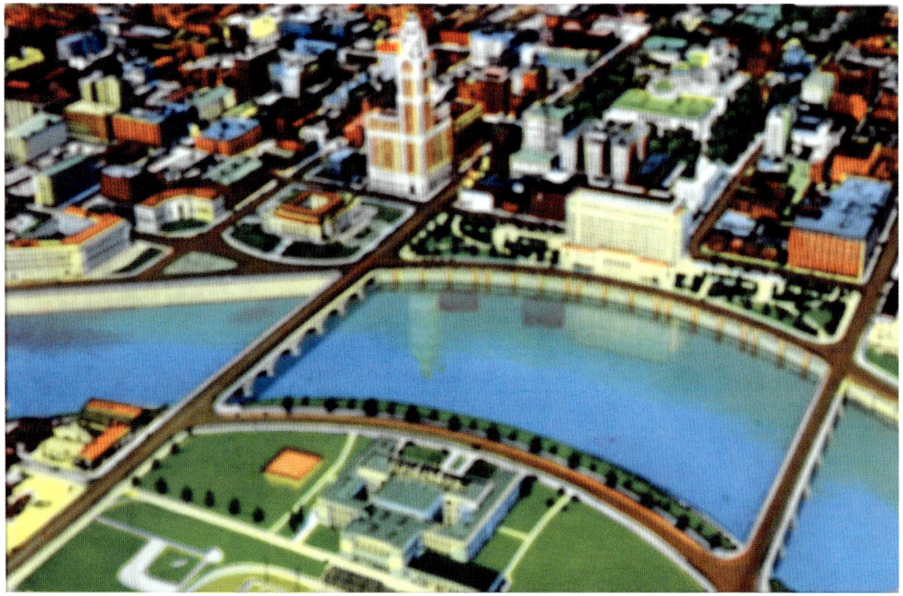

From the air, a view of the Civic Center group. Circa 1930s, $2-3.

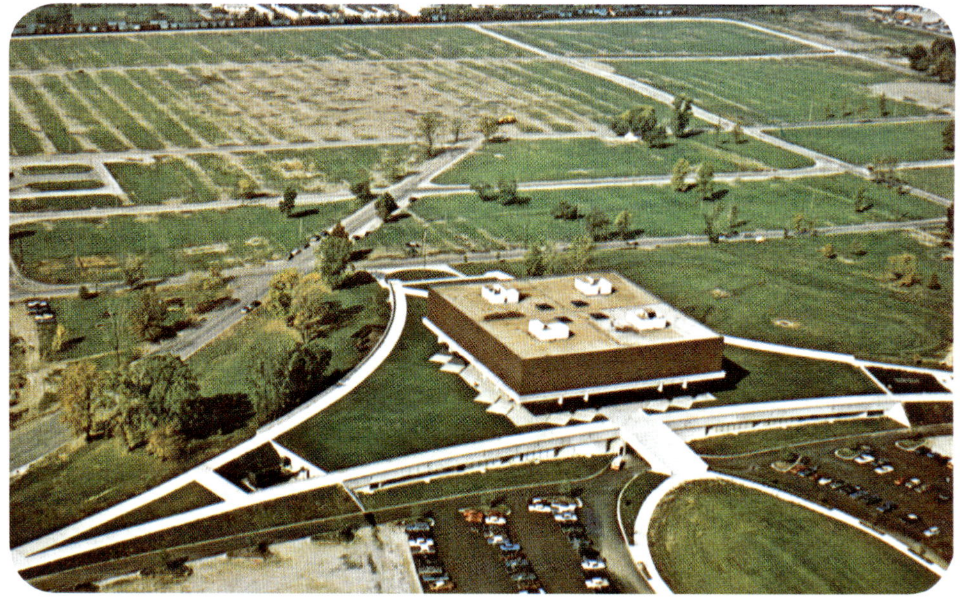

New Home of the Ohio Historical Society. Circa 1960s, $3-4.

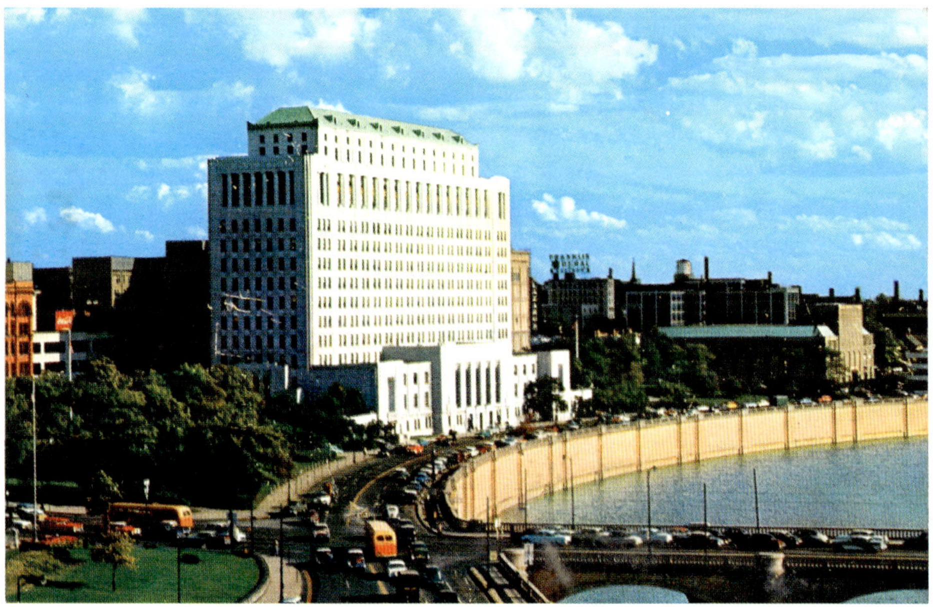

Traffic near State Office Building. Circa 1960s, $3-4.

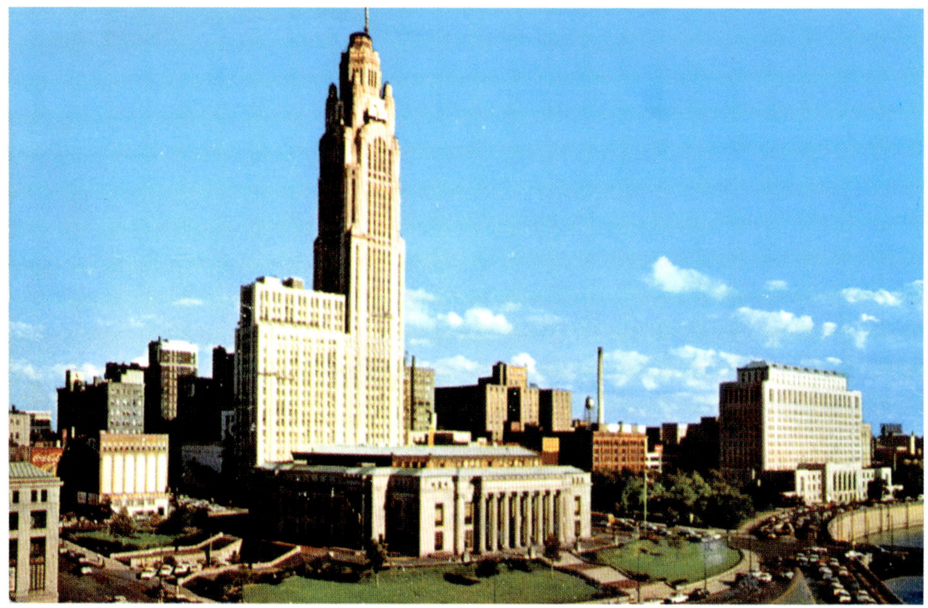

Heart of the city. City Hall, State office building in view. Circa 1960s, $2-3.

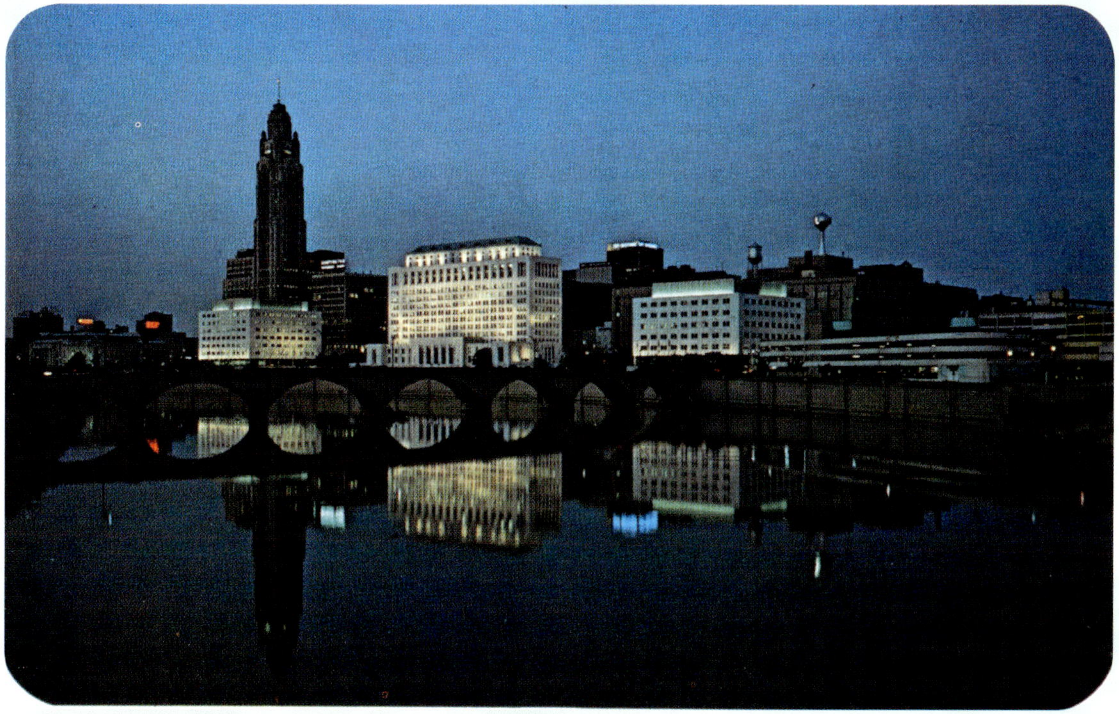

Columbus Civic Center.
Circa 1960s, $2-3.

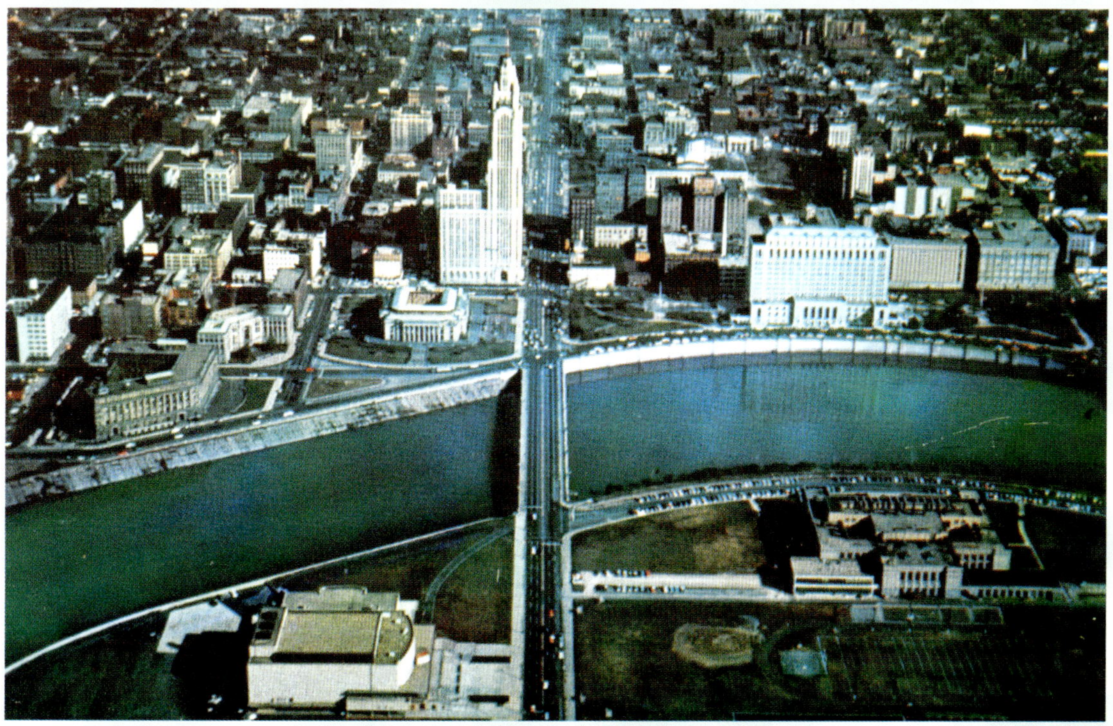

Skyline view of Columbus.
Circa 1960s, $3-4.

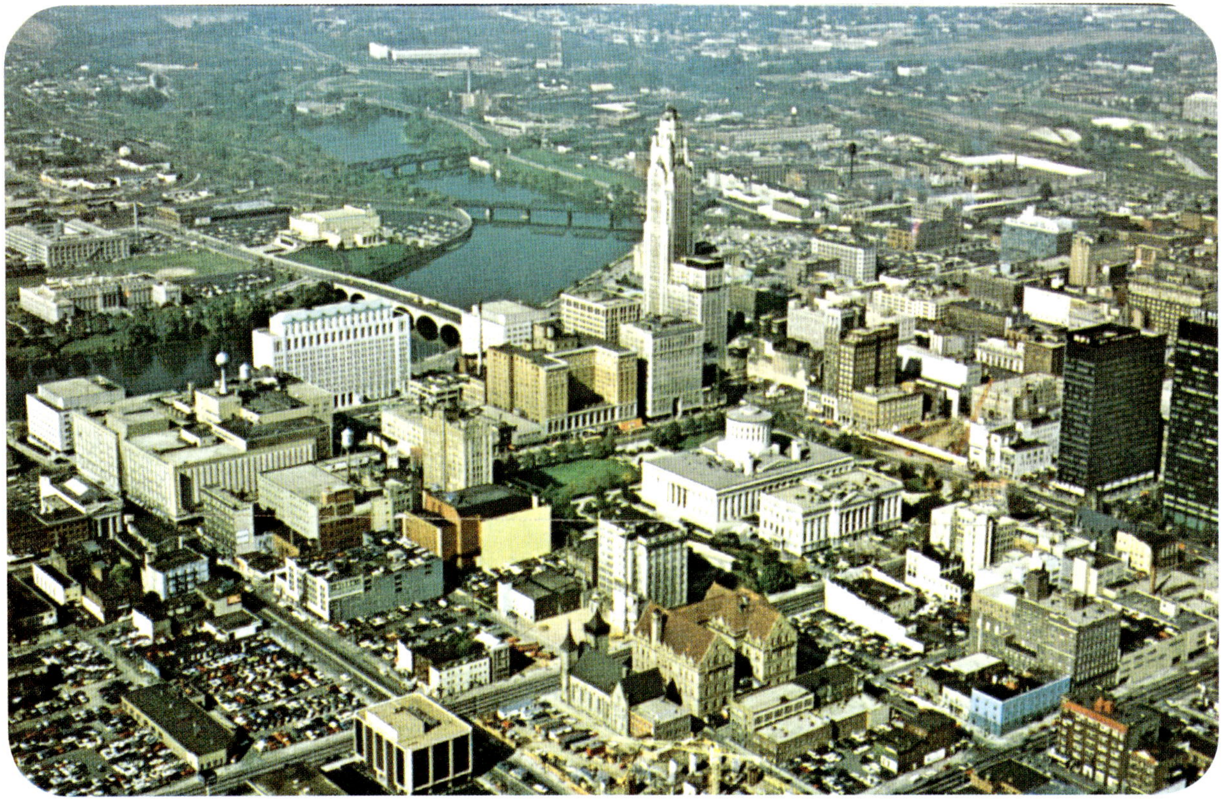

In the air over Columbus. Circa 1960s, $3-4.

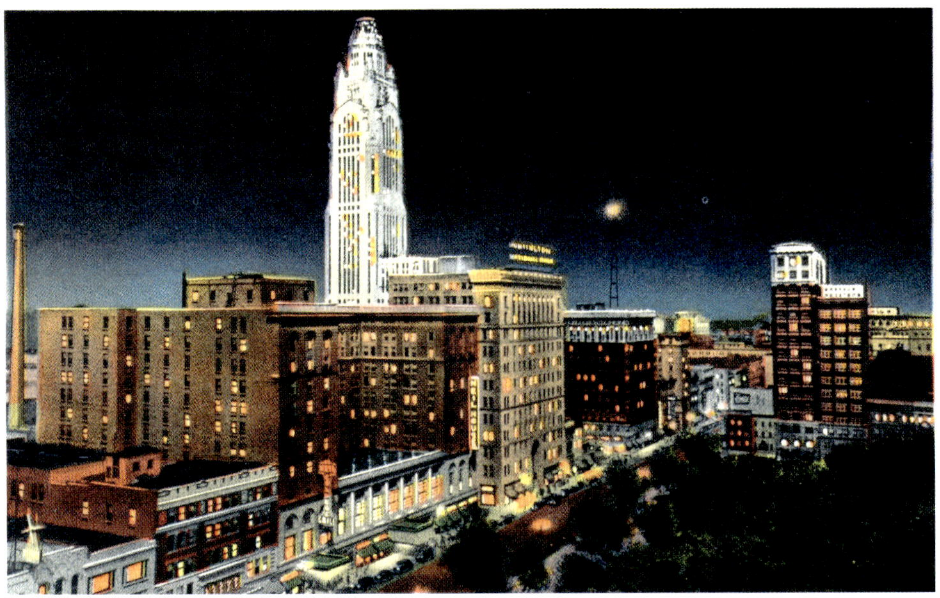

Columbus at night .Circa 1930s, $3-4.

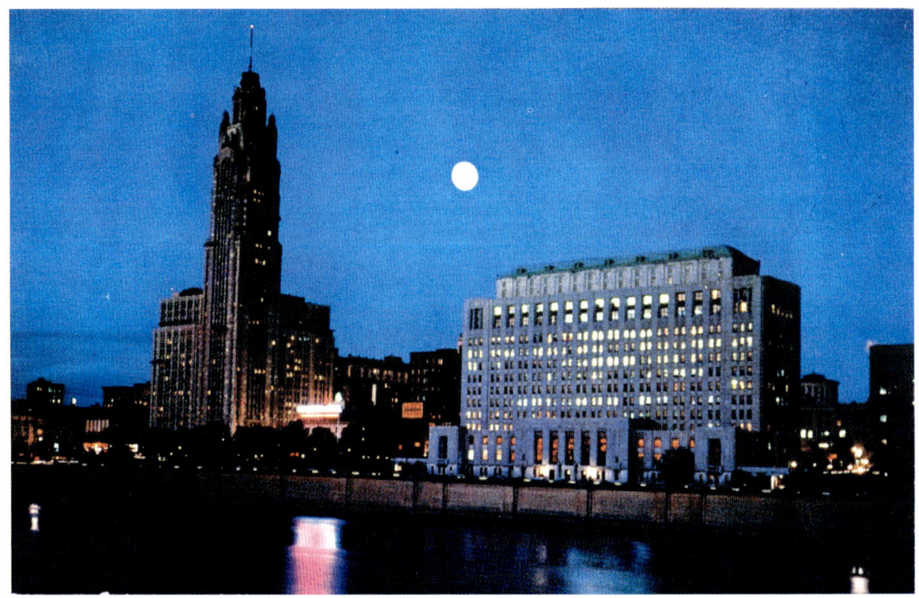

Full moon over Columbus. Circa 1950s, $3-4.

Storage dam, early view. Dated July 1907, $2-3.

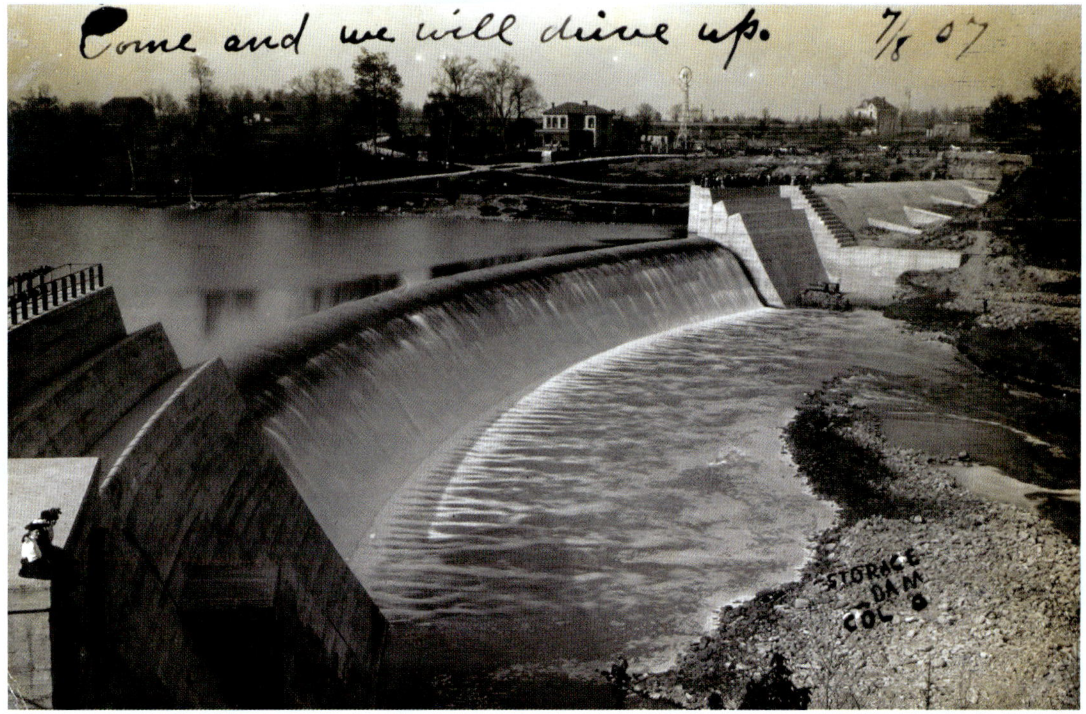

View of Storage Dam. Postmarked 1911, $3-4. Hand-written message reads: ***"Dear Aunt, may you live long and come over and I will take you to see this dam."***

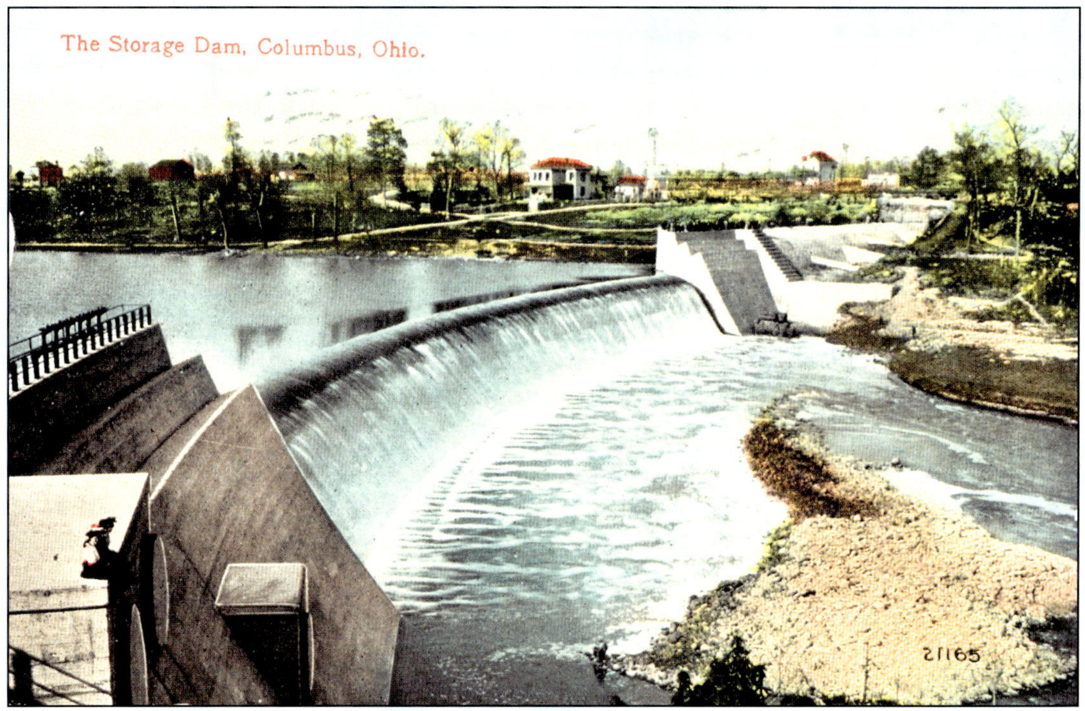

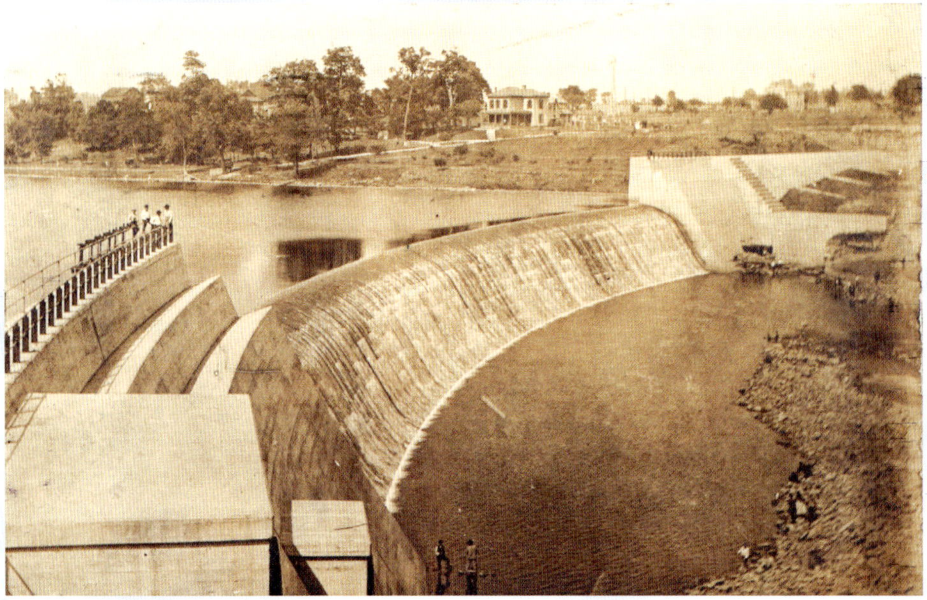

Four atop dam. Postmarked 1912, $2-3.

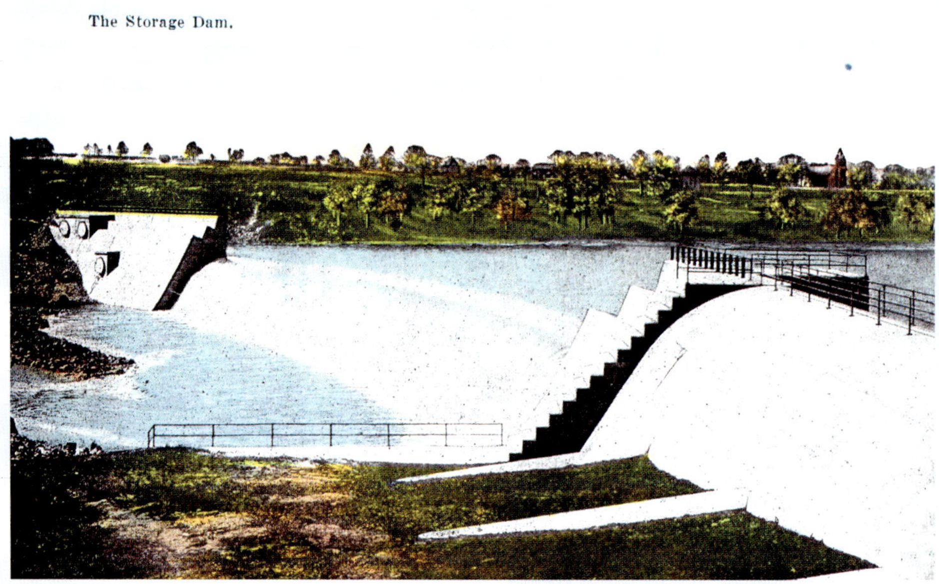

Columbus storage dam. Postmarked 1920, $2-3.

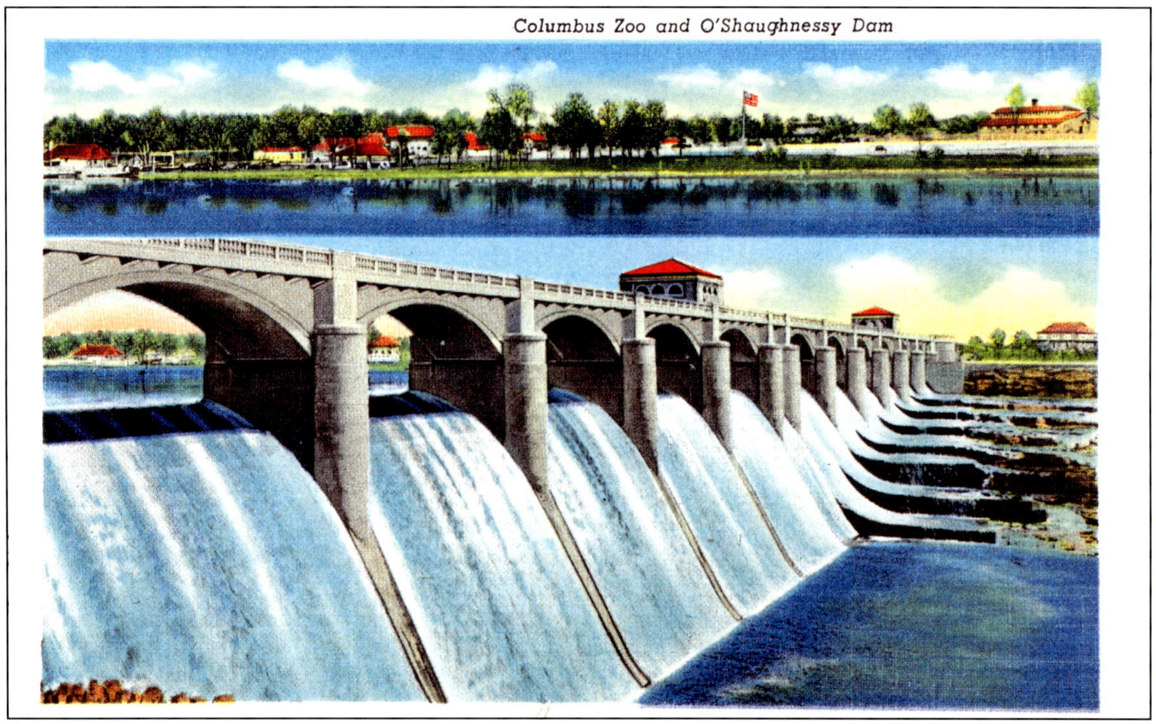

Columbus Zoo and O'Shaughnessy Dam. Circa 1930s, $3-4.

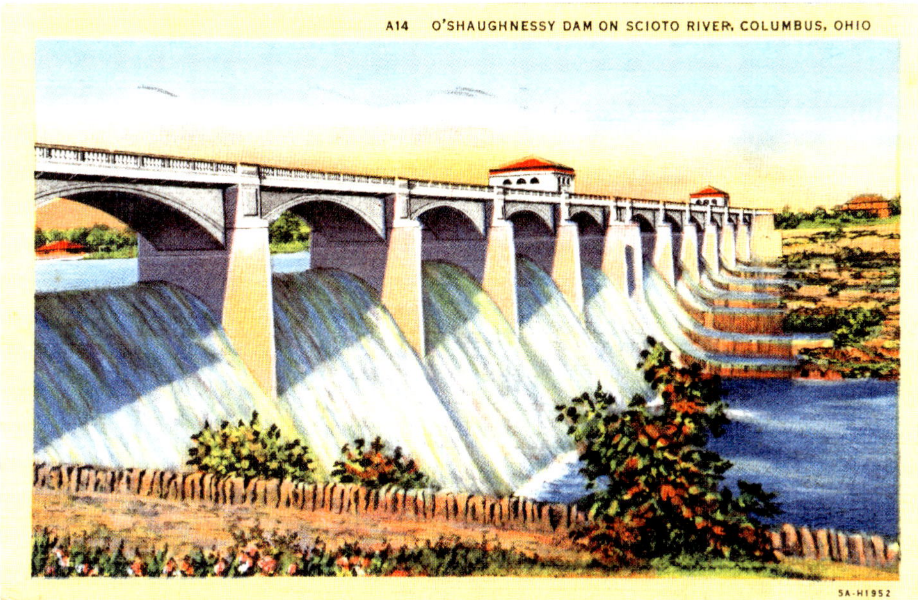

O'Shaughnessy Dam on Scioto River. Postmarked 1946, $2-3.

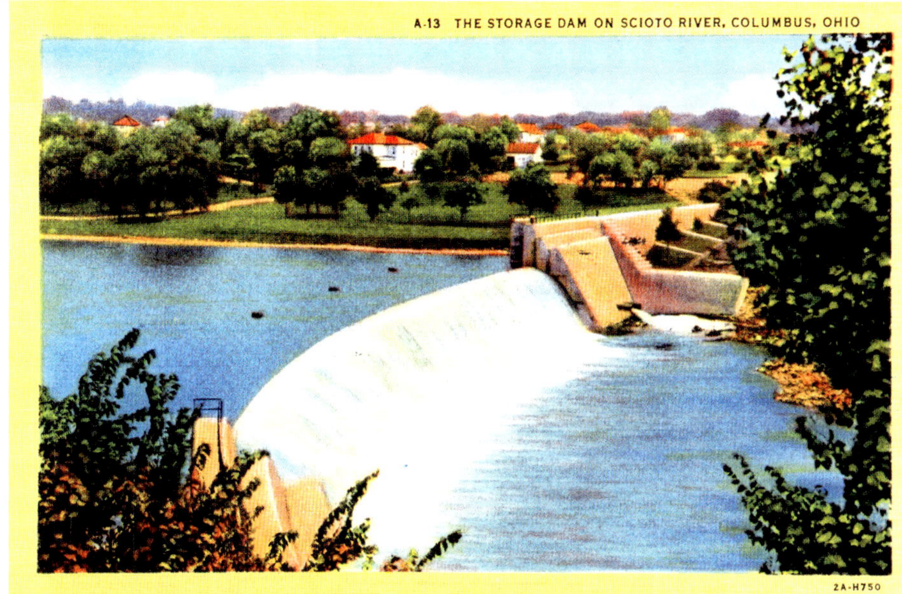

Storage Dam on Scioto River. Postmarked 1948, $2-3.

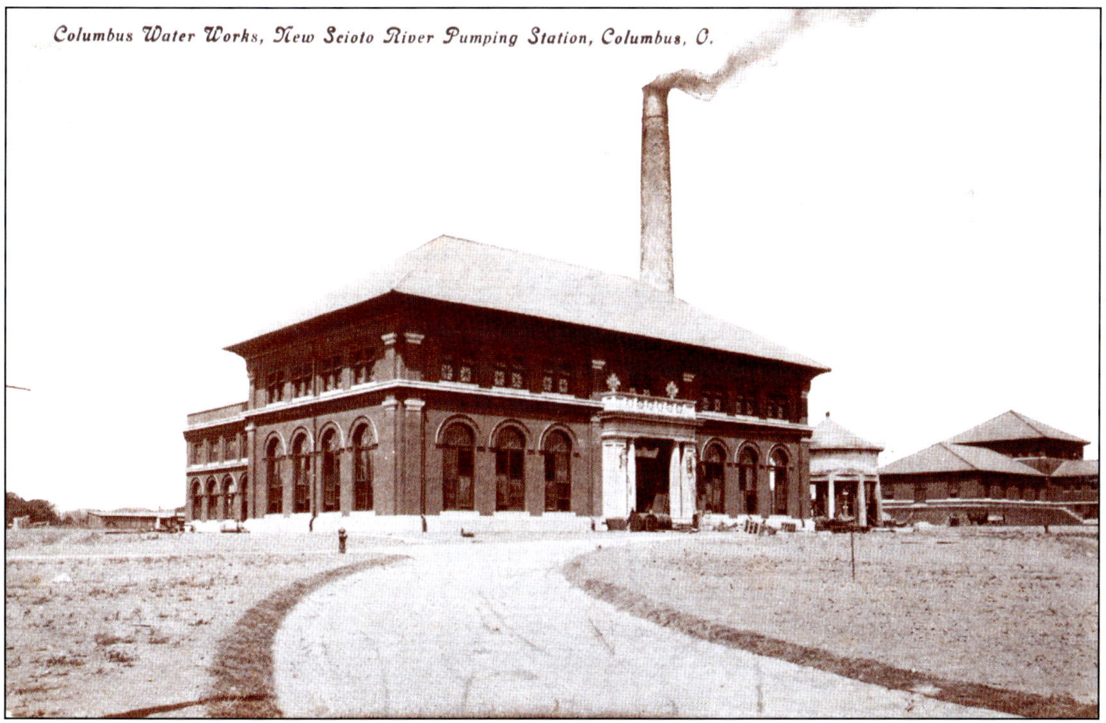

Columbus Water Works, New Pumping Station. Postmarked 1909, $3-4.

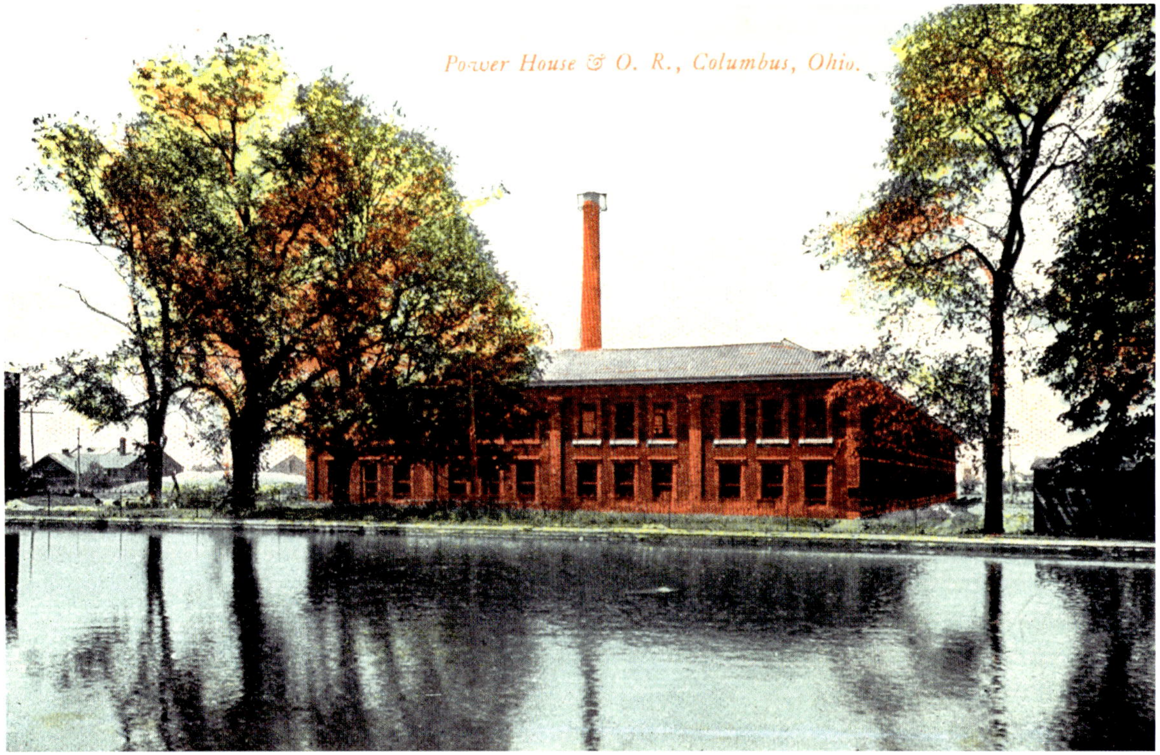

Columbus Power House. Circa 1900s, $3-4.

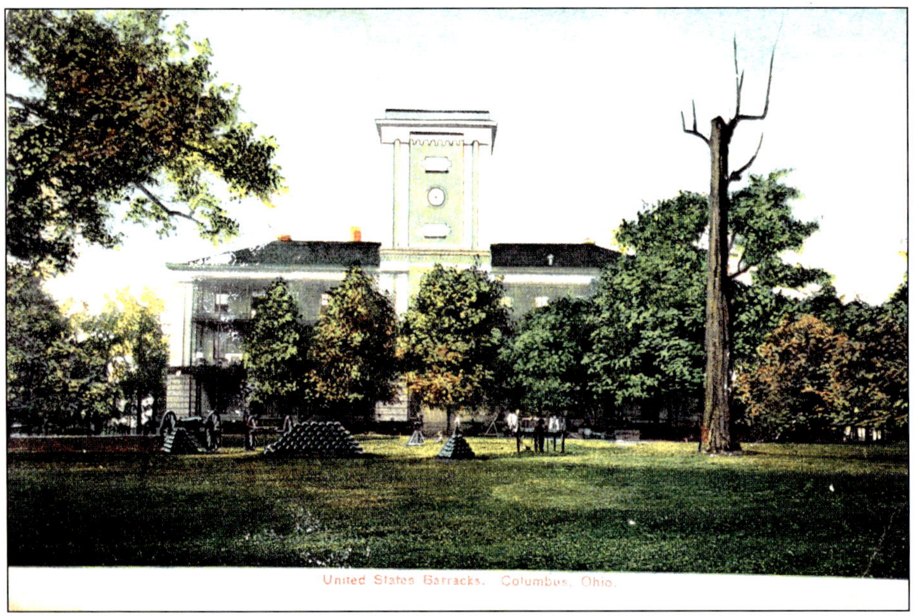

United States Barracks, Columbus. Postmarked 1908, $3-4.

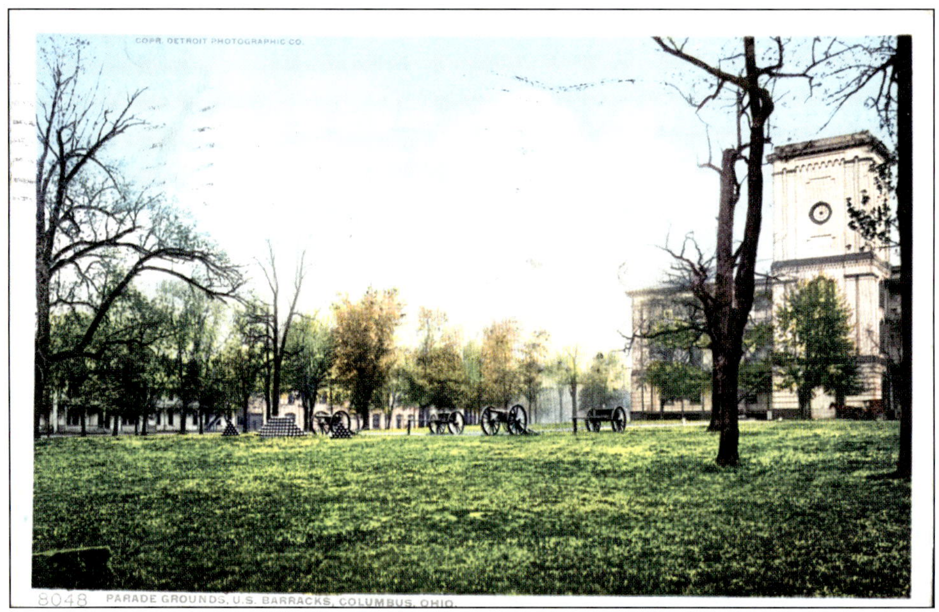

Parade grounds, U.S. Barracks. Postmarked 1910, $3-4.

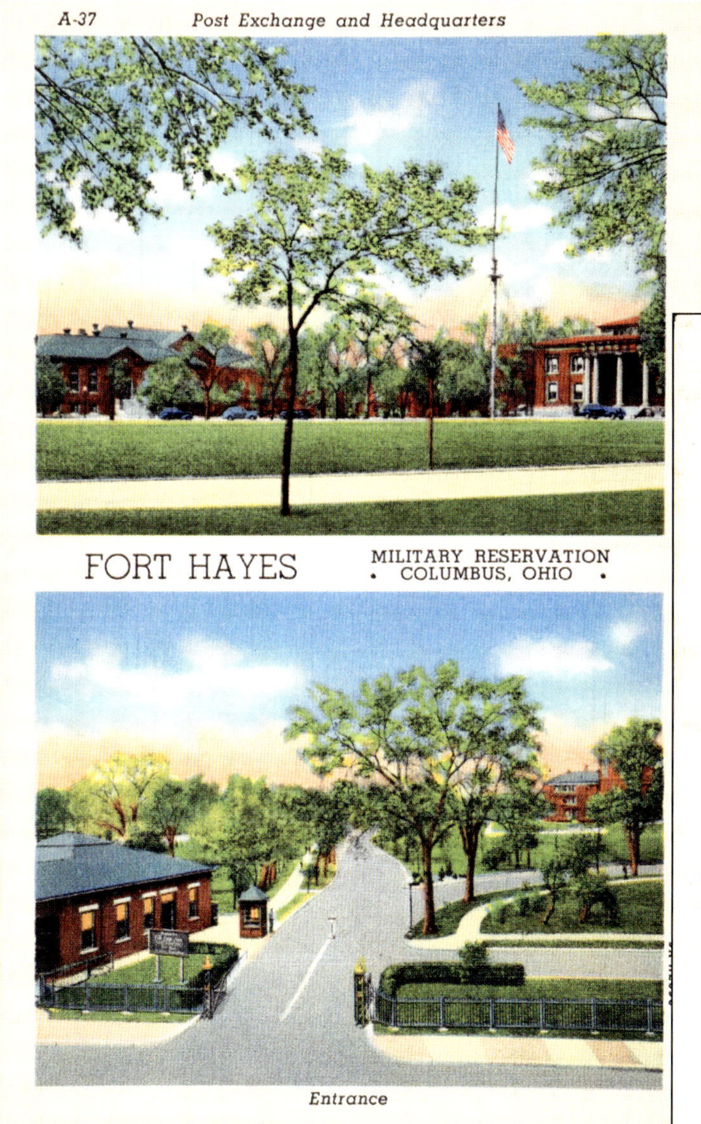

Fort Hayes, Military Reservation. Circa 1930s, $2-3.

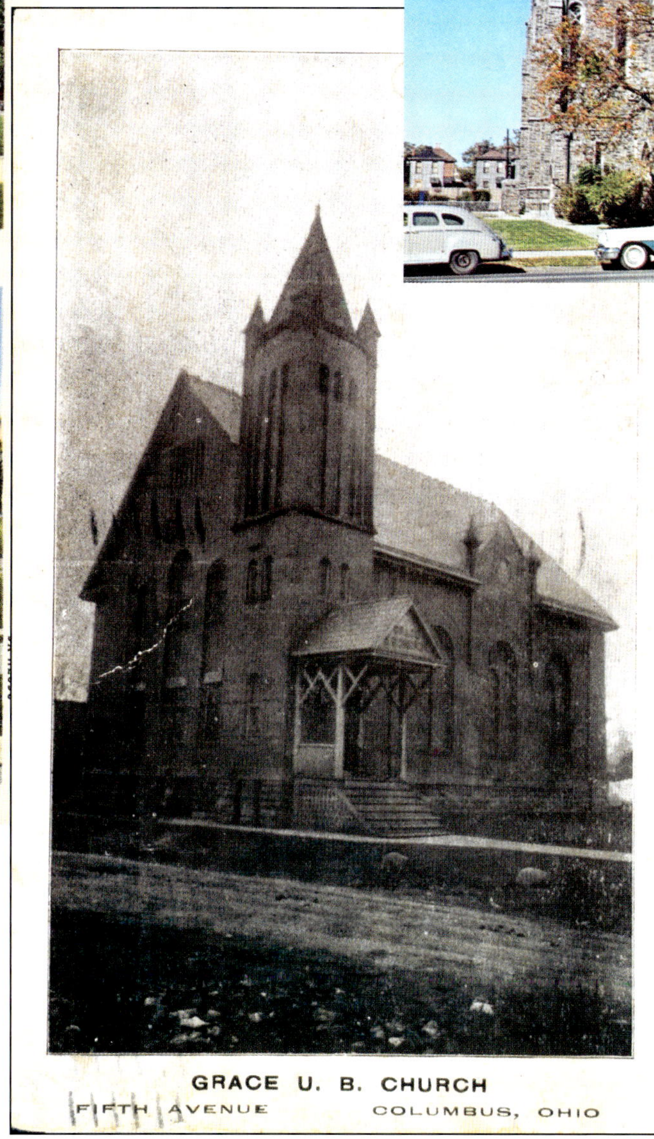

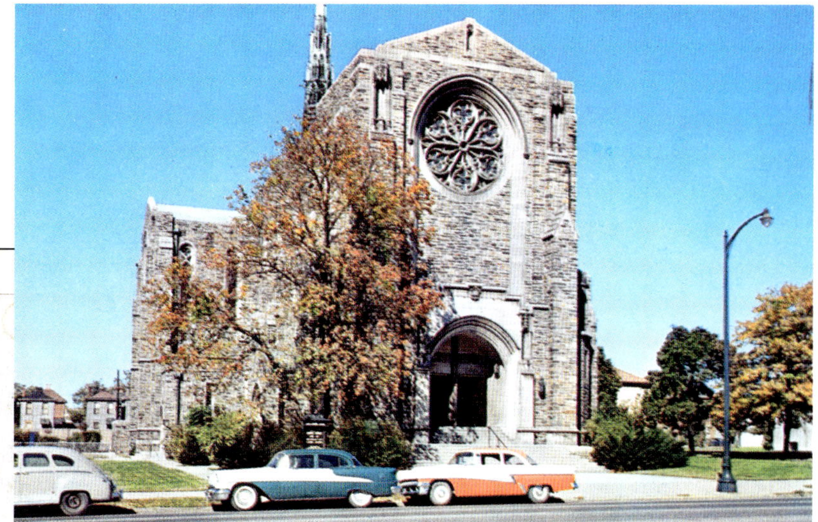

First Congregational Church. Located on East Broad Street. Circa 1950s: $3-4.

Grace U.B. Church, Columbus. Located on Fifth Avenue. Postmarked 1911, $2-3.

Bibliography

Alsberg, Henry G. *The American Guide*. New York, New York: Hastings House, 1949.

Andrist, Ralph K. *The American Heritage History of the 20s & 30s*. New York, New York: American Heritage Publishing Co., Inc. 1970.

Brigham, Albert. *Geographic Influences In American History*. Boston, Massachusetts: Ginn & Company, 1903.

Brubacher, Abram Royer, PH.D. *The Volume Library*. New York, New York: Educators Association, 1930.

Frontier Press Company. *The Standard Dictionary of Facts*. Buffalo, New York: The Frontier Press Company, 1919.

Frontier Press Company. *The. The Lincoln Library of Essential Information*. Buffalo, New York: The Frontier Press Company, 1949.

Gunther, John. *Inside U.S.A.* New York, New York: Harper & Brothers, 1947.

Hammond, C. S. & Co. *Great Cities of the World*. Maplewood, New Jersey: C. S. Hammond and Company, 1958.

Jenkins, Elmer. *Guide To America*. Washington, D.C.: Public Affairs Press, 1949.

Platt, Suzy. *Respectfully Quoted – A Dictionary of Quotations*. New York: Barnes and Noble Books, 1993.

Russell, Thomas. *Story of the Great Flood and Cyclone Disasters*. New York, New York: Thomas Morrison Publishing, 1913.

Torricelli, Robert. *Quotations For Public Speakers*. New Brunswick, New Jersey: Rutgers University Press, 2001.

Wecter, Dixon. *The Age of the Great Depression: 1929-1941*. New York, New York: The MacMillan Company, 1948.

Wisel, Alice. *Great Lakes Mobil Travel Guide*. New York, New York: Fodor's Travel Publications, Inc., 1995.

Articles

Columbus Post-Dispatch, 1926

Periodicals

This Week In Columbus, February 26-March 11, 1954; Columbus, Ohio.

Index

Arcade, 32

Bliss College, 63, 66
Broad Street, 58
Burnham & Co., 32

Camp Chase, 70
Chittenden Hotel, 23
'City of Columbus', 32
Clintonville, 15
Coral Reef, 79, 83
College of St. Mary, 63
Columbus Auto & Manufacturing, 32
Columbus Clippers, 54
Columbus Dispatch, 86, 93, 96
Columbus High School, 63
Columbus Jets, 54
Columbus Motor Vehicle Co., 32
Columbus Red Birds, 54, 57

Downtown, 8
Dumon, Santos, 32

Fort Hayes Hotel, 23, 27
Franklinton, 4

Gunther, John, 8, 40

Indianola Junior High, 63, 65

King Avenue, 70
Kitty Show Bar, 79, 83

Latin Lounge, 79, 83

Margetti's, 79
McKinley, William, 70
Methodists, 101

National Road, 4
Nationwide Arena, 32
Neil House, 23
New Southern Hotel, 23
North High School, 63

O. Henry, 20
O'Shaughnessy Dam, 108, 109
Ohio Agricultural & Mechanical College, 40
Ohio Dominican College, 63
Ohio Penitentiary, 20, 32
Ohio State, 40
Ohio State stadium, 54, 55, 57
Ohio Theatre, 79
Olentangy Park, 15

Port Columbus Airport, 36, 37, 38
Porter, William, 20

Rollerland, 79, 82

Sandusky Runabout, 33
Santos Dumont automobile, 32
Scioto River, 4, 9, 14
Seafood Bay, 79, 83
Seed & Evans, 33
Studebaker Stanhope, 32

Tremont, The, 79, 85